D0207860

MASTERING
OBJECT-ORIENTED
DESIGN IN C++

MASTERING OBJECT-ORIENTED DESIGN IN C++

CAY S. HORSTMANN

San José State University

John Wiley & Sons, Inc.

New York ▪ Chichester ▪ Brisbane ▪ Toronto ▪ Singapore

ACQUISITIONS EDITOR	Steve Elliot
DEVELOPMENTAL EDITOR	Sean Culhane
MARKETING MANAGER	Susan Elbe
PRODUCTION EDITOR	Publication Services
DESIGN	Ann Marie Renzi
MANUFACTURING MANAGER	Susan Stetzer
ILLUSTRATION	Sigmund Malinowski

COVER   Art from the triptych: *The Draughtsman, The Woodcutter, The Printer*, c. 1900, by Emil Orlik, © Sterling & Francine Clark Art Institute, Williamstown, Mass. Cover designed by Nancy Field.

This book was set in Palatino by Publication Services and printed and bound by Courier Stoughton. The cover was printed by Phoenix Color Associates.

Recognizing the importance of preserving what has been written, it is a policy of John Wiley & Sons, Inc. to have books of enduring value published in the United States printed on acid-free paper, and we exert our best efforts to that end.

Copyright © 1995, by John Wiley & Sons, Inc.

All rights reserved. Published simultaneously in Canada.

Reproduction or translation of any part of this work beyond that permitted by Sections 107 and 108 of the 1976 United States Copyright Act without the permission of the copyright owner is unlawful. Requests for permission or further information should be addressed to the Permissions Department, John Wiley & Sons, Inc.

Library of Congress Cataloging-in-Publication Data:
Horstmann, Cay S., 1959–
    Mastering object-oriented design in C++ / Cay S. Horstmann,
        p.   cm.
    Includes bibliographical references.
    ISBN 0-471-59484-9 (pbk. : acid-free paper)
    1. Object-oriented programming (Computer science)   2. C++
(Computer program language)   I. Title.
QA76.64.H67   1994
005.13'3—dc20   94-39841
                                            CIP
Printed in the United States of America

10 9 8 7 6 5 4 3 2 1

PREFACE

This book covers three topics:

1. The discovery and design of classes that model real-world problems
2. The feature set of a modern object-oriented programming language
3. Getting from item 1 to item 2: implementing the classes by using the language features effectively

It is intended for students in a one-semester undergraduate-level course in object-oriented design and programming. It should also be of interest to programmers working individually or in small teams who want to learn how to put C++ to work.

I wrote this book for use in a course in object-oriented programming at San José State University, having found other texts unsuitable for our environment. C++ language texts such as [Lippmann] necessarily cover all aspects of C++, and coverage of topics is proportional to their complexity, not their importance. A number of language-independent books on object-oriented programming are available, such as the excellent text [Budd]. However, for pragmatic reasons it was felt desirable that our students gain sufficient expertise in C++ rather than being exposed to a sampling of various object-oriented languages. Books on object-oriented analysis and design, such as [Booch] and [Rumbaugh], provide outstanding guidance for object orientation in the development process, but undergraduate students rarely have sufficient experience in large-scale software development to envision the complexities that these methodologies address.

At the risk of satisfying nobody, I therefore set out to write a book that is neither a C++ language manual, nor a comparative study of object-oriented programming languages, nor a guide to object-oriented analysis and design methodologies. I combine an introduction into the subset of C++ that is of most practical use; guidance to the effective usage of the language; common abstractions in object-oriented programming; and an introduction into formal design methods.

At the design level, I do not present a comprehensive methodology. Instead, a "mini-methodology" that combines the CRC card approach ([Beck]) with the "Booch lite" graphical notation ([Booch]) and a format for recording design information that migrates naturally to C++ code. It has been my experience that keeping it simple is the key to motivating both students and practitioners to actually use these tools in their work. There is no coverage of object-oriented analysis.

The realization of an object-oriented design in any object-oriented programming language is a nontrivial activity that does not get as much respect as it should. Analysis and design texts lump it into "implementation", and programming language texts don't cover it because they concentrate on "features". This book contains a large number of "design hints" to guide the programmer. The word "design" here refers not just to object-oriented design but to the multitude of design decisions that a programmer must make to map the discovered classes onto language features. Most of these design hints are independent of C++ and hold for any strongly typed object-oriented programming language, such as Eiffel, Modula 3, or Ada 9X. Most design hints are not absolute rules, just sound advice that works in 99.44% of all cases. Quite a few of these rules are *opinions* that I consider reasonable, but you may well have good reasons to disagree with them. I believe it is more valuable for the reader to have a design rule worded as a strong and memorable statement rather than lifeless verbiage that is qualified with endless exceptions.

On several occasions, I chose a bottom-up approach, first presenting the low-level mechanics of a new concept before discussing rules for good high-level design. For example, I show how encapsulation works in C++ before discussing its design impact. While perhaps not "politically correct", it does make for better learning. Without a concrete understanding of the implementation to which it leads, design advice has a tendency to sound trivial or ponderous. In teaching a programming-intensive course from this book, there is also a pressure to get quickly to the point where meaningful programming assignments are possible. If you disagree, you can reverse the sequence of some chapters. In particular, Chapters 3, 4, and 5 can be covered in any order. For teaching a one-semester course from this book, I recommend assigning most of the material in Chapters 11 through 15 for independent reading and spend class time on Chapters 16 through 19 instead.

The one area where C++ falls short when compared to other languages is the lack of automatic memory management. I follow a pragmatic approach to keep students and programmers from chasing pointer bugs all semester. The use of pointers is minimized by using a string class and a dynamic array template. Copy construction and reference counts are later introduced as tools for building low-level classes, and we rely on memberwise copying and assignment for high-level classes. Pointers are used only when necessary: for structural sharing and for polymorphism. Using the preprocessor, we define self to be *this, thereby making the implicit argument of a class operation into a reference, as it should be, because no & is applied in the call. Smart pointer templates are covered but are considered too avant garde to be used as a general strategy.

Knowledge of the C language is not a prerequisite for using this book. Students with a firm grounding in Pascal or Modula-2 will find the C syntax strange and unpleasant but typically have no great difficulty adapting to it. Chapter 2 provides a crash course that should be accessible to programmers in any procedural language. I never use the more forbidding C features, such as *p++, goto, or union, and I also stay away from a good number of C++ features that I consider of marginal value (such as private inheritance or pointers to member functions).

C++ is a complex language, partially because of its heritage and partially because it aims to span a wide array of programming styles and idioms. In this book, I have made an effort to crystallize a relatively small subset that is most useful to object-oriented programming. I have purposefully ignored quite a few complexities. There are several good language references (such as [Stroustrup] or [Ellis & Stroustrup]) that lay down the exact rules, and the reader is encouraged to consult them when clarification is needed.

I use a very strict style of coding. No class will ever have public data, and the const attribute is rigorously applied. Pointers are never used when there is an alternative. Global functions are rare, and global variables even rarer. A naming convention makes it easy to identify constants, variables, and types. Of course, such coding and style preferences are the subject of intense debate, and I do not expect every programmer to agree with my choices. The appendix contains a formal description of the guidelines. Instructors and programmers should feel free to modify them according to personal or local taste.

The exercises are placed throughout the text, not at the end of each chapter. While admittedly inconvenient for the instructor, it is a benefit to the reader. Some exercises are designed to make the reader think about the concepts introduced at a given point. Others show what can be accomplished with the newly introduced technique. Of course, one can choose to skip right over the exercises.

My thanks go to my students at San José State University, for suffering through courses based on various unfinished versions of this book; to my editors, Steve Elliot and Sean Culhane of John Wiley & Sons, for their encouragement and support for this project; to the reviewers, Ron McCarty of Pennsylvania State University at Erie and Gary L. Craig of Syracuse University, for their welcome and helpful suggestions; to an anonymous reviewer, for the savage criticism that was very unwelcome but equally helpful; to Charles Miller, for his tireless work on the source code; and to Jerome Colburn of Publication Services, for the excellent copyediting.

Cay S. Horstmann

CONTENTS

OBJECTS AND CLASSES

In this chapter we define the central entities of this book, namely objects and classes. We discuss the main relationships between classes. We present rules for discovering classes, operations of classes, and relationships between classes. Finally, we contrast object-oriented design with traditional design methods.

1.1. WHAT ARE OBJECTS AND CLASSES?

1.1.1. What Are Objects?

The central notion of object-oriented programming is, not surprisingly, the *object*. From the object-oriented point of view, a program is populated by objects, which communicate with each other to solve a programming task cooperatively. By delegating specific and narrow responsibilities to each object, the programmer can break down the programming problem into chunks and thus manage its complexity more easily.

Because of their generality, objects are necessarily hard to define. Consider the example of an electronic mail system. One may find a number of distinct entities, such as mailboxes, messages, passwords, and menus. What makes them *objects*?

Objects are commonly characterized by the following three properties:

- State
- Operations
- Identity

Let us examine these characteristic properties.

An object can store information that is the result of prior operations. That information may determine how the object carries out operations in the future. The collection of all information held by an object is the object's *state*. An object's state may change over time, but not spontaneously. State change must be the consequence of operations performed on the object.

1

Consider the mail system example. A mailbox may be in an empty state (as immediately after its creation), or full (as after receiving a large number of mail messages). This state affects the behavior of the mailbox object: A full mailbox may reject new mail messages, whereas an empty mailbox may give a special response when asked to list all new messages.

Objects permit certain *operations* and do not support others. For example, a mailbox can add a mail message to its collection or list its stored messages, but there are other tasks that it cannot carry out, for example, "translate this mail message into Lithuanian" or "solve this system of linear equations".

Object-oriented programs contain *statements*, in which objects are asked to carry out certain operations. Since not all operations are suitable for all objects, there must be a mechanism for rejecting improper requests. Object-oriented programming systems differ in this regard. Some systems attempt to weed out unsupported operations at compile time, while others generate run-time errors. In either case, the collection of admissible operations is an important attribute of an object.

The momentary state and the collection of admissible operations do not fully characterize an object, however. It is possible for two or more objects to support the same operations and to have the same state, yet to be different from each other. Each object has its own *identity*. For example, two different mailboxes may, by chance, have the exact same contents, yet the execution environment can tell them apart, and as the result of further operations their states may again differ.

Some researchers define objects as entities that have state, behavior, and identity. This definition is somewhat unsatisfactory—what, after all, is an "entity"? The definition is also quite broad. As has been pointed out by one computer scientist, it then follows that a cat is an object: It has a rich internal state (hungry, purring, sleeping); it reacts to certain operations (eat, catch a mouse) while not supporting others (solve this system of linear equations); and it has an identity that differentiates it from its twin brother. Of course, in computer programming we consider objects that have an existence in the computation system and that are, by necessity, models of real or abstract entities. While we would not consider the physical cat as an object, a software product (perhaps the software controlling a vacuum cleaning robot) may well contain objects that simulate certain relevant aspects of real cats. We do not attempt to give a rigorous definition of an object and instead rely on intuition and experience in recognizing them. It should be pointed out that the narrower question— "What is an object in programming language X?"—can be answered with precision. We will see in Chapter 3 what objects are in the context of C++.

Exercise 1.1.1. An object familiar to many programmers is the standard input file stdin. Discuss states, some typical operations, and the identity of this object.

Exercise 1.1.2. Is the number 5 an object? Discuss whether it has states, operations, and identity.

Exercise 1.1.3. Consider a traffic simulation project. There are some obvious objects: cars and traffic signals. Traffic signals are easy; discuss states and operations. Assume that the state of a car includes its position, velocity, and acceleration. What operations can you find that are relevant to the problem domain? (As in all computer programs, one models only those properties that are of interest to the task at hand. Real cars have colors and may need an oil change, but we ignore that for the purpose of traffic simulation.)

1.1.2. What Are Classes?

A *class* describes a collection of related objects. Although there are exceptions, most object-oriented programming systems support the grouping of similar objects into classes. Objects of the same class support the same collection of operations and have a common set of possible states. A class description must therefore list

- The operations that are allowed on the objects of the class
- The possible states for objects of the class

Consider, for example, a class MailBox that describes those aspects that are common to all mailboxes. All mailboxes support the same operations (add a mail message, list all stored messages, delete a message, and so forth). The state of an individual mailbox is not arbitrary but fulfills certain constraints. The set of all legal states is a property of the MailBox class.

Objects that conform to a class description are called *instances* of that class. For example, my mailbox in the departmental mail system is an instance of the MailBox class. The message that the department chair sent me yesterday is an instance of class Message. Each object is constrained by the properties of its class. It supports only those operations that the class lists as admissible, and its legal states must stay within the range that the class permits.

Exercise 1.1.4. What do the following objects have in common: stdin, stdout, config.sys, win.ini? (Unix users: Use /etc/passwd and .mailrc instead of the last two objects.) Find at least two classes to which they might belong.

Exercise 1.1.5. Consider a word processor. Find at least five classes of objects that the word processor manipulates.

Exercise 1.1.6. Consider the class Printer that abstracts a typical dot-matrix or laser printer with text and graphics capabilities. What operations might this class support? List at least five.

1.1.3. Inheritance

A very important aspect of object-oriented design is to exploit similarities between classes. It often happens that one class is a specialized version of another class, with most operations identical or similar, but a few differences.

For example, consider a system administrator in an electronic mail system. Administrators receive messages and manage their message collections in the same way as all other users do. In addition, administrators have special privileges, namely, being able to create new accounts. The set of all administrators is a subset of the set of all users.

Some voice mail systems support special broadcast messages that are sent by a privileged user, such as the university president, to all users. In most regards, these messages are identical to regular messages. They can be stored in mailboxes and played. However, they cannot be deleted until they are listened to at least once. (The voice mail system at the author's university actually has such a feature.) The set of all privileged messages is a subset of the set of all messages.

Object-oriented programming languages support a direct modeling of this subset relationship, called *inheritance*. A class, called the *subclass* or *derived class*, inherits from a class, the so-called *superclass* (or *parent* or *base class*), if its objects form a subset of the base class objects. The objects in the subclass must support all operations that are supported by the superclass, but they may carry out these operations in a special way. They may also support additional operations.

A subclass object must be legally usable in all situations in which a superclass object is expected. For example, a privileged message object can be played, just as any other message. But a greeting in a voice mail system, even though it is in many respects similar to a message, is not usable in the same contexts as messages are—users cannot forward their greeting to another user. We conclude that `PrivilegedMessage` may inherit from `Message` but that `Greeting` may not.

Exercise 1.1.7. Consider checking and savings accounts in a bank. Do they differ in any way? Should one model them as separate classes, or as instances of the same class? If you agree with the former, what common operations could be shared by a common base class `Account`? Which of these operations are carried out differently by `CheckingAccount` and `SavingsAccount`?

1.2. FROM PROBLEM TO CODE

This book discusses the design and implementation of computer programs from the object-oriented point of view. We focus on small and medium-sized problems. Although much of what we say remains valid for very large projects, there are added complexities that we do not address.

Programming tasks originate from the desire to solve a particular problem. The task at hand may be simple, such as solving the eight-queens problem (see [Wirth], p. 143 or [Budd], p. 75, for a statement and solution), or complicated, such as writing a word processor. The end product is a working program. Toward this end, it is traditional to break up the development process into three phases:

- Analysis
- Design
- Implementation

This section briefly discusses the goals and methods of these phases. Of course, it is simplistic to assume that development is a simple linear progression through these three phases, as is suggested by the so-called waterfall model (see [Ghezzi], p. 360). Successful software products evolve over time. Implementation experiences may suggest an improved design. New requirements are added, forcing another iteration through analysis and design. Experience seems to suggest that object-oriented design leads to software that withstands the evolution phase better than software developed with traditional procedural design does, because the objects that underlie a problem domain tend to be more fundamental and stable than the procedural requirements.

1.2.1. The Analysis Phase

In the analysis phase, a usually vague problem understanding is transformed into a precise description of the tasks to be solved. The result of the analysis phase is a detailed textual description that is

- A complete definition of the tasks to be solved
- Free from internal contradictions
- Readable both by experts in the problem domain and by software developers
- Reviewable by diverse interested parties
- Testable against reality

Consider for example the task of writing a word processing program. The analysis phase must define terms, such as fonts, footnotes, multiple columns, and document sections, and the interaction of those features, such as how footnotes in multiple-column text ought to look on the screen and the printed page. The user interface must be documented, explaining, for example, how the user is to enter and move a footnote or specify the font for footnote numbers. One can think of an analysis document as a combination of a user manual and a reference manual, both very precisely worded to remove as much ambiguity as possible.

The analysis phase concerns itself with the description of what needs to be done, not how it should be done. The selection of specific algorithms, such as those that insert page breaks or sort the index, will be handled in the implementation phase. It should be pointed out that, especially for larger projects, a textual description of the analysis results may not be adequate. Formal methods for structured and object-oriented analysis (for example, [Coad]) exist to direct the analysis phase. However, these methods are beyond the scope of this book.

Exercise 1.2.1. Write an analysis of the *n*-queens problem. Define all terms and state what indicates a solution. Indicate what user interface you expect a program to have. How is *n* specified? How do you expect the output to be formatted? How are multiple solutions presented? What should happen if no solutions exist? Do not discuss any algorithms to attack the problem.

Exercise 1.2.2. Write an analysis document for a program that is to simulate a bank teller machine. Be as specific as you can be about the capabilities that you intend to have implemented and how you want the user interface to look. Assume that you write a contract. You must accept any program that conforms to your specifications, and hand over the agreed-on fee.

Exercise 1.2.3. Read the document that a friend prepared for the preceding exercise. Find at least one loophole in the document: some capability on which an implementor can cut corners without contradicting the given requirements, but whose functionality is less than what would reasonably be expected.

Exercise 1.2.4. Analysis documents of real programs are very long and detailed, and one cannot expect a student to replicate such a task in a week. In this exercise, you will perform an analysis subtask. Consider the formatting of footnotes in a word processor. Starting from the fuzzy idea that footnotes are that text on the bottom of some pages, progress to a precise description. Address the following:

- Footnote numbers (fonts, position, special symbols [*,†])
- Separator lines
- Splitting footnotes over two (or more) pages
- Footnotes inside footnotes, headers, footers, and tables
- Footnotes in multicolumn text

1.2.2. The Design Phase

The program designer must structure the programming tasks into classes and class clusters. Each class must be specified precisely, listing both its operations and its relationship to other classes in the system. We will cover this process in this book in some detail.

The designer must strive for a result in which the classes are crisply defined and class relationships are of manageable complexity. The exact choice of data structures, for example, hash tables or binary search trees for a collection, is not of concern in the design phase but is deferred until implementation. Even the choice of programming language is not a design issue. It is possible to map an object-oriented design to a programming language without object-oriented features, albeit with some degree of unpleasantness.

The result of the design phase is typically a collection of descriptions of each class and each class operation and diagrams showing the relationships between the classes. Depending on the tool support, this description may be stored on paper, in text files, or in a CASE (computer-assisted software engineering) tool database.

Exercise 1.2.5. Perform a design for the n-queens problem. First find classes. Queen comes to mind. There must be some way for the queens to communicate, or there must be an object that can see all queens at once. In the latter case, you need another class for that object. This is an interesting question of responsibility. Come up with class operations. Try to give the queens as much responsibility as you can to solve the problem. The end product of the exercise is a short description for each class that defines the class purpose, all operations with descriptions, and the class state.

Exercise 1.2.6. Perform a design for a program that simulates a bank teller machine. For simplicity, assume that each user has one checking and one savings account, that there is no access card, that users enter their account numbers and passcodes using the keyboard, and that the machine can only dispense cash, transfer money between accounts, and give account balance information.

1.2.3. The Implementation Phase

In the implementation phase the classes and class operations are coded, tested, and integrated. Much of this book concerns itself with the problems of translating an object-oriented design into C++.

Traditional programming methods rely on completion and unit testing of procedural units, followed by an integration phase. This integration tends to be frustrating and disappointing. Few programs are born according to plan out of a successful "big bang" integration. Object-oriented development encourages the gradual growth of a program by successively attaching more working class clusters and repeated testing.

It is quite common to defer the implementation of some operations and build a rapid prototype that displays some functionality of the final product. Such a prototype can be extremely helpful to influence the design or even the problem analysis, especially in cases where a problem was so incompletely understood that seeing a prototype do some work gives more insights into the solutions that are really desired.

One should not rush the analysis and design phase just to get to a working prototype quickly, nor should one hesitate to reopen the previous phases if a prototype yields new insight.

Object-oriented design is particularly suited for prototyping. The objects supporting the prototype are likely to be the same that need to be present in the final product, and it can be quite feasible to grow the prototype into a complete program. Some researchers welcome this; others caution against it, because prototypes are often rushed and nobody may take the time to work them over carefully. In fact, it is not uncommon to implement a prototype in a language such as Smalltalk and then write the final product in C++. It is our experience that for small to medium-sized products, a prototype can well expand into a complete product, provided the transition phase is accompanied by frequent "walk-throughs" and enough time is allocated to fix mistakes and implement newly discovered superior solutions.

Exercise 1.2.7. Build a prototype of the bank teller machine simulation. A prototype should not skip over essential functionality. For example, it would be a poor idea to implement a program that can handle only a single user.

Allow the system to handle ten users with simple account numbers, but ignore the passcode and cash dispensing for now. (Use any programming language, such as Pascal or C, to build the prototype. Model classes as records or structures.)

Exercise 1.2.8. Grow the prototype into a product. Add the missing functionality and make the user interface appealing.

Exercise 1.2.9. Bank teller machines take deposits. Revisit your analysis, design, and implementation to handle deposits of single checks.

Exercise 1.2.10. Implement the *n*-queens problem. First make a prototype to test that you get the right solutions; then format the output to look good. Or, if you prefer, do it the other way around—have your prototype produce snazzy output, then get the solutions right. The latter approach can be recommended only if you are certain that you can solve the problem in the time allotted. Most users prefer a program that does the job with ugly output over a glamorous shell that does nothing.

1.3. OBJECT-ORIENTED DESIGN

1.3.1. Classes and Operations

The goal of object-oriented design is to decompose a programming task into data types or classes and to define the functionality of these classes. Consider, for example, a mailbox. A message system contains a number of mailboxes, each of which may contain a different collection of messages. But all mailbox objects share a common functionality: They belong to the same data type or class.

What can one do with a mailbox object? A number of operations come to mind:

- Add a new message to it.
- Play its current message.
- Delete its current message.

The operations suggest that each mailbox object carries some state information, namely a notion of the "current" message that is distinguished from the other messages held in the mailbox.

Once one object is established, others become apparent. We referred to messages in the description of the mailbox, suggesting that a Message class might be useful. Messages clearly support one operation:

- Play it.

It is not clear at this point whether the Message class supports other operations. This question needs to be settled in the design phase.

1.3.2. The Object-Oriented Design Process

Clearly, a structured approach to find classes and their features will be helpful. We follow [Booch], who identifies the following goals within the design phase:

- Identify the classes.
- Identify the functionality of these classes.
- Identify the relationships between these classes.

These are goals, not steps. It is usually not possible to find all classes first, then give a complete description of their functionality, then elaborate on their relationships. The discovery process is iterative—the identification of one aspect of a class may force changes or lead to the discovery of others.

Recall that a class is simply a data type. It corresponds to the notion of an "abstract data type" in computer science (see for example [Louden], p. 250). It is typically implemented as a record or structured type in a programming language. Operations correspond to functions and procedures that operate on these types.

The end result of the design process is a list of class descriptions and an overview of the class relationships. For each class we explain its purpose, list its operations, and describe how it is composed of other classes. These class descriptions can be recorded on paper, in a text file, or in a special database tool. The class relationships are customarily expressed in a graphical notation. See Chapter 5 for examples of class descriptions and class relationship diagrams.

The information gathered in this phase becomes the foundation for the implementation of the system in an actual programming language. Typically, the design phase is more time-consuming than the the actual programming, or—to put a positive spin on it—a good design greatly reduces the time required for implementation and testing.

1.3.3. Finding Classes

A simple rule of thumb for identifying classes is to look for nouns in the problem analysis. Here are some candidates:

- `Mailbox`
- `Message`
- `User`
- `Passcode`
- `Extension`
- `Administrator`
- `MailSystem`
- `Menu`

Many, but not necessarily all of them, are good choices for classes. Other classes will become necessary, even though they are not explicit in the problem description. For example, consider the storage of messages in a mailbox.

Messages are inserted and retrieved in a FIFO (first in, first out) fashion. A `MessageQueue` class can store the messages and support the FIFO retrieval. (However, the exact implementation of the queue, as a linked list or a circular array, is of no interest in the design phase.)

Exercise 1.3.1. Consider a word processor. It processes documents, which are made up of sections. Each section has headers and footers, paragraphs, figures, tables, and footnotes. When printed, the document is sequenced into pages. Find at least fifteen classes that have to do directly with the problem domain. Find another five classes that describe the user interface of a word processor with which you are familiar.

1.3.4. Finding Operations

Just as classes correspond to nouns in the problem description, operations correspond to verbs. Messages are *recorded*, *played*, and *deleted*; users *connect* to a mailbox; the administrator *adds* a mailbox. A central role of object-oriented design is to group each operation with *one* class. Each operation must have exactly one class that is responsible for carrying it out.

For some classes finding operations is quite easy, because we are familiar with the territory. For example, any textbook on data structures will tell us the operations of the `MessageQueue` class:

- Initialize to an empty queue.
- Add a message to the tail of the queue.
- Remove a message from the head of the queue.
- Return the message from the head without removing it.
- Test whether the queue is empty.

With other classes, finding the right operations is more difficult. Consider, for example, the `Message` class. We found one operation:

- Play it.

Playing a message (listing the message text on the screen) is an obvious operation. But what other operations should be defined? Here is a bad idea:

- Add it to a mailbox. (no)

What is wrong with the operation? Let us think through how a message could perform it. To add itself to a mailbox, the message would have to know to what mailbox it should be added. That is not a problem; operations can have arguments, and the add operation may receive a mailbox object as an argument. The message could indeed add itself to a mailbox if it knew the internal structure of the mailbox. If the mailbox contained an array of messages and an integer index denoting the last received message, the add operation could copy the message text into the array and update the index. If the mailbox contained a linked list of messages, a different manipulation would be required. Therefore, this approach is not recommended. We will always assume that an object has no insight into the internal structure of another object. All activities on objects other than itself must be achieved by performing an operation, not by direct manipulation of internal data.

In our situation the responsibility of adding a message to a mailbox lies with the mailbox, not with the message. It is the mailbox that has sufficient understanding of its structure to perform the operation. When discovering operations, it is quite common to make wrong guesses and assign the responsibility to an inappropriate class. For that reason, it is helpful to have more than one person involved in the design phase. If one person assigns an operation to a particular class, another can ask the hard question, "How can an object of this class possibly carry out this operation?" The question is hard because we are not yet supposed to get to the nitty-gritty of implementation details. But it is appropriate to consider a "reasonable" implementation, or, better, two different possibilities, and make it plausible that the operation can be carried out. Following this process makes us realize that "add a message to a mailbox" is an operation of the `Mailbox` class.

Exercise 1.3.2. Consider an `Account` class in an automated bank teller program. Describe all operations that should be supported. Should there be a "transfer to account" operation? If not, what other class might take on the responsibility of managing transfers?

Exercise 1.3.3. Consider page layout in a word processor. Is a `Page` object responsible for fitting `Paragraph` and `Figure` objects inside? Or should `Paragraph` and `Figure` objects support operations "add myself to a page"? What knowledge about internal structure is required in either situation?

1.3.5. Finding Class Relationships

Three relationships are common between classes:

- *Use* or awareness
- *Aggregation* or containment
- *Inheritance* or specialization

The *use* relationship is the most general one. For instance, class A uses class B under any of the following circumstances:

- An operation of A receives or returns an object of class B.
- In the process of an operation of A, an object of class B must be inspected or created.
- Objects of A contain objects of class B or references (pointers) to objects of class B.

It is almost easier to understand when A *doesn't* use B. If A can carry out all of its tasks without being aware that the class B even exists, then A does not use B. For example, the `Message` class does not need to use the `Mailbox` class at all.

Messages need not be aware that they are stored inside mailboxes. However, the Mailbox class uses the Message class. Mailbox operations receive and return messages, and mailboxes store messages.

One important design goal is to minimize the number of use relationships; that is, to minimize the coupling between classes (see [Ghezzi], p. 50). If class A is unaware of the existence of class B, it is also unconcerned about any changes in B. A low degree of coupling not only reduces the possibility of errors in the implementation but, more importantly, eases future modifications.

The *aggregation* relationship is very concrete. If objects of class A contain objects of class B or references to objects of class B, then A uses B for aggregation. (References could be actual pointers to B objects in memory or other mechanisms, such as keys, indexes, or handles, that lead to B objects.) For example, Mailbox objects contain Message objects. Aggregation is often informally described as the "has-a" relationship. If A objects contain B objects, it is useful to ask how many. There may be a 1 : 1 or 1 : n relationship. For example, each mailbox has exactly one passcode (1 : 1), but each mailbox may contain many messages (1 : n).

Aggregation is a special case of usage. Of course, if A objects contain B objects, then the class A is acutely aware of the existence of the class B. When classes are implemented as records or structures of a programming language, containment maps easily into the layout of the structured type: The structure A contains one or more fields of type B (or pointer to B).

Inheritance, or specialization, is a less familiar relationship, because traditional programming languages do not permit a direct way of expressing it. Class A inherits from class B if all objects of class A are also objects of class B. In particular, all B operations must be valid for A objects, although the implementation of these operations may differ. We say these operations are inherited from B. However, the A objects support additional operations or enhance the inherited operations in some way. We will learn later how the "correct" operations for a specific object are selected.

Inheritance is often called the "is-a" relationship. This intuitive notion makes it easy to distinguish inheritance from aggregation. For example, a system administrator is a user (inheritance) and has a password (aggregation).

As we will see, exploiting inheritance relationships can lead to very powerful and extensible designs. However, it must be pointed out that inheritance is much less common than the use and containment relationships. Many designs can best be modeled by employing inheritance in a few selected places only.

Exercise 1.3.4. Consider all classes that were discovered in the automated teller example in the preceding exercises. Find all the relationships between them. You may just list them, or draw a diagram as described in Chapter 5.

Exercise 1.3.5. Perform the task of the preceding exercise with the classes discovered in the mail messaging example.

Exercise 1.3.6. Perform the task of the preceding exercise with the classes discovered in the word processing example.

1.4. CONTRAST WITH TRADITIONAL DESIGN TECHNIQUES

1.4.1. Procedural Decomposition

One of the first problem-solving skills acquired in an introductory computer science course is the identification, combination, and decomposition of tasks. Tasks are modeled as procedures or functions in a programming language. There are two fundamental ways of finding solutions to complex tasks. One can first write procedures to solve simple tasks and compose them into more sophisticated procedures until the desired functionality is implemented. This is the bottom-up approach. Or one can decompose the task to be performed into subtasks, and recursively decompose those subtasks, until the subtasks are simple enough to be implemented directly. This is the top-down approach. Of course, we usually use a mixture of the top-down and bottom-up strategies to solve a programming problem.

A rule of thumb for discovering procedures is to look for verbs or actions in the problem description. In this regard, procedures are quite similar to the operations we discussed previously. However, operations have an important difference: Each operation is associated with a class, which is responsible for carrying out the operation. The operation is invoked by an object of that class.

For small problems the decomposition into procedures works very well, but for larger problems, classes and operations have two advantages. The classes provide a convenient clustering mechanism. A simple word processor may require 2000 functions for its implementation, or it may require 100 classes with an average of 20 operations per class. The latter structure is much easier for a programmer to grasp. Classes also hide their data representations from all code except their own operations. If a program bug messes up a data item, it is easier to search for the culprit among the 20 operations that had access to that data item than among 2000 procedures.

In this sense, classes are more powerful than procedures. You can always transform a procedural program into an object-oriented program: Make a single class called `Application` whose state is all global data, and make each procedure into an operation of `Application`. Naturally, this is rarely a good idea. It just shows that object-oriented programs are at least as powerful as procedural programs.

In summary, procedural decomposition has two drawbacks. Procedures are small, and a great many of them are needed to solve a nontrivial task. Furthermore, procedures do not regulate the access to data fields. In contrast, classes are larger entities, and their data is protected from modification by other procedures.

Exercise 1.4.1. Break down the automatic teller simulation into a set of functions and procedures, each of which is no longer than 30 lines when implemented in Pascal or C. What global data structures do these procedures operate on?

Exercise 1.4.2. The traditional approach to the n-queens problem ([Wirth], p. 143) involves a procedure that recursively places queens on the board and checks whether the resulting configuration is legal. The object-oriented approach outlined in [Budd], Chapter 5, gives the queens more responsibility. They check for themselves whether or not they fit. Discuss the changes one would need to make to either program if the problem were modified by placing knights on the board or by changing the shape of the board.

1.4.2. Module Decomposition

A second course in computer science typically introduces the concept of *modularization*. Programming tasks are broken up into modules, which communicate with each other through procedure calls only, not by sharing data. There are two advantages. Users of the module need not understand how the module achieves its tasks, and users cannot accidentally damage the data local to the module.

The traditional definition of a module has, however, one great limitation. Consider a typical module implementing a queue. There is a private circular array, with an index into the head and the tail. Functions such as `add`, `remove`, `isfull`, or `isempty` are exported and can be called by other modules. Look in [Horowitz], p. 71, for a typical example.

The limitation is this: There is only one queue. A program that requires two queues cannot simply link in the module twice. (You may think that few programs ever need more than one queue, but consider the mail message program. Each mailbox has a separate message queue. In fact, each mailbox has two queues: one for the unread messages and one for the saved messages.)

Classes do not have this limitation. Once a class has been defined, any number of objects can be constructed. Classes can be thought of as factories for objects, each of which acts like a module. In this sense, classes are more powerful than modules. You can always translate a traditional module into a class, translate its functions into operations of that class, construct a single object, and export it to the client code.

Exercise 1.4.3. Look into the stack implementation of your introductory data structures book. Does the push function take one argument (the quantity to be pushed) or two arguments (a stack record and the quantity)? The former makes the stack into a module, the latter into an object.

Exercise 1.4.4. Most DOS C compilers define a collection of graphics calls to draw lines, circles, text, and so forth on the PC screen. On Unix machines, the Xlib library does the same. The collection of these graphics calls forms a module. The module manages private state variables, such as the current color or font. Look at your graphics library and identify the maintained graphics state. Is there only one copy of all this information, or can you have more than one graphics state? Would you want more than one?

1.4.3. Opaque Types

An *opaque type* is a data type whose nature is hidden from the user, together with a collection of functions. Opaque types are usually represented as handles or pointers to structures with unknown layout. A creation function returns a new handle, and other functions take that handle as an argument. Of course, the implementation of these functions is hidden inside a module.

The typical example is the file interface in C. To open a file, the programmer calls fopen and receives a "magic cookie" value that must be passed to subsequent calls to fscanf, fgetc, or fread. The value is of type FILE* (pointer to a structure of type FILE), but most mortals have no idea what is inside the FILE record.

An opaque type is very similar to a class. Any number of instances can be provided simultaneously. The functions that know what to do with an argument of the opaque type correspond to operations of a class. If you always organize your program into a collection of modules, each of which is responsible for managing one opaque type, you have practiced object-oriented programming, perhaps without knowing it. Well, almost. There is one feature of object-oriented programming that is quite difficult to imitate in a traditional programming language, namely inheritance.

Exercise 1.4.5. Consider the standard C library. Besides FILE*, can you find other opaque types? (Hint: char* is not an opaque type for strings, since you can read and modify strings directly through the pointer without going through functions. In fact, there is no library function for reading or writing an individual character in a string.)

Exercise 1.4.6. Explain why malloc/realloc/free form the public interface of a module, not an opaque type, in C. (Hint: Could you have two allocators? Would you ever want two?)

1.5. DESIGN HINTS

1.5.1. Classes Model Sets of Objects

The keyword here is *set*. You should not use a class to describe a single object. This sounds simple, but even experienced designers sometimes have trouble with it.

Here is an example from [Wiener and Pinson], p. 176, slightly modified for a more natural string set. A finite-state machine reads an input string to test whether it satisfies a certain property. As characters are read, the machine state changes according to the transition rules of the machine. A transition rule has the form: "If the current state is s, and the current input character is c, move to state t." Some states are marked as accepting states. If the machine ends up in an accepting state when all input characters are read, the input string is accepted. Figure 1.1 shows a finite-state machine to test whether a string is a legal C floating-point number. For example, +.5E-3 is accepted, but -3E+.5 is not. State 1 is the start state. Final states are bold.

Pinson and Wiener discover a class State and an operation transition, which reads the next input character and returns the next state. They then

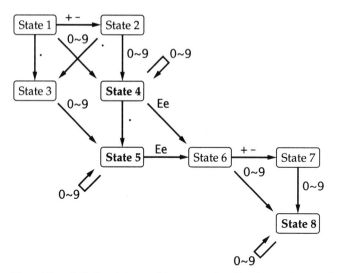

Figure 1.1.   A finite-state machine accepting floating-point numbers.

derive eight classes, State1...State8, from State. Each implements its own transition operation. For example, the transition operation of State1 returns an object of class State4 when it reads a character 0...9.

There is no question that State is a legitimate class to describe the set of states in finite-state machines. The class State1, however, is problematic. What objects does it describe? Only one: the first state of the particular finite-state machine depicted in Figure 1.1. It is generally not useful to write a class to describe a behavior of a single object. Classes should collect objects with similar behavior.

Of course, it is easy to come up with a better design for finite-state machines. Let us assume that an object of class State carries with it a table of the correspondence between input characters and successor states. The transition operation simply performs a lookup in this table. One additional operation is required: namely, to set the entries in the table.

Now we have designed a much more useful abstraction. This State class can be used for any finite-state machine, not just a particular one.

1.5.2. Classes Need Meaningful Operations

Classes should be large enough to describe a significant set of objects, but they should not be too large, either. It is tempting to design classes of glorious generality, but that is not usually helpful.

Consider the mailbox example. How does a message get into a mailbox? The boring answer is that class Mailbox has an operation append, which takes an object of type Message as an argument. Here is a much more exciting alternative. Suppose that Mailbox is derived from a class Component, that components are connected to one another with objects from a class Connection, that connections can carry objects of type Data, and that the class Message is inherited from class Data.

This architecture was seriously proposed by a senior designer on a voice mail project. And after all, why not? Perhaps the system would need to carry fax and computer data in addition to voice. And how about color graphics and full-motion video? Integration with other equipment, such as photocopy machines and mail-sorting equipment, is also covered by the design.

The problem with the design became apparent when it turned out to be very difficult to be specific about the *operations* of the discovered classes. It was not at all clear what operations made sense for Component or Data.

If the task at hand is very broad, to develop a general system for transporting arbitrary information to devices ranging from supercomputers to toaster ovens, the design may well be appropriate. If the problem to be solved is simply the linkage of existing telephones with a message delivery system, then the generality is completely inappropriate and of little help in developing the software.

A CRASH COURSE INTO BASIC C++

This chapter contains a very rapid introduction of basic C++ language features. We assume that the reader is already familiar with a procedural language such as Pascal, C, Ada, or Modula-2. This chapter is not intended to be a complete discussion of all language constructs. We restrict ourselves to a small subset of those features that are indispensable for writing programs. Our emphasis is on simplicity and safety, not speed. In particular, we greatly simplify the discussion by using an array template and string class. This allows us to bypass the inconvenient and error-prone built-in arrays and strings.

Look into the standard C and C++ reference books ([Kernighan and Ritchie], [Stroustrup]) for greater detail. The delightful book [Koenig] is particularly recommended for help with the pitfalls of C programming, and much of it applies to C++ as well.

This chapter covers the following topics:

- Numeric types
- Operators
- Arrays
- Strings
- Control structures
- Functions
- Input and output with the stream library

Since C++ is essentially a superset of C, most of this material will be familiar to the C programmer. The sections on function arguments, arrays, strings, and stream I/O contain new information.

2.1. HEADER FILES

Virtually every C++ program file needs to include one or more header files to inform the compiler about predefined constants, data types, and procedures. The `#include` preprocessor directive is used for this purpose.

```
#include <iostream.h>
#include <math.h>
#include "chisetup.h"
```

These directives cause the compiler to read in the standard header files iostream.h and math.h, as well as the local header file chisetup.h. Standard header files are delimited by `<...>` and located in the "standard places" for such header files. Local files are delimited by `"..."`, and the compiler first looks into the current directory before searching the standard places. Once a header file has been included, the features that it advertises can be used in a program.

We supply a header file, chisetup.h, that defines types and functions that are commonly used in this book.

Exercise 2.1.1. Find out what your compiler considers the "standard places" for header files. How can you add directories to the list of standard places? Would you add such directories *before* or *after* the existing ones?

Exercise 2.1.2. Once in a while it is necessary to look inside header files. Locate and read the standard header file math.h. Some of it is likely to be quite unreadable and technical—just ignore it. Find the declarations of the functions `sin` and pow.

2.2. COMMENTS

There are two styles of comments. Any text from `//` to the end of the current line

```
// like this
```

is ignored. This comment style is useful only if you are sure that the comment will never grow beyond one line. It is painful to modify //-style comments that extend over multiple lines. Use /*...*/ for multiline comments

```
/* like
     this
*/
```

Unfortunately, the /*...*/ comments do not nest. If you need to comment out a large block of code that itself contains comments, surround it with the #if...#endif preprocessor directives.

```
#if 0
code to be masked out
#endif
```

2.3. OUTPUT

Here is our first complete C++ program, which prints the message "Hello, World" on the screen. The code is contained inside a function main, the customary starting point in many programming environments.

```
#include <iostream.h>

int main()
{ cout << "Hello, World" << endl;
  // return 0 to indicate normal completion
  return 0;
}
```

The iostream.h header file must be included in all source code using stream input and output operations. This header file defines, among others, an object cout representing the standard output. Any data sent to cout is displayed on the terminal or sent to a file if standard output is redirected. Sending an output stream the special object endl (also defined in iostream.h) prints a newline character and flushes the stream buffer, causing the display of the buffered characters on the output device.

The << operator is used to send data to a stream. Integers, floating-point numbers, characters, and strings can be printed.

```
cout << "The value of pi is approx. ";
cout << 3.14159;
cout << endl;
```

Output operations to the same stream can be *chained*:

```
cout << "The value of pi is approx. " << 3.14159 << endl;
```

Data can be sent to a file instead of standard output.

```
#include <fstream.h>

ofstream os("output.dat");
os << "The value of pi is approx. " << 3.14159 << endl;
```

2.4. TYPES AND VARIABLES

C++ has the following numeric types.

Name	Description
int	Integers in a size most convenient for the processor (usually 2 or 4 bytes)
char	Integers to hold character values (usually 1 byte)
float	Single-precision floating-point numbers (usually 4 bytes, only 6 to 7 significant digits)
double	Double-precision floating-point numbers (usually 8 bytes, 13 significant digits)

Types can be modified with the short, long, and unsigned modifiers to yield types such as unsigned char and long int. The keyword int can be dropped if a modifier is present: long is the same as long int.

Exercise 2.4.1. Not all combinations of unsigned, long, and short with char, int, float, and double are legal. Consult a C or C++ reference to find all legal combinations.

New types can be constructed as enumerated types:

```
enum Color { BLACK, BLUE, GREEN, CYAN, RED, PURPLE, YELLOW,
   WHITE };
```

The typedef construct introduces a type synonym, a new name for an existing type. For example, the standard header file stddef.h defines size_t to be a type suitable to describe the size of memory blocks, typically

```
typedef unsigned int size_t;
```

More importantly, we will see in Chapter 3 how to define class types.

Variables are declared by listing the type, then the variable name and an optional initializer. Constants are prefixed by const.

```
unsigned int n = 1;
char ch = 'A';
String s = "Hello";
Color c = PURPLE;
Employee joe;
const double pi = 3.14159265358979323846;
```

Character constants are enclosed in single quotes. The constant '\n' denotes the newline character, which separates lines in a text file. String constants are enclosed in double quotes.

There is no true character type. char is simply a subrange of int, and characters are represented by their codes in some encoding scheme, usually ASCII. International users will find that eight-bit extended character codes greater than 127 are no end of trouble, because some implementations treat char as a signed quantity, others as an unsigned quantity. This makes a difference when char values are promoted to int.

At the time of this writing, C++ does not have a Boolean type. Instead, zero is considered false and any nonzero value (of integer, floating-point, or pointer type) is considered true in logical conditions. Throughout this book, we use the following explicit names:

```
typedef int Bool;
const int FALSE = 0;
const int TRUE = 1;
```

These are defined in chisetup.h. The committee that standardizes the design of C++ is contemplating the addition of a true Boolean type to the language. That change is expected to be largely transparent to C++ programmers.

2.5. OPERATORS

2.5.1. Arithmetic Operators

The usual arithmetic operators + - * / are used in C++. The / operator denotes integer division if both arguments are integers and floating-point division otherwise. Integer remainder is denoted by %. For example, 11 / 4 is 2, 11 % 4 is 3, and 11.0 / 4 is 2.75. There is no operator for raising a quantity to a power; use the pow function in math.h.

The increment and decrement operators ++ and -- add or subtract 1 to a variable. For example, the code

```
int n = 5;
n++;
```

changes n to 6. Because these operators change the value of a variable, they cannot be applied to constants. For example, 4++ is not legal. There are actually two forms of these operators, a prefix and a postfix form. Both have the same side effect of changing a variable by 1. Their difference becomes apparent only if they are used inside expressions. The prefix form evaluates to the new value after the increment or decrement operator, whereas the postfix form evaluates to the old value of the variable.

```
int m = 5;
int n = 5;
int a = 2 * ++m; // now a is 12, m is 6
int b = 2 * n++; // now b is 10, n is 6
```

We recommend against using ++ inside other expressions. Of course, it is the ++ operator that gives the C++ language its name. (Perhaps ++C would have been a more appropriate choice—after all, we want to use the language after it has been improved.)

2.5.2. Relational and Boolean Operators

Values can be compared with == (equality; note that this is *not* the same as =), != (inequality) and the usual <, >, <=, and >= operators.

C++ uses && ("and"), || ("or"), ! ("not") for the Boolean operators. The && and || operators are evaluated in "short-circuit" fashion: Once the truth value of an expression has been established, further subexpressions are left unevaluated. For example,

```
if (x != 0 && f(1 / x) > 0) // ...
```

does not evaluate 1 / x if x is zero.

There are bitwise operators & ("and"), | ("or"), ^ ("xor"), ~ ("not") that work on the bit patterns of their arguments. The >> and << operators shift a bit pattern to the right or left. These operators are intended for bit fiddling. They are occasionally useful for setting and clearing single-bit flags. The >> and << are also used for stream input and output.

Exercise 2.5.1. Write a Boolean expression that is true if and only if a year y is a leap year. Recall that years after 1582 that are divisible by 4 are leap years, except those that are divisible by 100; however, those divisible by 400 are again leap years.

2.5.3. Assignment

Assignment is denoted by a single =. Assignment has a value, namely the value that has been assigned. That means that assignment expressions can be nested inside other expressions. A typical example is

```
while ((y = f(x)) > 0)
{ // do something with y
   x++;
}
```

This is advantageous, since it avoids coding the function call twice:

```
y = f(x);
while (y > 0)
{ // do something with y
   x++;
   y = f(x);
}
```

Assignment associates right to left. In the expression

```
z = y = f(x);
```

the assignment y = f(x) is executed first, and its value (namely the new value of y) is assigned to z. In other words, both y and z are set to f(x).

Binary arithmetic operators can be combined with assignment. For example,

```
x += 4;
```

is equivalent to

```
x = x + 4;
```

2.6. ARRAYS

C++ uses the same array construct as the C language, and it is not particularly powerful or convenient. Fortunately, there is an alternative. It is possible to write so-called *templates* for "smart" arrays. Writing the code to implement templates is not easy; we will cover the details in Chapter 14. *Using* templates, however, is straightforward and requires no knowledge of the implementation details.

In this section we describe a template for *dynamic* arrays, which grow on demand as more elements are inserted. Many compiler and library vendors offer array templates of various capabilities. However, there is, at the time of this writing, no standard for C++ array templates. The code necessary to use the template described here is included in the companion disk to this book.

The declaration

```
Array<X> a;
```

specifies a "smart" array of any type X. The array is initially empty and must be grown to make space for elements. For example,

```
Array<double> a;
a.grow(1, 10);
```

declares an array of 10 floating-point numbers, a[1] ... a[10]. Accessing an element outside this range, such as a[11], yields a run-time error.

The curious ".grow" syntax is very common in C++, as we will see shortly. It is the syntax for applying an operation (grow) to an object (the array a).

Array bounds can be determined with the low and high operations.

```
for (int i = a.low(); i <= a.high(); i++)
   // do something with a[i]
```

The number of elements in an array is a.length().

Arrays of the same type can be copied with the = operator.

```
Array<double> b;
b = a;
```

Any existing elements in b are discarded, and all elements of a are copied into the corresponding slots in b.

Very occasionally, we will use the arrays that are built into C++. A built-in array a of n elements of type X is defined as

```
X a[n];
```

Here n is a compile-time constant. Built-in arrays always have a low bound of 0. The high bound is $n - 1$. They cannot be copied or resized. However, they are more efficient than array templates, and they are easier to initialize. For example,

```
int days_per_month[12] =
   { 31, 28, 31, 30, 31, 30, 31, 31, 30, 31, 30, 31 };
```

2.7. STRINGS

The basic C++ support for strings is weak, but it is possible to implement a string class that offers easy and safe string handling. Such a string class is likely to become a part of the standard C++ library at some point. The library accompanying this book has a simple string class that is likely to be very similar to the eventual standard. Its usage is described in this section.

Strings can be initialized with quoted strings or left uninitialized, in which case they are constructed as empty strings.

```
String s = "Hello";
String t;
```

Strings can be copied with the = operator. The + operator concatenates strings.

```
String u = s + ", World";
```

The relational operators == != < <= > >= represent lexicographic comparison.

```
if (s <= t) // ...
```

The [] operator provides access to individual characters in a string. The starting character of a string has index 0. (This is inconvenient, but it keeps compatibility with C strings.) The length operation returns the length of the string. The substr operation extracts a substring with given starting index and length.

```
String s = "Hello, World";
int n = s.length(); // n is 12.
char ch = s[0]; // the starting character 'H'
   // s[11] is 'd', and s[13] is illegal.
t = s.substr(0, 4); // substring s[0]...s[3], "Hell"
```

Sometimes string objects must be passed to library functions that require C-style character arrays. This happens commonly with file names. Apply the c_str operation to a string object whenever a C string is expected.

```
String filename = "input.dat";
ifstream is(filename.c_str());
```

2.8. BLOCKS

In C++, statement blocks are delimited by {... }.

When a variable is declared local to a block without an initializer, its value is random. Explicit initialization on declaration is therefore highly recommended. Fortunately, variables can be declared *anywhere* within a block, and it is usually possible to defer their declaration until the initializer value is computed. Consider this example.

```
double x1 = x0 - xc;
double y1 = y0 - yc;
// some computations
x1 = x1*x1 / a;
y1 = y1*y1 / b;
// now we are ready to compute r
double r = x1 + y1;
```

2.9. CONTROL FLOW

The conditional statement has the form

```
if (condition) block₁ else block₂
```

The else part is optional. An else groups with the closest if. That is,

if (C_1) B_1 else if (C_2) B_2 else B_3

is the same as

if (C_1) B_1 else { if (C_2) B_2 else B_3 }

There are two similar forms of repeating loops:

while *(condition)* *block*

and

do *block* while *(condition)* ;

These execute a block while a condition remains true. The do . . . while loop executes the block at least once. The while loop may never execute if the condition is false at the outset.

C++ has a very general construct to support iteration. Typical examples are

```
for (int i = 1; i <= 10; i++) a[i] = 0;
for (i = 0; i < 10; i += 2) a[i] = 2 * i;
```

Note that it is possible to define a variable in the first slot of the for statement. The scope of such a variable extends until the end of the block enclosing the for statement. A for loop

for *(statement₁; expression₂; expression₃) block;*

is completely equivalent to

statement₁;
while *(expression₂)*
{ *block;*
  expression₃;
}

It is an unwritten rule of good taste that the three slots of a for statement should only initialize, test, and update a variable. One can write very obscure loops by disregarding this rule. For example,

```
for (p = head; p != 0; p = p->next) // ...
```

is acceptable, but

```
for (i = a[0] = 0; i < 8; a[i] = 2 * i) i += 2; // DON'T
```

is not.

The multiple selection statement offered by C++ is somewhat cumbersome. Execution starts at the case label matching the value of the expression in the switch and continues until the next break or function return or the end of the switch. Here is an example that shows a number of typical situations:

```
switch (s[i])
{ case '0':
  case '1':
  case '2':
  case '3':
  case '4':
  case '5':
  case '6':
  case '7':
  case '8':
  case '9':
    v = 10 * v + s[i] - '0';
    i++;
    break;
  case '-':
    sign = -1;
    // FALL THROUGH
  case '+':
    i++;
    break;
  case '\0':
  case '\n':
  case ' ':
    return sign * v;
  default:
    verr = TRUE;
    break;
}
```

The default clause is optional. A range of constants can be specified only by listing all elements of the range explicitly. If the break or return at the end of a case is omitted, execution "falls through" past any case labels to the next statement group. This is a very common cause of programming errors. In the extremely rare situation in which this behavior is desired, it ought to be clearly commented.

2.10. FUNCTIONS

2.10.1. Function Definitions

A function definition lists the type of the returned value, the name of the function, and the types and names of its arguments, followed by the implementation code. Here is a typical example, a function that computes the binomial coefficient, which is

$$\binom{n}{k} = \frac{n!}{k!(n-k)!}$$

```
long int binom(int n, int k)
{ if (2 * k > n) k = n - k;
  if (k < 0) return 0;
  long r = 1;
  for (int i = 1; i <= k; i++)
  { r = r * n / i;
    n--;
  }
  return r;
}
```

When a function is called, local variables for all function arguments are allocated on the run-time stack and initialized with the values of the call expressions. In the example, local variables n and k are initialized with the call values and modified during execution of the function. This modification has no effect on the values supplied in the function call.

Function arguments can be of any type. In particular, class and array template arguments are permitted. These are copied field by field from the caller into the local argument variables. (Naturally, for large class objects and arrays, that copy can be inefficient. We will later learn how to minimize the associated cost.) For example, here is a function that computes the average of an array of floating-point numbers:

```
double average(Array<double> a)
{ double sum = 0;
  for (int i = a.low(); i <= a.high(); i++)
    sum += a[i];
  int n = a.length();
  if (n == 0) return 0;
  else return sum / n;
}
```

Functions with no arguments are declared and called with an empty argument list.

```
int rand() { /*...*/ }
x = rand();
```

In C++ there is no distinction between functions and procedures. Proce-dures are simply functions with the special return type void.

Exercise 2.10.1. Write a function

```
int median(Array<int> a);
```

that computes the median value of an array in $O(a.length())$ time. Do not sort or otherwise modify the array in the process, and do not make another copy of it. Hint: [Bentley 1988], ch. 15.

2.10.2. Reference Arguments

Consider the task of writing a function swap that is to swap two integers. The following code does not work:

```
void swap(int x, int y) // NO
{ int temp = x;
    x = y;
    y = temp;
}

int a = 1;
int b = 2;
swap(a, b);
// a is still 1, b is still 2
```

When the swap function is called, its argument variables x and y are initialized with the values 1 and 2, and their contents are interchanged. When the swap function terminates, the local variables x and y are abandoned. At no time are a and b affected.

A mechanism is required that communicates to the swap function the location, not merely the value, of the arguments. This is usually referred to as "call by reference" (see [Louden], pp. 213–220, for a discussion on parameter passing). In C++ an argument is passed by reference by declaring it as a reference type:

```
void swap(int& x, int& y)
{ int temp = x;
    x = y;
    y = temp;
}
```

```
int a = 1;
int b = 2;
swap(a, b);
// now a is 2, b is 1
```

Pascal programmers can consider reference arguments the equivalent of **var** parameters. C programmers should think of references as pointers with "syntactic sugar": when using a reference, the compiler provides a *, and when initializing a reference, the compiler automatically takes the address.

A function that changes an argument of array template or string type must use call by reference as well. Examples are

```
void sort(Array<double>& a);
void reverse(String& s);
```

Call by reference is the most common and straightforward application of reference types in C++, but a number of other important uses exist that will be discussed later. By the way, int& is usually pronounced as "int ref."

Exercise 2.10.2. Write the function void sort(Array<double>& a). Use quick-sort.

Exercise 2.10.3. Write the function void reverse(String& s).

2.10.3. Return Values

C++ functions can return a result of any type except built-in arrays. In particular, class objects and array templates can be returned as function values. Examples are

```
Employee find(Array<Employee> staff, String name);
Array<Employee> find_all(Array<Employee> staff, String regex);
```

The return statement causes an immediate exit from the function. The expression following the return keyword is the function result.

Return values are copied from the scope of the function to a temporary location in the scope of the caller. For large class objects or arrays, this copy can be somewhat expensive. We will discuss possible remedies later.

Functions need not return any value. In that case, the return type is void. Such functions are commonly referred to as procedures.

Exercise 2.10.4. Write a function String rev(String s) that returns a reversed string without modifying the original.

2.10.4. Function Declarations

Before a function can be called, the C+ + compiler must know its argument and return types. This is necessary because the compiler may need to generate code to effect type conversion. Moreover, it allows the compiler to generate error messages if the argument types of the function do not match the arguments used in the call.

For many short programs this requirement can be easily fulfilled by placing the code of any function before its first usage. This arrangement breaks down for mutually recursive calls and for calls to functions defined in another module.

For that reason, one can declare a function by supplying only its *prototype*. A function declaration or prototype is the first line of the function definition, listing the return type, name, and argument types. Argument names are optional but recommended for clarity. The function code is omitted. Examples are

```
int find(String s, char ch);
void sort(Array<double>&);
```

The *declaration* of a function is merely an advertisement of its existence somewhere, in the same module, another module, or a library. The actual code is supplied in the function *definition*. A function can be declared multiple times in a program but must have one and only one definition.

2.10.5. Name Overloading

In C++ the same name can be used for different functions as long as the function argument types are different. For example, find can name both a function to find a character in a string and a function to find an employee in an array. This phenomenon is called function *overloading*.

```
int find(String s, char ch);
Employee find(Array<Employee> staff, String name);
```

Of course, the code for each function is completely unrelated.

In any specific call to find,

```
r = find(a, x);
```

the compiler checks the types of the arguments and selects the correct function. In the example, if a is of type String and x of type char, the first function is called. If no matching function exists, an error is reported. The function return type is not used for matching.

If no exact match for an overloaded function can be found, some type conversions are attempted. This might result in a match or an ambiguous situation, which is reported as an error. The exact rules are somewhat arcane (see [Ellis and Stroustrup], ch. 13). It is best to stay away from situations that depend on the intricacies of these rules. If the compiler has a hard time figuring out which function to call, programmers will have an even harder time understanding and maintaining the code.

2.10.6. The `main` Function

In traditional command line environments, C++ program execution begins in the function called `main`. This function must process the command line arguments, call other functions as necessary, and eventually terminate the program. The prototype for `main` is

```
int main(int argc, char* argv[]);
```

This means that `main` receives two arguments: an integer `argc`, reporting the number of command line arguments, and an array of character pointers `argv`, one for each command line argument. In order to avoid C strings, we supply a convenient class `Args` to parse command line arguments. Initialize an `Args` object with `argc` and `argv`, then read the arguments with the `option` operations.

```
int main(int argc, char* argv[])
{ Args args(argc, argv);
  // ...
}
```

For example, if a program named `sort` is invoked on the command line as

```
sort -v -s10 input.dat
```

then `args.prog_name()` is the string `"sort"`, `args.bool_option('v',b)` sets b to TRUE, `args.int_option('s', n)` sets n to 10, and `args.arg(1)` is the string `"input.dat"`.

If you have no interest in processing command line arguments, you can declare `main` as

```
int main();
```

The `main` function returns a value that may be processed by the calling environment, usually the operating system shell. It is traditional to return 0 for success and a nonzero value to report an error condition.

Nontraditional operating environments may use a different function to start a program. For example, Windows programs start with `WinMain` and receive arguments that make sense only in a Windows program, such as handles to the current and previous instance of the program task.

Exercise 2.10.5. Write a program echo that does nothing but print out its command line arguments. For example, echo hello cruel >world will write the words "hello cruel" to the file world.

Exercise 2.10.6. Many programs use command line options that start with the "-" character. Modify the echo program from the previous assignment to write the command line arguments in reverse order if the -r option has been specified. Do not echo any options starting with "-". For example, echo hello world -r prints "world hello".

2.11. INPUT

The iostream.h header file defines an istream class and an object cin to read from standard input (either the keyboard or a redirected file). The >> operator is used for reading data.

```
double x;
String s;
cin >> s >> x;
```

In reading any object with the >> operator, any leading white space is skipped. To read a single character without skipping the preceding white space (that is, to read the white space itself, if present), use the get operation:

```
char ch = cin.get();
```

We supply a function to read an entire line into a string.

```
String s;
s.read_line(cin);
```

You can peek at the next character of an input stream without actually reading it. This is useful to make decisions on the upcoming input. For example:

```
double x;
String s;
char ch = cin.peek();
if (isdigit(ch) || ch == '+' || ch == '-')
  cin >> x;
else
  cin >> s;
```

Input operations can fail for two reasons. If the characters in the input do not match the data type, the stream state is set to "fail" *and all subsequent operations fail*. This happens most frequently in trying to read a number in when the stream does not contain a sequence of digits. There are techniques for detecting and resetting the stream state, but it is easiest not to get into this situation in the first place. You can read all input as strings and use the to_long or to_double function to convert them into numbers at your leisure. Or you can peek at the next character before you read.

More importantly, input fails at the end of the file. It is best to test that the stream is still in a good state after each input operation.

```
cin >> s;
if (cin.fail()) return FALSE;
```

If the stream has reached the end of file, or an operation has failed, all subsequent input operations will fail as well. When an input operation fails, it never changes the value of the item to be read.

Note that fail() is never a predictor of future success; it is just an indicator of past failure. You must first try to read and then check whether the input succeeded.

Here is a loop that reads in numbers from standard input and computes their average. The loop may terminate either at the end of file or at an input string that is not a number.

```
double t = 0;
int n = 0;
while (!cin.fail())
{ double x;
  cin >> x;
  if (!cin.fail()) { t += x; n++; }
}
if (n > 0) cout << "average: " << t / n << endl;
```

Instead of reading from standard input, you can read from any file.

```
#include <fstream.h>

ifstream is("input.dat");
is >> s >> x;
if (is.fail()) return FALSE;
```

C programmers may wonder why we are not using the scanf/printf functions for input and output. The stream library has two advantages over the stdio routines with which C programmers are familiar: It is type-safe, and it is extensible. There can be no mismatch between formatting instructions and data values, and the formatted input/output capabilities can be extended for any user-defined types. We will discuss this library in detail in Chapter 12. In this chapter we covered just the basics that suffice for simple programming tasks.

Exercise 2.11.1. Write a program that reads input of the form *number operator number operator* . . . where *number* is any floating-point number and *operator* is one of + - * / =. Whenever a = is encountered, print the current result. As with a cheap calculator, there is no operator precedence or parentheses. For example, 1 + 2*3 = 1*-2+3= prints 9 and 1. Quit upon end of file, and quit with an error message on illegal input.

Exercise 2.11.2. Write a program that reads a C++ program, whose file name is specified on the command line, and prints out to standard output all // and /*...*/ comments that are contained in it. Beware of quoted strings "...".

2.12. ASSERTIONS

The assert macro, defined in assert.h, tests a condition and generates a run-time error reporting the condition, the file, and the line number if it fails. Assertions are used to check against conditions that "cannot" happen and cause program failure if, due to a programming error, they do occur.

```
#include <assert.h>
#include <math.h>
// ...
y = f(x);
assert(y >= 0);
z = sqrt(y);
```

If you know that the function f is never supposed to compute negative numbers, you can easily protect against coding or data error with the assertion.

To turn assertions off, you need to define the NDEBUG preprocessor variable for compilation. On a command line compiler, this is typically done by using the compiler's -D switch and invoking the compiler as:

cc -DNDEBUG *sourcefile*

Integrated development environments have some other way to specify definitions. You can also simply place the line

```
#define NDEBUG
```

into the source code or a common header file.

Exercise 2.12.1. Write a small program in which you purposefully trigger an assertion failure to see how your system reports it.

Exercise 2.12.2. Write a program that runs a loop generating random numbers by calling rand. Test for an assertion that you know to be always true, namely that the return value is nonnegative. (The rand function returns integers in the range 0 . . . RAND_MAX.) Then compute and discard the square root. Time 100,000 iterations of the loop, first with assertions enabled and then with them disabled. If your system has a profiler, use it. Otherwise, print out the system time before and after the loop. What is the cost of performing the assertion check?

IMPLEMENTING CLASSES

This chapter presents the mechanics of implementing classes and operations in C++. We present the mechanics of the public and private interface, accessor and mutator operations, and construction. This is a language chapter. If you prefer to learn about the why before the how, read Section 3.1 and then Chapters 5 and 4 first before returning here. The chapters are written in such a way that their order can be reversed.

3.1. CLASSES IN C++

Three steps are necessary to implement a class in C++:

- Declare operations in the public section of the class definition.
- Define data fields in the private section of the class definition.
- Define the implementation of the operations following the class definition.

It sounds simple, and it actually is. (Well, actually C++ lets you make more complicated arrangements, but this one is by far the most useful.)

3.1.1. Declaring Operations

Here is a partial definition of a C++ class implementing a mailbox:

```
class Mailbox
{
public:
  void add(Message);
  Message get_current();
  void delete_current();
  // ...
};
```

The operations are declared public, because they can be applied to mailbox objects anywhere in a program.

In C++ objects are simply variables whose type is their class. An object of class `Mailbox` can be defined like this:

```
Mailbox mbox;
```

Here is some code that gets the current message from a mailbox and plays it:

```
Message msg;
msg = mbox.get_current();
msg.play();
```

Operations can have arguments; for example:

```
mbox.add(msg);
```

As you can see, an operation is applied to an object using the dot (.) notation:

object.operation(arguments);

We will soon see how to specify the implementation of the operations.

3.1.2. Declaring Fields to Represent Object State

In C++ the state of an object is described by the values of one or more *data fields*. For example, here is an (incomplete) description of objects representing calendar dates:

```
class Date
{
public:
   // ...
private:
   int _day;
   int _month;
   int _year;
};
```

The data fields are declared `private` to ensure that they can be accessed only by the operations of the `Date` class. They are hidden from all other program code. (We will see the significance of the _ prefix in Section 3.2.2.)

The state of a date object is characterized by three values: the settings for the day, month, and year. Actually, the set of legal states is only a *subset* of the set described by the class definition. There are additional restrictions on the data fields. For example, it is expected that _day ≤ 31. In this case, the C++

class definition gives an incomplete description of the set of legal states. We will see later how *class invariants* can be utilized to sharpen the definition.

The Date class, as described here, is similar to a C structure (or Pascal record):

```
struct date
{ int day;
   int month;
   int year;
};
```

But C structures provide no privacy. The data fields of the structure can be inspected and modified freely anywhere:

```
struct date birthday = { 31, 3, 1961 };
// ...
birthday.day = birthday.day + 1;
```

The corresponding code in C++ will not compile.

```
Date birthday;
birthday._day = birthday._day + 1; // ERROR
```

Only operations of a class can inspect and modify its private data.

Exercise 3.1.1. Write the data declaration of a class Employee. Each employee has a name, hire date, employee ID number, and monthly salary.

3.1.3. Defining Operations

A worthwhile operation on a date is to advance it by a certain number of days. For example, after the call

```
b.advance(30);
```

the date stored in b is 30 days after the original date. To implement this operation, two steps are required. First, the operation must be declared in the definition of the Date class:

```
class Date
{
public:
   void advance(int nday);
   // ...
};
```

Next, the function itself must be defined.[1]

```
void Date::advance(int nday)
{ // convert to Julian day
   long j = dat2jul(_day, _month, _year);
   // add  n days
   j += nday;
   // convert back from Julian day
   jul2dat(j, _day, _month, _year);
}
```

Note the *scope resolution* Date:: in the definition of the function. Other classes may also have an advance operation, and since in C++ operations are defined outside the class definition, it is necessary to specify both the class and the operation name.

The details of the computation are not important now. Just observe that the operation reads and modifies the _day, _month, and _year values. But *which* _day, _month, and _year values? There may be many Date objects, and each of them has _day, _month, and _year values. The operation modifies the values belonging to that object that invoked the operation. For example, if the call is

```
b.advance(30);
```

then the data fields b._day, b._month, b._year are modified, and after the call the object b has a different state.

But isn't access to these fields restricted? Indeed, it is—to operations of the class. Since advance (or, more precisely, Date::advance) is an operation of the Date class, it does have the privilege to access and modify the data fields.

In C++, an operation of a class is very similar to a regular function. However, an operation is always applied to an object, the so-called *implicit argument* of the operation. In addition, the operation may have no, one, or more *explicit arguments*, which are listed inside parentheses in the usual way. For example, the call

```
b.advance(30);
```

has two arguments: the implicit argument b and the explicit argument 30.

C++ programmers often refer to operations as *member functions*, because they are declared inside classes just as data fields (which they call *data*

---

[1]We make use of two functions long dat2jul(int, int, int) and void jul2dat(long, int&, int&, int&), which convert between calendar dates (day/month/year) and the *Julian day number*, the number of days from Jan. 1, 4713 B.C. (for example, the calendar date May 23, 1968, beginning at noon Greenwich time, corresponds to the Julian day 2,440,000). Julian day numbers are much more convenient for date arithmetic than calendar dates. The functions are taken from [Press].

members) are.[2] The dot (.) is used to select both data members and member functions.

Exercise 3.1.2. Write an operation void Employee::raise(double p) that raises the employee salary by p percent.

Exercise 3.1.3. Classes and operations can be implemented in C, albeit without the benefit of privacy. Classes become structures, and operations become functions whose first argument is always a pointer to the implicit argument. For example, the advance operation is implemented as

```
Date date_advance(Date* current, int n)
```

and called as

```
Date d = date_advance(&b, n);
```

Perform this translation on the Date class and recode the date_advance function. Note that field access inside an operation must be expressed explicitly, for example current->_day.

3.2. THE IMPLEMENTATION OF OPERATIONS

3.2.1. Constant Operations

In C++ it is important to make a distinction between *mutator* operations, which change an object, and *accessor* operations, which merely read its data fields. The latter need to be declared as const operations.

Consider the declarations of two operations advance and print in the Date class.

```
class Date
{
public:
  void advance(int);
  void print() const;
  // ...
};
```

---

[2]If two names for the same concept are good, surely three are even better. Programmers using the Smalltalk language ([Goldberg and Robson]) call operations *methods*, and they refer to member function calls as *messages* ("send the advance(30) message to the object b"). Here is a dictionary for the savvy object traveler:

C++	Smalltalk	Other common terms
Member function	Method	Operation
Call a member function	Send a message	Apply an operation
Data member	Instance variable	Field, attribute

The keyword const at the very end of the declaration indicates that the print operation leaves the calling object unchanged. The absence of const in the advance operation indicates that it may modify its implicit argument.

The const keyword is replicated in the definition of the operation:

```
void Date::print() const
{ //...
}
```

If advance and print were regular functions, they would have best been declared as

```
void Date_advance(Date&, int);
void Date_print(Date);
```

But the implicit argument of an operation is, unlike all other function arguments, always passed by reference. The const attribute is necessary to specify whether or not an operation takes advantage of the chance to modify its implicit argument.

If code in a const operation modifies a data field of the implicit argument, the compiler reports an error. This is an excellent feature. For example, date arithmetic (*date ± integer*) could be implemented in a nondestructive manner by returning the result as a value:

```
Date Date::add_days(int n) const;

Date b = a.add_days(30);
   // b is  a + 30 days, a not changed
```

Suppose you are implementing this operation. If you misunderstand the intended semantics and perform a modification, the compiler will catch the mistake. The const attribute is important because it lets the compiler check the preservation of a *design* property.

Conversely, what happens if you omit the const in a nondestructive operation like print? At first, nothing. The compiler will not check that the const is missing, even though you never modified any data field. However, as we will explain shortly, omitting the const attribute makes your code *unusable* to those programmers who use and believe in const.

Suppose Date::print is not declared as const. A programmer implementing an Employee class will then find that the following code does not compile.

```
void Employee::print() const
{ cout << _name << " " << _id << endl;
  _hiredate.print();
  // ERROR—attempt to modify a const object
}
```

The compiler does not understand your Date::print and assumes that it *will* modify its implicit argument, because it is *not* declared const. That leaves the programmer using your Date class three options:

· Drop the const from Employee::print().
· Play tricks with pointer casts to "cast away constness."
· Find another Date class.

None of this will bring you glory or admiration.

  Like ([Coplien], p. 38), this book recommends a *canonical form* for class declarations in which the mutator operations (non-const) are listed before the accessor functions (const). The rationale is that you want to know first what you can do to an object, and then how you can find out what you did.

Exercise 3.2.1. Write a constant operation String Date::zodiac() const that returns the zodiac sign name ("Gemini", "Virgo", and so forth) of a given date. (Consult the astrology section of your newspaper for the dates of the various signs.)

Exercise 3.2.2. Write a constant operation void Employee::print (ostream&) const that prints an employee record onto a stream.

3.2.2. Field Accessors and Mutators

Consider a Date class with fields for the day, month, and year. As always, we implement the fields as private data.

  Given a date, a programmer may well need to access the month entry. But the private data field is not accessible except through class operations. It therefore makes sense to supply an operation to compute the month:

```
class Date
{
public:
  int month() const;
  // ...
private:
  int _day;
  int _month;
  int _year;
};

int Date::month() const
{ return _month;
}
```

The operation is trivial—it simply reports the value of the month field. The month operation is declared constant, because the call d.month() does not change the object d.

Many classes have operations that simply report on the value of a private field. Such functions are called *field accessors*. For the class implementor it is more trouble to write both a private field and a public accessor function rather than simply a public data field. But programmers using the class are not greatly inconvenienced—they simply write d.month() instead of d._month. Now the value has become "read-only" to the outside world. Only operations of the class can modify it. In particular, should the value ever be wrong, only the class operations need to be debugged.

Now we can explain why we named the month field _month. C++ requires that the name of the field be distinct from the name of the operation month(). Because this situation commonly arises, many programmers use a standard convention to cope with it mechanically. Prefixes or suffixes for all data fields (_month, xmonth, m_month, month_) are a popular device. An alternative is to call all field accessors get...(), such as get_month() (see [Plum and Saks], pp. 22–23). That convention requires iron discipline. For example, you may design a String class with a length() operation and later decide to add a length data field to cache the length value and improve the performance of the operation. Oops, you should have called the function get_length(). Once a class is out in the field, it is too late to rename public features. Are you prepared to prefix all const operations with get_? Some class libraries do just that. We prefer to give the operation the most convenient and succinct name and uglify the private field data instead. Naturally, all this is a matter of taste. Find a scheme you like and stick to it.

Now suppose a programmer needs to change the month of a given date, say increment it by 1. Of course, d.advance(30) will do the trick. Well, not quite—if d is January 1 or July 31, it won't work correctly. We can provide an operation set_month to set the private field. Its implementation is trivial in the day/month/year representation:

```
void Date::set_month(int m)
{ if (1 <= m && m <= 12)
     _month = m;
}
```

The set_month operation is not declared as const, since it modifies its implicit argument. A function like set_month, whose purpose is to modify a field, is called a *field mutator*.

Of course, most private data fields of most classes are of a technical nature and of no interest to anyone but the implementor of the operations. But small classes especially, such as our Date example, contain fields in which class users have a legitimate interest. In this case, class implementors find it quite tedious to implement *three* items:

- A private data field _property
- A public const accessor property()
- A public modifier set_property(...)

instead of a single public data field. The tedium is undeniable, but there are considerable benefits.

The internal implementation can be changed without affecting any code other than the operations of the class. Of course, the accessor and mutator functions may need to do real work—translating between the old and the new representations rather than simply reading and writing a single field. In a large program, the code for the operations of a single class is relatively short and well localized, making such a change feasible, whereas updating the usage pattern of a public data field is usually extremely difficult.

The mutator functions can perform error checking; assignment to a field does not. For example, b.set_month(13) can be trapped by error checking code in the mutator, but b._month = 13 would have to be unearthed by a program trace. Read-only data values can be implemented by not supplying a mutator at all.

Actually, the Date class is a good example of a class that should *not* have mutators for each field. Consider the code

```
d.set_day(31);
d.set_month(3);
d.set_year(1961);
```

If d was previously February 1, then the set_day operation sets it to the invalid date February 31. In this case, of course the situation is remedied in the set_month operation, but having three separate mutators makes error checking much more difficult than it should be. It is better to supply a single set_date function instead.

```
d.set_date(31, 3, 1961);
```

Exercise 3.2.3. Write field accessor and mutator classes for the Employee class. You may assume that we never want to change the name or hire date of an employee, as those will be set by the constructor (see Section 3.4). But address and salary are changeable.

3.2.3. Inline Functions

Those readers who count processor cycles will have been horrified by the suggestion of replacing a simple data access with a function call. Calling a function is *much* more expensive than accessing data. A return address must be pushed and popped, and the branching to the function code slows down the prefetch queue in the instruction-decoding mechanism of the processor.

Fortunately, C++ has a convenient answer to these concerns: inline functions. Consider this simple function that squares an integer.

```
int square(int x) { return x * x; }
```

Calling square(a) is certainly less efficient than evaluating a * a, but calling

```
square(x[i] - y[i])
```

may be better than evaluating

```
(x[i] - y[i]) * (x[i] - y[i])
```

depending on the compiler's ability to recognize common subexpressions. The function call certainly is easier to read.

C++ allows the programmer to declare the function as inline.

```
inline int square(int x) { return x * x; }
```

This instructs the compiler to translate square(*expression*) into *expression* * *expression*, provided the expression is simple and has no side effects. Otherwise the expression is stored in a temporary location temp, and temp * temp is evaluated.[3]

This feature is particularly useful, for very simple operations:

```
inline int Date::month() const { return _month; }
```

A call d.month() is compiled as a direct field access d._month, not as a function call. The compiler can generate an access to the private field, even though the programmer cannot!

Inline functions give the protection and legibility of regular functions yet avoid the performance overhead of function calls. Of course, inline functions should be used only for very short functions. Program code size increases dramatically if longer functions are inline-replaced. The inline attribute is only a recommendation to the compiler. Compilers will refuse to inline overly complex code.

There is an alternate method of defining inline functions: by including their code inside the class declaration.

```
class Date
{
public:
  int day() const { return _day; }
  // ...
private:
  int _day;
  // ...
};
```

---

[3]C programmers often use the preprocessor to implement inline functions (#define square(x) (x)*(x)). This is error-prone (consider square(x[i++])) and should be completely avoided in C++.

This method saves keystrokes but is not recommended, for several reasons:

- It clutters up the public interface with the implementation of some operations.
- It reveals implementation details to the reader of the public interface.
- It is more difficult to revoke the `inline` attribute for debugging or profiling purposes.

It is seductively easy to add a one-line accessor function to a data field—even one that perhaps should not be accessible to the public. However, use of this feature is not recommended, even though the explicit definition of operations outside the class definition requires tedious typing. We will not use it except for trivial constructors and destructors.

Exercise 3.2.3. Do a performance analysis that measures the impact of inlining. Write a loop that squares numbers, both with an inline and a regular version of `square`, and use the execution profiler to time both loops.

Exercise 3.2.4. Inspect the assembly code that your compiler generates for a field lookup d._day, a call to an operation d.print(), and an inline operation d.day().

3.2.4. Private Operations

When implementing a class, we made all data fields private and all operations public. Public data is not useful, but private functions occur quite frequently. These functions can only be called from other operations of the class.

To implement operations, one may wish to break up the code or to factor common code into separate functions. These functions are typically not useful to the public. They may be very close to the implementation or require a special protocol or calling order. Such functions are best implemented as private operations.

Consider, for example, a `Date` class that, as a part of its date arithmetic implementation, requires a function to test whether a year is a leap year.

```
class Date
{
public:
  // ...
private:
  Bool is_leap_year() const;

  int _day;
  // ...
};
```

By making the function private, we are under no obligation to keep it available if we change to another implementation, such as the Julian date representation discussed in Chapter 4. The function may well be *harder* to implement, or *unnecessary* if the data representation changes. As long as the operation is private, we can be assured that it was never used outside the other class operations, and we can simply drop it. Had the function been public, we would be forced to reimplement it on change of representation, because other code might have relied on it.

Choose private operations for those functions that are of no concern to the class user and for those functions that could not easily be supported if the class implementation changes.

3.2.5. Class-Based Access Privileges

In C++, class operations have the privilege of accessing private data and functions of any object of their class, not just the implicit argument. (In other object-oriented languages, such as Smalltalk, access is more restricted. Operations can access the private features only of the object on which they operate. See [Budd], p. 225, for a comparison.)

Consider, for example, an operation that compares two dates for sorting purposes. The call d1.compare(d2) returns a negative number if d1 comes before d2, zero if they are the same, and a positive number otherwise. (The function is declared const, since the object invoking compare is not changed by the computation.)

```
int Date::compare(Date b) const
{ int d = _year - b._year;
  if (d != 0) return d;
  d = _month - b._month;
  if (d != 0) return d;
  return _day - b._day;
}
```

The compare function is permitted to access both the fields of its implicit argument (_year) and the fields of its explicit argument (b._year).

Some programmers consider this perfectly natural; others find it surprising. [Ellis and Stroustrup], p. 257, discusses the design rationale.

3.3. OBJECT CONSTRUCTION

3.3.1. Constructors

Since all data fields of an object are private, special functions are required to initialize the data whenever an object is allocated. For example, the following code will not compile:

```
Date d;
d._day = 31; d._month = 3; d._year = 1961; // ERROR
```

In Section 2.2.5 we discussed a `set_date` operation that can be used to set the date fields:

```
Date d;
d.set_date(31, 3, 1961);
```

This is a good way of doing it, but in C++ you can do better by placing the `set_date` functionality inside a *constructor*. A constructor is a special operation that is automatically invoked whenever an object is created.

Constructors have the same name as the class name. A `Date` constructor can be declared like this:

```
class Date
{
public:
  Date(int d, int m, int y);
  // ...
};
```

In the definition of the constructor the name `Date` occurs twice, first to denote the class name, then as the name of the constructor:

```
Date::Date(int d, int m, int y)
: _day(d),
  _month(m),
  _year(y)
{}
```

The constructor initializes the data fields of the object. The curious notation `_day(d)` indicates that the `_day` field is constructed using d. In this case, it is equivalent to an assignment `_day = d`. Similarly, the month and year fields are constructed by initializing them with the values m and y. There is nothing else to be done to initialize a `Date` object; hence, the function body of the constructor is empty. Although it looks strange at first, this is the simplest and most common case. Some constructors require additional work beyond construction of their data fields, or their data field initialization is too complex to fit in the initializer list. In that case, additional code is placed inside the constructor body.

Note that the `Date::Date` constructor, like all constructors, has no return value. Constructors are special functions whose task is not to compute a value but to initialize an object.

This constructor is invoked automatically when a date object is declared in the following fashion:

```
Date d(31, 3, 1961);
```

The notation is perhaps unfortunate. Although in fact d is an object of type `Date`, it looks as if d were a function, to be called with arguments 31, 3, and 1961.

In fact, a function *is* called with those arguments—namely, the constructor. It initializes the object d.

There is an important difference between constructors and operations. A constructor is invoked exactly once on an object, at the time of creation. It cannot be called again to "reinitialize" the object. For example, the call

```
d.Date(17, 8, 1959); // ERROR
```

is illegal. You cannot invoke a constructor on an existing object. In fact, you cannot explicitly call a constructor. You merely cause it to be invoked by supplying its arguments in an object definition.

Exercise 3.3.1. Write a constructor for the Employee class.

3.3.2. Argument Overloading and Default Arguments

A great advantage of constructors is the elimination of uninitialized variables— or, more accurately, variables that are initialized with random leftover bytes. Once a constructor has been declared for a class, it is no longer possible to define objects that avoid construction. For example, after adding a constructor Date(int, int, int) to the Date class, attempting to define a Date object without supplying construction values is an error:

```
Date d; // ERROR
```

This is actually a good feature. If we don't know the values of the fields of d, are we really happy to leave them to completely random bit patterns? On the other hand, if we do know the field values, there is nothing wrong with using them in the constructor. Since in C++ variables can be defined anywhere in a function, the definition of an object can be deferred until the values required for construction are computed.

Classes can have more than one constructor. For example, a constructor Date(String) could translate a string into a date:

```
Date d("March 31, 1961");
```

A constructor with no arguments can be used to initialize an object when no construction information is supplied. If a constructor Date() with no arguments is included in the Date class, it is invoked when a variable is defined as

```
Date d;
```

Such a constructor is called a *default constructor*. Most classes have a default constructor as well as one or more constructors with arguments. In fact, default constructors are necessary to allocate arrays of objects. The default constructor is invoked on each array element. It is an error to allocate an array of objects of a class that has one or more constructors but lacks a default constructor.

Actually, one can argue that constructing a date without values for the day, month, and year makes little sense. For numbers, zero is a good choice for a default value, but there is no good default for dates. Should the default constructor initialize a date to today's date, the beginning of time (1/1/4713 B.C. or 1/1/1980?), or maybe to an invalid date like 1/1/0? (In the Julian/Gregorian calendar, there is no year 0—the year 1 B.C. is immediately followed by 1 A.D.) In the latter case, all date functions must be able to recognize that invalid date and act appropriately. Nevertheless, classes without a default constructor are rare, since it is a great inconvenience for class users if array allocation is blocked.

Exercise 3.3.2. Look at the class library supplied by your compiler vendor and find whether the date class has a default constructor, and if so, check what it does.

If a class has more than one constructor, the compiler must be able to choose the correct one whenever an object is allocated. The compiler checks the types of the arguments in the constructor call. For example, suppose Date has three constructors:

```
class Date
{
public:
  Date();
  Date(int d, int m, int y);
  Date(String);
  // ...
};
```

Then the compiler can easily decide which constructor to invoke in any object definition:

```
Date d(31, 3, 1961); // Date(int, int, int)
Date e; // Date()
Date f("March 31, 1961"); // Date(String)
Date g(31, "March", 1961);
  // ERROR—no Date(int, String, int)
Array<Date> h(1, 10); // invokes Date() ten times
```

This facility of the C++ compiler is called *overloading*. Overloading occurs if several functions have the same name (in our case Date) but different argument types. The compiler has to engage in *overloading resolution* and pick the correct function by matching the argument types of the various functions with the types of the values supplied in the call. A compile-time error occurs if no match can be found or if more than one constructor matches. In addition to constructors, C++ permits overloading of operations, regular functions, and operators.

The number of overloaded constructors can often be minimized by another C++ device: default function arguments. Consider, for example, a constructor

```
class Date
{
public:
  Date(int d, int m, int y = 0);
  // ...
};

Date::Date(int d, int m, int y)
  : _day(d),
    _month(m),
    _year(y)
{ if (_year == 0) _year = current year;
}
```

If the constructor is called with only two integer arguments, the compiler automatically supplies the default value as the third one:

```
Date d(31, 1);
```

is equivalent to

```
Date d(31, 1, 0);
```

and the latter is implemented to set the year to the current year. Note that the default arguments are provided only in the constructor declaration inside the class definition. They are not replicated in the constructor definition. More than one default can be provided:

```
class Date
{
public:
  Date(int d = 1, int m = 1, int y = 0);
  // ...
};
```

In this example,

```
Date d(31);
Date e;
```

is equivalent to

```
Date d(31, 1, 0);
Date e(1, 1, 0);
```

Default arguments are used only for those slots that are not supplied in the call. Default arguments are always filled in from the back. It is not possible to obtain defaults in the middle of a call, such as

```
Date(31, ,1961); // ERROR
```

All C++ functions, not just constructors, may supply default arguments. They are a useful feature to reduce the number of overloaded functions.

Exercise 3.3.3. Write a default constructor for the `Employee` class.

Exercise 3.3.4. Write the `Date::Date(String)` constructor.

It is helpful to keep in mind how an object can be constructed. There are three possibilities:

- With explicit construction arguments, `Date d1(1, 8, 1989)`
- With the default constructor, `Date d2`
- As a copy of an existing object, `Date d3 = d1`

3.3.3. Anonymous Objects

One characteristic of built-in types is the fact that constants are readily available without having to store them in a variable. For example,

```
int y = x + 10;
```

can be used instead of the long-winded

```
int temp = 10;
int y = x + temp;
```

Constructors can be used in a similar fashion to generate objects that are used in a computation and then go away.

```
Date d = Date(31, 3, 1961).advance(x);
```

This is more concise and less cluttered than the equivalent

```
Date temp(31, 3, 1961);
Date d = temp.advance(x);
```

Just as we think of 10 as the integer constant ten, we can think of `Date(31, 3, 1961)` as the date constant March 31, 1961. We leave it to the compiler to allocate an anonymous temporary object.

Anonymous objects are particularly convenient for constructing function results:

```
Date quarter_end(int q, int y)
/* PURPOSE:  returns the end of a calendar quarter
     RECEIVES: q = 1, 2, 3, 4 — the quarter
               y — the year
     RETURNS:  the date of the quarter end
*/
{ if (q == 1 || q == 4)
     return Date(31, 3 * q, y);
  else
     return Date(30, 3 * q, y);
}
```

There is no need to give a name to the object that the function returns—we simply instruct the function to construct an object with certain properties and to return it as the function result.

3.3.4. Construction of Subobjects

All objects of a class must be constructed, including those that are contained inside other objects. An important role of a constructor is to direct the construction of its subobjects. Here is a constructor for the Employee class that invokes constructors for subobjects.

```
Employee::Employee(String n, int hd, int hm, int hy)
: _name(n),
  _hiredate(hd, hm, hy)
{}
```

This constructor passes arguments on to the constructors of the various subobjects. Those fields that are not explicitly listed in the initialization list (such as _address) are initialized with the default constructor of their class. Their contents may be changed later in the body of the constructor or through another operation such as set_address. Fields that belong to a class without a default constructor *must* be initialized explicitly, or the compiler will report as an error that it is unable to construct the subobject. However, fields of numeric or pointer type that are missing from the initializer list are quietly left uninitialized.

The syntax for constructing subobjects in a constructor is somewhat peculiar. The colon (:) syntax is valid only in constructors, not in any other operation (in class declarations the : signifies inheritance). The constructor invocation *fieldname*(*arguments*) makes *fieldname* look like the name of a function. The syntax is fundamentally the same as that used to construct a variable, such as

```
Date hiredate(31, 3, 1961);
```

but the type name is omitted, because it can be inferred from the class definition. Fields of numeric or pointer type can be initialized with the same syntax:

```
Date::Date(int d, int m, int y)
: _day(d),
  _month(m),
  _year(y)
{}
```

In this case, there are no constructor calls involved: numeric and pointer types are not classes and have no constructors. The values are simply copied into the fields. The constructor

```
Date::Date(int d, int m, int y)
// poor style—no initializer list
{ _day = d
  _month = m;
  _year = y;
}
```

has the same effect. However, it is considered poor style to defer initialization until the body of the constructor. On the contrary, constructors that simply build up their fields in the initializer list and have an empty body are considered ideal.

Exercise 3.3.5. Add a _birthday field to the Employee class and provide a constructor Employee(String n, Date b, Date h). Use the : syntax to initialize the fields. Set the salary to 0 but leave the address initialized by the default constructor.

Exercise 3.3.6. Write an Address class that you consider useful for a reasonably wide range of standard applications. Write a test program that reads addresses in, places them in an Array<Address>, sorts that array (with the qsort operation of the array template), and prints the sorted array. Sort first by country, then by postal code.

3.4. DESIGN HINTS

3.4.1. Always Keep Data Private

It is technically legal in C++ to place a data field in the public section of a class. In practice, you should never use public data. Always keep data private and use operations to read and change it. Chapter 4 discusses the rationale for data hiding. In a nutshell, experience has shown that the data representation used in the class implementation tends to change over time as the class evolves. When data is private, it can be changed without affecting the class users.

There is sometimes the temptation to code public data fields just to get on with the task at hand, promising to make the data private later. Don't do it. Making data private after the fact usually leads to awkward code.

Coding a set of field accessors and mutators can be a bother, but if you look at the big picture, it is a minor issue. In a nontrivial programming problem the vast majority of operations do real work, and even if you could somehow skip all accessors and mutators, it would not make much of a difference.

3.4.2. Class Types Are the Norm; Challenge Basic Types

Ultimately, all classes are composed of numbers and strings. But only low-level classes are directly composed from these types. The majority of classes have fields that are themselves of class type.

You should challenge class fields that are merely of `int` or `String` types. Consider this example of a poorly designed class in which all data fields have basic types:

```
class Employee
{
public:
    // ...
private:
    String _lname;
    String _fname;
    char _middle_initial;
    String _street;
    String _city;
    String _state;
    long _zip;
    // ...
};
```

It is much better to group the fields that describe an address into a single object of type `Address`. That way, you can easily cope with changes to addresses in countries with nonnumeric postal codes for cities, addresses with additional fields for organizations and departments, or separate home and work addresses. Additionally, the software package is likely to contain other addresses, such as the addresses of customers or vendors. Code that is common to all address handling, such as formatting or sorting by postal code, can be shared rather than replicated. The same idea holds for the employee name. An improved data organization looks like this:

```
class Name
{
public:
    // ...
private:
    String _lname;
    String _fname;
    char _middle_initial;
    // ...
};
```

```
class Address
{
public:
  // ...
private:
  String _street;
  String _city;
  String _state;
  long _zip;
  // ...
};

class Employee
{
public:
  // ...
private:
  Name _name;
  Address _address;
  Date _hiredate;
  // ...
};
```

3.4.3. Not All Fields Need Individual Field Accessors and Mutators

You should not supply accessors and mutators to individual fields unless they are really necessary. Low-level classes, such as Date or Point, need to reveal the settings of all fields. Higher-level classes typically do not. Consider a User class of a mail system. Each user has a mailbox, a collection of messages.

```
class User
{
public:
  void add_message(Message);
  void remove_message(int);

  void list_messages() const;
  void print_message(int) const;
  // ...
private:
  Array<Message> _mailbox;
  // ...
};
```

There is no need for the `User` class to reveal the `_mailbox` field with `mailbox()` and `set_mailbox()` operations. All mailbox access and modification takes place through the public operations.

3.4.4. Declare Accessor Operations as `const`

Always use the `const` attribute with accessor operations that just read from the data fields without modifying them. If you don't, you limit the utility of your operation and, ultimately, of your class.

Suppose you supply a class `Address` but don't declare `Address::print` to be `const`. If another programmer uses your class to implement `Employee`, `Employee::print` won't compile.

```
void Employee::print() const
{ // ...
  _address.print(); // ERROR—attempt to modify a const object
}
```

This will not endear you to your customer, the author of `Employee`, who may well search for a more competent supplier.

The `const` attribute is useful for finding errors.

```
int Employee::compare(Employee b) const
{ _name.to_upper(); // ERROR—attempt to modify a const object
  b._name.to_upper();
  // ...
}
```

This `compare` operation first forces the name to uppercase, thereby modifying it. Yet the operation promises, as it should, that comparing an object with another does not change it. The compiler catches this contradiction.

3.4.5. Use a Canonical Form for Class Definitions

Use a standard order for presenting the features of a class. As we will see later, classes can have more features than just operations and fields. The coding guidelines in the Appendix give a complete description of the canonical form that we recommend. Here is the short version:

- First list the public section, then the private section. The readers of your class (including yourself) are more interested in the public interface than the details of the private implementation.
- In the public section, first list the constructors, then the mutators, then the accessors. This tells the class readers the answers to the three questions they are likely to have. How do I make an object of this class? Once I have an object, what can I do with it? Once I did it, how can I find out the result?

- In the private section, list the private operations (mutators, then accessors), and then the fields.

Here is an example:

```
class Date
{
public:
  Date();
  Date(int d, int m, int y); // construct from day, month, year

  void advance(long n); // advance this date by n days

  int day() const;
  int month() const;
  int year() const;
  Weekday weekday() const;
  Date add_days(long n) const; // computes n days from this date
  long days_between(Date b) const;
    // number of days between this date and  b
private:
  int _day;
  int _month;
  int _year;
};
```

3.4.6. Supply a Default Constructor

Most classes should have a default constructor. To declare an array of class objects, the class *must* have a default constructor.

It is usually easy enough to supply a default constructor: Initialize all numeric and pointer fields to zero and use the default constructor on all fields of class type.

Sometimes it appears desirable to compute a better default object. For example, a Date default constructor may want to set the date to today's date. That is not necessarily a good idea. Computing today's date has some cost. If a large array of dates is allocated, does it really make sense to expend computational effort to initialize each array element with today's date?

It is best if an object created by the default constructor is a valid object. For example, an employee object whose name and address are blank is not likely to do any harm.

This does not always work. If you initialize the day, month, and year fields of a date object with zero, the resulting object is not a valid date. Such objects should not be used until they are set to a valid state as the result of some other operation. Managing this situation is always awkward.

If no valid default object can be found, and if the cost of monitoring to ensure that no invalid object enters a computation is considered too high, then you need not supply a default constructor. Of course, you then lose the ability to declare arrays.

3.4.7. Construct All Subobjects
Before the Constructor Body

A constructor consists of two parts: the initializer list and the constructor body. By the time the constructor body is entered, all fields that are not explicitly constructed in the initializer list are constructed with their default constructor.

```
Employee::Employee(String n, int hd, int hm, int hy)
{ // _name, _hiredate already constructed with default constructor
  _name = n;
  _hiredate = Date(hd, hm, hy);
}
```

There is no point in first running the default constructors and then overwriting the fields with the intended value. Use the initializer list to construct the fields the way you want them.

```
Employee::Employee(String n, int hd, int hm, int hy)
: _name(n),
  _hiredate(hd, hm, hy)
{}
```

INTERFACES

4.1. ENCAPSULATION

4.1.1. Impact of Private Data on the Programmer

In the previous chapter we studied the mechanics of making all data fields of a class private, hiding the implementation details from public scrutiny. This process is called *encapsulation*. We will now discuss the rationale behind it.

In C++ the programmer actually has the choice of placing data fields into the private or public section. However, *it is always a bad idea to make data public*. Style guides and programming rule books usually prohibit public data outright. You should program as if the private section were the only legal place for data fields.

On the face of it, this appears to be a minor inconvenience to the programmer. After all, if the value of a data field is required in a computation, one can always add an operation to the class that performs the computation. Or, if private data of an object needs to be modified, one can write an operation that effects this modification.

This is indeed true, but it nevertheless comes as a surprise to most programmers just how often they are tempted to access data fields of objects casually as they code along.

Furthermore, it is not a good idea to wait until the implementation phase to determine what operations to add to a class. Adding operations as the need arises typically leads to a cluttered collection of operations that is overly large, unintuitive to use, and difficult to maintain as the class functionality evolves over time. It is particularly important to *design* a complete and usable set of operations before starting to code.

Of course, nobody has perfect foresight, and design flaws may well surface in the implementation phase. When you find that you cannot carry out a task because you lack access to private data, you should first realize that this indicates a failure of the class design. You then have the following choices.

- Revisit the design. *(OK.)*
- Add the problem task as an operation. *(Maybe.)*

- Add an accessor or mutator operation for a data item. *(Maybe.)*
- Make the data public. *(Don't!)*

Public data and cluttered interfaces must be avoided. You have no good choice but to stop coding your immediate task and to reexamine the overall class design. You may then discover new operations or a rearrangement of responsibilities. Before implementing the changes, it is particularly important that you take the time to write clear documentation for the new or changed features. If you cannot explain the altered interface in words that you would not be embarrassed to read six months later, more design work appears to be required.

4.1.2. Why Private Data?

Having seen that private data is actually inconvenient for the programmer during coding, we may well wonder why programmers consider it such an essential feature. Writing code is only one of the tasks of software production, and it is not the most time-consuming one. Debugging and testing must be considered as well. Most importantly, successful software products evolve over time. New user requirements must be implemented, and obsolete features are sometimes retired. The existing code must be modifiable. It would be too slow and expensive to rewrite all code for every product release. (This aspect of software can be hard for a novice programmer to envision—in college, the lifetime of a program is typically between a week and a semester, and indeed then the coding phase dominates all other aspects.)

Successful software products, by the very nature of their success, are long-lived and require a great deal of modification during their lifetime. Data hiding is one strategy that can contribute to making program modification technically feasible.

Suppose a programmer changes the implementation of a data structure in a working program to speed up an algorithm or to support added functionality. What other changes are necessary to make the program compile and run again? If no protection mechanisms are in place, the programmer might have to inspect each line of the program to see whether it is affected by the change. More likely, the programmer will update all known references to the changed data but be surprised by some unexpected interactions during debugging. In a large program this approach is simply not feasible.

Data encapsulation provides a mechanism for restricting the range of the program that is affected by a change to a small subset. Once that subset has been updated to track a change, one can state with confidence that no other portion of the program needs attention in this regard.

Let us consider a very simple example of how problems can arise with unencapsulated data. Suppose we defined a data type Date with fields day, month, year. If our program performs a lot of *date arithmetic* (date + integer = date, date − date = integer), it would benefit from a different data representation:

the *Julian date*, which is simply a (long) integer counting the number of days from some fixed date.[1] Clearly, date arithmetic is trivial in the Julian representation, but other operations (printing a date as month/day/year) are not. Let us suppose that the tradeoff is beneficial in our case. What changes need to be made? We change Date; remove the day, month, and year fields; and add a field long julian instead. Of course, if we used public data, now our program will no longer compile. That is good—at least we know where we must fix up the code. We must supply functions to compute the day, month, and year values from the Julian date, and call them whenever the field values were used previously. For example,

```
d = b.day;
```

would be replaced with

```
d = b.day(); // now computes day from Julian date
```

But what if the fields are modified? One could replace

```
b.month = 1;

b.year++;
```

with

```
b = Date(b.day(), 1, b.year() + 1);
```

This gets complex, and it also gets to be extremely inefficient. Instead, it is really necessary to revisit the way in which the dates are used in each instance. What should be a simple change of representation turns into a major effort.

In this scenario, we were lucky that the compiler located all expressions that needed to be changed. Consider a slightly more complex situation in which we keep the day, month, year fields and then add a julian field and a flag to indicate which of the two representations is the most current. Now the compiler will accept code containing b.day, but the code may be wrong, since the day field may not be currently active. It is easy to make mistakes, obtain corrupted data, and require time-consuming debugging sessions.

---

[1]This is not to be confused with the Julian calendar enacted by Julius Caesar. The 16th century historian Joseph Scaliger used the recurrence interval for leap years beginning on Sunday and having the moon phases on the same days of the month, together with the 15-year Roman tax cycle, to find a synchronization point, Jan. 1, 4713 B.C., to use as a zero for mapping every event in written history reliably to a positive day number ([Parise], p. 318). Scaliger named this day number after his father Julius ([Moore], p. 219).

Exercise 4.1.1. Reimplement the Date class to use the Julian day representation. Replace the integer day, month, year fields with a `long _julian`. Rewrite the days_between, advance, and add_days operations (which get easier) and the day, month, year operations (which get harder).

Exercise 4.1.2. For this exercise only, make the _day, _month, _year of the Date class public. Write a program that reads a sequence of dates, sorts them, and prints them. Feel free to access the public data fields whenever it seems easier. Then rewrite your program, replacing the integer day, month, and year fields with a long Julian day number. What is the impact on the code?

Exercise 4.1.3. Write the declaration of a Date class that employs a caching strategy, keeping both the day, month, and year fields and a field for the Julian date. How can you indicate which of the two is currently valid?

Exercise 4.1.4. Write operations for the class of the previous exercise. Assume that there are two operations: to set the day, month, year field from the Julian date, and vice versa. Write operations print and advance that work with the more convenient representation, possibly temporarily invalidating the other one.

4.2. PUBLIC INTERFACES AND PRIVATE IMPLEMENTATIONS

4.2.1. The Roles of Class User and Class Designer

The design and implementation of classes must be approached from two points of view simultaneously. Classes are designed and implemented by programmers, to be used in code by other programmers, who are often referred to as *class users*. These are different from the end users of the final software application, who, of course, wish to know nothing about the application code. The customer of the class designer is another programmer, the class user. As in any relationship between service providers and customers, the service provider must consider the needs of the customer.

The class designer has certain objectives, such as efficient algorithms and convenient coding. Those programmers who use the classes in their code have different priorities. They want to be able to understand and use the operations without having to comprehend the internal data representations. They want a set of operations that is large enough to solve their programming tasks yet small enough to be comprehensible.

It is often difficult for beginning programmers in an object-oriented language to separate these two aspects, because in their first programming projects they are both the class designer and the class user. If the learning environment permits this, it is very helpful to get together with a colleague for a project. Each of you designs the necessary classes, then you switch roles and complete the assignment with the other programmer's classes. Of course, no substantial changes to the classes should be made after the switch. This gives you a feel for the difficulty both of anticipating the needs of another programmer and of working with classes that were produced with less-than-perfect anticipation of these needs. An excellent way of continuing this exercise is to switch roles once again and to have the original class designer change the internal implementation—for example, using linked lists instead of arrays or a binary instead of a linear search. The class user code should not be affected by these changes. Of course, you may attend a course where group work is not possible, and then you must play Dr. Jekyll and Mr. Hyde and envision both roles yourself.

4.2.2. The Class User Perspective

The class users see the public interface of a class. While they may peek at the private data, they often do not. The data may not be straightforward to understand, especially in complex or highly optimized representations. At any rate, it is subject to change at any time. The public interface must contain sufficient operations to enable the class user to comprehend the class and to use it effectively. For example, here is a complete interface of a Date class:

```
class Date
{
public:
  Date(int d, int m, int y);

  void advance(int);

  Date add_days(int n) const;
  long days_between(Date b) const;
  int day() const;
  int month() const;
  int year() const;
  Weekday weekday() const;

private:
  // ...
};
```

This interface is complete—anything that you may wish to do with dates can be done—but it is perhaps not convenient. For example, printing a date requires getting the day, month, and year; perhaps translating the month into a string; and printing the data in some order. Should this functionality be included in a date class? It is highly locale-dependent. Even without the complexity of month names in various languages, the order of printout differs from country to country. Americans use *month/day/year*, whereas Germans use *day.month.year*.

Of course, these are just the issues that class users don't want to think about, and it might be a good idea to delegate them to a class, either the Date class or another class whose specific focus is locale-dependent formatting.

The interface of the Date class is small. It is not uncommon for a class to have twice as many operations, but classes with 50 or more operations are rare.

Exercise 4.2.1. Consult the manual for the class library that your compiler vendor provides. Look at the public interface for the Date or Directory class. Perform a simple programming task such as printing a calendar, figuring out how many days elapsed since your date of birth, or printing a nested directory listing. Was it easy? Did you get the services you deserve? What improvements would you like to see in the interface?

4.3. DESIGNING AN INTERFACE

This section contains a checklist of criteria to determine the quality of a class interface. Note that some of the goals are in conflict with others.

4.3.1. Cohesion

A class describes *a single abstraction*. All class operations must logically fit together to support a single, coherent purpose.

Consider this mailbox class:

```
class Mailbox
{
public:
   void add_message(Message);
   void remove_message(int);
   String get_command();

   void print_message(int) const;
   void list_messages() const;
   int count() const;

private:
   // ...
};
```

The get_command operation sticks out as being different from all other operations. The other operations deal with a single abstraction: a mailbox that holds messages. The get_command operation adds another wrinkle to it, the ability to get commands. From where? In what language? It would be better to have a different class deal with commands and leave the mailbox to do what it does best: store messages.

Exercise 4.3.1. [Kernighan and Ritchie], p. 242, describe the C standard library interface to the file system. These are not operations of a single class, but the criterion of cohesion can be applied to a collection of library functions as well. The functions that are described as "file operations" are fopen, freopen, fflush, fclose, remove, rename, tmpfile, tmpnam, setvbuf, and setbuf. Find out what these functions do and discuss whether the interface is cohesive. If not, can you split it up into two or more sets, each of which is cohesive?

Exercise 4.3.2. Repeat the previous exercise with the functions that [Kernighan and Ritchie] list for the C string-handling interface: str[n]cpy, str[n]cat, str[n]cmp, str[r]chr, str[c]spn, strpbrk, strstr, strlen, strerror, strtok.

4.3.2. Primitive Operations

Operations of a class should be *primitive*, not decomposable into smaller operations.

For example, consider an operation Bool List::advance(int& x) in a linked-list class, taken from a real class library. Its purpose is to advance a list cursor (a pointer to one element of the list) to the next element. But it also reports whether the cursor was able to advance or whether it was already at the end of the list and, if the cursor did move, sets x to the element under the new cursor position.

The fact that the explanation of this operation is so complex should make one pause. There really are three primitive operations that make up this operation:

- Get the list element under the cursor.
- Test whether the cursor is already at the end of the list.
- Advance the cursor to the next list element.

Each of these should become a separate operation.

Of course, ultimately each operation is implemented by decomposing it into sequences of statements, but these statements act on the implementation of the class and are not defined on the interface level.

When primitive operations are supplied, programmers using the class can mix and match them in the order that is relevant to their problem.

Exercise 4.3.3. Consider the functions declared in the C header file time.h. Which of them are primitive, and which could be generated from others?

4.3.3. Completeness

A class interface must be complete. All operations that make sense on the abstraction that the class represents must be supported.

Consider this class that represents a list of integers (taken from [Stroustrup], p. 269, with operations renamed). It is incomplete.

```
class List
{
public:
   List(); // makes an empty list
   void insert(int x); // insert at head
   void append(int x); // insert at tail
   void remove(int x); // remove from head
   void set_current(int x); // set element under cursor
   void advance(); // advance list cursor
   int current() const; // report element under cursor
   Bool at_end() const; // is cursor at tail of list?
private:
   // ...
};
```

There is no way of inserting and removing elements in the middle of the list. For example, there is no way of changing the list (1 4 9 16 25 36) to (1 9 25).

Exercise 4.3.4. The C header file string.h defines operations that can be carried out on built-in character arrays. Suppose that you were not allowed to access the contents of a character string directly; that is, you could not access or modify s[i]. Is the interface given by the functions declared in string.h complete? Or can you think of a natural operation on strings that could not be performed with just that interface?

4.3.4. Convenience

An interface that is complete and consists of primitive operations is always serviceable, but it may not be convenient. As a secondary goal, it is a good idea to look at typical usage patterns and supply additional operations for the convenience of programmers.

Consider the String class. The operation String::field(i) considers a string to be composed of fields separated by white space and returns the ith field of a string.

```
String s = "Hello cruel world";
String t = s.field(2); // t is "cruel"
```

This is obviously convenient, but it is also not a primitive operation. There are other ways to solve this task; for example, with find and substr.

It is important not to overdo this. A class with a great number of convenience operations is itself inconvenient to use, because the programmer must first find the appropriate operation.

A good strategy is first to start out with no convenience operations; to watch the patterns in which other programmers use the class; to solicit feedback; and then add only those convenience operations that the class customers really demand.

Exercise 4.3.5. Consider the `fseek` operation in stdio.h. It is not a primitive operation, because it can be composed from more basic operations (`fclose`, `fopen`, `fread`). How? Do you think `fseek` is a necessary part of the `FILE*` interface, or a frill that should be eliminated?

Exercise 4.3.6. The BIOS (basic input/output services) interface for the IBM PC contains a function to draw a pixel on the graphics screen at any specified (x,y) location. Nevertheless, all serious programs that render graphics bypass this function and instead perform a direct write into the graphics adapter memory. Is the BIOS interface complete? Is it convenient?

4.3.5. Consistency

The operations in a class should be consistent with each other with respect to

- Names
- Arguments and return values
- Behavior

The objective is to avoid programmer surprises and misunderstandings. Confused programmers write buggy code.

Inconsistencies in operation names are irritating to class users. They are surprisingly common, even though they can be easily avoided. Stick to a common pattern for capitalization: Don't call one function `set_speed` and another one `setWeight`. Use uniform prefixes: Don't mix `set_speed` and `put_weight`. Be consistent with concepts: If you have an accessor `speed`, don't call the mutator `set_velocity`.

For example, consider our `Array` and `String` classes. A number of operations take a pair of integer arguments, such as `String::remove`, `Array<T>::remove_range`, `Array<T>::insert_range`. The first argument is the starting index, and the second one is the *length*. One could equally well have chosen the *ending index* as the second argument, as long as that choice was consistently applied. (We chose the former for compatibility with the proposed ANSI libraries.) On the other hand, if some operations followed one convention, others the other, programmer confusion would be inevitable.

Exercise 4.3.7. Actually, there are two operations in the `Array` class template that do not conform to the *(starting index, length)* convention, namely the `Array<T>(int, int)` constructor and the `grow` operation. They take a starting and ending index. There is a reason. When declaring an array, specifying the lower and upper bound is a convention in many programming languages. Consider

```
Array<double> a(-10, 10);
```

Under the *(starting index, ending index)* convention, this is an array of 21 elements with indexes ranging from −10 to 10. Under the *(starting index, length)*

convention, it would be an array of 10 elements with indexes ranging from -10 to -1. Which do you think is more natural? Do you think that it would be a better choice to have `insert_range` and `remove_range` use the ending index as well?

Pay attention to return values. When returning a Boolean value, always return TRUE on success, FALSE on failure. When returning an integer, does 0 mean failure, or -1, or INT_MAX? It doesn't matter, as long as you stick to one convention.

The C++ iostream library supports three ways of formatting integers: decimal, octal, and hexadecimal. To pick which one you want, you turn on decimal, octal, or hexadecimal mode. The library also supports three formats for floating-point numbers: fixed, scientific, and general. If you want fixed or scientific, you turn them on. But if you want general format, you must turn both fixed and scientific *off*. This is a confusing inconsistency in behavior.

Exercise 4.3.8. Consider the functions operating on FILE* in stdio.h: fopen, fread, fprintf, fgets, and so on. Describe the inconsistencies in the arguments and return values.

4.4. CATEGORIES OF OPERATIONS

In this section we present the most common categories of operations found in classes. This is not meant to be an exhaustive list. Many classes have operations that do not fall into any of these categories. Not every class needs operations from all the categories, either.

4.4.1. Constructors

The purpose of constructors is to initialize *every* data field in an object. Every class should have at least one constructor, and most classes should have a default constructor. More than one constructor can be provided.

4.4.2. Destructors

A destructor releases any resources (such as heap memory, open files, or fonts) that the object has acquired when it was constructed or as the result of an operation. If the class manages no external resources, no destructor is necessary. We will discuss destructors in Chapter 13.

4.4.3. Accessors

Accessors compute a value from an object without modifying it. The simplest form is the *field accessor*, which simply reports the value of a data field. Other accessors carry out a computation of some complexity to arrive at a result. Sometimes accessors *cache* the result of a computation, simply returning the previously computed value if the accessor is called twice with no intervening change of the object. Some accessors take no arguments, using only the information stored in the object to compute the result. Others take arguments, which enter into the computation.

4.4.4. Comparison Operators

Comparison operators compare an object with another object of the same type to determine whether the objects are identical or whether one is less than the other, according to some ordering relation.

Here is an operation for ordering employees by their ID number. As is common with comparison operators, this one returns a negative integer if the first object comes before the second, zero if the objects have identical contents, and a positive integer otherwise.

```
int Employee::compare(Employee b) const
{ return _id - b._id;
}

Employee e, f;
// ...
if (e.compare(f) < 0) // e comes before f
```

Comparison operations look awkward, because of the asymmetric syntax for invoking an operation on an object. We must arbitrarily choose one of the two objects to be compared as the active agent that carries out the computation.

Comparison operations are a special case of accessors, because comparing an object with another does not change the object that carries out the comparison.

4.4.5. Mutators

A mutator is any operation that modifies the object in some way. Field mutators just change the value of a single field. Other mutators carry out more general computations that can change one or more fields. Very occasionally, a class has no mutators; the values of its objects are completely set at construction time and can only be inspected, never changed.

4.4.6. Iterators

Some classes manage a collection of items. Depending on the nature of the data structure, access to these items can be either through a key or through an iteration protocol. In the latter case, the state includes the notion of a current item, and there are operations to look at the current item and to move on to the next.

Here is an example of a class that returns the names of files in a directory, using an iteration protocol.

```
class Directory
{
public:
  Directory(String path);

  void reset(); // restart iteration
  void next(); // move to next file
  String current() const; // return current filename
  Bool at_end() const; // at end of iteration?
  // ...
private:
  // ...
};

Directory dir("\\WINDOWS\\SYSTEM");
dir.reset();
while (!dir.at_end())
{ cout << dir.current() << endl;
  dir.next();
}
```

The operations facilitating the iteration (reset, next, current, at_end) are collectively called *iterators*. The reset and next operations are mutators—they modify the internal state of the object.

4.4.7. Copying and Cloning

For objects that do not manage external resources, copying can be simply performed by assignment and initialization. Objects that have complex responsibilities need to supply their own functions for this purpose. We will discuss this in detail in Chapter 13.

An object can carry out copying in two ways: It can set itself to be a copy of another object, or it can return a copy of itself. The latter process is called *cloning*.

4.4.8. Input and Output

An output operation simply renders the object onto some output device, such as a file, screen, or printer. The operation receives a handle to the output device as as an argument. Output does not modify the object performing it.

An input operation similarly receives a handle to an input device. The input operation, when successful, overwrites all fields of the object with those settings read from the input device. If the input operation is not successful, it is desirable that the object be unchanged. If that cannot be achieved, care should be taken that it is at least in a well-defined state.

Exercise 4.4.1. Classify the operations of the Date class according to the categories just given.

Exercise 4.4.2. Classify the operations of the Array class template according to the categories just given.

4.5. DESIGN HINTS

4.5.1. Too Many Operations?

Some basic classes, such as the string and stream classes, have about 50 operations. Most classes have far fewer. If your class has an unusually large number of operations, first check for cohesion. Are all operations really related to one abstraction? If not, split up the class into two or more classes and distribute the operations over them. Then check for simplicity. Mark those operations that are primitive—not decomposable into other operations. The others are then presumably for the convenience of the class user. Talk to some typical users. Try taking out operations and see who complains. Keep only those that are really appreciated.

4.5.2. In How Many Ways
Can the Class User Achieve a Task?

There has to be at least one way to achieve any task that makes sense with the class, and in most cases there should be exactly one way. That keeps it simple for the class user. However, sometimes you need to add operations that make a common task easier. When doing that, keep track of the number of ways in which a task can be achieved. Is there one that is obviously better? If not, programmers using the class can spend too much time agonizing over which way to choose.

4.5.3. Is This Class Reusable
in Another Context? Should It Be?

Some classes are built to be reused in a wide variety of different contexts, such as Date or String. Others are for a specific purpose, such as Mailbox. A class with a wide usage range must obviously be designed with a great deal of care. On the other hand, a class that has a specific purpose for only one project should concentrate on those services that are essential to get its job done. Some programmers overengineer classes by adding lots of operations that far exceed any reasonable future use. One should always keep reuse in mind, but not to the extent of gold-plating. Actually, reuse is often facilitated by keeping classes as simple as possible.

4.5.4. On How Many Other
Classes Does This Class Depend?

The fewer, the better. Any class that does input and output depends on the input/output device. A class that is geared toward terminal input and output may be difficult to use in a graphical user interface, where input and output go through dialog boxes. Consider the `Mailbox::print(int)` operation, which prints a message to standard output. Certain devices that deliver mail, such as some hand-held communicators, have no notion of streams or standard output. The `Mailbox` class would be better off replacing `print` with an operation `get`, which simply returns a message, and leave it to another part of the system to render the message on the screen. Then `Mailbox` no longer depends on `ostream`.

4.5.5. No Class Is Perfect

There are inevitable conflicts in designing a class. The quest for a minimal interface competes with the desire for convenience. Naming and usage of operations should be consistent but also reflect traditional usage. We don't want a class with just one operation, but that one operation may not coherently fit anywhere else. As in any engineering task, it is the job of the class designer to understand the conflicts and to resolve them by making the necessary compromises.

OBJECT-ORIENTED DESIGN

This chapter introduces a miniature version of a typical object-oriented design methodology. This approach is not intended to replace an industrial-strength methodology. It is our goal to provide the guidance of a formal method while reducing some of the cumbersome mechanics and detail. This makes it more appealing to complete program designs, even for small projects, rather than starting to code right away. We spend some time explaining the mechanics of the tools (when to use paper and pencil, when to use software, how to run a group discussion). Many of these points may be obvious, but we feel it is important that you be comfortable with the activities.

5.1. DESCRIPTION OF THE MAIL MESSAGE SYSTEM

To walk through the basic steps of the object-oriented design process, we will consider the task of writing a program that simulates a telephone voice mail system, similar to the message system that is in use in many companies.

In a voice mail system a person dials an extension number and, provided the other party does not pick up the telephone, leaves a message. The other party can later retrieve the messages, keep them, or delete them. Real-world systems have a multitude of fancy features: Messages can be forwarded to one or more mailboxes; distribution lists can be defined, retained, and edited; and authorized persons can send broadcast messages to all users. Some features deal with the physical characteristics of voice. An electronic mail message can be displayed as a page of text on a computer screen, and it is easy to glance at it and scroll forward and backward. For voice messages, scrolling is not so easy. Special commands are necessary to move back or skip ahead by a few seconds. The system in use at the author's university has a particularly obnoxious feature: You cannot fast forward or delete a broadcast message from the university president until you have listened to it in its entirety.

We would like to write a program that simulates a voice mail system. It is not our interest to have a completely realistic working phone system. At the time of this writing, few of us have computers with easily programmable voice capture and storage. We will simply represent voice mail by text that is entered through the keyboard. We will also ignore the complexities of simultaneous access to the system by multiple users. Our simulation will handle sequential access events only.

Are we ready to start coding? Definitely not. Major decisions have yet to be made. What features will we actually implement? How will we distinguish simulated voice input from simulated input of telephone number keys (1 ... 9, #, *)? How will we denote the act of hanging up and picking up the receiver? Are there system limits on the length of a message, the number of messages per mailbox, or the number of mailboxes? How do mailboxes get created and deleted?

A surprisingly popular approach, practiced both by students and industry programmers, is to start programming and to solve these problems as they come up. The end result *can* be quite acceptable *if* produced by a single individual with a good understanding of user needs, good judgment, and good code organization. More likely, it will be an awful mess that is unintuitive to use and impossible to enhance and maintain. We are interested in a process that does not take chances but predictably delivers a good program.

The first formal step in the process that leads us toward the final product (the mail message program) is the analysis phase. Its role is to answer the questions that were just raised. We will perform a sample analysis in the next section.

5.2. ANALYSIS OF THE MAIL MESSAGE SYSTEM

5.2.1. Reaching an Extension

At the outset, the mail message system awaits the input of a four-digit extension number. Some numbers belong to active extensions; others do not. We will see subsequently how active extensions are created. If an inactive extension has been dialed, an error message is generated, and the system reverts to its initial state. If an active extension has been reached, the mailbox greeting is played. Unless changed by the owner, the greeting is

```
You have reached extension xxxx. Please leave a message now.
```

At this point the caller can type in a message by entering the message text on the keyboard. At the end of the message, an "H" should be entered on a single line to denote hanging up the telephone. Only nonempty messages should be stored.

Alternatively, callers can press the "#" key to access their own mailboxes.

5.2.2. Accessing a Mailbox

To restrict access to a mailbox to its owner, the system prompts for a passcode. After the mailbox owner has entered the correct password, it is possible to retrieve messages from the mailbox or to change mailbox settings. The user options menu is displayed:

```
You have n new messages and s saved messages.
Press 1 to retrieve your messages.
Press 2 to change your greeting.
Press 3 to change your passcode.
```

(The first command prompt is shown only when messages are pending.) When "1" is pressed, the system enters the message retrieval loop.

If the caller presses "2" to change the greeting, the system prompts to record a new greeting. If the caller presses "3" to enter a new passcode, the system prompts to enter a new passcode. Passcodes must be four digits long. Invalid passcodes cause an error message. On completion of a greeting or password change, the main menu is displayed again. If the user hangs up instead of entering a greeting or passcode, no change is recorded.

5.2.3. Retrieving Messages

The first message is displayed. Then the message options menu appears:

```
Press 1 to delete the current message.
Press 2 to save the current message.
```

After the selection is processed, the next message is played. This repeats until all messages are played. Then the user options menu appears again. At any time, the caller may hang up by pressing "H". New messages are played in the order in which they were received. After all new messages are played, the saved messages are played in the order in which they were saved.

5.2.4. Adding New Mailboxes

When first started, the mail system has one special mailbox, with extension 9999 and passcode 1728, belonging to the administrator and no further active extensions. The administrator mailbox works the same way as all other mailboxes, but it has an additional option in the main menu:

```
Press 4 to add a new extension.
```

When "4" is pressed, the system prompts to enter the new four-digit extension number and then prompts for a four-digit passcode. The extension is activated, and the main menu is played again.

5.2.5. Simulation of Voice Data and Telephone Equipment

In our program, we need to simulate the three distinct input events that occur in a real telephone system: speaking, pushing a button on the telephone pad, and picking up and hanging up the telephone. We use the following convention for input: An "H" on a line by itself denotes hanging up the telephone. A sequence of keys "1"..."9" on a line with no further characters denotes a dialed number. A "#" or "*" on a line by itself denotes pushing one of the command keys on the pad. Any other text denotes voice input.

To quit the program, access mailbox 0000.

5.2.6. System Limits

We need to set some limits on system resources. The following limits are admittedly unrealistic, but they enable us to concentrate on the object-oriented features rather than memory management during the programming phase. We set limits of 10 active mailboxes in addition to the administrator mailbox, and up to 20 new and 10 saved messages per mailbox. Attempts to generate more active accounts are rejected. If a mailbox with 20 new messages is called, the message

```
You have reached extension xxxx.
The mailbox is currently full.
```

is displayed instead of the greeting, and no new message can be stored. If the saved message area is full, the mailbox owner can only discard new messages. Messages and greetings may be of any length. They may span multiple lines.

5.3. CRC CARDS

5.3.1. Card Layout

An effective technique for discovering classes, functionality, and relationships is the so-called CRC card method, described by [Beck]. A CRC card is simply an A5 or A6 size index card (4" by 6" or 3" by 5" will do fine if you live in a nonmetric country) that describes one class and lists the class responsibilities (operations) and collaborators (related classes). Index cards are a good choice, for a number of reasons. They are small, discouraging you from piling too much responsibility into a single class. They are stiff and can be handed around and rearranged by a group of designers in brainstorming sessions. Of course, many people have used regular sheets of paper or documents in a multiwindow editor, with good success.

You make one card for each discovered class. List any discovered operations on the front, together with any classes that are used in some way to carry out these operations. On the back you may list any data fields.

Class: `Mailbox`
Operations (Responsibilities)   Relationships (Collaborators) get current message   `Message, MessageQueue` play greeting

Fields (on back of card) queue of new messages queue of kept messages greeting extension number passcode

Figure 5.1. Front and back of a typical CRC card.

The front of the CRC card shown in Figure 5.1 indicates that we have discovered two operations of the mailbox: to get the current message and to play the greeting. The "get current message" operation collaborates with the `Message` and `MessageQueue` classes. That is, it needs to interact with message and message queue objects in some unspecified way.

5.3.2. An Example of CRC Card Evolution

CRC cards are quite intuitive for an analyst "walking through" a sequence of steps that solve one task. Consider, for example, the behavior of the message system when a user sends a message to another user's mailbox. The scenario begins when "someone" processes the dialing of an extension number. We find the need to specify a responsible agent and create a new index card, shown in Figure 5.2.

In our program we will have only one object of type `MailSystem`: "the" voice mail system. That is fine—it is typical for top-level objects to be the sole instance of their class. The `InputReader` is a class that can handle the separation of simulated telephone keys and message input.

The next logical step is to find the mailbox that belongs to the extension. This sounds like an appropriate task for the `MailSystem` class, since the system knows where all mailboxes are. We add an operation (see Figure 5.3).

Class: `MailSystem`
Operations (Responsibilities)   Relationships (Collaborators) dial extension   `InputReader`

Figure 5.2. An initial CRC card for the mail system.

Class: MailSystem	
Operations (Responsibilities)	Relationships (Collaborators)
process dialing	InputReader
locate mailbox	Mailbox

Figure 5.3.   Evolving the CRC card for the mail system.

"Someone" has to find out whether the next step in the input is a message for the dialed extension or a login command. This could be done either by MailSystem or Mailbox. We let the "processing dialing" function handle it and give two separate operations, "receive message" and "login", to the Mailbox class. The updated CRC cards are shown in Figure 5.4.

5.3.3. Hints for Using CRC Cards

Try to keep cards physically close to their collaborators. The visual arrangement of the cards can give clues to simple or overly complex relationships. You should not be afraid to tear up cards or to erase, modify, or reorganize operations. Experienced designers will cheerfully admit that they rarely hit upon an optimal division of responsibilities at the first try, and that a fair amount of trial and error is necessary even in seemingly simple cases.

Group discussion can be particularly successful with class design. Get two or three designers together. Here is a good way to "break the ice" and get started. Let all participants use the "noun and verb" technique described in Chapter 1 to come up with a pool of candidates for classes and operations. Then consider the first important task that comes to mind, and perform a scenario

Class: MailSystem	
Operations (Responsibilities)	Relationships (Collaborators)
process dialing	InputReader
locate mailbox	Mailbox

Class: Mailbox	
Operations (Responsibilities)	Relationships Collaborators)
get current message	Message, MessageQueue
play greeting	
receive message	Message, MessageQueue
login	InputReader

Figure 5.4.   Updated CRC cards for the mail system and mailbox.

walk-through. Have one person play protagonist. The protagonist proposes a responsible agent and a method for carrying out the task. Invariably the description will be somewhat vague, and it is easy for the other participants to ask for clarification, or to suggest different preferences. Rotate the protagonist role. You are done when all nontrivial tasks have been played through to the satisfaction of all participants.

Resist the temptation of adding operations just because they can be done. Keep in mind that implementation details are not supposed to be prescribed in the design, but it is certainly fair to consider sketches of possible implementations. In fact, participants should criticize approaches that unnecessarily force a particular data structure. Conversely, belief in the validity of an operation is strengthened when it is shown that it can be carried out under two different plausible implementations.

You do not necessarily need a group of people for effective class discovery. But if you work on your own, it helps if you have a "Jekyll and Hyde" personality and can play your own devil's advocate.

CRC cards are a good tool for discovering designs, but they are not particularly suited for documenting them. The visual arrangement and movement of the cards is ephemeral. As the design evolves over time, it is inconvenient to update a stack of paper cards. For this reason, the cards are usually discarded after a design has been found. We will discuss more permanent documentation tools in the next sections.

In summary, index cards are a popular mechanism to discover classes and operations. It is easy to make a new card for each class as the need arises and to mark new operations on the cards. Scenarios can be "played out" by moving the cards around while tracing the control flow.

5.3.4. CRC Cards for the Mail System Problem

Figure 5.5 shows a complete set of CRC cards for the mail system example. The solution presented here is only one of many possible divisions of responsibility. The exercises suggest other alternatives.

Class: MailSystem	
Operations (Responsibilities)	Relationships (Collaborators)
process dialing	InputReader, Message
locate mailbox	Mailbox
create mailbox	Mailbox

Fields (on back of card)
collection of mailboxes
administrator mailbox

Figure 5.5.   A complete set of CRC cards for the mail system.

Class: Mailbox	
Operations (Responsibilities)	Relationships (Collaborators)
receive message	Message, MessageQueue
login	InputReader
get current message	Message, MessageQueue
delete current message	Message, MessageQueue
change greeting	InputReader
change passcode	InputReader
retrieve messages	
activate	

Fields (on back of card)
queue of new messages
queue of kept messages
greeting
extension number
passcode

Class: AdminMailbox	
Operations (Responsibilities)	Relationships (Collaborators)
receive message	Message, MessageQueue
login	InputReader
get current message	Message, MessageQueue
keep current message	Message, MessageQueue
delete current message	Message, MessageQueue
change greeting	InputReader
change passcode	InputReader
activate	
create mailbox	MailSystem

Fields (on back of card)
queue of new messages
queue of kept messages
greeting
extension number
passcode

Class: Message	
Operations (Responsibilities)	Relationships (Collaborators)
play	

Fields (on back of card)
message text

Figure 5.5.   *(continued)*

Class: MessageQueue	
Operations (Responsibilities)	Relationships (Collaborators)
length of queue	
get message at head	Message
remove message at head	Message
append message at tail	Message

Fields (on back of card)
collection of messages

Class: InputReader	
Operations (Responsibilities)	Relationships (Collaborators)
type of pending input	
get next item	

Fields (on back of card)
buffered input line

Figure 5.5. *(continued)*

Exercise 5.3.1. In our design for the voice mail system, the MailSystem class only handles user login. As soon as a user has logged in, the user's Mailbox class gains control. Change the responsibilities so that the MailSystem is responsible for all user interaction. What differences do you see in the collaboration patterns?

Exercise 5.3.2. Modify the design for the voice mail system to make the Message class responsible for reading its own text. What differences do you see in the collaboration patterns?

Exercise 5.3.3. Play the following scenario with the CRC cards and record in detail the sequence of active classes and the operations they perform: A user leaves a message for the other user. The other user logs in, plays the message, and keeps it.

Exercise 5.3.4. Discover classes and operations for a program that controls an automatic bank teller machine, using CRC cards.

Exercise 5.3.5. Use CRC cards for the design of a simple line-oriented text editor. Here is a minimal set of commands that you should support.

- list n_1 n_2: List all lines between n_1 and n_2.
- insert n s: Insert the text s (which may contain spaces) before line n.

- cut n_1 n_2: Remove all lines between n_1 and n_2 and place them into the paste buffer.
- copy n_1 n_2: Copy all lines between n_1 and n_2 into the paste buffer.
- paste n: Paste the contents of the paste buffer before line n.
- search s: Print all lines containing s.

Exercise 5.3.6. Extend the voice mail system by supporting privileged messages. A privileged message must be played once in its entirety before it can be deleted. Only the administrator can send privileged messages.

5.4. CLASS PATTERNS

It is not possible to give a complete categorization of classes, but classes do fall into common patterns. The following patterns cover the most frequent cases, and you may find them helpful in the class discovery process. A given class may fall into more than one of these patterns.

5.4.1. Tangible Things

These are the easiest classes to discover since they are visible in the problem domain. We have seen many examples: Mailbox, Message, Document, Footnote.

5.4.2. System Interfaces and Devices

These are also easy to discover by considering the system resources and interactions of the system. Typical examples are DisplayWindow and InputReader.

5.4.3. Agents

Sometimes it is helpful to change an operation into an agent class. For example, the "compute page breaks" operation on a document could be turned into a Paginator class, which operates on documents. Then the paginator can work on a part of a document while another part is edited on the screen. In this case, the agent class is invented to express execution parallelism.

The InputReader class is another example. Rather than having the message read its input, the input reader gets text, which is used to construct the message. The agent class decouples the Message class from input mechanisms and separates the abstraction levels of input processing and controlling message contents.

5.4.4. Events and Transactions

Event and transaction classes are useful to model records of activities that describe what happened at a time in the past or what needs to be done at a later time. A low-level example is a MouseEvent class, which remembers when and where the mouse moved or a button was clicked. A high-level example is a `CustomerArrival` class, which specifies when and where what kind of customer is scheduled to arrive.

5.4.5. Users and Roles

User and role classes are stand-ins for actual users of the program. An `Administrator` class is an interface to the human administrator of the system. A `Reviewer` models a user in an interactive authoring system whose role is to add critical annotations and recommendations for change. User classes are common in systems that are used by more than one person or where one person needs to perform distinct tasks.

5.4.6. Systems

System classes model a subsystem or the overall system being built. Their roles are typically to perform initialization and shutdown and to start the flow of input into the system. The `MailSystem` is a typical example.

5.4.7. Containers

Containers are used to store and retrieve information. An example is a `Mailbox` that stores messages or an `Invoice` that stores items and quantities ordered. At the design phase, one should not be overly concerned with the low-level nature of a container (hash table or balanced tree), and one should assume that the standard data structures (lists, queues, maps, and so forth) are readily available.

5.4.8. Foundation Classes

These are classes such as `String`, `Date`, `Vector`, `Matrix`, `Rectangle`, `PostalAddress`, or `Semaphore`. They encapsulate data types with well-understood properties. At the design stage, one should simply assume that these classes are readily available, just as the fundamental types (integers and floating-point numbers) are. These classes can often be acquired from library vendors. They can be reused easily in many projects.

5.4.9. Collaboration Patterns

Sometimes, classes group together to achieve a goal. The container/iterator pattern is characteristic. A container holds data, and an iterator can attach itself to the container and sequentially step through the data in the container. This way, data can be inspected one item at a time. Another common pattern is the model/view pattern, in which a so-called model holds information and one or more views can present the data in different formats. An example is a model class, holding financial data, with one view displaying the information as a graph and another presenting it as a table.

Exercise 5.4.1. Consider the classes that we discovered for the voice mail system. Into which patterns do they fall?

5.5. RECOGNIZING CLASS RELATIONSHIPS

5.5.1. Recognizing Usage

Usage is easiest to recognize. Simply look at the "collaboration" part of the CRC card. Collaboration is equivalent to usage. For example, the Mailbox class collaborates with, or uses, Message, but Message does not use InputReader.

5.5.2. Recognizing Aggregation

Aggregation is the "has-a" relationship. It is fulfilled if each object of one class either contains or exclusively manages objects of another class. For example, each Mailbox has, or aggregates, Message objects.

We distinguish between aggregation and simple attributes. If an object consists of a field of a numeric basic type, such as integer or floating-point values, or of a foundation class, such as date or string, it is considered merely an attribute, not aggregation.

The fields that are noted on the back of a CRC card denote either attributes or aggregation. Of course, no concerted effort is made in the design phase to determine all fields of a class. You should therefore check to capture all aggregation relationships.

5.5.3. Recognizing Inheritance

Inheritance is the "is-a" relationship. If every object of a class logically conforms to another class but has additional special properties, then the first inherits from the other. For example, the AdminMailbox class inherits from Mailbox, because an administrator mailbox is a special case of a mailbox.

Sometimes inheritance is difficult to see because you did not yet discover a common base class. If you observe that several classes have shared responsibilities, check whether it is possible to define a base class that can assume those responsibilities.

Recognizing common base classes is particularly important for the implementation. Common code need only be provided once in the base class and is automatically inherited by the derived classes—hence the term *inheritance*. Chapter 7 describes how this code sharing is carried out in C++.

Here is an example for discovering shared behavior. Consider a computer system that can deliver faxes, voice messages, or electronic mail. The user sees a listing of the received messages on the screen, showing type, arrival time, and sender. Faxes can be printed, deleted, saved, and forwarded with attachments. Voice messages can be played over the computer speaker, deleted, saved, and forwarded with added recordings. Electronic mail can be displayed on the screen, deleted, saved, or edited and forwarded. What is the common abstraction, and what are its properties? The common abstraction is `Message`. A mailbox holds a collection of messages, which may be fax, voice, or email. The mailbox can keep, delete, or forward them. Each message can be inspected and edited. Derived classes are `FaxMessage`, `VoiceMessage`, and `EmailMessage`. The method of inspection and editing is different for each of these classes, but the operational interface is the same.

Exercise 5.5.1. Determine usage, aggregation, and inheritance for the classes that we discovered for the voice mail system.

Exercise 5.5.2. Consider an extension of the voice mail system that supports privileged messages. A privileged message must be played once in its entirety before it can be deleted. Only the administrator can send privileged messages. What class relationships exist between `PrivilegedMessage` and other classes in the voice mail system?

5.6. CLASS DIAGRAMS

5.6.1. Common Diagramming Conventions

Graphical presentation methods to convey design information are very popular, for a good reason. It is easier to extract relationship information by looking at a diagram than by reading documentation. On the other hand, there is a limit to the information contents of graphs (see [Tufte]). The best approach is to use the graph to convey an overview of the design and to use text for the details.

To express class relationships, some convention is required. We are all familiar with flowcharts that use rectangles for steps and diamonds for decisions. Of course, there is no logical reason why decisions couldn't be denoted by triangles or circles. The diamond is just the traditional choice. Unfortunately, there is no similar tradition for class diagrams. A number of diagramming conventions have been proposed, among them those described in [Booch], [Rumbaugh], and [Coad]. These notation systems are in active use, and there are software tools supporting each one of them. The notations are well thought out and provide tools to express a large amount of detail information in a graphical form. There are symbols for class relationship, object behavior under transactions, timing and scheduling, modules, and templates. For our modest goals, it is sufficient to concentrate on class relationship notation only.

Unfortunately, the various notations differ greatly in their visual appearance. Figures 5.6, 5.7, and 5.8 show the same relationships, as drawn following the Booch, Rumbaugh, and Coad-Yourdon notations. Classes are easy to recognize. They are denoted by boxes or cloud shapes containing the class name and (if you like) the names of the major operations. The class relationships are frustrating to decipher. To the uninitiated, the small circles, squares, and diamonds used as annotations for connecting lines are completely meaningless. One author ([Martin], p. 121) recommends that "tools using strange diagrams are best avoided" and then turns around and explains his own diagrams, which look just as strange.

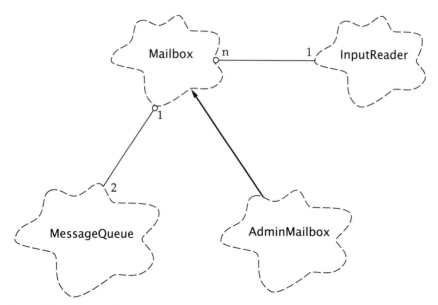

Figure 5.6.   A class relationship diagram in the Booch notation.

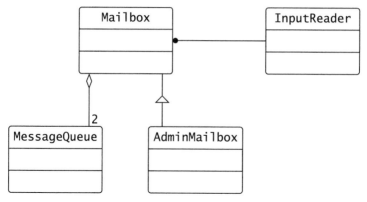

Figure 5.7.   A class relationship diagram in the Rumbaugh notation.

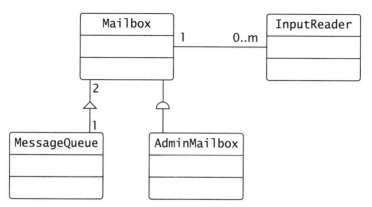

Figure 5.8.   A class relationship diagram in the Coad-Yourdon notation.

It should be pointed out that the sophisticated methodologies of [Booch] and [Rumbaugh] use many more diagrams to display other design information. Furthermore, there is more to a methodology than just diagramming rules. In order not to overwhelm the reader, we just use the most important subset, which is common to a number of methodologies.

5.6.2. Simplified Class Diagrams

In this book, we will use the following trick. We will draw all diagrams using the notation of Booch, using a software tool supporting the notation. (We don't claim that the Booch notation is superior to another notation, but it is fairly well known in the C++ community.) However, we will always write the relationships on the arrows, using this simple convention:

Annotation	Meaning
uses	Use relationship
has	Aggregation relationship
is	Inheritance relationship

Figure 5.9 shows an example of the annotations. This is simple common sense, long practiced by the designers of traffic signs. Consider Figure 5.10: The sign conveys the same information both textually and visually by using a characteristic shape. The sign is comprehensible to those familiar with the shape convention but unable to read as well as to literate visitors from outside the United States. Figure 5.11 shows how mysterious an unfamiliar sign without textual annotation can be.

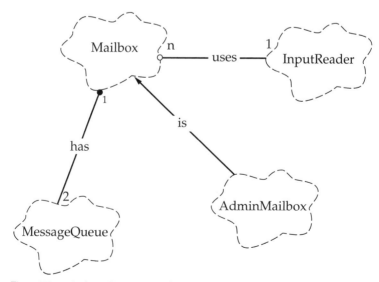

Figure 5.9.   A class diagram in the annotated Booch notation.

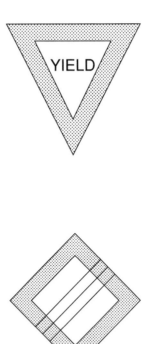

Figure 5.10. An American "yield" traffic sign.

Figure 5.11. A European "no right of way" traffic sign.

We encourage you to use the same method. You can use pencil and paper or any drawing software that can draw boxes and lines and that can place text inside boxes and along lines. The shape of the classes is not important. If your drawing software doesn't support the fancy clouds, just use rectangles. In handwritten diagrams, ovals tend to work best.

For the "has" relationship, we also write the cardinality (1 : 1 or 1 : n) on the end points of the connection.

We cannot overemphasize the importance of the "uses" relationship in class diagrams. A class A uses another class B if any A operation needs to access a B object. In that case, any change in B could have a potential impact on A. For that reason, well-clustered usage relationships greatly increase the stability of a design.

5.6.3. Diagramming the Mail System Design

We discovered the following class relationships:

- `AdminMailbox` inherits from `Mailbox`.
- A `MailSystem` has one admin mailbox and $n \geq 0$ other mailboxes.
- A mailbox has two message queues.
- A message queue has $n \geq 0$ messages.
- `MailSystem` and `Mailbox` each use `Message` and `InputReader`.

Figure 5.12 displays these facts graphically.

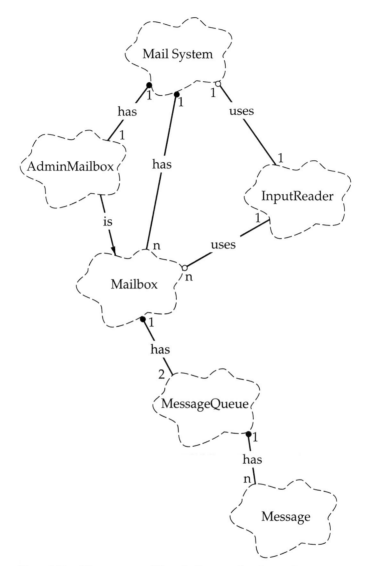

Figure 5.12.   The annotated Booch diagram for the mail system.

Exercise 5.6.1. Look at Figure 5.12. If the interface of the Message class changes, which other classes may be affected? If MailSystem changes, which other classes may be affected?

Exercise 5.6.2. Add the PrivilegedMessage class to the class diagram.

Exercise 5.6.3. Draw the class diagram for the classes of the automatic teller machine in Exercise 5.3.4.

Exercise 5.6.4. Draw the class diagram for the classes of the simple text editor in Exercise 5.3.5.

5.7. CLASS DESCRIPTION FORMS

5.7.1. Forms for Classes and Operations

CRC cards contain very limited information about classes: their names, the names of all operations, and the names of related classes. Class diagrams add information on the nature of the relationship. A more detailed description is necessary to aid the programmer charged with implementing the class.

Name	
Base class(es)	
Purpose	
States	
Constructors	
Operations *Mutators* *Accessors*	
Fields	

Figure 5.13.   A class description form.

Prototype	
Purpose	
Receives	
Returns	
Remarks	

Figure 5.14.   An operation description form.

The information is gathered in forms. ([Booch] calls them templates, but in the context of C++ templates mean something completely different.) You can think of a form as a questionnaire, asking about important features of the class. As with all forms, there may be fields that do not apply to a particular situation and that can be left blank.

Actually, there is one form for the class and a separate form for each operation. Figure 5.13 shows the class form. For each operation, fill out a form like the one shown in Figure 5.14.

The implementation details for fields should be left as vague as possible. Should a passcode be an `int` or a `String`? Either way, it won't have an impact on the design, and the decision can be deferred. The nature of a link may be kept open, and during implementation a pointer, reference, handle, or other location mechanism may be selected. The exact nature of a collection (that is, whether it is an array, linked list, hash table) should not be specified.

5.7.2. Preparing Forms

Some programmers like to plan everything with pencil and paper before starting to code. For those programmers it is best to make photocopies of the forms and fill them in by hand, as in Figure 5.15.

However, it actually makes a lot of sense to type the descriptions into the computer, using a programming editor. You can use a word processor, but if you do, don't bother with fonts or fancy boxes. The goal is to get an ASCII file that becomes the basis for code in the implementation phase. We assume that the implementation language will be C++. It is a good idea to use C++ syntax to describe functions, arguments, and fields and to use C++-style comments to bracket text sections.

Name	`Mailbox`
Base class(es)	
Purpose	A mailbox contains messages that can be listed, kept or discarded.
States	empty | full | neither
	inactive | active
Constructors	default: makes inactive mailbox
Operations *Mutators*	`receive_message(Message)`
	`login()`: process password and commands
	`retrieve_messages()`
	`delete_current()`
	`change_greeting()`
	`change_password()`
	`activate(int extension, int passcode)`
Accessors	`Message get_current()`
Fields	`MessageQueue _new_messages`
	`MessageQueue _kept_messages`
	`String _greeting`
	`_extension`
	`_passcode`

Figure 5.15.   A class form for the `Mailbox` class.

The information in Figure 5.15 might look like this in an editor:

```
class Mailbox
/* PURPOSE: A mailbox contains messages that can be listed,
            kept, or discarded.

    STATES:  empty | full | neither
             inactive | active
*/
// CONSTRUCTION
   default // makes inactive mailbox

// OPERATIONS -- Mutators
   receive_message(Message)
   login() // process passcode and commands
   retrieve_messages()
   delete_current()
   change_greeting()
   change_password()
   activate(int extension)
// OPERATIONS -- Accessors
   Message get_current()
// FIELDS
   MessageQueue _new_messages
   MessageQueue _kept_messages
   String _greeting
   _extension
   _passcode
```

Figure 5.16 shows a form containing the information about an operation. When entered in a programming editor, the information should be formatted to look like this:

```
Bool MailSystem::add_mailbox(int extension)
/* PURPOSE:  Add a new mailbox to the system.
   RECEIVES: extension - the extension number of the mailbox
   RETURNS:  TRUE iff the operation succeeded

   REMARKS:  The operation may fail if the extension number is
             already in use or if there is no space to add
             another mailbox.
*/
```

The tabular form is easier to read, but the ASCII form is easier to convert to code, and the code will be modified as time goes on. We are therefore interested

Prototype	`Bool MailSystem::add_mailbox(int extension, int passcode)`
Purpose	Add a new mailbox to the system.
Receives	`extension` – the extension number of the mailbox
	`passcode` - the passcode number
Returns	TRUE iff the operation succeeded
Remarks	The operation may fail if the extension number is already in use or if there is no space to add another mailbox.

Figure 5.16.   A form describing a class operation.

in code that is as self-documenting as possible. For small- and medium-sized projects, it is feasible to keep most documentation in the code, thereby avoiding the considerable difficulty of keeping code and external documentation synchronized. At some point in the future, there may well be tools that produce both compilable code and good-looking documentation, perhaps in the spirit of the WEB system invented by Donald Knuth (see [Sewell]). In the meantime, it seems best to migrate as much documentation as possible into the actual code.

Exercise 5.7.1. Write descriptions for all classes and operations in the voice mail system. You may use photocopies of the forms or a text editor.

Exercise 5.7.2. Write descriptions for all classes and operations of the automatic teller machine from Exercise 5.3.4.

Exercise 5.7.3. Write descriptions for all classes and operations of the simple text editor from Exercise 5.3.5.

5.8. C++ IMPLEMENTATION

In many cases it is easy to produce a code outline from the forms described in the previous section. Some issues need to be resolved in the coding phase:

- Specific data structures need to be selected for containers.
- Object links must be implemented as pointers, references, handles, or other mechanisms.
- Code must be written for all operations (of course).

- Additional private operations and data fields may need to be added to carry out these operations.
- Memory management functions may be required (see Chapter 13).

Here is the code for the `Mailbox` example form from the preceding section:

```
class Mailbox
/* PURPOSE: A mailbox contains messages that can be listed,
              kept, or discarded.
    STATES:  empty | full | neither
             inactive | active
*/
{

public:
   Mailbox(); // makes inactive mailbox

   void receive_message(Message);
   void login(); // process passcode and commands
   void retrieve_messages();
   void delete_current();
   void change_greeting();
   void change_password();
   void activate(int extension, int passcode);
   Message get_current() const;

private:
   MessageQueue _new_messages;
   MessageQueue _kept_messages;
   String _greeting;
   int _extension;
   int _passcode;
};
```

Note that accessor functions are declared as `const` and that all data is in the `private` section. All comments are retained.

The comments describing operations should also be retained when the implementation code is added:

```
Bool MailSystem::add_mailbox(int extension, int passcode)
/* PURPOSE:   Add a new mailbox to the system.
   RECEIVES:  extension - the extension number of the mailbox
              passcode - the passcode number
   RETURNS:   TRUE iff the operation succeeded
   REMARKS:   The operation may fail if the extension number is
              already in use or if there is no space to add another
              mailbox.
```

```
*/
{ if (_nused > NMAILBOX) return FALSE;
  int i = locate_mailbox(extension);
  if (i > 0) return FALSE; // duplicate
  _nused++;
  _mailbox[_nused].activate(extension, passcode);
  return TRUE;
}
```

Exercise 5.8.1. Using the class and operation descriptions, implement the automatic teller machine in C++.

Exercise 5.8.2. Using the class and operation descriptions, implement the simple text editor in C++.

5.9. DESIGN HINTS

5.9.1. Consider Reasonable Generalizations

Every problem is just one instance in a larger range of similar problems. Permute the task that you are modeling in reasonable ways. What features might the next update contain? What features do competing products implement already? Check that these features can be accommodated without radical changes in your design.

5.9.2. Minimize Coupling between Classes

A class is *coupled* with another if there is a relationship (is, has, uses) between them. A class that is not coupled with any other classes contributes nothing to the system and can be dropped. Classes that are coupled with too many other classes are a sign of trouble ahead. The inevitable evolution of the highly coupled class will force changes in the other classes.

Reducing coupling can require major reorganization, discovery of new classes, and reassignment of responsibilities, but this is time well spent. Make every effort to minimize coupling at the design stage. Once you get to the implementation, it is too late to make substantial reductions in coupling.

5.9.3. Challenge Counts of One

It is an essential advantage of object-oriented design that it is just as easy to create multiple objects as it is to create one object. You should double-check all aggregations that specify a count of 1.

Does the word processor really edit just one document? Is there only one window on the screen? Does the mail system really have just one administrator mailbox? Does a message have just one sender? Sometimes, a count of 1 is an integral part of the problem to be solved. More often, it is just a temporary limitation that may need to be lifted later. Make sure that your design can withstand this generalization.

5.9.4. Split Up Classes with Too Much Responsibility

Sometimes a top-level class such as MailSystem ends up with far too many operations because all commands are simply added to it. Rethink classes with too much responsibility and split them up.

5.9.5. Eliminate Classes with Too Few Responsibilities

A class with *no* operations is surely not useful. What would you do with its objects? A class with only one or two operations may be useful. You should convince yourself that there is really no better way of distributing the responsibilities. If another existing class can meaningfully carry out the task, move the operations and eliminate the class.

5.9.6. Eliminate Unused Responsibilities

Sometimes responsibilities seem natural for a class, but they are never used in the scenario walk-throughs. For example, someone may have suggested a Mailbox operation "sort messages."

It makes little sense to implement an operation that is unused. It is not even a good idea to promise to implement the operation should there ever be a need for it. That promise may restrict the evolution of the class.

Nevertheless, the fact that an operation can be supported adds confidence that the design is strong and generalizable.

5.9.7. Reorganize Unrelated Responsibilities

Does your class contain an operation that sticks out like a sore thumb, being completely unrelated to the others? Move it to a different class, or add a new class that can handle it.

5.9.8. Express Repeated Functionality with Inheritance

Is the same responsibility carried out by multiple classes? Check whether you can recognize this commonality by finding a common base class and have the other classes inherit from it.

5.9.9. Keep Class Responsibilities at a Single Abstraction Level

Every software project exhibits a layering of abstraction levels. At the lowest levels, we have file systems, memory allocation, keyboard and mouse interfaces, and other system services. At the highest levels there are classes that tie together the software system, such as MailSystem or SpreadsheetApplication.

The responsibilities of a class should stay at one abstraction level. A class MailUser that represents a mid-level abstraction should not deal with implementing queues, a low-level responsibility, nor should it be concerned with the initialization of the system, a high-level responsibility.

5.9.10. Names of Classes and Operations

Class names should be nouns, in the singular form: Message, Mailbox. Sometimes the noun needs to be prefixed by an adjective or gerund: ConvexPolygon, ReceivingBuffer. Don't use Object in the class name (MailboxObject)—it adds no value. Unless you are solving a very generic problem, stay away from generic names such as Agent, Task, Item, Event.

Names of operations should be verbs or short sequences of words containing one verb. In the first steps of design, operation names can be longer and informal: "get input from terminal." In the implementation, names should be shortened to one or two words. Take advantage of the added information given by the types of the arguments: "add message" can become add(Message m).

Keep implementation names consistent. Don't mix get_message with give_name.

INVARIANTS

6.1. A REFRESHER ON LOOP INVARIANTS

Consider the task of computing the nth power of a floating-point number a for a positive integer n. It would be inefficient to multiply a to itself n times (an $O(n)$ algorithm). The repeated squaring algorithm can perform the same task in $O(\log n)$ time:

```
double pow (double a, int n)
{ double r = 1;
  while (n > 0)
  { if (is_even(n))
    { a = a * a;
      n = n / 2;
    }
    else
    { r = r * a;
      n = n - 1;
    }
  }
  return r;
}
```

Why does it work? One can run through a few cases to see that it indeed seems to come up with the right answer every time. In that process, one may well gain an intuitive understanding that gives sufficient confidence to put the matter to rest.

But there is a better way to demonstrate that the function performs the correct computation. One can establish a *loop invariant*, use simple algebra to check that the loop indeed preserves the invariant, and then derive a guarantee of correctness. Let a_{in}, n_{in} be the input values to the function. The "in" subscript is required because the function modifies a, n. The invariant of the while loop is

$$r \cdot a^n = a_{in}{}^{n_{in}} \qquad (I)$$

(In logical conditions we write $=$ for equality, not for assignment.) To show that (I) is indeed a loop invariant, we must show (1) that it holds before entering the loop for the first time and (2) that the statement continues to hold after one iteration through the loop provided it was true on entering the loop. Before entering the loop for the first time, we have

$$r = 1$$
$$a = a_{in}$$
$$n = n_{in}$$

and (I) clearly holds. Suppose that (I) holds at the beginning of the loop. We label the values of r, a, n as "old" when entering the loop and as "new" when exiting the loop. We assume that on entry

$$r_{old} \cdot a_{old}{}^{n_{old}} = a_{in}{}^{n_{in}}$$

In the loop we have to distinguish two cases: n even and n odd. If n is even, the loop performs the following transformations:

$$r_{new} = r_{old}$$
$$a_{new} = a_{old}{}^2$$
$$n_{new} = n_{old}/2$$

Therefore,

$$
\begin{aligned}
r_{new} \cdot a_{new}{}^{n_{new}} &= r_{old} \cdot (a_{old})^{2 \cdot n_{old}/2} \\
&= r_{old} \cdot a_{old}{}^{n_{in}} \\
&= a_{in}{}^{n_{in}}
\end{aligned}
$$

On the other hand, if n is odd, then

$$r_{new} = r_{old} \cdot a_{old}$$
$$a_{new} = a_{old}$$
$$n_{new} = n_{old} - 1$$

Therefore,

$$
\begin{aligned}
r_{new} \cdot a_{new}{}^{n_{new}} &= r_{old} \cdot a_{old} \cdot a_{old}{}^{n_{old}-1} \\
&= r_{old} \cdot a_{old}{}^{n_{old}-1} \\
&= a_{in}{}^{n_{in}}
\end{aligned}
$$

In either case, the new values for r, a, and n fulfill the loop invariant. Therefore, we can conclude two facts when the loop condition becomes false and the loop is exited for the last time. By the loop invariant, we know that

$$r \cdot a^n = a_{in}{}^{n_{in}}$$

Because the loop terminated, we know that

$$n = 0$$

Combining those two facts, we see that

$$r = r \cdot a^0$$
$$= a_{in}{}^{n_{in}}$$

Hence r indeed computes the nth power of the original a.

This technique is quite useful, because it can explain an algorithm that is not completely obvious, without a trace of a doubt. The general argument has this form. Consider a loop

```
// invariant I
while (C )
{ T
}
// I ∧ ¬ C
// that is, I is true and C is false.
```

To show that I is an invariant, we must see that it holds before the loop and that the transformations T in the loop preserve it. The benefit is then that we know $I \wedge \neg C$ upon loop termination. If I and C are chosen skillfully, we may be able to deduce correctness of a computation.

Exercise 6.1.1. Technically speaking, in the example of the pow function, we only know that $I \wedge n \leq 0$ upon the exit of the loop, but we actually used $n = 0$ in the argument. Show that the loop invariant can be extended to be

$$r \cdot a^n = a_{in}{}^{n_{in}} \text{ and } n \geq 0 \tag{I}$$

and show why that implies that $n = 0$.

When the technique of loop invariants was first discovered, computer scientists had high hopes that it would lead to a revolution in programming in which programs would routinely be supplied with correctness proofs. Unfortunately, this has not happened, for a number of reasons. It is often difficult to come up with the right invariants. You can see that from the pow example: Once the invariant was formulated, its verification involved only simple algebra. But try to explain it to a friend tomorrow without looking it up, and you may well fumble a bit before hitting upon the right equation. In cases involving more complex data structures, it turns out to be quite difficult to carry out the algebraic verification steps. See [Reynolds] for more information. From a practitioner's standpoint, one can view correctness proofs as one tool in the toolbag that is very useful in some situations. [Bentley 1986], ch. 4, explains this point of view.

Exercise 6.1.2. Show that

$$r = \binom{n + i - 1}{i - 1}$$

is a loop invariant for the loop in the binom function of Chapter 2. Use this fact to show the correctness of that function.

Exercise 6.1.3. Consider this loop for binary search to locate the position p of an element t of a *sorted* array a. Assume that it is known that exactly one of the elements of a is t. (In particular, a is nonempty.)

```
int l = a.low();
int h = a.high();
while (l < h)
{ int m = (l + h) / 2;
   if (a[m] < t) l = m + 1;
   if (a[m] == t) l = h = m;
   if (a[m] > t) h = m - 1;
}
p = l;
```

Verify that

$$t \in \{a[l] \ldots a[h]\}$$

is a loop invariant. Explain why that shows the correctness of the algorithm. Where do you require that the array be sorted?

Exercise 6.1.4. Enhance the algorithm of the previous exercise by removing the restriction that exactly one of the entries of a is known to equal t. If at least one entry equals t, set p1 to the lowest, p2 to the highest array index containing t. If t is not present in the array, set p1 to a.high() and p2 to a.low() - 1. Formulate an invariant for the loop in your modified algorithm.

6.2. CLASS INVARIANTS

Just as loop invariants are aids in studying the behavior of a single loop, *class invariants* are logical conditions to ensure the correct working of a class. Loop invariants are to hold before the loop starts and are preserved by the transformation that the loop carries out on the function variables. Similarly, class invariants must hold when an object is created, and they must be preserved under all operations of the class.

We distinguish between *interface invariants* and *implementation invariants*. Interface invariants are conditions that involve only the public interface of a class. Implementation invariants involve the details of a particular implementation. Interface invariants are of interest to the class user, because they give a behavior guarantee for any object of the class. Implementation invariants can be used by the class implementor to ensure the correctness of the implementation algorithms.

Consider, for example, a bounded stack of floating-point numbers.

```
class Stack
{
public:
    void push(double);
    double pop();
    Bool is_empty();
    Bool is_full();
private:
    // ...
};
```

We may formulate several interface invariants. After an element is pushed onto a stack, the stack is no longer empty. In logical notation, we write

$$\{s.\texttt{push}(x)\}\neg s.\texttt{is\_empty}()$$

If a stack is not full and we push an element on a stack, then calling pop retrieves the same element:

$$\neg s.\texttt{is\_full}()\{s.\texttt{push}(x); y := s.\texttt{pop}()\}x = y$$

Here we use the notation

$$C_1\{A_1; A_2; \ldots; A_n\}C_2$$

to mean the following: Provided that the condition C_1 holds, the actions $A_1, A_2, \ldots, A_n$ are carried out in sequence. Afterwards, the condition C_2 must hold. If C_1 does not hold, we make no further assertion. The logical conditions cannot involve mutator operations—only accessors and logical comparisons. The actions can involve mutators and assignments. (For clarity, we use := for assignments.)

One can give a complete algebraic description of a stack in this fashion. Other data types, such as queues or sets, can be characterized in a similar fashion (see [Cleaveland], ch. 13). However, this algebraic specification does not spell out any implementation strategy, and it is completely silent on the performance aspect of the operations. Many practical data structures can implement the same abstract data type, with varying efficiency tradeoffs. Invariant relations are necessarily silent on these issues. Nevertheless, interface invariants can be a useful tool to spell out the guarantees that any conforming implementation of a class must uphold, and they can aid the user of unfamiliar classes.

An implementation invariant makes an assertion about one particular implementation. Consider, for example, the following implementation of the bounded Stack class as an array that does not grow:

```
class Stack
{
public:
    Stack();
    void push(double);
    double pop();
    Bool is_empty();
    Bool is_full();
```

```
private:
  int _sptr;
  Array<double> _data;
};

Stack::Stack() : _data(1, MAXDATA), _sptr(0) {}
```

We may wish to assert that the stack pointer is always within a certain range:

$0 \leq s._sptr \leq$ MAXDATA
$s._sptr = 0 \Leftrightarrow s.is\_empty()$
$s._sptr =$ MAXDATA $\Leftrightarrow s.is\_full()$

These conditions make sense only if a stack is implemented as an array. If a stack is implemented as a linked list, there is no integer stack pointer field.

Exercise 6.2.1. Give interface invariants for a queue class. Assuming a circular array implementation, give an implementation invariant.

Exercise 6.2.2. Give an interface invariant for a priority queue. A priority queue is a container into which elements are inserted in any order, but the remove operation removes the smallest element that is currently present.

6.3. PRESERVATION OF CLASS INVARIANTS

Class invariants must be preserved by all operations of the class. For example, all Stack operations are responsible for maintaining $0 \leq$ _sptr $\leq$ MAXDATA. All Date operations are responsible for maintaining $1 \leq$ day() ≤ 31 and, in fact, the more complete condition describing all legal dates.

Exercise 6.3.1. Write down an interface invariant that completely describes legal dates.

For this reason, it would be difficult to have a set_day operation of the Date class. The sequence of instructions

```
Date d(20, 2, 1992);
d.set_day(31);
```

would leave the d object in a state that violates the Date invariant—February 31 is not a legal date. Of course, the next operation is likely to be set_month, but class invariants must always be maintained for all objects. In the middle of an operation the invariant might be temporarily violated, but it must be restored when the operation is completed. This leaves us with two choices—weaken the class invariant and thereby weaken protection, or abandon the idea of a set_day operation. A set_date operation that simultaneously sets day, month, and year can be implemented to preserve the class invariant. The operation would simply reject any attempt to set an invalid date.

Invariants are a useful guarantee for the class user, but they are also useful for the implementation of operations. If a condition is known to be true when an operation starts, the operation need not spend time checking it. For example, when looking up the string name ("January", and so forth) for a month in a table, the operation need not perform a range check on _month.

To verify that a condition really is an invariant of the class, one must verify that

- The condition holds at the end of every constructor.
- The condition holds at the end of every mutator (non-const) operation.

Class invariants are only meaningful for classes with constructors. In the absence of a constructor, fields may be initialized with random values, and it is unlikely that any meaningful invariants can be established.

Exercise 6.3.2. Implement the Stack class and verify that the conditions

$$\neg s.\texttt{is\_full}()\{s.\texttt{push}(x); y := s.\texttt{pop}()\}x = y$$

and

$$0 \leq s.\texttt{\_sptr} \leq \texttt{MAXDATA}$$

are indeed interface and implementation invariants of your implementation. Pay particular attention to empty and full stacks.

In practice, class invariants are a useful tool but not a complete guarantee against all problems. It is usually difficult to formulate a complete set of interface invariants that uniquely defines the abstract data type. A partial set of conditions that spells out the nonobvious conditions is more helpful to the class user. Similarly, the most useful invariant conditions for the class implementor are those that set out rules for the more subtle implementation aspects. Invariants that guarantee the validity of certain pointer variables or the range of certain index variables are often useful. They form a convenient checklist of conditions that every operation must restore.

Exercise 6.3.3. Recall that a binary search tree is a tree all of whose subtrees have the property that all left children are smaller in value than the root of the subtree, and that all the right children are larger. This is an implementation invariant. Show how the usual insert operation preserves that invariant. What happens if the tree is empty?

6.4. PRECONDITIONS AND POSTCONDITIONS OF OPERATIONS

The interface invariants of the Stack class say nothing about pushing yet another element on a stack that is already full. It is simply not covered by the rules. We say that ¬isfull() is a *precondition* of the push operation. Conversely, after pushing an element on the stack, we know that ¬isempty() must necessarily hold. This is a *postcondition* of the push operation.

In particular, all class invariants are both pre- and postconditions for all operations of the class.

An operation is not responsible for doing anything sensible if its precondition fails to hold. Conversely, an operation will guarantee its postcondition whenever it is invoked when the precondition is true. [Meyer], p. 115, views operations as agents fulfilling a *contract*. Contracts between persons or legal entities spell out responsibilities of two partners. Similarly, pre- and postconditions spell out the responsibility of the caller of an operation and the operation itself. The caller is responsible never to invoke the operation when the precondition fails. The operation is responsible for ensuring the postcondition when invoked correctly. It may rely on the correctness of the precondition and need not spend time checking it. For example, if the Stack class properly advertises that ¬isfull() is a precondition for the push operation, the code for push need not bother to check against the condition. Pushing onto a stack that is already full is the caller's fault, not the fault of Stack::push.

In practice, the purpose of programming is not to apportion blame but to get the job done. It does not usually pay to write operations with lots of preconditions. Most operations should spend some time in making consistency checks and gracefully performing some default action rather than creating real damage. [Koenig] describes a dialog between two programmers in which one asks the other what should happen if a certain condition fails, and the other responds, "I don't care—that can never happen." The first programmer then asks whether he can corrupt the entire database file in that case, and the second programmer concedes that he does care after all. Corruption of the entire database is too great a risk to take. Failures that can theoretically never occur do happen with distressing regularity in practice.

On the other hand, checking against errors in operations that occur very frequently can be very expensive. Consider, for example, range checking of arrays. Our Array template generates code that checks every array access a[i], in effect generating code

```
if (a.low() <= i && i <= a.high())
    use a[i];
```

This is great for trapping programmer errors, but it also makes code that works correctly quite a bit slower. The C language takes the position that it is the caller who must ensure that i is within the correct range, and indeed chaos will ensue if it is not. As every C programmer knows, memory overwrites and challenging debugging sessions are the consequence of violating this precondition.

Is the arbitrary corruption of memory an adequate penalty for failing to live up to one's contractual obligations? Would you enter a contract that gives you great rewards in most cases but a terrible punishment if you mess up, or would you prefer a different deal that asks less of you but gives you less performance? In real life there is no one answer—some people drive race cars, others sedans. Similarly, programmers must constantly make similar tradeoffs between safety and speed. The notion of pre- and postconditions is valuable because it makes the tradeoff visible and explicit. To use Meyer's metaphor, documented pre- and postconditions are a written agreement and thus superior to implicit understandings or verbal agreements.

Exercise 6.4.1. Can constructors have preconditions? Can they have postconditions that are stronger than the class invariant?

Exercise 6.4.2. Add a postcondition to the `Employee` constructor. Check `_name`, `_birthdate`, `_hiredate`, and `_salary` against impossible situations.

Exercise 6.4.3. Describe preconditions and postconditions for the operations of a `Queue` class. Discuss both a bounded and an unbounded queue.

Exercise 6.4.4. Describe preconditions and postconditions for the following operations of the `Array` template used in this book: `get`, `set`, `[]`, `insert`, `remove`, `qsort`.

Exercise 6.4.5. We have distinguished between interface and implementation invariants. Are pre- and postconditions part of the interface or part of the implementation? Would it make sense to have both kinds of pre- and postconditions?

6.5. TESTING FOR INVARIANTS AND CONDITIONS IN C++

The C++ language supports no constructs to attach logical conditions to classes or operations for automatic checking. We will use conditional compilation and the `assert` facility.

Checks against null pointers or range errors take little time to perform. Other invariants, such as the correctness of a date or the sortedness of an array, can be expensive to check. We must therefore have a way of turning checking on for testing and off for production code. (This technique has been derided as akin to wearing a life vest while sailing close to the shore and throwing it overboard in the middle of the ocean. True enough, but the life vest is uncomfortable and there is no chance of being rescued anyway when washed overboard in the middle of the ocean.)

The simplest method for conditional check is the `assert` macro defined in the assert.h header file. Insert the code

   `assert(` *condition that should be true* `)`

into your code, and if the condition fails, the program exits with an error message that contains the text of the condition, the name of the source file, and the line number in the file. For example,

```
assert(den != 0);
double x = (double) num / den;
```

For better error reporting, we supply three macros

```
ASSERT_INVARIANT
ASSERT_PRECOND
ASSERT_POSTCOND
```

When triggered, these macros either produce an error message and abort the program, or, if your compiler supports exception handling, raise an exception. (Exceptions are discussed in Chapter 15.)

To test for a class invariant, add a private operation

```
Bool Class::check_invariant() const
```

that tests the invariant. As the invariant conditions are refined, they need to be updated only in one location. Then add the line

```
ASSERT_INVARIANT(check_invariant());
```

at the end of each constructor and at the end of each mutator operation. You may even wish to avoid generating code for the invariant check if assertion checking is turned off. To achieve that, surround both the declaration and the definition of the check_invariant() function with preprocessor directives

```
#ifndef NDEBUG
```

and

```
#endif
```

Similarly, pre- and postconditions of individual operations can be checked by adding ASSERT statements at the beginning and end of operations. For example,

```
void Stack::push(double x)
{ ASSERT_PRECOND(!isfull());

  _sptr++;
  _data[_sptr] = x;

  ASSERT_INVARIANT(check_invariant());
}
```

Exercise 6.5.1. Add invariant checking to the Stack class. Pop off an empty stack intentionally and see how the assertion failure is triggered.

Exercise 6.5.2. Study the assert macro, as implemented in the assert.h header file. It uses some less known features of the preprocessor, such as "stringizing" and the __FILE__, __LINE__ macros. Read about them in the preprocessor documentation. What mechanism is involved to avoid code generation when NDEBUG is defined?

6.6. DESIGN HINTS

6.6.1. Typical Interface Invariants

The most common interface invariants are:

- Restrictions on state, as observed through accessors
- State change, caused by a mutator
- Relationships between two mutators

The invariant that a date is legal is of the first kind.

$$1 \le d.day() \le 31$$
$$d.day() = 31 \Rightarrow d.month() \in \{1, 3, 5, 7, 8, 10, 12\};$$
. . .

Only accessors are used.

The statement that a stack is no longer empty after an element has been pushed onto it expresses the state change of the push mutator.

$$\{s.push()\} \neg s.is\_empty()$$

The push and pop mutators of a stack are related by the statement that they are inverses to each other:

$$\neg s.is\_full()\{s.push(x); y := s.pop()\}x = y$$

6.6.2. Typical Implementation Invariants

Implementation invariants make statements about data fields. Common examples are assertions that an index is within certain bounds or that a pointer is not null.

Implementation invariants can spell out the relationships between several data fields. For example, in a linked list we may keep pointers to both a current element and its predecessor. The fields are related by the invariant

$$\_pre \neq 0 \Rightarrow \_pre\text{->}\_next = \_cur$$
$$\_pre = 0 \Rightarrow \_cur = \_head$$

This is a subtle but important invariant, and it is well worth checking that it is preserved by each mutator operation.

6.6.3. Typical Preconditions

A precondition is a condition that the class user guarantees when calling an operation. Preconditions fall into two categories:

- Validity of the arguments of the operation
- Compatibility between object state and the operation

Consider a hypothetical `File` class:

```
class File
{
public:
  void open(String name);
  unsigned char get();
  // ...
};
```

For this class, a precondition for `open` is that `name` corresponds to an existing file. Here we require that the argument of the operation be valid. A precondition for `get` is that the file has been previously opened. Here we require that the state of the object is not in conflict with the operation.

6.6.4. Typical Postconditions

A postcondition is a condition that an operation guarantees on completion. Postconditions fall into two categories:

- A statement about the result
- The state of the object upon completion

For example, a postcondition of the `get` operation on a priority queue is that the returned item be smaller than all others held in the queue. This is a statement about the result.

The `push` operation of a stack has as postcondition a guarantee about the state of the stack: It is definitely not empty. These postconditions are valuable, because they can turn into preconditions to other operations. After a `push`, we are assured that a `pop` may be applied to the stack.

6.6.5. Preconditions Must Be Verifiable

Consider the `File` class of Section 6.6.3. Would you want to use it? Consider that the precondition of the `open` operation is that the filename correspond to an existing file name. Since it is a precondition, the `open` operation is permitted to take any action if you invoke it with an illegal filename. It may terminate the program or just mess up in some way. Termination of the program (or continuation with flaky behavior) seems like a high price to pay for invoking the operation with an invalid filename.

A precondition is a strong contractual statement. The caller of the operation *must* fulfill it or lose the program.

Suppose we are given another function to test whether a file with a certain name exists. Then we could invoke it first, before calling open, and be assured that the operation will succeed.

```
File f;
if (file_exists(filename))
{ f.open(filename);
  // ...
}
```

Not quite. Between the execution of file_exists and open, another process might have removed or renamed the file, causing our program to die.

We conclude that requiring the existence of a file is an *inappropriate* precondition for the open operation, because there is no way for the programmer to *guarantee* its validity. We should drop the precondition, allow open to take any filename, and have it return the success or failure of the operation.

```
class File
{
public:
  Bool open(String name); // no  precondition
  unsigned char get(); // precondition: file open
  // ...
};
```

Contrast that with the precondition for get, namely that the file must be opened. This is objectively verifiable by the class user.

```
if (f.open(filename))
{ unsigned char ch = f.get();
  // ...
}
else
  // don't call get—it may terminate or corrupt your program
```

6.6.6. Preconditions vs. Defensive Programming

The advantage of a precondition is that it allows a more efficient implementation. Since the caller guarantees it, the operation need not spend time to check it. For example, the File::get operation may go right to the file buffer and get the next character without bothering to check whether the file is opened and its file buffer is correctly initialized.

Of course, if get is called on a file that has not been opened, the pointer to the file buffer is invalid, and accessing the file buffer through it either gives random results or causes a processor fault.

The alternative to a precondition is *defensive programming*, allowing the invocation of the operation on objects of any state, with any arguments. Then the operation must spend time checking the validity of the object and all arguments, and proceed only if they are in order.

We recommend the following approach. For infrequent operations, program defensively. The savings of not performing a check are not worth the risk of having the program die. For operations that are carried out frequently, especially in loops, such as putting elements into a container or getting input from a file, preconditions are effective. Formulate preconditions that the class user can verify.

As a class user, try to verify that the preconditions must hold for logical reasons. Monitor them during debugging. Measure the speed-up that results from dropping the check. If it is substantial, consider the remaining risk and make a decision to drop the check or to leave it in place in the release version.

INHERITANCE

In this chapter we discuss the important class relation of *inheritance*. A class (the so-called *derived* class) inherits from another class (the so-called *base* class) if the derived class describes a specialized subset of those objects characterized by the base class. Liskov formulated the following rule for inheritance: Any object of the derived class must be usable in place of a base class object (see [Bar-David], p. 59). For example, a class `Truck` may derive from a class `Vehicle`. All operations that apply to vehicles (moving, computing weight, license plate number) also apply to trucks. But trucks are more specialized, since they have operations that are not applicable to vehicles in general. For example, computation of road taxes applies to trucks but not to bicycles.

As we saw in Chapter 3, classes can be be modeled in any language supporting structured data types. The support of class operations and encapsulation (private and public features) is a useful benefit of object-oriented language. However, the principal advantage that an object-oriented language offers is the direct support of inheritance as a language construct.

In the first two sections of this chapter, we will introduce a collection of classes for displaying graphics on the computer screen. While this may seem a long digression, it is worth the effort, because classes representing graphical shapes lend themselves very well to the study of inheritance. We then learn how this collection of classes can be extended and organized through the inheritance mechanism.

7.1. GRAPHICS CONTEXT

Consider the task of writing the words "Hello, World" in the center of the screen and surrounding it with a box, like this:

Hello, World

Here is the code required to perform this task using the Borland Graphics Interface (BGI) under DOS, and using Microsoft Windows. BGI is an extremely primitive set of graphics routines. The Windows support for graphics is good, although it does fall short of the sophisticated interface of PostScript or Xlib.

The exact code is not important at this point. Just observe the considerable differences between the two program segments.

Here is the BGI version.

```
#include <stdlib.h>
#include <graphics.h>
#include <bios.h>

// Note: The .BGI file should be in the current directory.
// Be sure to link in graphics.lib.

int main()
{ int gdriver = DETECT;
  int gmode;
  initgraph(&gdriver, &gmode, "");
  int errorcode = graphresult();
  if (errorcode != grOk) exit(1);
  // initialization error—most likely missing .BGI file
  setfillstyle(1,getmaxcolor());

  String msg = "Hello, World";

  int msg_x = textwidth(msg.c_str());
  int msg_y = textheight(msg.c_str());

  int disp_x = getmaxx();
  int disp_y = getmaxy();

  int text_x = (disp_x - msg_x)/2;
  int text_y = (disp_y - msg_y)/2;

  outtextxy(text_x, text_y, msg.c_str());

  int dist_x = 5;
  int dist_y = 5;

  rectangle(text_x - dist_x,
     text_y - dist_y,
     text_x + msg_x + dist_x,
     text_y + msg_y + dist_y);

  while (!bioskey(0))
     /* wait */ ;
  closegraph();
  return 0;
}
```

Here is the Windows version. Stock code for `WinMain` and the window procedure are omitted.

```
#include <windows.h>
#include <stdlib.h>
#include <string.h>

void paint(HWND hwnd)
{ PAINTSTRUCT paintstruct;
  BeginPaint(hwnd, &paintstruct);

  HDC hdc = paintstruct.hdc;

  String msg = "Hello, World";
  int msglen = msg.length();

  DWORD dw = GetTextExtent(hdc, msg.c_str(), msglen);
  int msg_x = LOWORD(dw);
  int msg_y = HIWORD(dw);

  RECT rect;
  GetClientRect(hwnd, &rect);
  int disp_x = rect.right;
  int disp_y = rect.bottom;

  int text_x = (disp_x - msg_x) / 2;
  int text_y = (disp_y - msg_y) / 2;

  TextOut(hdc, text_x, text_y, msg.c_str(), msglen);

  int dist_x = 5;
  int dist_y = 5;

  SelectObject(hdc, GetStockObject(EMPTY_BRUSH));
  Rectangle(hdc, text_x - dist_x,
    text_y - dist_y,
    text_x + msg_x + dist_x,
    text_y + msg_y + dist_y);

  EndPaint(hwnd, &paintstruct);
}
```

There is a good reason why we would like to find a way to unify the
code. It would allow us to easily write applications that run under both DOS
and Windows. In fact, we have that problem in this textbook. We need to present

code for rendering graphics, not knowing the graphics interface favored by the readers.

As a first approximation, we might try to map functions with common purposes, such as `textWidth/GetTextExtent` and `rectangle/Rectangle`, to functions with common names. To some degree, this can be done. However, different graphics systems manage the graphics state, such as the current font or fill pattern, in different ways. What is required is a combination of data reflecting the current state, together with a collection of functions providing graphics services. As we know, these combinations of graphics operations and graphics state can be represented by classes. Such a class is usually called a *graphics context* or *device context*.

Having classes that manage access to a graphics device has yet another advantage. Applications often need to render graphics on more than one device, typically to both the screen and a printer. On systems that have no common device support, the code for controlling the screen can be quite different from that for the printer, and it is easy to have divergent results because of programming errors. Having the same interface for both devices enables the programmer to share code and avoid such mistakes.

We supply a graphics context class for each graphics system. (See the documentation on the Companion Disk on selecting the class appropriate to your system.)

```
class GraphicsContext
{
public:
  GraphicsContext();
  void close();
  void text(String s, double x, double y) const;
  // ...
private:
  // ...
};
```

To be independent from the resolution of a particular graphics device, the graphics context classes use by default the coordinate system shown in Figure 7.1. The coordinate system reflects the fact that most graphics displays have a 4:3 aspect ratio. The graphics context class has an operation (`set_window_coords`) to change to other coordinate systems.

The code to display "Hello, World" in a box is then

```
double win_x = 20;
double win_y = 15;
GraphicsContext gc;

String msg = "Hello, World";
double msg_x, msg_y;
gc.text_extent(msg, msg_x, msg_y);
```

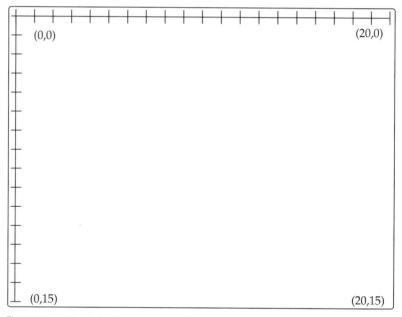

Figure 7.1.   The default screen coordinate system.

```
double text_x = (win_x - msg_x) / 2;
double text_y = (win_y - msg_y) / 2;
gc.text(msg, text_x, text_y);

double dist_x = 0.15;
double dist_y = 0.15;
gc.rectangle(text_x - dist_x,
    text_y - dist_y,
    text_x + msg_x + dist_x,
    text_y + msg_y + dist_y);

gc.close();
```

It is not important to understand the implementation of the graphics context class. You can use a graphics context in the same way that you use a file: Construct an instance, write to it, and close it when you are done. When you write to a file or graphics context, you need not concern yourself with the exact mechanics of the data transfer and system calls that go on behind the scenes.

Exercise 7.1.1. To gain experience with the graphics context class, write a program that reads in a set of data items, each of which has a name and a numeric value (such as California 40.3), and produces a pie chart. Draw a circle of suitable radius, use lines to subdivide it, and place the text labels next to the segments. Put some care into the text placement: The bisector of the segment should meet the closest corner point of the rectangle enclosing the text.

7.2. GRAPHICAL SHAPES

7.2.1. Points

We start with a simple class for points.

```
class Point
{
public:
  Point(double x = 0, double y = 0);

  void move(int dx, int dy);
  void scale(Point center, double scalefactor);

  double x() const;
  double y() const;
  void plot(GraphicsContext&) const;
  void print(ostream&) const;
  // ...
private:
  double _x;
  double _y;
};

inline double Point::x() const { return _x; }
inline double Point::y() const { return _y; }
```

To move p closer to a point center (see Figure 7.2), use the scale function.

```
void Point::scale(Point center, double scalefactor)
/* PURPOSE:   Moves the point toward or away from a center point
     RECEIVES: center        - the center of the scale operation
               scalefactor   - the ratio by which to move the point
*/
{ _x = _x * scalefactor + center._x * (1 - scalefactor);
  _y = _y * scalefactor + center._y * (1 - scalefactor);
}
```

To plot a point, we have to specify the graphics context.

```
GraphicsContext bgi;
```

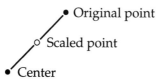

Figure 7.2.   Scaling a point.

```
Point p(5.0,5.0);

for (int i = 1; i <= 20; i++)
{ p.plot(bgi);
  Point c(1.0, 0.0);
  p.scale(c, 0.9);
}
```

Try out this code to get a visual feeling for the scaling operation.

Exercise 7.2.1. Write a program to generate a random cloud of points. Then pick a random center of scaling. Make a loop that moves the points 10% farther away from the center, erasing the old points. (Set the raster operation mode of the graphics context to XOR and draw the points over themselves to erase them.) Generate a few extra random points in each loop to account for those that get moved outside the screen boundaries.

7.2.2. Rectangles

We will design a Rectangle class that holds the coordinates for a rectangle given by two corner points, as in Figure 7.3. We have two choices for the data layout: Place the points inside the Rectangle class:

```
class Rectangle
{
public:
  Rectangle(Point, Point);

  void move(double dx, double dy);
  void scale(Point center, double s);

  void plot(GraphicsContext& gc) const;
  // ...
private:
  Point _corner1;
  Point _corner2;
};
```

Figure 7.3.   Specifying a rectangle from two corner points.

Or place individual *x*- and *y*-coordinates:

```
class Rectangle
{
public:
  // ...
private:
    double _x1;
    double _y1;
    double _x2;
    double _y2;
};
```

As a rule of thumb, always use the highest level of abstraction possible. This leads us to adopt the first solution.

The Rectangle constructor looks like this:

```
Rectangle::Rectangle(Point p, Point q)
: _corner1(p),
  _corner2(q)
{}
```

Consider the implementation of the scaling operation.

```
void Rectangle::scale(Point center, double s)
{ _corner1.scale(center, s);
  _corner2.scale(center, s);
}
```

This confirms the wisdom of our decision to use the *higher abstraction*, Points rather than doubles, to implement rectangles. We were able to leverage the higher *functionality* of points.

Exercise 7.2.2. Write a program that reads a sequence of floating-point numbers and makes a simple bar chart: a sequence of rectangles with the same base width whose height is proportional to the data points.

Exercise 7.2.3. Make the bar chart of the previous exercise into a class. Write a program that reads in four bar charts (from four input files whose names are supplied on the command line) and displays them in four quadrants of the screen. *Hint:* Reuse the code that builds a bar chart filling the entire screen, and then scale the bar charts to move them into quadrants.

7.2.3. Polygons

We now turn to a class to display polygons. In this case, we cannot write a Polygon constructor that accepts the vertex points, since there may be an arbitrary number. Instead, we will use the following interface:

```
Polygon q(4); // a quadrangle
q.set_vertex(1, Point(13.0, 12.0));
q.set_vertex(2, Point(9.5, 12.5));
q.set_vertex(3, Point(9.0, 9.5));
q.set_vertex(4, Point(12.0, 8.0));
```

The vertex points are stored in an array

```
class Polygon
{
  public:
  Polygon(int);

    void set_vertex(int i, Point p);
    void move(double dx, double dy);
    void scale(Point center, double s);

    void plot(GraphicsContext& gc) const;
    Point vertex(int) const;

    // ...
  private:
    Array<Point> _vertex;
};
```

We supply a constructor

```
Polygon::Polygon(int n)
: _vertex(1,n)
{}
```

and an operation to set a vertex.

```
void Polygon::set_vertex(int i, Point p)
{ ASSERT_PRECOND(1 <= i && i <= _vertex.high());
  _vertex[i] = p;
}
```

The plot function simply joins adjacent points by a line.

```
void Polygon::plot(GraphicsContext& gc) const
{ for (int i = 1; i <= _vertex.high(); i++)
  { int j = i + 1;
    if (j > _vertex.high()) j = 1;
    gc.line(_vertex[i].x(), _vertex[i].y(),
      _vertex[j].x(), _vertex[j].y());
  }
}
```

Exercise 7.2.4. Write a function

```
Polygon regular_polygon(Point c, double r, int n)
```

that returns a regular n-gon with center c and radius r.

7.3. IMPLEMENTING INHERITANCE

7.3.1. Inheritance for Code Reuse

Let us design a class to store triangles. Rather than replicating all code, we will take advantage of the existing polygon code.

We use a new programming paradigm and *inherit* from the Polygon class.

```
class Triangle : public Polygon
{
public:
  Triangle(Point, Point, Point);
};
```

This code means that a triangle is a special case of a polygon. Triangles behave in exactly the same fashion as polygons, except for construction. All operations of polygons (such as plotting or scaling) are automatically applicable to triangles.

```
Point p(3.0, 2.0);
Point q(0.5, 2.5);
Point r(4.0, 1.0);
Triangle t(p, q, r);

for (int i = 1; i <= 20; i++)
{ t.plot(bgi);
  t.scale(Point(1.0, 1.0), 0.9);
}
```

We refer to Triangle as the *derived class* and to Polygon as the *base class*. The process of forming a derived class is called *derivation* or *inheritance*.

When inheriting from a base class, one only needs to declare the *difference* between the derived and base classes. Reuse of the base class operations is automatic.

The keyword public in the syntax for inheritance,

```
class Derived : public Base { /* ... */ };
```

is required for technical reasons. It is a common error to omit it. If you do, the compiler will complain about inaccessible base class operations. (If the keyword public is omitted, inheritance defaults to private inheritance. Private inheritance is not useful for object-oriented design and only marginally useful in some implementation scenarios. We do not cover it in this book.)

7.3.2. Constructing Base Classes

We need to supply the code for the Triangle constructor:

```
Triangle::Triangle(Point a, Point b, Point c)
: Polygon(3)
{ set_vertex(1, a);
  set_vertex(2, b);
  set_vertex(3, c);
}
```

The : notation is used to call the *base class* constructor. Base classes are identified by their *type*, such as Polygon.

Compare this constructor with the recently discussed Rectangle constructor.

```
Rectangle::Rectangle(Point p, Point q)
: _corner1(p),
  _corner2(p)
{}
```

Here the : notation is used to call the *field* constructors. The data fields are identified by their *name*, such as _corner1.

In general, derived-class constructors may need to invoke both base class constructors and data field constructors.

Exercise 7.3.1. Derive a class Square from Rectangle. Write the constructor and try scaling and plotting squares.

Exercise 7.3.2. Implement the Triangle class directly, without inheriting from Polygon, by having it store three vertices. Write all operations that the original Triangle inherited from Polygon.

7.3.3. Simulating Inheritance

C++ directly supports inheritance as a language construct. It is instructive to see what one must do to simulate the effect of inheritance with traditional means.

Instead of inheriting from Polygon, we can use aggregation. The polygon information can be stored in a data field.

```
class A_Triangle
{
public:
  A_Triangle(Point, Point, Point);
  void scale(Point center, double s);
  void plot(GraphicsContext& gc) const;
  // ...
private:
  Polygon _poly;
};
```

The constructor is similar, but of course it needs to construct the data field, not the base class. Note that the set_vertex functions are now applied to the explicit data field, not to the implicit argument.

```
A_Triangle::A_Triangle(Point a, Point b, Point c)
: _poly(3)
{ _poly.set_vertex(1, a);
  _poly.set_vertex(2, b);
  _poly.set_vertex(3, c);
}
```

All operation functions must be *recoded* to make them available to the new class!

```
void A_Triangle::plot(GraphicsContext& gc) const
{ _poly.plot(gc);
}

void A_Triangle::scale(Point center, double s)
{ _poly.scale(center, s);
}
```

Of course, the recoding is completely trivial. The functions are just reapplied to the polygon object.

Real inheritance makes this recoding unnecessary.

Exercise 7.3.3. Write a class A_Square that implements square shapes by containing a Rectangle subobject rather than inheriting from Rectangle. Recode all Rectangle functions for A_Square by routing them to the rectangle subobject.

7.3.4. Adding Operations to the Base Class

Suppose we add a print function to Polygon:

```
void Polygon::print(ostream& os) const
{ os << "Polygon " << _vertex.length();
  for (int i = 1; i <= _vertex.high(); i++)
  { os << " ";
    _vertex[i].print(os);
  }
}
```

For example, q.print(cout) prints

```
Polygon 4 (13, 12) (9.5, 12.5) (9, 9.5) (12, 8)
```

The Triangle class picks up this operation automatically. But if inheritance is simulated, as in the A_Triangle class, an A_Triangle::print function must be added manually to track the increased functionality.

This is particularly important from a code management point of view. The fact that Triangle inherits from Polygon indicates that *any* operation that is applicable to polygons, whether it is implemented today or will be added at a later point in time, is applicable to triangles. Indeed, if an operation is later added to the Polygon class, it is then automatically available to Triangle, whereas in the simulation of inheritance the operation would have to be added manually to all simulated derived classes. In practice, it may be difficult to determine all such classes! One can read off the base classes of a class simply by looking at the class declaration, but a class has no knowledge of what classes derive from it. (This is no different from functions. You can find out what other functions a specific function calls, but it is much harder to find out who calls it.)

Exercise 7.3.4. Add an operation circumference that computes the circumference of a polygon (by adding up the lengths of the sides). Verify that the operation is available to Triangle objects.

7.3.5. Adding Data in the Derived Class

To display text on the screen, let us start with a simple Text class.

```
class Text
{
public:
  Text(Point, String);
  void scale(Point center, double s);
  void plot(GraphicsContext& gc) const;
private:
  Point _start;
  String _text;
};
```

```
Text::Text(Point p, String s)
: _start(p),
  _text(s)
{}

void Text::plot(GraphicsContext& gc) const
{ gc.text(_text, _start.x(), _start.y());
}

void Text::scale(Point center, double s)
{ _start.scale(center, s);
}
```

This text class is fine for labeling figures, but it does have one problem. The position of the text is changed by the scaling operation, but the size of the characters is not. Let us fix this deficiency by deriving from Text.

```
class ScalableText : public Text
{ ScalableText(Point, String);
  void plot(GraphicsContext& gc) const;
  void scale(Point center, double s);
private:
  double _size;
};
```

An object of type ScalableText has the data layout shown in Figure 7.4. Here is the constructor:

```
ScalableText::ScalableText(Point p, String s)
: Text(p, s),
  _size(1.0)
{}
```

Note the construction of the base class (Text(p, s)) vs. construction of the data field (_size(1.0)).

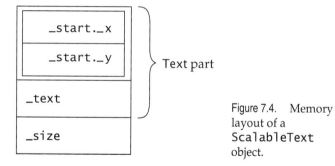

Figure 7.4. Memory layout of a ScalableText object.

Exercise 7.3.5. Write a class Employee that contains the name, hourly wage, and ID number of an employee. Supply a constructor and an operation to print the employee information. Then derive a class Manager from Employee. A manager is just like an employee, but also has a secretary. Store the ID number of the secretary as an added data field. Supply a constructor.

7.4. OPERATIONS IN BASE AND DERIVED CLASSES

There are three actions that a derived class D can take with respect to an operation f() of a base class B:

1. The derived class can *inherit* the function B::f() without change.
2. The derived class can *replace* B::f() by a function D::f() performing a different action.
3. The derived class can *extend* B::f() by a function D::f() calling B::f() and performing other tasks.

We have seen an example for the first case: The Triangle class inherits the plot and scale operations without change. We will see examples for the other cases in this section.

7.4.1. Extending a Base Class Operation

The scale operation of the derived class ScalableText *extends* the action of the corresponding base class operation.

```
void ScalableText::scale(Point center, double s)
{ Text::scale(center, s);
  _size = _size * s;
}
```

The derived-class function calls the base class function and performs additional work. Note the scope resolution in the call Text::scale. It is easy to forget the Text::. If it is omitted, then scale refers to the scale operation in the current scope: ScalableText::scale. The result is an infinite recursion.

7.4.2. Replacing a Base Class Operation

In C++ a derived-class operation can perform any task whatsoever. There is no requirement that it call the corresponding base class operation.

For example, we may not be happy that triangles are printed out as

```
Polygon 3 ...
```

In this case, we may wish to replace the base class operation.

```
class Triangle : public Polygon
{
public:
  Triangle(Point, Point, Point);
  void print(ostream& os) const;
};

void Triangle::print(ostream& os) const
{ os << "Triangle ";
  vertex(1).print(os); os << " ";
  vertex(2).print(os); os << " ";
  vertex(3).print(os);
}
```

Some object-oriented languages (such as Beta) do not allow replacement, because it alters the character of the derived objects. In such languages all operations must be either inherited or extended.

Exercise 7.4.1. Write the print function of the Manager class of Exercise 7.3.5. Call Employee::print and then print the ID number of the secretary.

Exercise 7.4.2. Supply a function Employee::raise(double p) that raises the hourly wage by p percent. Does it have to be reimplemented for Manager, or can it be inherited?

Exercise 7.4.3. Write a function Employee::weekly_pay(double h) that pays the employee for working h hours in a given week. Any work in excess of 40 hours must be paid at the overtime rate, one and one-half times the regular rate. Then compute the weekly wage for a manager. If the manager worked less than 30 hours, the weekly wage is the same as that of an employee, that is, hours worked multiplied by the hourly wage. Otherwise, the manager's weekly wage is $40 \times$ hourly wage.

7.5. ACCESS RIGHTS TO THE BASE CLASS

Consider again the operation

```
void ScalableText::scale(Point center, double s)
{ Text::scale(center, s);
  _size = _size * s;
}
```

The following code would have saved a function call:

```
void ScalableText::scale(Point center, double s)
{ _start.scale(center, s); // ERROR
  _size = _size * s;
}
```

However, this code does not compile: ScalableText does not have the right to access the _start data field.

This appears to contradict the data layout diagram, according to which ScalableText has three data fields: _start and _text (inherited from Text) and _size (added in ScalableText). Nevertheless, _start and _text are private to Text and not accessible from classes deriving from Text.

It is important not to confuse the *presence* of the data with the *right to access* the data. If the derived class needs to access private base class data, it must go through the public protocol, just like everyone else. Derived-class operations have no special privileges to access base class data.

There is no difference between inheritance and aggregation in this regard. Consider the simulated inheritance

```
class A_ScalableText
{
public:
  // ...
private:
  Text _text;
};
```

Then _text._start is not accessible either.

Exercise 7.5.1. Reimplement Rectangle by deriving from Polygon. Note that Rectangle has quite a few more operations than Polygon. Supply them all. Use the Polygon::vertex operation as the public protocol to gain access to the private polygon data.

7.6. WHEN NOT TO USE INHERITANCE

7.6.1. Points and Circles

Recall that inheritance is used to model an "is-a" relationship. Use aggregation (data fields) for "has-a" relationships.

For example, each rectangle *has* two corner points. Each triangle *is* a polygon. A car *has* a tire (in fact, it has four, or five counting the spare). A car *is* a vehicle.

It is easy to get this wrong. For example, a popular C++ tutorial derives Circle from Point:

```
class Circle : public Point // DON'T
{
public:
  void plot() const;
  // ...
private:
  double _radius;
};
```

It does them little good—only one of the operations of Point (move) is applicable for Circle. Nothing of value is inherited, and, except for move, all operations need to be coded again. A circle *has* a center point—it isn't a point.

```
class Circle
{
public:
  void plot() const;
  // ...
private:
  Point _center; // OK
  double _radius;
  // ...
};
```

The same example goes on to derive Rectangle from Point. That doesn't work any better. In fact, it is downright weird.

```
class Rectangle : public Point // DON'T
{
public:
  void plot() const;
  // ...
private:
  Point _other;
};
```

One of the corner points is stored in the base class; the other is a data field. None of the operations can be inherited.

Exercise 7.6.1. Would you derive Point from Circle (with radius 0)?

7.6.2. Lists and Stacks

Consider a linked list class with the following interface:

```
class List
{
public:
  List(); // makes an empty list
  void insert_head(int x); // insert at head
  int remove_head(); // remove from head
  void insert_tail(int x); // insert at tail
  int remove_tail(); // remove from tail
```

```
    int head() const; // return head
    int tail() const; // return tail
    int length() const; // number of links
    // ...

private:
    // ...
};
```

Some authors recommend using the linked list as the base class for a Stack class:

```
class Stack : public List // DON'T
{
public:
    void push(int x);
    int pop();
    Bool is_empty() const;
};

void Stack::push(int x) { insert_head(x); }
int Stack::pop() { return remove_head(); }
Bool Stack::is_empty() const { return length() == 0; }
```

This is not a good idea. A stack isn't a special case of a list. There are things that you can do to a list that make no sense for a stack. When using inheritance, the stack class inherits all operations of the list class, whether appropriate or not. The code

```
Stack s;
s.push(x);
s.insert_tail(y);
```

is legal but obviously makes no sense for a stack. The appropriate solution is to use aggregation, not inheritance.

```
class Stack
{
public:
    void push(int x);
    int pop();
    Bool is_empty() const;
private:
    List _list;
};
```

```
void Stack::push(int x) { _list.insert_head(x); }
int Stack::pop() { return _list.remove_head(); }
Bool Stack::is_empty() const { return _list.length() == 0; }
```

Exercise 7.6.2. [Dewhurst and Stark], p. 106, recommend deriving `Pathname` from `String` to describe the name of a directory path. Why is this a bad idea? (*Hint:* Find an inherited operation that changes a pathname into a string that is not a pathname.)

7.6.3. Students, Professors, and Staff

Here is an example from [Wiener and Pinson] (for consistency, we replaced `char*` pointers with `String` objects). The purpose of this example is to model students, faculty, and staff at a university, presumably for some database application.

```
class DataRec
{ // ...
  String _lastname;
  String _firstname;
  String _street;
  String _city;
  String _state;
  String _zip;
};

class Student : public DataRec
{ // ...
  String _major;
  int _id_number;
  int _level;
};

class Professor : public DataRec
{ // ...
  String _dept;
  float _salary;
};

class Staff : public Professor
{ // ...
  float _hourly_wage;
};
```

Figure 7.5 shows the class relationships.

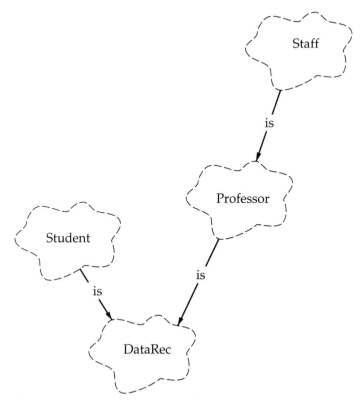

Figure 7.5.   Diagram for university classes.

There are some real problems with this design:

- Is a student, or a professor, a `DataRec`? Hardly. A student *has* a name and an address.
- Is a secretary a special case of `Professor`? Hardly. Just because `Staff` can inherit the `_dept` field doesn't mean it should derive from `Professor`. And what good are the two fields `_salary` and `_hourly_wage` in `Staff`?

Here is a possible remedy.

- The `DataRec` class seems artificial. It seems clearer to have two classes `Name` and `Address`.
- Professors and staff members are both employees. A base class `Employee` captures the common elements, such as the department. But professors are salaried employees, staff are not. (Admittedly, this is not realistic, but we are fixing the design, not the analysis.)
- Students and employees are persons. Each person has a name and address.

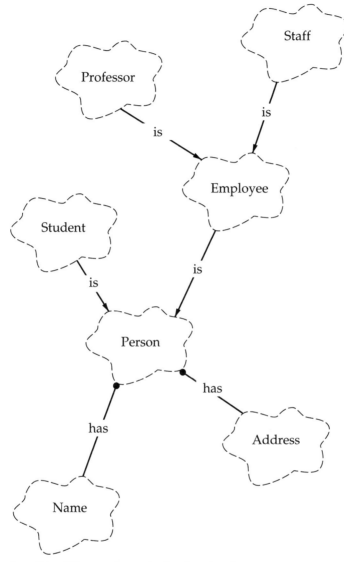

Figure 7.6. Diagram for revised university classes.

This leads us to the classes and relationships shown in Figure 7.6.

```
class Name
{ // ...
  String _lastname;
  String _firstname;
};
```

```
class Address
{ // ...
  String _street;
  String _city;
  String _state;
  String _zip;
};

class Person
{ // ...
  Name _name;
  Address _address;
};

class Employee : public Person
{ // ...
  String _dept;
};

class Staff : public Employee
{ // ...
  float _hourly_wage;
};

class Student : public Person
{ // ...
  String _major;
  int _id_number;
  int _level;
};

class Professor : public Employee
{ // ...
  float _salary;
};
```

7.7. SUBOBJECTS AND SUBCLASSES

Each car *has* a motor. An individual motor is therefore a *subobject* of an individual car, as shown in Figure 7.7. We model this as aggregation.

```
class Car
{ // ...
private:
  Motor _motor;
};
```

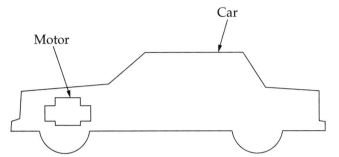

Figure 7.7. Aggregation means object containment.

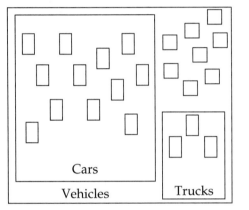

Figure 7.8. Inheritance means class containment.

Each car *is* a vehicle; in other words, the class of cars is a *subclass* of the class of vehicles, as shown in Figure 7.8. We model this subset relationship as inheritance:

```
class Car : public Vehicle
```

Sometimes differentiating between "is-a" and "has-a" relationships is complicated by the language we use. We usually talk about objects when we mean classes, saying "*a* car" when we mean "*each* car" or the class of all cars.

Note that we only look for the "is-a" relationship between two *classes*. For example, "Chevrolet is a car" means that every Chevrolet is a car. That is a relationship between classes (the class of Chevrolets and the class of cars). But "Chevrolet is a division of General Motors" is a relationship between an object (the Chevrolet division) and a class (the divisions of General Motors).

Class derivation is often referred to as *subclassing*. Beginners are sometimes confused that *objects* get *bigger* (or at least stay the same size) when performing subclassing. The "sub" prefix expresses the fact that the subclass models a smaller collection of objects. These more specialized objects indeed need a richer state to perform their operations and hence have a larger size.

Exercise 7.7.1. What relationships exist between the following pairs? In which order? Your choices are is-a, has-a, or neither.

- Sun, Planet
- Sun Microsystems, Manufacturer
- Sun SPARCstation, Workstation
- Sunday, Date
- Year, Date
- Date, Person
- Person, Employee
- Secretary, Employee
- Secretary, Manager
- Manager, Employee
- Triangle, Polygon
- Triangle, Rectangle
- Circle, Point

7.8. DESIGN HINTS

7.8.1. Place Common Operations and Fields into the Base Class

Consider a class `Vehicle` with derived classes `Car` and `Truck`. Suppose we simulate cars and trucks moving along a road. Position, speed, and acceleration are common to cars and trucks, indeed all vehicles, and should be placed in the base class.

Consider the operation `update_position`, which computes the position after a time interval from the current position, speed and acceleration. The laws of physics dictate that $s(t + \Delta t) = s(t) + v\Delta t + \frac{1}{2}a(\Delta t)^2$, independent of the kind of vehicle. Hence, this operation can be placed in the base class.

7.8.2. Use Fields for Variations in State, Operations for Variations in Behavior

Suppose trucks have a maximum legal speed of 55 miles per hour, but cars may drive up to 65 miles per hour. Do not define operations

```
double Car::max_speed() const { return 65; } // DON'T
double Truck::max_speed() const { return 55; } // DON'T
```

Instead, add a field `_max_speed` to `Vehicle` and a `Vehicle` accessor operation reporting its value. Set the field in the constructors of `Car` and `Truck`.

Reserve operations for variations in *behavior*. For example, the method for computing road tolls may differ for cars (with a charge per passenger) and trucks (with a charge depending on weight). Both Car and Truck need to define a road_toll operation.

7.8.3. Derived Class Operations
Must Preserve Base Class Invariants

An operation of a derived class must not put an object in a state that violates an invariant of the base class.

Here is an example: Consider the Message class holding an electronic mail message. Let Message::lines() compute the number of lines in the message by counting newline characters in the message text. A class EncryptedMessage derives from Message. Ignoring 2,000 years of better algorithms, we encrypt with the method known to Caesar, by adding a fixed number to each character.

```
String encrypt(String s, char key)
{ String r = s;
  for (int i = 0; i < s.length(); i++) r[i] += key;
  return r;
}
```

For example, encrypt("Hello", 8) is "Pmttw". The original string is retrieved with a key of −8. The constructor of EncryptedMessage first encrypts the string, then passes it to the Message constructor. The EncryptedMessage::play function first asks the recipient for the key, on which the sender and recipient presumably agreed. It then decrypts and displays the message.

The inherited lines operation produces nonsense results for encrypted messages, since newline characters are no longer recognizable. The derived class has failed to preserve a subtle invariant of the base class, namely that newline characters in the message text denote line terminators.

It is actually difficult to come up with an example for this problem if all fields of the base class are private and all base class operations preserve the class invariants. As long as the derived class must use the public interface of the base class, it has no better chance of violating the class invariant than any other client of the base class.

However, some programmers do access protected base class data fields from the derived class. (See Chapter 10 for a discussion of the protected attribute.) It is then important to ensure that the derived-class operations preserve the base class invariants.

7.8.4. Derived Classes Must Be
Preserved by Inherited Operations

The objects of a derived class form a subset of the objects of the base class. The operations that the derived class inherits from the base class must map that subset into itself. In other words, the derived class must be closed under the inherited operations. If not, one or more operations transform derived-class objects into invalid objects. In that case, the derived class needs to redefine the offending base class operations, or else we must conclude that inheritance is not an appropriate relationship for the classes involved.

Consider a class `Filename` deriving from `String`, describing a DOS file name. A DOS file name is a string containing a name, with up to eight characters, and an optional extension, with up to three characters, as in whatnot.cpp. Since `Filename` derives from `String`, any `String` operation can be applied to a `Filename` object. But there are plenty of `String` operations that, when applied to a `Filename`, yield a string that is not a legal file name. Just append more than 12 characters, or insert extra . characters. This shows that inheritance from `String` is not appropriate for the `Filename` class. Instead, `Filename` should use aggregation to gain a `String` field, and define only those class operations that make sense for manipulating file names.

POLYMORPHISM

8.1. A FILLED RECTANGLE
CLASS FOR PLOTTING BAR CHARTS

For plotting bar charts, we would like to display rectangles that are filled with
a pattern, like the one shown in Figure 8.1. We will derive from the existing
Rectangle class:

```
class FilledRect : public Rectangle
{
public:
  FilledRect(Point, Point, GraphicsContext::Brushstyle);
  void plot(GraphicsContext& gc) const;
private:
  GraphicsContext::Brushstyle _pattern;
};
```

The type FillPattern is an enumerated type; it is defined in the graphics
context module, together with a number of patterns.

Here is code for a simple bar chart, shown in Figure 8.2.

```
FilledRect chart1(Point(1.0, 7.0), Point(2.0, 2.0),
  GraphicsContext::FDIAG_BRUSH);
Rectangle chart2(Point(2.0, 7.0), Point(3.0, 1.0));
FilledRect chart3(Point(3.0, 7.0), Point(4.0, 3.0),
  GraphicsContext::HORIZ_BRUSH);
Rectangle chart4(Point(0.5, 0.5), Point(4.5, 7.5));

chart1.plot(gc);
chart2.plot(gc);
chart3.plot(gc);
chart4.plot(gc);
```

Figure 8.1.   A filled rectangle.   **143**

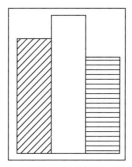

Figure 8.2. A bar chart.

This isn't terribly useful. In a practical application the number and height of the bars varies at run time and is not known at compile time. In the next sections we will see how to write a program that can display an arbitrary mix of rectangles and filled rectangles.

Exercise 8.1.1. Write a program that reads in a set of floating-point numbers and draws a bar chart as just described, made up entirely of filled rectangles whose patterns cycle through the available brush styles.

8.2. CONVERSION BETWEEN BASE AND DERIVED-CLASS OBJECTS

Figure 8.3 shows the data layouts in a `FilledRect` object and a plain `Rectangle` object. Each `FilledRect` object inherits the `_corner1` and `_corner2` fields from `Rectangle` and adds a `_pattern` field.

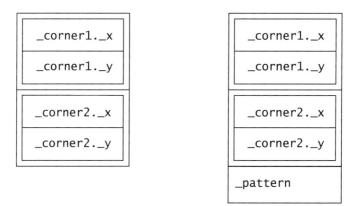

Figure 8.3. Memory layout of base and derived-class objects.

Note that derived-class objects have as least as many data items as objects from the base class, because fields can only be added, not taken away, in the derivation process.

A derived-class object can be assigned to a base class object. However, since the base class object has fewer fields, some information is lost during such an assignment.

```
FilledRect d(ul, lr, GraphicsContext::HORIZ_BRUSH);
Rectangle b = d; // OK, but information lost
b.plot(gc); // plots as Rectangle only
```

A derived-class object can be passed as an argument to a function that expects a base class object. Since the function argument is a variable that can only hold base class information, the additional fields are not transferred.

```
void plot(Rectangle r) { r.plot(gc); }

FilledRect d(ul, lr, GraphicsContext::HORIZ_BRUSH);
plot(d); // plots as Rectangle only
```

Conversely, a base class object cannot be assigned to a derived-class object.

```
Rectangle b(ul, lr);
FilledRect d = b; // ERROR
```

The reason is clear: The derived-class object has more fields than the base class object, and it is not obvious how they should be set.

Exercise 8.2.1. Here is a naïve procedure to carry out the assignment d = b. Simply assign those fields that are common to both the derived and base class, and leave the remaining ones unchanged. Discuss how this concept is in conflict with the notion of class invariants.

It is common to have a mix of objects—some of the base class and some of a derived class. Storing such a collection is a problem. A simple array does not suffice. Suppose we use an array of base class objects:

```
Array<Rectangle> chart;
chart.grow(1,4);
chart[1] = FilledRect(Point(1.0,7.0), Point(2.0,2.0),
  GraphicsContext::FDIAG_BRUSH);
chart[2] = Rectangle(Point(2.0,7.0), Point(3.0,1.0));
chart[3] = FilledRect(Point(3.0,7.0), Point(4.0,3.0),
  GraphicsContext::HORIZ_BRUSH);
chart[4] = Rectangle(Point(0.5,0.5), Point(4.5,7.5));
```

```
for (int i = chart.low(); i <= chart.high(); i++)
   chart[i].plot(gc);
```

This is not useful. All objects are truncated to the base information only.

Conversely, one cannot use an array of derived-class objects. There may not be a unique derived class, and at any rate, base class objects cannot be stored in derived-class array entries.

We will see in the next section how this problem can be overcome by storing *pointers* to objects instead.

Exercise 8.2.2. Try out the foregoing code that uses an Array<Rectangle> to store the chart components. Verify that it compiles and that the fill patterns are sliced away when FilledRect objects are stored in Rectangle slots.

8.3. A QUICK INTRODUCTION TO POINTERS

Pointers are a mechanism to share ownership of objects. In C++, objects are copied as values. That is, a copy of an object has its own distinct identity. Modifying the copy has no influence on the original. In many cases, this behavior is desirable. However, there are situations in which objects need to be inspected or changed by more than one agent.

For any type X, there is an associated pointer type X*. For example, pointers of type Employee* are used for accessing Employee objects. Pointer variables are declared like this:

```
Employee* pe;
```

Actually, because of a syntactical oddity of the C declaration syntax, it is important to declare only *one* pointer variable in each line. The declaration

```
Employee* pe, pf; // DON'T
```

does not do what the code suggests—pe is a pointer, pf is an employee. See, for example, [Koenig] for more information. In practice, this is not usually a problem, since each variable ought to be initialized and followed by a short comment anyway, thereby greatly reducing the temptation of declaring multiple variables together.

There are three methods for obtaining pointer values. The & operator returns a pointer to an existing object; the new operator creates an object on the heap and returns a pointer to it; and the value 0 denotes a pointer value that currently points to no object.

```
Employee joe("Joe Isuzu");
Employee* pj = &joe;
Employee* ph = new Employee("Harry Hacker");
Employee* pn = 0;
```

Storage obtained from the heap must be recycled, by invoking the `delete` operator, when it is no longer used.

```
delete ph;
```

The unary ＊ operator transforms a pointer into the value to which it points.

```
Employee e = *ph;
```

This transformation is called *dereferencing* the pointer. Applying ＊ to a 0 pointer or an uninitialized pointer has results that are random, disastrous, or both.

By copying a pointer, you gain two access paths to the same object.

```
Employee* p = new Employee("Harry Hacker");
Employee* q = p;
(*p).set_salary(40000); // sets Harry Hacker's salary
(*q).raise_salary(.10); // raises Harry Hacker's salary
```

The parentheses in the function call

```
(*p).f();
```

are necessary because the member access operator (.) binds more strongly than the pointer-dereferencing operator (＊). That makes ＊p.f() implicitly parenthesized as ＊(p.f()), which is an error: p is a pointer, not a structure, and the "." operator cannot be applied.

Because pointers to class objects are so common, and expressions like (*p)._x and (*p).f() are cumbersome to write and read, C has another operator -> ("dereference and access member"). The code

```
p->_x
```

performs the same operation as (＊p)._x, and

```
p->f()
```

is equivalent to (＊p).f().

Many programmers initially find that the -> operator looks strange when used to invoke an operation.

```
Employee* p = new Employee("Harry Hacker");
p->set_salary(40000); // sets Harry Hacker's salary
```

Keep in mind that `set_salary` has two arguments: the implicit argument ＊p and the explicit argument 40000.

Other languages, such as Pascal, do not have the -> operator, because they do not need it. In Pascal, pointer dereferencing (^) is a *postfix* operator, and **p^.x** accesses a member without the need for additional parentheses.

Generally, pointers are implemented as memory addresses. You may think of the value stored in a pointer variable as the starting address of the associated object in memory.

8.4. CONVERSION BETWEEN BASE AND DERIVED-CLASS POINTERS

In C++ a pointer to a derived-class object can be converted to a base class pointer:

```
FilledRect* pd =
    new FilledRect(ul, lr, GraphicsContext::HORIZ_BRUSH);
Rectangle* pb = pd;
```

The memory layout, shown in Figure 8.4, makes it clear why this works. The base class pointer is used only to access fields that are present in the base class. Those fields are also present in the derived class, in the same locations. The fact that there are other fields beyond is of no interest when using the base class pointer.

This explains why operations can be inherited without recoding them. The base class operation receives a pointer to a base class object as its implicit argument, but it can equally well receive a derived-class pointer instead. For example, if the scale operation of Rectangle is called with the address of a FilledRect object, it simply transforms the fields in the Rectangle portion and leaves the others alone.

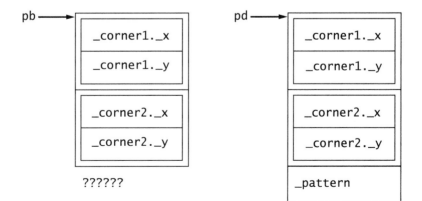

Figure 8.4.   Pointers to base and derived-class objects.

It is possible to convert a base class pointer to a derived-class pointer. Of course, this makes sense only if it originated as a pointer to that derived class. Because of the inherent danger, such conversions always require a *cast*:

```
FilledRect* pd = ...;
Rectangle* pb = pd;
// ...
FilledRect* pe = (FilledRect*) pb; // OK, because we remember
```

The cast mechanism forces the compiler to change the pointer type, although it is not necessarily safe to do so. While casts cannot always be avoided, their use should be minimized. The results of dereferencing an improperly cast pointer are undefined and usually disastrous.

Pointers offer us a solution to the problem of storing a collection of related objects. While objects of base and derived classes may have different sizes, pointers to them have the same size. This is an important consideration that frequently comes up in C++ programs.

The following loop builds an array of pointers and calls the plot function for each array element.

```
Array<Rectangle*> chart; // an array of pointers
chart.grow(1,4);
chart[1] = new FilledRect(Point(1.0, 7.0), Point(2.0, 2.0),
  GraphicsContext::FDIAG_BRUSH);
chart[2] = new Rectangle(Point(2.0, 7.0), Point(3.0, 1.0));
chart[3] = new FilledRect(Point(3.0, 7.0), Point(4.0, 3.0),
  GraphicsContext::HORIZ_BRUSH);
chart[4] = new Rectangle(Point(0.5, 0.5), Point(4.5, 7.5));
for (int i = chart.low(); i <= chart.high(); i++)
  chart[i]->plot(gc);
```

Unfortunately, that doesn't work. All rectangles come out plain (see Figure 8.5). The compiler translates the call chart[i]->plot(gc) into a call to Rectangle::plot, because the *static* (compile-time) type of chart[i] is Rectangle*.

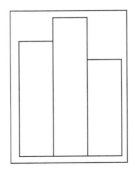

Figure 8.5. The fill patterns are not plotted.

We would like to select the appropriate `plot` function according to the *dynamic* (run-time) type of each `chart[i]`. In C++, this is possible by making the `plot` function into a *virtual* function. Virtual functions are discussed in the next section.

Exercise 8.4.1. Try out the foregoing code, which uses an `Array<Rectangle*>` to store the chart components. Verify that it compiles and that the fill patterns are not rendered when `FilledRect` objects are plotted through `Rectangle` pointers. Verify that the fill patterns themselves are not sliced away by trying out

```
FilledRect* fr = (FilledRect*)chart[1];
fr->plot(gc);
```

8.5. DYNAMIC BINDING

8.5.1. Static and Dynamic Binding

To enable the selection of the correct version of `plot` at run time, we make `plot` into a *virtual* function. The compiler translates a virtual-function call into code that selects the correct operation at run time, depending on the actual type of the object making the call.

For example, if `plot` is a virtual function, the code

```
chart[i]->plot(gc);
```

will call the correct version of `plot`, either `Rectangle::plot` or `FilledRect::plot`, depending on the actual contents of `chart[i]` for various values of `i`.

This call mechanism is more complex than a regular function call. It is referred to as *dynamic binding* or *dynamic dispatch*. The regular function call mechanism is called *static binding*, because the actual operation to be executed is determined completely at compile time.

Static binding depends on the type of the *pointer* that invokes the operation. Dynamic binding depends on the type of the *object*. For example, in the call `chart[i]->plot(gc)`, the type of `chart[i]` is `Rectangle*`. If `plot` is a nonvirtual operation, it is bound statically and `Rectangle::plot` is invoked. If `plot` is a virtual operation, then either `Rectangle::plot` or `FilledRect::plot` is invoked, depending on the object to which `chart[i]` points.

8.5.2. Declaring Virtual Functions

To enable dynamic binding, the operation must be declared as `virtual` in the base class.

```
class Rectangle
{
public:
  Rectangle(Point, Point);
  virtual void plot(GraphicsContext&) const;
  // ...
};
```

The keyword `virtual` is not replicated in the function definition.

```
void Rectangle::plot(GraphicsContext& gc) const
{ gc.rectangle(_corner1.x(), _corner1.y(),
  _corner2.x(), _corner2.y());
}
```

In the derived-class declaration, the keyword `virtual` is optional. It is, however, considered good style to provide the keyword for the benefit of the human reader.

```
class FilledRect : public Rectangle
{
public:
  FilledRect(Point, Point, FillPattern);
  virtual void plot(GraphicsContext& gc) const;
  // ...
};
```

Once a function is defined as virtual, it remains virtual in all derived classes.

Exercise 8.5.1. Try out the foregoing code that uses an `Array<Rectangle*>` to store the chart components. Make `plot` virtual. Verify that the fill patterns are rendered exactly for those objects whose dynamic type is `FilledRect`, even though they are plotted through `Rectangle` pointers.

8.5.3. Recognizing Dynamic Binding

Because C++ uses the same syntax for static and dynamic binding, it takes some effort for the compiler and, more importantly, the human reader to find out which mechanism is used for a particular invocation of an operation.

If an *object* invokes an operation, the call is always statically bound.

```
Rectangle r;
r.plot(gc); // static binding, calls Rectangle::plot
```

If a *pointer* invokes an operation, the binding depends on the nature of the operation. If the operation has been declared as `virtual`, then the binding is dynamic. Otherwise the binding is static. In the following example, assume that `scale` is not virtual:

```
Rectangle* r;
r->plot(gc);
  // dynamic binding, calls Rectangle::plot or FilledRect::plot
r->scale(p, 0.9); // static binding, calls Rectangle::scale
```

If a virtual function is invoked on the *implicit argument* of a class operation, the binding is dynamic. Consider this example:

```
class Window
{
public:
  virtual void paint(Rectangle r);
    // repaint the part of the window inside r
  void scroll(double dx, double dy);
  Rectangle size() const;
  // ...
};

void Window::scroll(double dx, double dy)
{ if (dy > 0)
  { // scroll window contents
    Rectangle s = size(); // static binding
    Point p = s.left_top();
    Rectangle r(p, Point(s.xright(), p.y() + dy));
    paint(r); // dynamic binding
  }
  else
    // ...
}
```

Note the call `paint(r)`. This invokes the virtual paint function. If the object invoking `scroll` is a plain `Window`, then `Window::paint` is called. But suppose that `GraphWindow` is derived from `Window` and inherits `Window::scroll`. Then the call

```
GraphWindow gw;
gw.scroll(0, dy); // static binding, calls Window::scroll
```

invokes `GraphWindow::paint`.

Calling a virtual function inside any operation makes that operation more flexible. A part of its code adapts itself to the actual type of the calling object. It is immaterial whether the operation itself is virtual or not. This is a powerful concept. It allows the base class to implement a general mechanism. The derived class merely needs to override specific subtasks, such as painting, that the base class cannot carry out.

To summarize, nonvirtual functions are always statically bound. Virtual functions are statically bound when they are invoked on an object and dynamically bound when they are invoked on a pointer or the implicit argument of an operation.

Unfortunately, it can be tedious to find out whether an operation has been declared as virtual. Consider the following class:

```
class GraphWindow : public ChildWindow
{
public:
  void paint(Rectangle r);
  // ...
private:
};
```

Is paint a virtual function? Our coding style mandates that each redefinition of a virtual function must be tagged as virtual. But the C++ language does not require it, and not everyone follows our style. The only way to find out for sure is to look at the parent class ChildWindow, its parent class FrameWindow, and *its* parent class Window to see whether any of them also defines paint, and if so, whether any of those definitions is tagged virtual. Only if no virtual ancestor is found anywhere can we be assured that paint is not a virtual function. This search process is less tedious if your compiler has a *browser*, a tool to inspect the class hierarchy visually.

Exercise 8.5.2. Make the weekly_pay function of Exercise 7.4.3 a virtual function. Write a second, nonvirtual function Employee::paycheck(double h) that prints the name, address, and amount paid for working h hours in a week. Make a call to weekly_pay inside paycheck, and verify that this is a virtual call by invoking paycheck on employee and manager objects.

Exercise 8.5.3. In some programming languages, such as Smalltalk, every operation is virtual. Discuss the advantages and disadvantages of that approach.

8.6. POLYMORPHISM

8.6.1. Heterogeneous Collections

For a real chart we also want to add text, lines, bitmaps, or other graphical elements.

We would envision some code that builds up the elements of the chart in an array. The chart can then be plotted with the code

```
for (int i = chart.low(); i <= chart.high(); i++)
  chart[i]->plot(gc);
```

scaled to a different size with the code

```
for (int i = chart.low(); i <= chart.high(); i++)
  chart[i]->scale(c, 0.5);
```

and saved to disk with the code

```
ofstream of("chart.dat");
for (int i = chart.low(); i <= chart.high(); i++)
  chart[i]->print(of);
```

But what is the type of chart[i]? Its type needs to be a pointer to a class that supports virtual functions plot, scale, and print. No such type currently exists in our system, and we must introduce a new type that is the *lowest common denominator* of the objects we wish to display, scale, and save. We will call it a Shape.

Here is the declaration for the Shape class.

```
class Point; // forward declaration

class Shape
{
public:
  virtual void plot(GraphicsContext& gc) const;
  virtual void print(ostream& os) const;
  virtual void scale(Point center, double s);
  virtual void move(double x, double y);
};
```

All other shape classes are derived from it:

```
class Point : public Shape { /* ... */ };
class Rectangle : public Shape { /* ... */ };
class FilledRect : public Rectangle { /* ... */ };
```

The complete inheritance tree appears in Figure 8.6. Now we may store and manipulate our chart as a collection of Shape* pointers:

```
Array<Shape*> chart;
// construct chart ...
for (int i = chart.low(); i <= chart.high(); i++)
  chart[i]->plot(gc);
```

The chart array is called a *heterogeneous collection*, because it collects objects of different types. In contrast, an Array<Rectangle> collection is homogeneous. All elements are of the same type Rectangle.

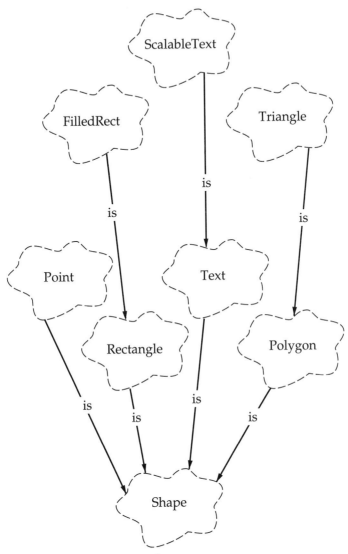

Figure 8.6. The shape hierarchy.

Exercise 8.6.1. Write a program that builds an array smiley of Shape* pointers. Populate it with a circle, two points inside for the eyes, and a horizontal line for the mouth. (OK, so it doesn't actually smile.) Scale and plot the figure 20 times, using a scale factor of 0.9 and the top right corner of the screen as the center.

Exercise 8.6.2. Write a program that reads in an arbitrary collection of shapes into an array figure of Shape* pointers. The input format for each shape is

shape name   shape data

for example

```
Point    (1.2, 13.0)
```

Use the type name to build a new object of that type, and then use the virtual read function to read in the data.

```
String s;
is >> s;
Shape* p = 0;
if (s == "Point") p = new Point;
else if (s == "Rectangle") p = new Rectangle;
else ...
if (p != 0) { p->read(is); figure.append(p); }
```

The figure description is followed by a description of commands

```
move x y
scale p s
```

Read the commands, execute them on all shapes, and plot the results. At the end, write out a textual description of the modified shapes.

Exercise 8.6.3. Populate an array e of Employee* pointers with a mixture of employees and managers. Invoke the nonvirtual raise_salary function and the virtual weekly_pay function on each of them. Use the debugger to trace through each call e[i]->raise_salary(...), e[i]->weekly_pay(...).

8.6.2. Forms of Polymorphism

The plot function in this code is an example for a *polymorphic* function. "Polymorphic" literally means "of multiple shapes." A polymorphic function is one that can result in different actions depending on context.

In C++, a function can be polymorphic for three different reasons:

- The same function name may be overloaded to denote several actual functions, leaving the compiler to pick the correct one. This is referred to as *overloading* or, occasionally, as *ad hoc* polymorphism.

- The name of an operation in a parameterized class, such as grow in the Array template, stands for different actual functions in instantiated types, such as Array<Employee> or Array<Shape*>. Again, the compiler locates the correct version. Some authors refer to this process as *parameterized* polymorphism.

- Most importantly for object-oriented programming, a virtual function call can invoke any number of actual functions, but the actual selection occurs as the program runs. This is called *pure* polymorphism. In object-oriented programming, most people mean pure polymorphism when they talk about polymorphism.

8.7. ABSTRACT BASE CLASSES

Consider the complete definition of the Shape class.

```
class Shape
{
public:
    virtual void plot(GraphicsContext& gc) const;
    virtual void print(ostream& os) const;
    virtual void scale(Point center, double s);
    virtual void move(double x, double y);
};
```

The shape class has *no data fields*, because there is no data in common with all derived classes.

The operations do nothing at all. Here is the plot operation.

```
void Shape::plot(GraphicsContext&) const
{}
```

After all, what could it plot? (Note the syntax trick: When the name of a function argument is omitted, as with the foregoing GraphicsContext&, the compiler doesn't warn about the unused function argument.)

All Shape* pointers that are generated in the program actually point to real shapes, such as rectangles and text. The base class Shape is only a unifying construction. The chart-drawing program is not expected ever to allocate actual shapes; in fact, such an allocation would be a conceptual error. Only objects of classes derived from Shape are allocated.

```
chart[1] = new Rectangle(Point(...),Point(...));
chart[2] = new Ellipse(Point(...), 0.5, 0.5);
chart[3] = new ScalableText(Point(...), "C++");
```

A class that is never instantiated (that is, of which no objects are allocated) is called an *abstract base class*. Its only purpose is to serve as a base class for derivations and as a place holder for virtual functions.

We could modify the plot code to find out whether a Shape object had been accidentally created and plotted.

```
void Shape::plot(GraphicsContext&) const
{ cerr << "Shape detected" << endl;
}

chart[4] = new Shape;
    // ERROR—run-time error when plotted
```

Even better, we can tell the compiler that we have no idea how to plot a shape and that it does not matter, because none are ever supposed to be created. We define plot as a *deferred* operation by appending "= 0" to the function declaration in the class definition. A deferred operation cannot have a definition. (In C++, deferred operations are sometimes called *pure virtual functions.*)

```
class Shape
{
public:
    virtual void plot(GraphicsContext& gc) const = 0;
    // ...
};

chart[4] = new Shape;
    // ERROR—cannot create object of abstract class
```

The compiler refuses to construct any object of a class with deferred operations. Of course, in the derived classes (Rectangle, Ellipse, and so forth) the plot function will be defined, and objects of those classes can be constructed.

Virtual functions of an abstract class are not necessarily condemned to do nothing. Functions can return a default response that is appropriate for many of the derived classes and can be overridden by others.

```
Bool Shape::is_closed() const { return FALSE; }
    // for flood fill test
```

This function can be retained by Point and Text and should be overridden to report TRUE by Rectangle and Polygon.

It is often tempting to add *some* actual data into an abstract class to make it look more real and less naked. However, that is usually not a good idea. We could add a Point _location, but this would be less than helpful for the Polygon class. Or we could add a _color field, but that would conflict with objects with more complex color descriptions, such as a bitmap.

Exercise 8.7.1. Add a virtual function circumference to the shape hierarchy that computes the circumference of each shape. This is easy for all shapes but Text. A graphics context is required to measure the size of the text string in a font. You may either return 0 for the circumference of a text field, or pass an argument of type GraphicsContext to the virtual function. How do you define the operation on the abstract class Shape? Can any derived classes reuse that definition?

8.8. Simulating Virtual Functions with Type Tags

The classical solution to selecting an appropriate function at run time is to use type tags. Each value contains one field, at a well-defined location, specifying its type. The code contains branches like the following:

```
char type = ...;
switch (type)
{ case 'P':
    // scale a point
    break;
  case 'R':
    // scale a rectangle
    break;
  // ...
}
```

Let us sketch an implementation using type tags for the shape hierarchy. We place a type tag in the base class T_Shape.

```
class T_Shape
{
public:
  void set_type(char);
    // called in derived-class constructors
  char type() const;
private:
  char _type;
};

char T_Shape::type() const { return _type; }

class T_Point : public T_Shape
{
public:
  void plot(GraphicsContext& gc);
  // ...
};

class T_Rectangle : public T_Shape
{
public:
  void plot(GraphicsContext& gc);
  // ...
};

class T_FilledRect : public T_Rectangle
{
public:
  void plot(GraphicsContext& gc);
  // ...
};
```

All objects are accessed as T_Shape* pointers. Once the type of an object is determined from the type tag, the pointer is cast to the correct type.

```
T_Shape* s = chart[i];
switch(s->type())
{ case 'P':
    ((T_Point*)s)->plot(gc);
    break;
  case 'R':
    ((T_Rectangle*)s)->plot(gc);
    break;
  case 'F':
    ((T_FilledRectpoint*)s)->plot(gc);
    break;
  // ...
}
```

Obviously, this is tedious and error-prone. It is also a maintenance headache, as we will explain in the next section.

Exercise 8.8.1. Carry out the implementation using type tags, at least to the degree that you can scale and plot bar graphs consisting of rectangles and filled rectangles.

8.9. INCREMENTAL GROWTH

Using virtual functions greatly improves program maintenance and growth. Consider the steps necessary to add a PieSegment to the object-oriented code with virtual functions.

- Derive a class PieSegment from Shape.
- Implement operations plot, scale, and so forth.
- Write code that constructs PieSegment objects.

The code can be placed in a separate file, compiled, and relinked with the existing code. *Not a line of existing code needs to be modified.* Calls such as

```
chart[i]->plot(gc);
```

now automatically work for PieSegment objects.

    Contrast that with the effort required to add a T_PieSegment class to code using type tags.

- Write the T_PieSegment structure.
- Implement operations plot, scale, and so forth.
- Write code that constructs T_PieSegment objects.
- Look for all code performing an if or switch test on the type tag and check whether it needs to be updated.

Looking for all branches on the type tags is not too bad if they are all encapsulated in `switch` statements. But in real life, control logic involving type tags is often cluttered:

```
char t = s->type();
if (t == 'R' || t == 'F') // ...
else if (t >= 'a') // ...
// where does the T_PieSegment code go?
```

Inheritance and virtual functions enable a mode of programming in which the application code spells out the general mechanisms, but the individual objects are responsible for carrying out the detail instructions. It is then possible to add on new classes of objects that conform to the same protocol, perhaps even classes that were never envisioned by the original designers, without changing the application code.

Exercise 8.9.1. Carry out the code evolution described in this section. Derive the `PieSegment` class from `Shape`. Observe what existing code needs to be modified.

Exercise 8.9.2. Now derive a `FilledPieSegment` from `PieSegment`. Some operations can be inherited. Implement the remaining ones. Again, observe the impact on the existing code.

Exercise 8.9.3. Use the type tag implementation and add classes `T_PieSegment` and `T_FilledPieSegment`. Document the amount of editing that was required to enhance the existing code.

8.10. INHERITANCE AND INVARIANTS

8.10.1. Class Invariants

The derived class D must maintain all class invariants of the base class B. It can, of course, strengthen them.

$$\text{invariant } (D) \Rightarrow \text{invariant } (B)$$

Consider a class `BalancedTree` that implements a balanced binary tree. A tree is balanced if all leaves have depth d or $d - 1$ for some integer d. The operations on the balanced tree preserve this property—it is a class invariant. Derive from it a class `Heap`. A heap is a balanced tree with the added property that the element stored in each node is no larger than any of its children. In particular, the root of the tree contains the minimum element. Such heap structures (see Figure 8.7) are used for sorting and to implement priority queues. (This notion of "heap" has nothing to do with the free store for dynamic allocation, which is also commonly referred to as a heap.) See [Aho, Hopcroft, and Ullmann], p. 87, for more details on heaps for sorting.

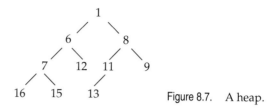

Figure 8.7.   A heap.

The heap has an invariant that is stronger than the balanced-tree invariant. Its operations not only keep the tree balanced; they also keep all elements smaller than their children. Heap may therefore inherit from BalancedTree.

There is a good reason why derived classes must respect their base class invariants. If a derived-class operation destroys the base class invariant, other base class operations may cease to function properly.

8.10.2. Preconditions

When a derived class redefines an operation f, its precondition must be no stronger than the precondition of the base class operation:

$$precond(B::f) \Rightarrow precond(D::f)$$

The derived-class operation may be invoked dynamically through a base class pointer. It must be possible to check at compile time that the derived-class operation can safely execute.

In particular, if the base class operation has no precondition, the derived-class operation may not have one either.

Here is a typical example. Consider the Text and ScalableText classes and their plot function. They actually have a subtle precondition, namely that the current font size in the graphics context is 1. This must be formulated as an invariant for Shape::plot, not just Text::plot. Invoking plot on a shape object that happens to be a Text object, with a faulty graphics context as argument, yields an erroneous plot.

8.10.3. Postconditions

When a derived class redefines an operation f, its postcondition must be at least as strong as the postcondition of the base class operation:

$$postcond(D::f) \Rightarrow postcond(B::f)$$

Suppose Shape::plot promises not to change the currently selected font in the graphics context (or to restore it if it has changed). Then all derived versions of plot must make the same promise.

8.11. DESIGN HINTS

8.11.1. Use Polymorphism, Not Type Information

Whenever you find code of the form

```
if (x is of type 1)
  action1(x);
else if (x is of type 2)
  action2(x);
```

think polymorphism. Depending on some property of x, a certain action was selected. Could it be that there are actually two kinds of x, each of which has a natural action associated with it? Then recognize the classes and make the action into a virtual function.

Code with virtual functions is *much* easier to maintain and extend than code with type tests.

8.11.2. Move Common Behavior to the Base Class

Of course, if all derived classes provide an *identical* definition for an operation, it is an easy matter to move it to the base class.

If *most* of them need one version of the operation, and a few need a different one, move the most common one to the base class and let only those that need a different one override it.

If the operations are *almost* identical, but not quite, see whether you can express the *difference* as a virtual function. Then move the code to the base class. The virtual function call will reach the correct code in each derived class.

Consider, for example, an operation Shape::floodfill that plots a shape and fills its interior with a color. Here are some versions.

```
void Ellipse::floodfill
(GraphicsContext& gc,GraphicsContext::Color c)
{ plot(gc); // plot the shape
  Point p = _center; // find a point in the inside
  gc.floodfill(p.x(), p.y(), c); // fill
}

void Rectangle::floodfill
(GraphicsContext& gc,GraphicsContext::Color c)
{ plot(gc); // plot the shape
  Point p = _corner2; // find a point in the inside
  p.scale(_corner1, 0.9);
  gc.floodfill(p.x(), p.y(), c); // fill
}
```

```
void Segment::floodfill
(GraphicsContext& gc,GraphicsContext::Color c)
{ plot(gc); // plot the shape
  // nothing to fill
}
```

Let us unify this. Floodfilling means

- Plot the outline.
- If it isn't a closed shape, give up.
- Find an interior point.
- Fill.

Here is the unified version in the base class.

```
void Shape::floodfill(GraphicsContext& gc, Color c)
{ plot(gc); // plot the shape
  if (!is_closed()) return; // nothing to fill
  Point p = center(); // find a point in the inside
  gc.floodfill(p.x(), p.y(), c); // fill
}
```

All specialized versions in the derived classes can be removed.

8.11.3. Abstract Classes Can Have Concrete Operations and Fields

Abstract classes cannot be instantiated. That is, no object of an abstract class can be allocated. It is a common misconception that abstract classes have no data fields. That is not so; abstract classes can have data fields and operations. The reason they cannot be instantiated is that there is at least one virtual operation whose implementation has been deferred to a derived class. It would not be safe to have objects of that class around. If the deferred virtual function were invoked, the behavior would be undefined.

It always makes sense to move as much functionality as possible into a base class, whether or not it is abstract. Only those operations that cannot be implemented in the base class should be deferred.

BINDING AND RUN-TIME TYPING

9.1. USAGE OF REFERENCES

The most obvious usage for references is for functions that modify their arguments. In C++, however, references are common in a number of other contexts, which are discussed in this section.

9.1.1. Constant Reference Parameters

When a function is called, the function parameters are allocated on the stack and initialized with the expressions in the function call. For large objects this process can be somewhat expensive. It is wholly unnecessary to give the function a copy of the call argument if that value is never modified. In that case, it suffices to transmit the location rather than the value. That is just what references are designed to do. It is important to declare such references as const to convey that the reference mechanism is used for efficiency, not to modify the function argument.

For example, the function

```
void print(Employee e, ostream& os);
```

could be recoded as

```
void print(const Employee& e, ostream& os);
```

Neither the call nor the function code needs to be changed. However, all modules that use this function must be recompiled.

This transformation is obviously just an optimization strategy, and one may well wonder why the compiler cannot carry it out automatically. The compiler would merely have to check that the parameter is never changed in the function and that the cost of an added level of indirection for each access is less than the cost of making a copy. Unfortunately, this optimization would force recompilation of all modules that call the function. The standard programming environments compile each module in isolation, making such intermodule optimization infeasible. For this reason, it falls to the C++ programmer to perform this optimization manually.

Exercise 9.1.1. Write a function

```
int compare(Employee a, Employee b)
```

that compares two employee records by performing a lexicographic comparison on their _name fields. Make a timing loop, calling this function a large number of times. Then replace the function with

```
int compare(const Employee& a, const Employee& b)
```

Observe that no further change to the implementation or the call is necessary. Measure the timing again, and determine the speed-up obtained by using a constant reference.

9.1.2. The Implicit Argument of an Operation

When an operation is invoked on an object, the implicit argument is transferred to the function, as are all explicit arguments. We know that the implicit argument must be a reference, not a value parameter, since an operation can modify its implicit argument.

```
Employee e;
e.raise_salary(0.05); // e modified
```

We normally have no need to refer by name to the parameter variable to which the implicit argument is bound, since any names of class features that are used in the code of the operation are automatically applied to the implicit argument.

```
void Employee::raise_salary(double p)
{ _wage *= 1 + p; // ( implicit argument)._wage
}
```

Any fields of the implicit argument can be accessed. However, the value of the implicit argument is occasionally needed in its entirety—for example, to make a copy or to pass it to another function as an explicit argument. In such cases, its name is important. The implicit argument is called self.

```
Date Date::add_days(long n) const
/* PURPOSE: Return self +  n days
*/
{ Date b = self;
  b.advance(n);
  return b;
}
```

The type of self in the add_days operation above is const Date&. In a mutator operation, such as

```
void Date::advance(long n)
/* PURPOSE: Add n days to self
*/
{ // ...
}
```

the type of self is Date&.

Actually, this is not entirely true. For historical reasons, a *pointer* to the implicit argument, called this, is defined in operations. The setup.h header file used for this book defines self as *this to give the implicit argument the same syntax as any other reference argument. For example, consider this operation:

```
long Date::days_between(const Days& b) const { /* ... */ }
```

The call

```
long n = d1.days_between(d2);
```

computes the number of days between d1 and d2. Both d1 and d2 are passed to the days_between function as constant references. It therefore makes sense if both self and b are of type const Date&.

You should be aware that this convention is not universally accepted, and you may need to translate between *this = self and this = &self when reading other code. In particular, to see self in the debugger, inspect *this. The name self was chosen because it is used in Smalltalk for the same purpose.

Furthermore, in some applications it is more natural to consistently use pointers, not objects, for variables and function arguments. Then it makes sense to use this as the name for the implicit argument, and we will do so. For example, consider an operation that tests whether two shapes meet (that is, have a nonempty intersection):

```
Bool Shape::meet(const Shape* b) const { /* ... */ }
```

Since shapes are polymorphic, they are likely to be allocated on the heap. A typical call is

```
Triangle* t = new Triangle(...);
Rectangle* r = new Rectangle(...);
if (t->meet(r)) // ...
```

In this case, meet has two arguments, this and b, both of type const Shape*. In general, we will use self or this, whichever is more natural.

Exercise 9.1.2. An object d of type Date can be printed on a stream with the << operator; for example, cout << d. Write an operation Date::print(ostream&) that calls <<.

Exercise 9.1.3. In your debugger, place *this into the watch window and step through a number of operations in a C++ program. Note the display of the current implicit argument.

9.1.3. Returning References

A function can return a reference. It is not immediately obvious why this is useful. There are two applications.

The most common case is an operation returning a reference to self.

```
Date& Date::advance(long n)
/* PURPOSE: Add n days to self
*/
{ // ...
    return self;
}
```

This allows *chaining* of operations:

```
d.advance(30).print(cout);
```

The return value of advance, namely a reference to d, becomes the implicit argument of print.

Exercise 9.1.4. What happens if the advance operation returns a Date object instead of a Date reference? Will the code compile? Will chaining work?

Some operations return a reference to a portion of their internal data. Consider a class encapsulating the efficient storage of *bidiagonal matrices*, which contain 0 except on the main diagonal and the diagonal above it (see Figure 9.1):

$$
\begin{bmatrix}
* & * & & & \\
& * & * & & \\
& & * & * & \\
& & & * & * \\
& & & & *
\end{bmatrix}
$$

Figure 9.1.   A bidiagonal matrix.

```
class Bidiag
{
public:
  Bidiag(int);
  double& elem(int, int);
  // ...
private:
  int _dim;
  Array<double> _diag;
  Array<double> _above;
};

Bidiag::Bidiag(int d)
: _dim(d),
  _diag(1, d),
  _above(1, d - 1)
{}
```

The following function returns the (i,j) element of a bidiagonal matrix.

```
double& Bidiag::elem(int i, int j)
{ if (1 <= i && i <= _dim && i == j)
    return _diag[i];
  if (1 <= i && j <= _dim && i == j - 1)
    return _above[i];
  static double z; // off the diagonals—entry is 0
  z = 0;
  return z;
}
```

For example:

```
Bidiag m(5);
// ...
double x = m.elem(1, 2);
```

But since the function returns a reference, it can also be used *on the left-hand side of an assignment:*

```
m.elem(1, 2) = 3.14;
```

How does it work? The `elem` function does not return a `double` value but the address of a `double`. The foregoing line stands for

```
*(returned address) = 3.14;
```

A common, and fatal, programming mistake is to return a reference to a local object:

```
double& Bidiag::elem(int i, int j)
{ if (1 <= i && i <= _dim && i == j)
    return _diag[i];
  if (1 <= i && j <= _dim && i == j - 1)
    return _above[i];
  double z = 0;
  return z; // DON'T
}
```

All stack variables are popped off before the function exits, and it makes no sense to return the address of a variable that no longer exists. For that reason, we declared z as `static` in the `elem` function. Static variables do not live on the stack but persist for the duration of the program.

Exercise 9.1.5. Consider the declaration of the `static` variable in the `elem` code. Explain what can go wrong when it is changed to

```
static double z = 0; // DON'T
return z;
```

It is legal, but extremely poor programming practice, to return a reference to a new object on the heap:

```
double& Bidiag::elem(int i, int j)
{ if (1 <= i && i <= _dim && i == j)
    return _diag[i];
  if (1 <= i && j <= _dim && i == j - 1)
    return _above[i];
  double* pz = new double;
  *pz = 0;
  return *pz; // DON'T
}
```

How can the allocated block be recycled to the heap?

9.2. OBJECTS AS VALUES

In C++, variables are used to hold object values, not to access objects. When an object value is copied into another variable, a copy of the object, distinct from the original, is created. Modifying the copy has no influence on the original.

```
Employee a("Joe User");
Employee b;
b = a;
b.raise_salary(0.05); // a is unchanged
```

This is not surprising to a programmer accustomed to the storage of structures in a language like Pascal or C. Both a and b have a collection of data fields, and the copy b = a makes a copy for each field.

In particular, it is the behavior we expect when generalizing from numeric types.

```
int a = 10;
int b;
b = a;
b += 15; // a is unchanged
```

Many object-oriented programming languages, such as Smalltalk, take a different point of view. Variables are not used for object storage but for object access. The objects themselves are stored in dynamic memory, and object variables hold their addresses. This is particularly convenient when managing collections of objects from different classes. All variables have the same size; hence, arrays and other containers can be built easily. Dynamic binding of operations (virtual function invocation) is the default.

The drawback in those languages is that a copy of a variable only creates another access to an existing object rather than creating a new object. To force a copy, a special copy operation must be called. This takes some getting used to, and it introduces a distinction between fundamental types (such as integers) and class types.

The C++ object model, in which objects are values, and copies create new objects, is well suited for abstractions that are conceptually like basic types, such as complex numbers or strings. It is less convenient for handling inheritance, since it requires the use of pointers to express polymorphism.

9.3. OBJECTS, POINTERS, AND REFERENCES

When an object is stored in a variable, the object is said to be *bound* to the variable. For example, the code

```
Employee e("Joe User");
```

binds an `Employee` object with name `"Joe User"` to the variable e. As the execution of the program progresses, other objects can be bound to e:

```
e = Employee("Karl Schiller");
```

All objects bound to e have the same type, namely `Employee`. While it is possible to assign an object of a derived type to e, that assignment copies only the `Employee` subobject into e.

```
e = Manager("Carol Smith"); // truncates object
```

In order to vary both the contents and the type of the objects bound to a variable, a pointer must be used.

```
Employee* pe = new Employee("Joe User");
```

The variable `pe` is bound to an employee object, but at some later point in the computation it may be bound to another object of class `Employee` *or any class derived from it:*

```
pe = new Manager("Carol Smith");
```

Two pointers can share an object.

```
Employee* pf = pe;
```

Pointer variables can be bound to no object at all:

```
pe = 0;
```

This is possible only for pointer variables. Object variables are always bound to some object, even if it is an uninteresting default one.

One should be careful to distinguish between the use of pointers for dynamic storage, for object sharing, and for polymorphism. Pointers are used for dynamic allocation of heap-based data structures, such as linked lists. Such data structures are possible because pointers can be bound to an object (such as the next link in a list) or to no object at all (at the end of a list). Object sharing takes place when access to the same object is required in distinct parts of a program, either for efficiency or for controlled access. It is achieved by binding two or more pointer variables to the same object. When pointers are used for polymorphism, objects are not necessarily shared, but pointers are bound to objects of some class or a derived class. It is worth noting that the same implementation mechanism, namely the pointer mechanism, is used to realize conceptually distinct design goals.

References are similar to pointers. They too can be bound to an object of a given class or any derived class thereof.

```
double salary(const Employee& e, Date from, Date to)
{ // ...
}

// ...
Manager m("Carol Smith");
double p = salary(m, d1, d2); // e bound to same object as m
```

There are a number of differences between references and pointers. First, references have the "syntactic sugar" of objects. That is, fields and operations are accessed with the dot (.) operator, not with ->. But there are more important conceptual distinctions.

As soon as a reference is created, it must be bound to an existing object. Once the binding is established, it cannot change for the lifetime of that reference. In particular, there is no null reference.

References are most commonly used for function parameters. When a function with a reference parameter is called, the reference is bound to the object in the call. When the function exits, the binding terminates and the reference variable goes out of scope.

Like pointers, references are used to realize various design goals. A function may receive a reference to an object because the code of the function needs to modify that object, or it may receive a reference because the reference is cheaper to establish than a copy of the object. Both of these reasons are examples of object sharing. A reference may also be desired to realize polymorphism. For example, the `salary` function previously shown does not modify the employee object but instead queries the object to compute pay information. The method for determining pay may differ between the base class and the derived classes.

Exercise 9.3.1. Write the salary function just described. For each week (or fraction of a week) between `from` and `to`, invoke the virtual `weekly_pay` function on `e`, and total up the results. Note how important it is that `Employee::weekly_pay` has been properly declared as `const`.

9.4. STATIC AND DYNAMIC BINDING

The type of an object variable coincides with the type of the object bound to it, but the type of an object bound to a pointer or reference may differ from the type of that variable. We refer to the type of the variable as the *static type*, and the type of the object as the *dynamic type*. Of course, the dynamic type is equal to the static type or a derived class thereof.

When invoking an operation on an object, we often wish to select the operation that is appropriate for the dynamic type. In C++ this is accomplished by a virtual function call.

Virtual function calls have a nontrivial overhead over regular function calls. The compiler therefore generates a regular function call whenever it can be assured that the static and dynamic type coincide; that is, when a call is carried out through an object. A virtual call is generated whenever the implicit argument is a pointer or reference.

```
Employee e("Joe User");
Employee* pe = new Manager("Carol Smith");
e.print(); // regular call of Employee::print
pe->print(); // virtual call

double salary(const Employee& e, Date from, Date to)
{ double d = e.weekly_pay(...); // virtual call
  // ...
}
```

In particular, if one operation invokes another operation on its implicit argument, that call is virtual, because the implicit argument is the self reference of the operation.

```
void Employee::print_paycheck(Date from, Date to) const
{ double d = weekly_pay(...); // virtual call, self.pay(...)
  print(); // virtual call, self.print()
  // ...
}
```

Occasionally, one must override the virtual call mechanism and call an operation of a specific class. This can be achieved by specifying the class name in the call. The most typical example is the invocation of the base class operation in a derived-class redefinition.

```
void Manager::print() const
{ Employee::print(); // regular call of Employee::print()
  // ...
}
```

Exercise 9.4.1. Suppose each manager object has an array _superv of the supervised employees. Which calls to print in the following code are virtual?

```
void Manager::print() const
{ Employee::print();
  for (int i = _superv.low(); i <= _superv.high(); i++)
    _superv[i]->print();
}
```

```
Manager m;
m.print();

Employee& e = m;
e.print();
```

9.5. RUN-TIME TYPES

9.5.1. Testing for a Type Match

It is possible to find out whether a base class pointer actually points to a derived class of a certain type. C++ provides the `typeid` operator for this test. (For the test to work properly, the class needs to have at least one virtual function.) The following tests whether a `Shape` pointer actually points to a rectangle.

```
Shape* s;
if (typeid(s) == typeid(Rectangle*))
    // s points to a Rectangle object
else
    // s points to an object of some other class
```

Older versions of C++ do not support the `typeid` operator. In that case, you can of course supply your own mechanism:

```
enum ShapeType { POINT, TEXT, RECTANGLE, FILLEDRECT, ... };

class Shape
{
public:
   virtual void plot(GraphicsContext& gc) = 0;
   virtual ShapeType type() const = 0;
   // ...
};

ShapeType Rectangle::type() const { return RECTANGLE; }
ShapeType FilledRect::type() const { return FILLEDRECT; }
// ...

Shape* s;
// compute area
if (s->type() == RECTANGLE)
   // s points to a Rectangle object
   // compute height × width
else
   // points and text have area 0
```

The type match test looks interesting, but it is actually practically useless. In the foregoing code the test fails if s points to a FilledRect or some other class derived from Rectangle, even though conceptually a filled rectangle *is* a rectangle.

The purpose of inheritance is to build objects that act exactly like the base class objects unless they themselves decide otherwise. Type matching defeats this.

We strongly recommend against testing for type matches, because it is incompatible with inheritance. Use virtual functions instead. We will see one legitimate use for type match testing in Section 9.6.

9.5.2. Testing for Downcasting

Very occasionally, there are situations in which virtual functions are not flexible enough, and a run-time type inquiry is required. Consider, for example, the task of computing the intersection of two geometric shapes that might be rectangles or polygons. In general, the intersection is a union of polygons, but the intersection of two rectangles is again a rectangle.

In this case, we must know whether a Shape pointer actually points to a Rectangle, or maybe a class derived from it. This test is sometimes referred to as a "kind of" test. If the test succeeds, we need to convert the Shape* pointer to a Rectangle* pointer to gain access to the rectangle features.

The process of converting a base class pointer to a derived-class pointer, provided that some information is available that guarantees the correctness of the cast, is often referred to as *downcasting*. The term originates from the habit of many computer scientists to draw the root of the inheritance tree on the top (in complete violation of biological facts, except perhaps in Australia) and the derived classes further down.

In C++, downcasting is performed with the dynamic_cast operator. Suppose we need to find out whether a Shape pointer actually points to a Rectangle of some kind: either a plain Rectangle, a FilledRect, or some other rectangle. The following code achieves this.

```
Shape* s;
// ...
Rectangle* r = dynamic_cast<Rectangle*>(s);
if (r != 0)
    // r equals s and points to an object that is a Rectangle
else
    // s points to an object that is not a Rectangle
```

The dynamic_cast performs both the test and the type conversion. (For dynamic_cast to work properly, the base class must have at least one virtual function.)

It is possible to cast references as well. But because there is no null reference, a failed reference cast causes an exception. See Chapter 15 for details.

Older versions of C++ do not support the `dynamic_cast` operator. If downcasting is required only for a few types (as it should be in practice), one can easily implement test operations.

```
class Shape
{
public:
  virtual void plot(GraphicsContext& gc) = 0;
  virtual Rectangle* is_rectangle();
  // ...
};

Rectangle* Shape::is_rectangle() { return 0; }
Rectangle* Rectangle::is_rectangle() { return this; }

Shape* s;
// ...
Rectangle* r = s->is_rectangle();
if (r != 0)
  // r equals s and points to an object that is a Rectangle
else
   // s points to an object that is not a Rectangle
```

There are two subtle points. First, note that the `is_rectangle` function is defined only in two classes. The `Shape` class defines it to return 0, and the `Rectangle` class to return `this`. All classes derived from `Rectangle` inherit the rectangle version, proclaiming that they too are rectangles. All other classes inherit the `Shape` version, stating that they are not rectangles. Next, note that the return value of `is_rectangle` is `Rectangle*`, not `Bool`. There is a simple reason. When the type test succeeds, the code needs to access the information as a rectangle. Rather than an ugly cast `(Rectangle*)p`, we can use the same returned pointer, properly typed as a rectangle.

This mechanism is not entirely satisfactory, because it requires one virtual function per type. If your compiler does not support dynamic casts, you may want to look at [Stroustrup], p. 442, for a description of a DYNAMIC_CAST macro. Unfortunately, it is complex and requires that the programmer insert certain other macros into class definitions to generate links representing the inheritance relationships.

Exercise 9.5.1. Write a function

```
Shape* intersect(const Shape* a, const Shape* b)
```

that returns the rectangle or polygon of intersection if a, b are rectangles or triangles (that is, polygons with three vertices), and returns a 0 pointer otherwise.

9.5.3. Shallow and Deep Copying

Suppose we want to make a copy of all entries in a container holding a collection of shapes. We can copy the pointers. Such a copy is called a *shallow* copy.

```
Array<Shape*> fig1;
// ...
Array<Shape*> fig2;
fig2.grow(fig1.low(), fig1.high());
for(int i = fig1.low(); i <= fig1.high(); i++)
  fig2[i] = fig1[i];
```

If the entries in fig1 are changed, then the fig2 pointers refer to the changed objects as well.

```
for(int i = fig1.low(); i <= fig1.high(); i++)
  fig1[i]->rotate(p, a);
// fig2 also contains rotated shapes
```

That is often undesirable. Suppose that we really want to have a new set of objects. A virtual clone function is required that creates a new copy of an object:

```
class Shape
{
public:
  virtual void plot(GraphicsContext& gc) = 0;
  virtual Shape* clone() const  = 0;
  // ...
};

Shape* Point::clone() const { return new Point(self); }
Shape* Rectangle::clone() const { return new Rectangle(self); }
```

The statement

```
return new X(self);
```

is roughly equivalent to

```
X* r = new X;
*r = self;
return r;
```

However, it is more efficient to construct the new object directly as a copy of self, rather than first using the default constructor, followed by assignment.

See Chapter 13 for more information on the process of constructing an object as a copy of another object of the same class.

The `clone` function can be used to make a true copy of each object, often called a *deep copy*.

```
for(int i = fig1.low(); i <= fig1.high(); i++)
  fig2[i] = fig1[i]->clone();
```

Because `clone` is virtual, the appropriate `clone` function is called for each object.

It is a good idea to plan for deep copies and include a `clone` function in an inheritance hierarchy. Of course, then each derived class must implement

```
Base* Derived::clone() const { return new Derived(self); }
```

In polymorphic C++ code, pointer variables act like object variables in Smalltalk or Eiffel. Copying the pointer gives another access to the same object, and a special operation must be invoked to make a true copy of the object. Sadly, the C++ programmer has the added obligation to delete the actual objects when they are no longer needed, a task that a garbage collector undertakes in Smalltalk and Eiffel.

Exercise 9.5.2. Make a figure (such as a bar chart) as an array f of shape pointers. Make a copy g = f. Move the elements in g to another portion of the screen. Plot both f and g. Explain the result.

Exercise 9.5.3. Make a figure (such as a bar chart) as an array of shapes. Then make a deep copy, using `clone` on each element. Move the original figure to another portion of the screen. Verify that the copy is not affected.

9.6. OBJECT EQUALITY

There are two concepts of object equality. Let us consider numeric types first. We may ask whether two integers have the same *value*:

```
int m, n;
// ...
if (m == n) ...
```

Given two pointers to int, we may again wish to test whether the integers to which they point have the same *value*:

```
int* p;
int* q;
// ...
if (*p == *q) ...
```

Or we may want to know whether they have the same *identity*:

```
if (p == q) ...
```

The latter is interesting if we need to know whether changing *p also changes *q.

Reference values are compared like object values:

```
void f(int& r, int& s)
{ if (r == s) ...
}
```

To test whether two references have the same identity, compare their addresses.

```
if (&r == &s)
```

For a class object, testing equalities of values is often meaningful. For example, two points are identical if their *x*- and *y*-coordinates are:

```
Bool Point::is_equal(const Point& b) const
{ return _x == b._x && _y == b._y;
}
```

Two rectangles are identical if their top left and bottom right corners are:

```
Bool Rectangle::is_equal(const Rectangle& b) const
{ return left_top().is_equal(b.left_top())
     && right_bottom().is_equal(b.right_bottom());
}
```

Exercise 9.6.1. Write an is_equal function for Polygon. It isn't as simple as you may think. You can't just test whether corresponding entries in the vertex array are the same points. The same points may be at different positions, permuted cyclically or in backwards order. That is, the polygon containing points p_1, p_2, p_3, p_4 should be considered identical to that containing p_4, p_3, p_2, p_1, or p_4, p_1, p_2, p_3, but not p_1, p_4, p_2, p_3. This exercise shows why testing for equality of values must be supplied by the programmer and cannot be recursively generated by the compiler.

Given two pointers to rectangle objects, it is now an easy matter to test whether they refer to the same object,

```
Rectangle* p;
Rectangle* q;
// ...
if (p == q) ...
```

or whether the objects to which they refer have the same value:

```
if ((*p).is_equal(*q))
```

Or is it? If q points to a FilledRect, the call to is_equal will return TRUE if its rectangle portion coincides with that of *p, even though intuitively a rectangle is never equal to a filled rectangle, and two filled rectangles are equal if their rectangle portions and fill pattern are.

More generally, we may want to test whether two arbitrary shape pointers point to objects of equal value—for example, to implement a *set* data structure that ignores duplicate values.

The simple answer is to make is_equal a virtual function, but the situation is not that simple: is_equal has *two* arguments, both of which vary in the type hierarchy. Virtual functions can only select an operation based on one argument, the implicit argument of the virtual function call. While that is sufficient for many applications, it breaks down for equality testing. This is one situation where an exact type match is useful.

```
Bool Rectangle::is_equal(const Rectangle& b) const
{ if (typeid(self) != typeid(b)) return FALSE;
  return left_top().is_equal(b.left_top())
    && right_bottom().is_equal(b.right_bottom());
}
```

Exercise 9.6.2. Add a virtual is_equal operation to the Shape hierarchy.

Exercise 9.6.3. Using the virtual is_equal function of the previous exercise, write a function to test whether two figures (array of Shape* pointers) are made up of equal shapes.

9.7. DOUBLE DISPATCH

As we have seen in the previous section, polymorphic equality testing is difficult because virtual functions allow run-time selection only on their first argument. For equality testing we were able to overcome that problem, because equality is defined only on objects of the same type. The problem is more difficult if an operation is defined on arbitrary combinations of two polymorphic arguments.

Consider the task of computing *regions* on the screen. Regions are defined as unions and intersections of shapes. Intersections of rectangles are again rectangles (or empty), but unions of rectangles are not. Suppose the class RectRegion denotes unions of rectangles (stored as an array of their constituents), and Region denotes general regions, formed by unions and intersections of rectangles and ellipses (stored as tree structures). These classes are to be derived from Shape. The following tables list the types of unions and intersections of the various regions. For simplicity, we ignore polygons and nongeometric shapes like Text in this example.

Intersection	Rectangle	RectRegion	Ellipse	Region
Rectangle	Rectangle	RectRegion	Region	Region
RectRegion	RectRegion	RectRegion	Region	Region
Ellipse	Region	Region	Region	Region
Region	Region	Region	Region	Region

Union	Rectangle	RectRegion	Ellipse	Region
Rectangle	RectRegion	RectRegion	Region	Region
RectRegion	RectRegion	RectRegion	Region	Region
Ellipse	Region	Region	Region	Region
Region	Region	Region	Region	Region

The method of carrying out intersection and union depends on the type of both arguments. To compute the intersection of two rectangles, one compares their coordinates. To intersect a rectangle with a rectangle region, one intersects the rectangle with all rectangles in that region and forms the union of the nonempty intersections.

Ideally, we would write separate virtual functions for each combination and rely on the virtual function mechanism to locate and execute the correct one, whenever we need to intersect two shapes. But, as we have observed, a virtual function call

```
s->intersect(t);
```

looks only at the type of s to select an operation. One could resort to explicit type inquiry to find the type of t and then carry out the appropriate action. But explicit type inquiry is always suspect and should be avoided.

Instead, we will use a technique called *double dispatch*. Consider for example

```
Shape* Rectangle::intersect(const Shape* t) const
```

which is executed as the result of the virtual function call

```
s->intersect(t);
```

if s points to a rectangle. The trick is now to launch a virtual function on t to have the virtual function mechanism act on its type. Of course, just calling

```
t->intersect(s); // DON'T
```

would get us nowhere. Instead, we take advantage of the fact that we know that s must point to a rectangle, and call

```
t->intersect_rectangle(this);
```

Suppose t pointed to a rectangle region. This call then executes the function

```
Shape* RectRegion::intersect_rectangle(const Rectangle* r)
const
```

In that function the types of both arguments are known: this (the original t) is a RectRegion*, and r (the original s) is a Rectangle*. We now have enough information to carry out the actual work.

That means, for each of the types X we have to define a virtual function

```
Shape* X::intersect(const Shape* t)const
{ t->intersect_X(this); }
```

and for each combination of types X and Y we define

```
Shape* Y::intersect_ X(const X * r) const
{ // this is a Y*
  // r is an X*
  // now compute the intersection
}
```

Of course, several of the operations perform identical work, and common code can be factored out into (nonvirtual) procedures.

The double dispatch approach performs run-time resolution on two arguments, but at a cost. Suppose there are n classes, with base class B (in our example, $n = 6$). We require

- A virtual function $B::f(\text{const } B*)$ const
- n virtual functions $B::f\_X(\text{const } X*)$ const
- n implementations $X::f(\text{const } B* \ t) \ \text{const} \ \{ \ t\text{->}f\_X(\text{this}); \ \}$
- n^2 implementations $Y::f\_X(\text{const } X* \ r) \ \text{const}$ that do the actual work of carrying out the operation involving X and Y objects.

Double dispatching is workable only for small and stable collections of classes. The code is difficult to maintain. The addition of a new class forces the addition of a new virtual function in the base class and $2(n + 1)$ new implementations of operations.

Double dispatch is used only when functionality can vary with both arguments. Comparison operations such as equality testing should not be implemented with double dispatch. That would implement $n^2 - n$ operations that simply return FALSE, and n operations that compute a nontrivial result when the argument types are identical.

Exercise 9.7.1. Derive the class `RectRegion` from `Shape` and supply the `plot`, `print`, `move`, and `scale` operations. Implement a rectangular region as an array of rectangles. You may plot them filled with a solid brush.

Exercise 9.7.2. Implement the `intersect` operation using double dispatch.

9.8. DESIGN HINTS

9.8.1. Use Objects Instead of Pointers When Possible

Objects have more intuitive copy semantics than pointers. There is no need for dynamic allocation and deallocation. Use objects instead of pointers when you can.

There are three reasons why you may need pointers:

- For sharing
- For polymorphism
- For 0|1 relationships

For example, consider a mailbox that holds messages. Should you use an `Array<Message>` or an `Array<Message*>`?

Let us look at the reasons for pointers in detail. Can two mailboxes share the same message, to the degree that editing one necessarily affects the other? Are there different message types, derived from a base class `Message`? Does a slot in the mailbox need to differentiate between a blank message and no message at all (that is, is there a 0|1 attachment)? If any one of these applies, use pointers; otherwise use objects.

9.8.2. Use References Instead of Pointers When Possible

References have one essential advantages over pointers: They always refer to something. There is no null or uninitialized reference. This eliminates a whole class of programming errors.

You can use a reference to model an association that does not change over its lifetime. Reference parameters of functions are just one example. Over the lifetime of the function invocation, the reference parameter is bound to the argument of the call. An object may contain a reference to a file or a graphics context that it uses throughout its lifetime.

There is one additional requirement: You must be able to initialize the reference at the beginning of its lifetime. For reference parameters of functions, this is automatic. Reference fields of classes must be initialized in the constructor. If an object is to contain a reference to a file object, that file object must be supplied at construction and cannot be supplied (or changed) later.

9.8.3. Don't Take the Address of an Object Except to Test for Identity

There is one legitimate reason to use the & operator: to test whether two pointers or references point to the identical object. All other uses are suspect.

Taking and storing the address of stack objects is not usually useful, because stack objects are so short-lived. Taking the address of a field yields a pointer to the inside of an object and breaks the encapsulation.

9.8.4. Avoid Returning Pointers or References to Internal Fields

In general, functions should not return pointers or references to data fields of objects. It violates the encapsulation. For example, the following would be an extremely poor idea:

```
class Date
{
public:
   int& day();
   // ...
private:
   int _day;
   // ...
};

int& Date::day() { return _day; } // DON'T
```

It sounds clever—day() can be used on the left-hand side of an assignment:

```
d.day() = 31;
```

But there is essentially no difference between this setup and public data. In particular, it is impossible to change the data representation.

There is one exception to this rule. Containers like arrays, lists, vectors, and matrices commonly return references to the elements that they store.

9.8.5. Minimize Operations That Return Pointers to New Heap Objects

In general, functions should not return pointers to newly allocated heap objects. Doing so requires that the caller (1) capture the returned pointer and (2) eventually delete it. This is a big burden to place on the caller.

However, an operation that computes a polymorphic result must build its return value on the heap. For example, to copy polymorphic objects, a clone operation must return a heap copy of self. When reading in a polymorphic object from a file, the read operation must determine the exact type of the object described in the file, allocate a heap object of that type, and return it. The Shape::intersect operation must return a heap result. In all three cases, the caller of the operation is responsible for eventually deleting the returned object.

9.8.6. Never Return a Reference
to a Stack or New Heap Object

Never return a pointer or reference to a local stack object. The object is gone when the function exits.

Never return a reference to a newly allocated heap object. The syntax for deleting it is too unintuitive.

In general, only return a reference to an object that existed before the call of the operation. For example, returning `self` is acceptable.

9.8.7. Avoid Type Inquiry

Whenever possible, use virtual functions rather than type inquiry. They lead to far more extensible and maintainable code.

Don't use the `typeid` operator except for equality testing. It is fundamentally incompatible with inheritance. Use `dynamic_cast` when there is no good solution using virtual functions.

NAME CONTROL

Every feature that is defined in one place of a program for usage elsewhere has a name. Classes, fields, operations, global variables, functions, types, and templates are identified by names. A programmer who defines a new feature must name it. When a program is composed of many components, written by many programmers and vendors, it is important to guard against name conflicts.

If two distinct features are inadvertently given the same name, construction of the program will fail. Of course, renaming one of them will remedy the problem, but renaming is rarely practical with code obtained from third-party vendors. The renaming would have to be carried out again with every new code release. Of course, if the source code is not available, renaming is plainly impossible.

This chapter discusses how name conflicts can be minimized by placing names into the scope of classes and name spaces. The last two sections cover access control and the decomposition of a program into separately compiled modules.

10.1. NAME LOOKUP

10.1.1. Variables

The name of a variable is searched first in the local scope; then, for operations, in the scope of the class; and then in the scope of the file. If a variable x is used in an expression, first the local scope is searched. Local scopes are nested and searched from the inside out:

```
void X::fun()
{  ...
    {  int x; // match
        ...
        {  ...
            ... x ...
        }
    }
}
```

Function arguments are local names in the outermost local scope:

```
void X::fun(int x) // match
{   ...
    {   ...
        {   ...
            ... x ...
        }
    }
}
```

If the variable is not found in any surrounding local scope, and it occurs in an operation of a class, the class scope is searched next:

```
class X
{   ...
    int x; // match
};
```

If the class X derives from another class, all parent classes are also searched for a name match.

```
class B
{   ...
    int x; // match
};

class X : public B { ... };
```

Finally, the file is searched for a definition or declaration of a global variable.

```
int x = 0; // match
static int x = 0; // match
extern int x; // match
```

The style convention in which we prefix class fields with an underscore is designed to keep the variables in class scope disjoint from those in local and file scope.

Exercise 10.1.1. Suppose there is a global variable named x, a class X with a data field named x, and an operation int X::f(int x) { ... }. Implement f to return the sum of the three variables named x without renaming any of them. *Hint:* Use scope resolution.

10.1.2. Functions

Unlike Pascal, C++ does not support the nesting of function definitions. Functions are looked up first in the class scope if they are invoked from an operation.

```
void X::fun()
{  ...
   f();
   ...
}

class X
{  ...
   void f(); // name match
};
```

If a match occurs, f denotes an operation with implicit argument self (unless f is a shared function; see Section 10.2.3).

Next, the file scope is searched for a definition or prototype with the same name.

```
void f() { ... }; // name match
static void f() { ... }; // name match
void f(); // name match
extern void f(); // name match
```

Due to name overloading, at each stage the compiler must look at all functions that were found and compare the arguments in the call with the argument types of the function to select an actual match (or to declare that no unique match was possible). This step is specific to functions (and operators) only.

10.1.3. Accessing a Specific Scope

It is always possible to bypass the search in the local and class scope, and refer to a global name, by prefixing the name with the :: scope resolution operator.

```
void Window::message_box(String msg, String title)
{  // call global message_box function
   ::message_box(_handle, msg, title, MB_OK);
}
```

Name lookup can be directed into the scope of a specific class with the scope resolution operator. This is commonly used to access a function in a base class:

```
class Manager : public Employee { ... };

void Manager::print(ostream & os) const
{  Employee::print(os);
   ...
}
```

10.1.4. Name Lookup and Access Control

In C++, name lookup is performed before access control. That is, first all names are searched, regardless of public or private attribute. Then the compiler checks whether the code has the privilege to access the found feature:

```
void f() { ... }

class X : public B { ... };

class B
{ ...
private:
  void f(); // name  match
};

void X::fun()
{ ...
  f();
  ...
}
```

Because fun is an operation of class X, first the scope of X and its ancestors is searched, and B::f is found to match. The global f is never considered. Then access control reveals that B::f is private to B, and hence the call in X::fun is illegal. Of course, if access to the global function is desired, it can be reached as ::f.

At first glance, it seems silly even to look at inaccessible features for name matching. However, it was noted that programmers in practice often change operations from public to private or vice versa. It would be undesirable if such a change could quietly change the meaning of an expression from one legal interpretation to a quite different one. For example, suppose that the call to init in GraphWindow::open really intends to call Window::init from the base class, but then the designer of Window makes init private. It would not be desirable if that change simply altered the meaning of GraphWindow::open, invoking the global function init that happens to have the same name. Having the compiler generate an error alerts the programmer to the problem.

From a theoretical point of view, it is unsatisfactory that private features are used for name matching. Private features are a part of the implementation, not the interface. Making a public operation private or vice versa is really a change in interface. When the public interface changes, the class designer and users should expect changes in behavior.

Exercise 10.1.2. What happens if the implementor of GraphWindow::open calls the global function close_window, and then the designer of the base class Window adds a private operation close_window? What if the added operation is public? Is either behavior reasonable?

10.2. CLASS SCOPE

10.2.1. Class Scope Enumerations

Enumerated (enum) constants can be placed inside class declarations:

```
class Date
{
public:
  enum Weekday
  { MON, TUE, WED, THU, FRI, SAT, SUN
  };
  // ...
};
```

Operations of the Date class refer to these constants simply as MON, TUE, and so forth. Since the enumeration is public, other functions can use them as well and must access them with the scope resolution operator

```
Date::MON
```

Enumerations can be private, in which case they are accessible only to the operations of the class defining them.

Enumerations in class scope are a powerful method for avoiding name clashes. Names of global constants are even more vulnerable to conflicts than names of functions, because there is no possibility of overloading resolution. Even seemingly unique choices like SAT and SUN for weekday names can collide with names from quite different domains:

```
enum Workstation { DEC, HP, SUN, };

enum Test { SAT, GRE, GMAT, };
```

Moving enumerations into a class whose operations or clients are most likely to use them removes them from the global name space and minimizes the risk of conflicts.

Exercise 10.2.1. The ios class in the iostream library defines local enumerations for a number of purposes. Locate them (by peeking inside iostream.h or consulting Chapter 12). Would any of their names be likely to generate functions if the prefix ios:: was not necessary to access them?

Exercise 10.2.2. Look inside some header files for your compiler to see whether they define constants that are just waiting to create name conflicts. The DOS and graphics libraries are usually better targets than the standard header files, whose designers have gone to some lengths to uglify names (SEEK_SET). For example, one well-known vendor defines FILENAME as 4 in dos.h.

10.2.2. Shared Data

Consider the array

```
int days_per_month[12] =
{ 31, 28, 31, 30, 31, 30,
  31, 30, 31, 31, 30, 31
};
```

for use in a Date class. Suppose we want to restrict access to this array only to Date operations. We could make it a member:

```
class Date
{ // ...
private:
  int days_per_month[12];
  int _day;
  // ...
};
```

But this would be very wasteful. Every *instance* of Date would have its own days_per_month array.

   We want to have only one copy of the array that is shared among all Date objects, yet has the same access restrictions as regular Date members.

   To declare such shared data, use the keyword static:

```
class Date
{ // ...
private:
  static int days_per_month[12];
  int _day;
  // ...
};
```

This declares a single array that is not part of any Date object. It is accessible by all operations of the Date class.

   The syntax for initializing a shared variable is similar to that of defining an operation. The following definition must be included in the module implementing the Date class:

```
int Date::days_per_month[12] =
{ 31, 28, 31, 30, 31, 30,
  31, 30, 31, 31, 30, 31
};
```

Even though the declaration of shared class variables appears similar to that of class fields (except for the keyword static), they have nothing in common.

Fields are parts of objects. Class variables are not—there is a unique, per-class instance.

Global variables and shared class variables behave identically except for name space control. Global variables are in the global scope and hence can clash with other variables of the same name. Shared class variables are in the scope of the class and hence have their names protected.

Exercise 10.2.3. Add shared variables to Date to keep track of the total number of date objects constructed in a program. Use a shared variable to count the dates, and increment it in each constructor. If you are already familiar with destructors and copy constructors (see Chapter 13), also count the number of date objects alive at any given time.

10.2.3. Shared Functions

As we saw in the preceding section, global variables can be placed inside classes as shared variables, to group them where they logically belong and to remove their names from the global name space. The same is possible for functions.

Consider a function that tests whether a year is a leap year, for use in date arithmetic.

```
Bool is_leap(int year)
{ if (year % 4 != 0) return FALSE;
  if (year % 100 != 0) return TRUE;
  if (year % 400 != 0) return FALSE;
  return TRUE;
};
```

This function is not an operation of the Date class, because it does not take an implicit argument. (Of course, we could write a different function Bool Date::is_leap() to test whether the _year field of self is a leap year.) Nevertheless, the function is logically related to the Date class. It can be inserted into the scope of Date by using the keyword static.

```
class Date
{
public:
  static Bool is_leap(int);
  // ...
};
```

As a public function, is_leap can be called by any other function. Functions outside the scope of Date must use scope resolution.

```
if (Date::is_leap(y)) ...
```

Shared functions have no implicit argument and hence cannot access class fields without specifying an object. They can, however, operate on shared data.

Unlike global functions, shared functions have the privilege of accessing private features of their class. This enables us to write comparison functions with two explicit arguments, of the form needed by Array<X>::qsort, as shared functions.

```
class Date
{
public:
    static int compare(const Date&, const Date&);
    // ...
};

int Date::compare(const Date& a, const Date& b)
{ int d = a._year - b._year;
  if (d != 0) return d;
  d = a._month - b._month;
  if (d != 0) return d;
  return a._day - b._day;
}

Array<Date> a;
a.qsort(Date::compare);
```

Exercise 10.2.4. Continue Exercise 10.2.3 by writing a shared function that prints the object counts to a stream.

Exercise 10.2.5. Make the jul2dat and dat2jul functions that are used in the implementation of the Date class into shared functions.

Exercise 10.2.6. A class with only static features is a *module*. Explain.

10.2.4. Array Sizes

It is surprisingly difficult to specify integer constants to specify sizes of buffers or other fixed-size arrays in a class scope.

The following looks reasonable:

```
class Stack
{ // ...
private:
    static const int SIZE = 20; // ERROR
    int _s[SIZE];
};
```

But it is a syntax error. A static variable must be initialized outside the class declaration:

```
class Stack
{ // ...
private:
  static const int SIZE;
  int _s[SIZE]; // ERROR
};

const int Stack::SIZE = 20;
```

That is useless—the definition of SIZE comes too late.

Of course, a global SIZE, declared before the Stack class, would solve the problem—at the cost of a near-certain name clash. Surely somewhere in any program, someone has the bright idea of defining a constant named SIZE.

The solution is curious and really ugly, but it works and has become a standard idiom. We take advantage of the fact that enum constants can be given specific values.

```
class Stack
{ // ...
private:
  enum { SIZE = 20 };
  int _s[SIZE];
};
```

The constant SIZE is not logically part of any enumerated type. For that reason, we did not give the enumeration any type name. Using anonymous enumerations to specify array sizes is quite common, but this feature should never be used to specify any other integer constants.

10.2.5. Nested Classes

A class can be nested inside another. This is most frequently done to hide a class that is relevant only for implementation:

```
class List
{
public:
  void insert(int);
  int remove();
  // ...
private:
  class Link
  {
  public:
    Link(int, Link* = 0);
```

```
    int _info;
    Link* _next;
  };

  Link* _head;
};
```

This does *not* mean that every object of type List contains a subobject of type Link. Placing Link inside the scope of the List class merely hides the definition of Link from the outside world. Apart from visibility, there is no difference between nested classes and separately defined classes.

Although all data members of Link are public, they are known only to the List class, because Link itself is declared in the private part of List. This is common and entirely permissible, because the encapsulation of the List class is not compromised.

Operations of the Link class require two scope resolutions:

```
List::Link::Link(int i, Link* n)
: _info(i),
  _next(n)
{}
```

It is legal to declare a nested class inside its enclosing class and defer the definition:

```
class List
{ // ...
private:
  class Link;

  Link* _head;
};

class List::Link
{
public:
  Link(int, Link* = 0);

  int _info;
  Link* _next;
};
```

That makes the enclosing class easier to read.

Exercise 10.2.7. Design a class Directory that can list all files in a directory, including file name, size, and date of last change. Make a nested class FileProperties to store these file properties.

10.2.6. Types in Class Scope

Nested classes define class types in the scope of a class. Type definitions in class scope perform the same for type synonyms.

```
class Directory
{
public:
  enum { FILENAME_LEN = 80 };
  typedef char Filename[FILENAME_LEN];
  // ...
};
```

The type `Directory::Filename` can be used publicly, but it is guaranteed not to conflict with other types named `Filename`.

10.3. NAME SPACES

10.3.1. Using Classes for Name Space Control

The technique of enclosing all names inside a class scope is a very attractive method of removing name collisions. For example, a program composed of many modules supplied by multiple vendors may employ various mutually incompatible list implementations. They cannot all be named `List`, or a link conflict will result. But suppose each vendor is careful to wrap the name `List` inside a class:

```
class Vendor_A { public: class List { ... }; ... };

class Vendor_B { public: class List { ... }; ... };
```

This removes the name conflict. Of course, it brings the added tedium of always referring to the classes as `Vendor_A::List` and `Vendor_B::List`, making the code harder to read and write.

To ensure uniqueness, the name prefixes must be long. If both Vince Adams and Vendor A have the bright idea to use VA as their vendor prefix, nothing is solved.

As an added impediment, the descriptions of the classes `Vendor_A` and `Vendor_B` are likely to be huge, because they must contain all features required in a vendor library. Parsing huge class descriptions, even though only a small subset is required for any particular compilation unit, can have a significant impact on the build time for large programs.

10.3.2. The Name Space Mechanism

In 1993 a new language mechanism was added to C++ to provide unique (and therefore long) names in the object code of libraries that can be abbreviated to concise source code names.

Feature declarations are entered into a *name space:*

```
namespace Vendor_A_Containers
{ template<class T> class List { ... };
  template<class T> class Queue { ... };
  ...
}
```

The implementor, that is, vendor A, must also wrap the implementation code in a namespace block:

```
namespace Vendor_A_Containers
{
  template<class T> T Queue<T>::remove() { ... };
  template<class T> int Queue<T>::length() const { ... };
  ...

}
```

This has the effect of generating object code in which all data and functions have long names. Names can be guaranteed to be unique as long as vendors can agree to use unique names, such as their legal name and tax identification number. It is assumed that the linker and dynamic link mechanism have no problems with long names.

Name spaces can contain the definitions of global variables and functions, types, classes, and templates.

Programmers can refer to these features by their full name, such as

```
Vendor_A_Containers::Queue<Employee> q;
```

Of course, that is very awkward. An essential feature of name spaces is that shorter aliases are available.

10.3.3. Using Name Spaces

The easiest and safest method for simplifying access to a name space is to give it a shorter alias.

```
namespace Cont = Vendor_A_Containers;
```

Now containers can be obtained by using the shorter alias as a prefix:

```
Cont::Queue<Customer> q;
```

It also eases the change from the container library by vendor A to a compatible library by another vendor.

The second method is to specify which features you would like to use. Their names are entered into the scope containing the using declaration and need not be qualified.

```
class Bank
{ using Vendor_A_Containers::Queue;
  ...
private:
  Queue<Customer> _waitingQueue;
  ...
};
```

A using declaration can be inserted into any class scope, local scope, or file scope:

```
void f(double mean)
{ using Vendor_A_MathLib::expdist;
  double x = expdist(mean);
  // ...
};
```

Finally, all names of a name space can be made available in a scope:

```
using Vendor_A_MathLib;

void f(double mean)
{ double x = expdist(mean);
  // ...
};
```

However, that seems dubious. Name spaces are likely to be large and somewhat fluid, because vendors tend to add new features periodically. Simply pouring the contents of one or more name spaces into a scope seems to invite name collisions.

10.4. ACCESS CONTROL

We have seen that C++ classes can control the access to their class features with the public and private attributes. As we know, data should always be private to a class, but we can decide to make operations, shared functions, enumerations, nested classes, and types either public or private.

In certain circumstances, this simple access control mechanism is too restrictive. It distinguishes only between two sets of clients: the class's operations and all other code. Occasionally it is desirable to grant access to private features to some, but not all, other functions.

10.4.1. Friends

A class may name another function or another class as its *friend*. That gives the named function, or all operations of the named class, the right to access all private features. This is a dangerous mechanism, and it should be used only when absolutely necessary.

Consider the following pair of Link and List classes.

```
class Link
{
private:
  Link(int, Link* = 0);

  int _info;
  Link* _next;

  friend class List;
};

class List
{
public:
  void insert(int);
  int remove();
  // ...
private:
  Link* _head;
};
```

The Link class declares that List is its friend. Hence, all List operations (insert, remove, and so forth) may access the private features of Link. In this case, Link has *no* public features, and only List operations can manipulate links. The effect is very similar to a Link class that is nested inside List, and the nested class is generally the superior solution. However, if two classes, say List and Queue, share the same links, then the link class cannot be nested in either. Instead, it must be a global class that declares both List and Queue as friends:

```
class Link
{ // ...
  friend class List;
  friend class Queue;
};
```

If a class wants to give access permission to a global function or a single operation of another class, it must name it as a friend.

```
class Vector
{ // ...
  friend Vector Matrix::multiply(const Vector&) const;
  friend int compare(const Vector&, const Vector&);
  friend ostream& operator<<(ostream&, const Vector&);
};
```

In this example three functions are permitted access to the private fields of the Vector class. The Matrix::multiply operation, which multiplies a matrix with a vector can be implemented more efficiently if it has access to the internal representation of vectors. The compare function is not declared as a class operation, because it is intended for use in certain templates that require a regular function. A better solution would be to make compare a static function of Vector, as described in Section 10.2.3. As we will see in Chapter 11, it is possible to map operators (+, *, ==, <<) to functions. The operator<< function implements the printing of a vector onto a stream, and for efficiency it is allowed access to the private vector data.

Exercise 10.4.1. Implement a 2 × 2 matrix class (holding four floating-point numbers) and a vector class (holding two floating-point numbers). Supply constructors, print operations, and an operation multiply of the Matrix class that multiplies a matrix with a vector. Make it a friend of Vector.

10.4.2. Protected Features

The operations of a derived class have no more right to access the private features of its base class than any other code does. For example, consider a base class Chart, which stores an array of numbers, and a derived class PieChart:

```
class Chart
{
public:
  virtual void plot(GraphicsContext& gc) const = 0;
  // ...
private:
  Array<double> _val;
};

class PieChart : public Chart
{
public:
  virtual void plot(GraphicsContext& gc) const;
  // ...
};
```

The plot operation of PieChart cannot access the _val field of the base class Chart. The obvious solution is, of course, to supply a public operation Chart::value(int) const to obtain the data values. But then everyone, not just charts, gets to see these values. Another solution is to make PieChart a friend of Chart. But that is not a good idea. There will be other chart types, such as BarChart, derived from Chart. Making them *all* into friends does not work in general. A base class cannot know all classes that may derive from it.

It can occasionally be useful to consider operations of derived classes as more privileged than other code and to give them special access privileges. This is achieved with *protected* access control. A protected feature of a base class is accessible by the operations of all derived classes. For example, if the _val field is declared protected instead of private, then the operations of PieChart and BarChart can access (and modify) it.

Protected data is actually never a good idea. We will study a protected operation:

```
class Chart
{
public:
  virtual void plot(GraphicsContext& gc) const = 0;
  // ...
protected:
  double value(int) const;
private:
  Array<double> _val;
};
```

Now classes that derive from Chart can find out about the data stored in the chart, but no other code can:

```
void PieChart::plot(GraphicsContext& gc) const
{ // ...
  double s = value(i);
  // ...
}

int main()
{ PieChart pc;
  // ...
  double s = pc.value(i); // ERROR
  // ...
}
```

As an added security measure, class operations can use protected features only on objects of their own class.

```
void PieChart::spy(BarChart& bc)
{ // ...
  double s = bc.value(i); // ERROR
  // ...
}
```

In using protected features, the belief is that derived classes have a better understanding of a base class and thus can be trusted more than others to access data or to call operations with the right arguments and in the right order. This is a somewhat dangerous assumption, since a class has no influence over who derives from it.

Exercise 10.4.2. Implement the base class `Chart` and derived classes `PieChart` such that there is a public interface to add data values, and a protected interface to retrieve the number of data points and their values.

Exercise 10.4.3. Consider the `Rectangle` class of Chapter 7. Discuss the advantages and the disadvantages of making the two corner points into protected data members. How would the derived class `FilledRect` benefit from direct access to the protected data? Suppose a class invariant was added that `_corner1` was always to the top and the left of `_corner2`, with suitable modifications in the constructor. What operations of what derived classes might jeopardize the invariant?

10.4.3. Impact on Encapsulation

Loosening access control can compromise the encapsulation of a class. If a class names a single function as a friend, this is not a problem. The friend function is listed in the class definition and thus becomes part of the interface. If the class implementation is changed, the friend function must track the change just as all other functions declared in the class definition.

However, if a class declares another class as a friend, it agrees that all operations of the friend class, whether they exist now or will be added later, have access to all private features. This should only be carried out to join closely related classes, such as `Link` and `List`. If the private section of the class granting friendship is modified, all operations of the friend classes must track the change.

When granting friendship, it is possible to enumerate all functions that are granted access to the private features. These are the explicitly named friend functions and all operations of friend classes. In contrast, it is impossible to enumerate all functions that are allowed access to protected features. Any class may derive from the base class that grants protected access, and the base class code contains no trace of the derivation.

For this reason, protected data fields are a bad idea. It is impossible to determine what code must be changed when the data representation is modified. Protected data fields have another problem: It is much more difficult to monitor that the derived-class operations preserve the base class invariants.

On the other hand, protected operations can be helpful to distinguish the interface that is of interest to class users from the interface that is necessary to refine the class behavior through derivation. Since a class has no control over who will derive from it, protected operations should be written with the same care as public operations.

10.5. SEPARATE COMPILATION

10.5.1. Compilation Units

In practice, it is not feasible to place all source code for a program into a single file for compilation. Compiling large programs is slow. Compilers have limits on the sizes of internal tables. It is awkward to have more than one programmer work on one file at a time.

For that reason, programs are broken up into compilation units, which are compiled separately into object files. A separate control mechanism may exist to produce object files containing the code for instantiated templates. The linker combines the object files to an executable file, resolving all references to data and functions that are defined in one compilation unit and used in others.

10.5.2. Declarations and Definitions

In C++, one distinguishes between declarations and definitions. A declaration advertises the existence of a feature, such as a variable or function with a given name and type. The definition specifies the actual implementation. Variable definitions allocate space and optionally provide initialization. Function definitions specify the function code.

Definitions must be unique in a program, but the same feature can be declared multiple times, even in the same compilation unit.

The following are definitions:

```
int x;
Employee harry("Harry Hacker");
int sq(int x) { return x*x; }
```

The corresponding declarations are

```
extern int x;
extern Employee harry;
int sq(int);
```

Variable declarations require the keyword `extern` to distinguish them from definitions.

Declarations for classes and enumerations simply advertise the name:

```
class Date;
enum Color;
```

The definitions give the complete descriptions:

```
class Date
{
public:
  Date();
  void advance(long n);
  // ...
};

enum Color { RED, GREEN, BLUE, ... };
```

The class *definition* contains *declarations* of the operations that themselves are defined elsewhere.

```
void Date::advance(long n) { ... };
```

The name of the keyword notwithstanding, `typedef` *declares* types.

```
typedef unsigned int Handle;
```

There are no separate type definitions.

10.5.3. Linkage of Global Variables and Functions

Global variables and functions can be reached from other compilation units (provided their declarations are supplied), unless their definitions are explicitly made private to the file containing them, with the keyword `static`. These variables and functions are public:

```
int x;
int sq(int x) { return x * x; }
```

Any compilation unit that wishes to access them simply includes their declaration:

```
extern int x;
int sq(int);
```

Prefixing the definitions with `static` makes them inaccessible outside their source file.

```
static int x;
static int sq(int x) { return x * x; }
```

This holds only for global variables and functions that are declared outside any classes. Anything declared inside a class follows the access specifications given by the public and private sections of the class.

10.5.4. Header Files

C++ provides no automatic mechanism to communicate declarations of features between the implementation module and the modules using them. Programmers must establish this correspondence through header files.

A module is distributed over two files. A header file (module.h) contains

- Definitions of classes, templates and enumerated types
- Declarations of type synonyms (`typedef`)
- Declarations of global variables
- Declarations of non-inline global functions
- Definitions of inline constants and functions

The source file (module.cpp or module.C) includes its own header file and supplies

- Definitions of shared class variables and global variables
- Definitions of non-inline operations and functions

These may be wrapped in `namespace` blocks, both in the header and source file.

Any module that wishes to use the features of another module includes that module's header file. A header file contains the definitions of those features that all client modules must know in detail for compilation. When the compiler merely needs to be assured of the existence of a feature, only the declaration is supplied in the header file.

In particular, the code for functions that are not inline replaced is given in exactly one source file. The header file communicates the existence of the function to all clients. But the code for inline functions must be supplied in the header file since each client module must perform the inline replacement. Similar to inline functions, template code must be accessible to all clients to permit instantiation of the class and its operations, and is hence placed in header files.

10.5.5. Header File Design

The cardinal rule for header files is that they should be self-reliant. If a header file defines a feature that depends on the interface given in another header file, it should include it.

manager.h:

```
#include "employee.h"
. . .
class Manager : public Employee { ... };
```

The clients of the manager module just want to include manager.h, not the collection of headers on which manager.h happens to depend.

If no detailed knowledge of a class is required, a header file may just declare its name rather than pull in another header. This happens when only pointers or references to a class are involved.

manager.h:

```
#include "employee.h"
class ostream; // no need to include iostream.h
. . .
class Manager : public Employee
{
public:
  void print(ostream&) const;
  . . .
};
```

This speeds compilation, and it may even be necessary to break circular dependencies.

As a consequence, the same header file may be included more than once during compilation of a module. The compiler will read in a header file repeatedly, since there is the theoretical possibility that the second parsing gives different results—a changed preprocessor variable might affect conditional compilation. Of course, any header files that are designed to provide a changed set of declarations when parsed twice ought to be taken out and shot.

Header files, however, contain definitions of classes, templates and inline functions. Definitions may not be repeated. To guard against multiple inclusion, the contents of header files are surrounded by directives:

manager.h:

```
#ifndef MANAGER_H
#define MANAGER_H
```

header file contents

```
#endif
```

Many programmers find it tedious to distribute the code of a module into two files. All interface changes force update of both the header and the source file. The Companion Disk contains a tool (called mdgen) that extracts header files automatically from source files, thereby cutting in half the number of files with which a programmer needs to deal.

Exercise 10.5.1. Design a module containing a class `Address` that describes a postal address. Add a global function to compare two addresses for sorting purposes. Print with an operation `Address::print(ostream&) const`. Make some operations inline. Distribute the classes, functions, and operations over header and source files. Make sure that your header file includes all necessary header files. Do you need to include iostream.h in the address.h header file, or can you get by with `class ostream`? Do you need to include it in the source file?

Exercise 10.5.2. Continue the previous exercise by placing all declarations and definitions in a single source file. Place the `EXPORT` tags where required by the mdgen utility, and generate the header file automatically.

Now add another field, `_country`, to the address. Compare the changes that are required if you have separate source and header files, or if you have a single source file from which the header file is generated.

Exercise 10.5.3. The date module provided in the code library uses the mdgen tool to automatically generate the header file. Split it up manually into a source and header file.

10.6. DESIGN HINTS

10.6.1. Don't Pollute the Global Namespace with Constants

Even the most unlikely-sounding name for a global constant invites a name conflict. Is WM_SIZE the window message for resizing, or the size of the widget map? Place all constants inside classes (WindowMessage::SIZE, WidgetMap::SIZE). That way, you have a conflict only if two *class* names clash. When that happens, you are in trouble anyway and must rename or use name spaces.

10.6.2. Eliminate Global Variables

Global variables can usually be eliminated by making them shared variables of an appropriate class. Of course, being data, they should always be in the private section of the class. If necessary, add public shared functions to inspect and update the variables.

10.6.3. Try to Change Global Functions into Shared Class Functions

Try to find a good home for the functions in a module. Often there is a class that is closely related to their functionality. If the function is private to the module (declared as static), place it in the private section of the class; you gain the benefit of access to the class implementation, should it be needed. If the function is public (not static and declared in the header file), place it in the public section of the class; you gain the benefit of name control. The function is now known to the public as *classname*::f().

10.6.4. Use Nested Classes for Auxiliary Abstractions

Some classes need auxiliary abstractions in their interfaces. For example, list iterators are objects that can be attached to linked lists to inspect their contents. An Iterator class can be defined in the public section of the List interface. It is known to the outside world as List::Iterator, eliminating any confusion with iterators from other container classes.

Implementation classes that are of no interest outside a class should be defined as nested classes in the private section. Typical examples are the links of a linked list or the nodes of a tree.

The following list interface shows both classes.

```
class List
{
private:
  class Link
  {
  public:
    Link(int, Link* = 0);
```

```
      int _info;
      Link* _next;
    };
  public:
    class Iterator
    {
    public:
      Iterator(const List&);
      void reset();
      void next();
      int current() const;
      Bool at_end() const;
    private:
      Link* _current;
    };

    void insert(int);
    int remove();
    // ...
  private:
    Link* _head;
  };
```

10.6.5. Don't Grant Friendship Lightly

Declaring a single function (typically an operator function) as a friend of a class is perfectly acceptable. That function becomes a part of the class interface, and it is easy to gauge the impact of change in the private representation.

A class should declare another class as a friend only if it intends to be completely subordinate to that other class. For example, a Link class may declare List and Queue as friends, because the sole purpose for links is to be carriers of information for lists and queues. But Date should not declare Employee as a friend. There is no telling how Date and Employee will evolve over time.

10.6.6. Don't Use Protected Data

The rationale for encapsulating class data is the observation that the data representation is subject to change over the lifetime of a class. By making data private, it is possible to enumerate all operations that need to be updated when such a change occurs. Protected data is accessible to all derived classes. A base class cannot tell who derives from it. The impact of a change in protected data can therefore not be gauged in the base class code. For this reason alone, protected data is a bad idea.

Furthermore, a base class can control the preservation of its class invariants by insuring that its constructors and mutators respect them. If a derived class can mutate the base class fields directly, this control is lost. Implementation invariants can be subtle, and it is not a good idea to blindly trust all derived classes to understand them.

Here is a slightly contrived example. Let us define operations of the Text class that return the height and width of the text shape. Unfortunately, those dimensions are not known until the text is first plotted, because they depend on a graphics context. We will initialize them with −1, because they can't be negative, but they could be 0 for the empty text. We set them in the plot operation if they have not previously been set.

```
void Text::plot(GraphicsContext& gc)
{ Rectangle r; // a default rectangle
  if (_xwidth == -1)
    gc.text_extent(_text, _xwidth, _yheight);
  gc.text(_text, _start.x(), _start.y());
}
```

Independently, the ScalableText::scale operation will scale the dimensions. The fields have been declared protected, making the access legal.

```
void ScalableText::scale(Point center, double s)
{ Text::scale(center, s);
  _size = _size * s;
  _xwidth = _xwidth * s; // protected access
  _yheight = _yheight * s;
}
```

This is incorrect. Scaling should not be performed if _xwidth is −1.

Of course, in this simple case it is easy to spot the problem and to fix it, but subtle properties of data fields are surprisingly common in real classes. It is not a good idea to assume that they are properly understood by the open-ended collection of operations of all derived classes, as they may come into existence over time.

OPERATOR OVERLOADING

11.1. OVERLOADING OPERATORS FOR MATHEMATICAL OBJECTS

11.1.1. The Reason for Overloading

C++ allows the redefinition of operators such as + - * / for user-defined data types. This is especially convenient for complex numbers, fractions, vectors, and matrices. Overloaded operators make mathematical expressions easier to read. For example, the area for a triangle with vertex vectors a, b, c (see Figure 11.1) is

$$A = \tfrac{1}{2}\sqrt{((b - a) \cdot (b - a))((c - a) \cdot (c - a)) - ((b - a) \cdot (c - a))^2}$$

Here · is the dot product of two vectors. The expression

```
A = 0.5 * sqrt(((b - a) * (b - a)) * ((c - a) * (c - a))
    - square((b - a) * (c - a)));
```

is confusing enough, but the equivalent, with functions, here called sub and sprod, is much worse:

```
A = 0.5 * sqrt(sprod(sub(b, a), sub(b, a)) *
    sprod(sub(b, a), sub(b, a) -
    square(sprod(sub(b, a), sub(c, a)))));
```

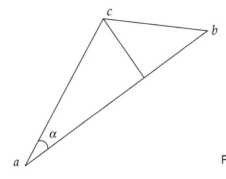

Figure 11.1.   A triangle.

211

11.1.2. Defining Overloaded Operators

In C++, operators are overloaded by defining special `operator` functions.

```
class Vector
{
public:
  // ...
    Vector operator-(Vector b) const;
    double operator*(Vector b) const;
};

Vector Vector::operator-(Vector b) const
{ return Vector(x() - b.x(), y() - b.y());
}

double Vector::operator*(Vector b) const
{ return x() * b.x() + y() * b.y();
}
```

The compiler translates the - and * operators in expressions involving `Vector` objects to calls of the `operator-` and `operator*` functions. For example,

```
u = v * (w - x);
```

becomes

```
u = v.operator*(w.operator-(x));
```

The `operator` functions are normal functions and can be called explicitly, as in the call above. Of course, nobody would seriously do that. The only reason to overload operators is to have a convenient way of invoking the functions.

Exercise 11.1.1. Fill in the details of the `Vector` class, and provide a constructor. These are vectors in the plane with an *x*- and *y*-component. In fact, they are very similar to `Point` objects. We use a vector class because mathematically it makes no sense to add and multiply points.

Exercise 11.1.2. Implement the vector subtraction and dot product. Test the operators by implementing the formula for the area of a triangle. Try it with some triangles for which you can determine or estimate the area.

Exercise 11.1.3. Supply an `operator+` to add two vectors. Supply an operator to scale a vector by a floating-point factor.

11.2. SYNTAX RULES FOR OPERATOR OVERLOADING

11.2.1. Operators That Can Be Overloaded

Essentially all operators may be overloaded. Here is a complete list:

```
+ - * / % ^ & | ~
! = < > += -= *= /= %=
^= &= |= << >> <<= >>= == !=
<= >= && || ++ -- -> ->*
[] () ,
```

Both the unary and binary forms of + - * & can be overloaded. For example, in addition to the binary

```
Vector Vector::operator-(Vector b) const
```

we may define a unary

```
Vector Vector::operator-() const
{ return Vector(-x(), -y());
}
```

The former is accessed as a - b, the latter as -a.

Only the following operators cannot be overloaded:

```
.  .*  ::  ?:
```

No new operators can be created. Sorry, no

```
|x|
y := x
y = x ** 2
```

An `operator` function must have at least one argument of class type. It is not possible to redefine operators applying just to numeric types (`int`, `double`, ...) or to pointer types (`char*`, `X*`, ...), or to define new operators for these types.

11.2.2. Precedence and Associativity

Precedence and associativity (left-to-right or right-to-left grouping) are the same for overloaded and standard operators. For example, it is not a good idea to overload ^ to denote raising a fraction to a power,

```
Fraction Fraction::operator^(int) const;
```

since the low precedence of the ^ operator will be surprising to most users. The operators in the expression

```
a ^ 2 + 1
```

bind as

```
a ^ (2 + 1)
```

Stick with the pow function—it is boring but predictable.

11.2.3. Increment and Decrement

The compiler will not automatically transform

```
v += w;
```

into

```
v = v + w;
```

Instead, an operator+= function must be defined. That is just as well, because a user-provided += operator can usually be coded more efficiently.
    Similarly,

```
x++;
```

is not automatically equivalent to

```
x = x + 1;
```

(In fact, if x is a vector, it makes no sense to add a scalar 1 to it.) Operator functions must be specially defined if the use of ++ and -- is desired. As an added complexity, there are both a prefix (++x) and a postfix (x++) form of these operators. A slightly bizarre mechanism is utilized to map the operators to two different functions. Two overloaded versions of operator++ can be defined:

```
Fraction Fraction::operator++(); // prefix increment
```

and

```
Fraction Fraction::operator++(int); // postfix increment
```

The int argument should be ignored—a 0 is always passed.

Exercise 11.2.1. Implement += and -= for vectors so that they directly modify the implicit argument. Measure the difference in speed between v += w and v = v + w.

Exercise 11.2.2. Define the two versions of ++ for the Date class. Of course, both operators increment the date by 1. They differ in their return value. The prefix ++ returns the new value of the date, after the increment. The postfix ++ returns the old value, before the increment.

11.2.4. Implementing Overloaded Operators as Functions

Most operators can be defined either as operations of a class or as regular functions. The exceptions are

```
= -> [] ()
```

which must be operations. For example, vector addition can be implemented as either

```
Vector Vector::operator+(Vector) const
```

or

```
Vector operator+(Vector, Vector)
```

The compiler translates

```
u + v
```

into either

```
u.operator+(v)
```

or

```
operator+(u, v)
```

Of course, it is an error to define both versions. As a rule of thumb, one should implement operators as operations of the class of the first argument whenever possible. We will consider exceptions to this rule in Section 11.6.5.

Exercise 11.2.3. Implement an operation to add a number of days to a date, yielding a new date. Implement it both as an operation of the Date class and as a function operator+(Date, long).

11.3. TYPE CONVERSIONS

11.3.1. Type Conversion on Operator Arguments

Consider a fraction class

```
class Fraction
{
public:
  Fraction(long n = 0, long d = 1);
  Fraction operator+(Fraction) const;
  // ...
private:
  long _num;
  long _den;
};

Fraction::Fraction(long n, long d)
: _num(n),
  _den(d)
{}

Fraction Fraction::operator+(Fraction b) const
{ return Fraction(_num * b._den + _den * b._num,
    _den * b._den);
}
```

The constructor can convert an integer into a fraction:

```
Fraction f = 2;
```

The same conversion is automatically carried out in arithmetic expressions:

```
Fraction g = f + 2;
// that is, g = f.operator+(Fraction(2,1));
```

However, the seemingly identical expression

```
2 + f
```

is not legal if operator+ is an operation of the Fraction class. The compiler does not perform a type conversion

```
Fraction(2).operator+(f)
```

The implicit argument is used for class selection, and no conversion on it is ever attempted.

This asymmetry is usually not desired for arithmetic operators of types that permit conversions from numeric types, such as fractions or complex numbers. Such operators are best defined as regular functions.

```
Fraction operator+(Fraction a, Fraction b);
```

Exercise 11.3.1. Implement the operator+ function that takes two Fraction arguments. Since it is not an operation of the Fraction class, it cannot access the private _num and _den fields of the fraction objects. It is probably not a good idea to supply accessors num() and den()—the numerator and denominator of a fraction are not well defined. For example,

$$\frac{-1}{2} = \frac{-2}{4} = \frac{1}{-2}.$$

Either make this operator a friend or make an inline call to an operation Fraction::add.

Exercise 11.3.2. Define a class Complex for complex number arithmetic. Supply a constructor Complex(double = 0, double = 0). This constructor serves as an automatic type conversion from a floating-point number to a complex number (with zero imaginary part). Implement + - * / += and -=. Which of these operations should be operations of the Complex class, and which should be global functions?

11.3.2. Defining Type Conversions

As we saw in the previous sections, constructors that accept a single argument also serve as type conversion functions. For example, a constructor

```
Fraction(int)
```

can automatically convert an integer into a fraction (presumably with denominator 1). Such constructors are the preferred method for defining automatic type conversions.

Exercise 11.3.3. Implement a type conversion from a float to a Fraction. This is quite tricky if you really want to find the closest fraction approximating a given floating-point number.

However, there are two cases in which a different method is required:

- When the target type is not a class
- When the target type is a class that you have no authority to modify

Consider, for example, a type conversion from fractions to floating-point numbers. Since double is not a class, no constructor can be defined for it. Instead, the fraction class must define a *type conversion operator*.

```
class Fraction
{
public:
  // ...
  operator double() const;
};

Fraction::operator double() const
{ return (double)_num / (double)_den;
}

Fraction f(1, 4);
y = sqrt(f); // that is, y = sqrt(f.operator double())
```

11.3.3. Conversion to a Truth Value

The stream classes have a conversion istream → void* that can be used to test the stream state.

```
istream::operator void*()
{ if (the state is not fail)
    return this;
  else
    return 0;
}
```

The actual returned pointer is immaterial, as long as a nonzero pointer is returned on success.

A typical usage is

```
cin >> x;
if (cin) // operation was successful
```

It would appear to be simpler to define an istream::operator Bool instead of a conversion to void*. But Bool is simply a type synonym for int, and having an automatic conversion from streams to integers would give legal but unintended meanings to many expressions.[1] For example, the erroneous

```
int x;
cin << x; // NO—meant cin >> x
```

would compile as a binary left shift of cin.operator int() by x bits. The void* type doesn't suffer from this problem, because the only legal operators

---

[1]Even the Boolean type, whose addition to C++ is planned at the time of this writing, would have similar problems.

on void* pointers are comparison and assignment. For this reason, a conversion to void* is a common idiom for testing the state of an object.

Exercise 11.3.4. Modify the Date class to permit both legal and illegal dates. The default constructor makes the illegal date 0/0/0. (There is no calendar year 0.) Create a type conversion Date → void* to test whether a date is legal. Add a test to each Date operation whether the date arguments are legal. That is made easy with the type conversion: assert(self), assert(b).

11.4. OVERLOADING THE [] OPERATOR

The [] operator is often overloaded for arrays, vectors, and matrices. Another interesting example is given by an associative array or map.

```
class Map
{
public:
   void add(String, double);
   double operator[](String);
private:
   class Pair
   {
   public:
     String _key;
     double _value;
   };

   Array<Pair> _assoc;
};
```

Pairs of strings and floating-point values can be inserted in the associative array. Values can be retrieved by their keys.

```
Map a;
a.add("Harry Hacker", 3.3);
x = a["Harry Hacker"];
```

Depending on the underlying data structure, it can be feasible to define the [] operator as an "lvalue", an expression that can be on the left-hand side of an assignment, by returning a reference.

```
a["Harry Hacker"] = 3.3;
```

However, this is an area filled with considerable technical difficulties, and we will not discuss it further.

Exercise 11.4.1. Implement the Map class and write a test program that manipulates student names and scores. For simplicity, perform a linear search through the array rather than hashing.

Exercise 11.4.2. Supply an overloaded [] operator for the Vector class that returns a *reference* to the _x field if the index is 1, a reference to the _y field if the index is 2, and a reference to a static dummy otherwise. If v is a vector, test that v[i] can be used both on the left-hand side and the right-hand side of an assignment.

11.5 OVERLOADING THE () OPERATOR

There are two good reasons to overload the () operator:

- To implement function evaluation on objects that behave in some way like functions
- To take advantage of the fact that () is the only operator that can take an arbitrary number of arguments

A polynomial class is a good example of a class whose objects behave like functions. Polynomials can be implemented by storing the coefficients of the powers of x in an array, letting _coeff[i] be the coefficient of x^i. For example,

$$2 - 3x^2 + x^3$$

corresponds to the array $\boxed{2\ |\ 0\ |\ -3\ |\ 1}$

A polynomial can be evaluated at an x-value. For example, if p is the polynomial just defined, then $p(4) = 2 - 3 \cdot 4^2 + 4^3 = 18$. We can exactly mimic the mathematical notation by overloading the () operator.

```
class Polynomial
{
public:
  // ...
    double operator()(double) const;
private:
    Array<double> _coeff;
};

double Polynomial::operator()(double x) const
{ double r = 0;
    for (int i = _coeff.high(); i >= 0; i--)
      r = r * x + _coeff[i];
    return r;
}

Polynomial p;
// ...
double x = p(4);
```

Occasionally, () is overloaded to take advantage of the fact that it can take more than one argument. A matrix class may overload () to access an element whose row and column index are specified as the arguments to ().

```
class Matrix
{
public:
  Matrix(int, int);
  // ...
  double operator()(int, int) const;
private:
  Array<double> _coeff;
  int _row;
  int _col;
};

double Matrix::operator()(int r, int c) const
{ if (1 <= r && r <= _row && 1 <= c && c <= _col)
    return _coeff[(r - 1)*_col + c];
  else return 0;
}

Matrix m(5, 5);
// ...
double x = m(3, 4);
```

Exercise 11.5.1. Implement the polynomial class. Naturally, you should overload + - * in addition to ().

Exercise 11.5.2. Implement the matrix class. Overload + - * in addition to ().

Exercise 11.5.3. Change the elem function of the Bidiag class of Section 9.1.3 to an overloaded () operator.

11.6. DESIGN HINTS

11.6.1. Avoid Surprises and Confusion

The C++ language enforces no semantics on overloaded operators. It is possible to define operator+ to denote addition of vectors and subtraction of matrices. Naturally, that is not a good idea. In general, it is best to stick to established mathematical conventions.

It is best to avoid cute or cryptic interpretations of operators. Abuses are common in published code.

```
Stack s;
s += 5; // DON'T—use s.push(5)
x = s--; // DON'T—use x = s.pop();
```

It is counterproductive to replace perfectly obvious function names like push and pop with cryptic operators += and -- that are, to say the least, mysterious to the uninitiated. Here is a surprisingly common example of an obscure device—can you guess what it does?

```
List lst;
ListIterator it(lst);
int* p;
while (p = it()) cout << *p << endl;
```

The expression it() is not a function call but the application of the () operator on the object it. That operator is implemented to return a null pointer if the iterator is at the end of a list, or otherwise to return a pointer to the current list item and advance the iterator. Redesigning the iterator interface is strongly suggested:

```
List lst;
ListIterator it(lst);

while (!it.at_end()) { cout << it.current() << endl; it.next();
```

Or, if one feels compelled to use overloaded operators, possibly

```
while (it) { cout << it.current() << endl; it++; }
```

11.6.2. Supply a Complete Set of Operators with Natural Interactions

When supplying + and - operators, also supply unary + and - as well as += and -= operators. Of course, the following relationships should hold:

- a = a + b ⇔ a += b, but the latter may be more efficient.
- a - b = a + (-b)
- -(-a) = +a = a

11.6.3. Minimize Type Conversions

If too many automatic type conversions are provided, the compiler can surprisingly often attach *some* unambiguous meaning that was never intended by the programmer. According to [Murray 1989], bidirectional automatic type conversions (such as double → Fraction, Fraction → double) are particularly suspect.

11.6.4. Beware of Constructors with a Single Integer Argument

Constructors with a single argument are type converters, whether this is appropriate or not. Suppose Array<X> had a constructor Array(int). (It actually, purposefully, has no such constructor—you need to specify both the lower and the upper bound).

```
Array<double> a(10); // an array with ten elements
// ...
a = 5; // NO—meant a[i] = 5;
```

The assignment a = 5 compiles to the type conversion a = Array<double>(5), which sets a to a newly constructed array of five elements. The old array is lost.

This behavior is very surprising to most users, and it is best to stay away from constructors that take a single integer as argument. Some class libraries introduce a class Size just for the purpose of specifying sizes in constructor arguments:

```
Array<double> a(Size(10));
```

Since the compiler refuses to carry out two user-defined type conversions automatically, this solves the problem of inadvertently invoking the constructor.

11.6.5. Choosing Between operator Functions and Class Operations

When you have the choice between defining an operator as an operation of a class or as a regular function, you should generally favor the class operation. It clearly makes the operator a part of the interface, and you get access to the implementation should you need it.

There are exceptions, in the following cases:

- The type of the first argument of the operator is not a class.
- The type of the first argument is a class that you have no authority to modify.
- Type conversion is desired on the first argument.

Then you must use a regular function for the operator. If access to the internal representation of either argument is required, make it a friend.

For example, the multiplication of a scalar and a vector must be a function:

```
Vector operator*(double, Vector);
```

The insertion operator to print a vector must be a function.

```
ostream& operator<<(ostream&, Vector);
```

It cannot be an operation of ostream, since you cannot modify the ostream class.

The multiplication of two fractions should be a regular function, because type conversion from int to fraction is desirable on the first argument.

```
Fraction operator*(Fraction, Fraction);
```

```
Fraction b = 2 * a; // OK
```

STREAMS AND PERSISTENCE

C programmers use the functions defined in the stdio library to perform input and output. C++ replaces stdio with the iostream library. That is the library that we have exclusively used in this book. Users familiar with the C library may feel some reluctance to switch, and it is indeed possible to write C++ code that uses stdio for all input and output. Nevertheless, the iostream library, despite its warts, is ultimately a superior design and should be used by C++ programmers.

12.1. USAGE OF THE << OPERATOR

Let us have a closer look at the C++ "Hello, World" program.

```
#include <iostream.h>

int main()
{ cout << "Hello, World" << endl;
  return 0;
}
```

Here cout is the ostream object attached to standard output. The << operator is overloaded to take an ostream on the left and another type on the right. The foregoing program uses

```
ostream::operator<<(const char[])
```

There are other << operators to output other data types:

```
double x = 3.14159;
cout << x;
```

This uses

```
ostream::operator<<(double)
```

Note that the << operators are not const. The calls change internal details in the ostream structure.

Of course, the header file iostream.h contains the definition of the class ostream and the declaration of cout.

Exercise 12.1.1. Look at the definition of ostream in iostream.h. For what types is the << operator defined?

The << operators can be *chained:*

```
double x = 3.14159;
cout << "The value of pi is approx. " << x;
```

This works because all << operators *return the stream reference they receive:*

```
ostream& ostream::operator<<(const char* s)
{ // print s
  return self;
}
```

Dissecting the foregoing statement yields:

```
cout << "The value of pi is approx. " << x
```

The first call to operator<< prints the string and returns (a reference to) cout. The second call cout << x prints the floating-point number.

The endl object is a manipulator object, defined in iostream.h. When a stream receives it, a newline character is printed and the stream buffer is flushed. We will discuss the implementation of manipulators in Section 12.4.

12.2. SAFETY AND EXTENSIBILITY

The iostream library has two principal advantages over the C stdio library. It is always safe to use, and the operations for input and output can be extended to new types.

12.2.1. Type Safety

The C stdio library uses two functions, printf and scanf, to write to standard output and read from standard input, as well as related functions for arbitrary files and strings. These functions make use of a special C feature: They can take a variable number of arguments of arbitrary type. Of course, the functions must then make sense of the bytes on the stack. The first argument, the format string, is used for this purpose. The format string contains embedded codes specifying the variable types and formatting information.

```
int n;
double x;
printf("Count: %6d Average: %10.4f", n, x);
```

In this example, %6d means that the next variable to be printed is an integer, to be printed in decimal in a field that is 6 characters wide. The code %10.4f specifies a floating-point number, a field width of 10, and 4 digits after the decimal point.

The format string is undeniably convenient. It gives a concise visual picture of the output. Unfortunately, it is not very safe. A common bug is a mismatch between the format string and the actual arguments:

```
printf("Count: %6d Average: %10.4f", x, n);
```

The compiler cannot detect this bug—it knows nothing about printf except the prototype

```
int printf(const char*, ...);
```

Even more insidious is the following

```
int n;
double x;
scanf("%f %d", &x, n);
```

which yields weird results. There are two mistakes. First, the & is missing from n, but an address is needed for storing the number. Second, the correct format to read in a double is %lf, for esoteric and historical reasons.

Stream operators are safe, because the compiler picks the correct operator<< or operator>> function. A mismatch is impossible, because there is no separate format string:

```
cout << "Count: " << n << " Average: " << x;
cin >> x >> n;
```

Especially for output, the drawbacks are clear. The output is harder to visualize, because it is broken up into little pieces. Furthermore, there is no specification of the format, such as field width and floating-point precision. In the next sections, we will learn how to address the latter problem and, unfortunately, exacerbate the former in the process.

12.2.2. Extensibility to New Types

It is not (easily) possible to extend `printf` to print other data types, such as fractions or vectors. To code

```
Vector v;
printf("Direction: %10.4v", v);
```

it would be necessary to rewrite `printf` and recognize a new %...v code. However, it is easy to enhance the stream facility to read and print new data types:

```
ostream& operator<<(ostream& os, Vector v)
{ os << "(" << v.x()<< "," << v.y() << ")";
  return os;
};
```

Now `Vector` objects can be printed like any other values:

```
Vector v;
cout << "Direction: " << v << endl;
```

To read vectors in from an input stream, one defines

```
istream& operator>>(istream& is, Vector& v)
{ char ch;
  is >> ch;
  if (ch != '(') ... // error
  double x, y;
  is >> x >> ch;
  if (ch != ',') ... // error
  is >> y >> ch;
  if (ch != ')') ... // error
  v = Vector(x, y);
  return is;
}
```

We have left error handling open. When there is an input error, the *error state* of the stream should be set, and v should not be touched. We will discuss this in Section 12.5.

To give the two operators access to the implementation, it would be helpful if we could implement them as operations of the `Vector` class, but that does not work, because the *first* argument is not a vector but a stream. Nor are we at liberty to add operations to the stream classes—we don't own them.

12.3. FORMAT STATE

The C programmer is used to a wealth of formatting options in `printf`. All those options, and a few more, are available in the stream library, but the access method is different.

The *field width* specifies the minimum number of characters for printing a value. If the character representation is shorter than the field width, spaces (or other *fill characters*) are inserted at the left or right, depending on the *alignment*.

12.3.1. Field Width

There are two ways of setting the field width: through a stream operation and through a stream *manipulator*. A manipulator is an object of some kind that is sent to a stream using the overloaded << or >> operator and that effects some state change in the stream object rather than character output.

Using stream operations is straightforward but requires breaking up the output statement:

```
cout.width(4);
cout << '(' << 12 << ',' << 34 << ')';
```

Manipulators are sent with the objects to be printed:

```
include <iomanip.h>

cout << '(' << setw(4) << 12 << ',' << 34 << ')';
```

Both commands print

```
(  12,34)
```

Unlike all other formatting commands, the field width affects only the *next* number or string to be printed and then reverts to 0.

The field width specifies the *minimum* field size. Larger items are printed at their full width:

```
cout << setw(4) << 32000;
```

prints 32000, not 2000. It is better to have the correct output poorly formatted than the wrong output looking pretty.

The accessor `cout.width()` and the mutator `cout.width(n)` return the current width. In theory, this allows you to save the width and restore it later. In practice, this is rarely important, because the width usually is zero. Of course, manipulators are inserted into the stream and cannot return the previous value.

12.3.2 Fill Character

The fill character can be changed from the default (space) to any other character. Again, both operator and manipulator are provided. Both

```
cout.fill('*');
cout.width(4);
cout << 12;
```

and

```
cout << setfill('*') << setw(4) << 12;
```

print **12.

The fill character, like all other formatting attributes except field width, remains set until changed. The accessor `cout.fill()` and the mutator `cout.fill(c)` return the current fill character. It is good practice to restore the fill character to its original state (which may or may not be the space character) after changing it. The same holds for all other format attributes except field width.

12.3.3. Alignment

Normally, values are right-aligned in their field. This is fine for numbers but not usually for strings.

The alignment is set through one of the many *flags* defined in the `ios` class. (`ios` is an abbreviation for "input/output state".) That class is a base class for both `istream` and `ostream`.

```
cout.setf(ios::left);
cout.width(10);
cout << "Month" << ':';
cout.setf(ios::right);
cout.width(4);
cout << 12;
```

or

```
cout << setiosflags(ios::left) << setw(10)
  << "Month" << ':'
  << setiosflags(ios::right) << setw(4)
  << 12;
```

print

```
Month     :  12.
```

There is also a strange option, `ios::internal`, that distributes the fill character between the sign and the number. It is only useful if the fill character is 0.

```
cout << setiosflags(ios::internal)
    << setw(6) << setfill('0') << -12;
```

prints -00012.

Exercise 12.3.1. Given n, print a table of the binomial coefficients $\binom{n}{k}$ (in other words, Pascal's triangle):

```
    1
   1 1
  1 2 1
 1 3 3 1
1 4 6 4 1
```

Pay attention to formatting and alignment.

12.3.4. Integer Format

Integers can be formatted in decimal, hexadecimal, or octal.

```
int n = 12;
cout << hex << n << ' ';
cout << oct << n << ' ';
cout << dec << n << endl;
```

prints c 14 12. To show the base and print the letters in uppercase, use

```
cout.setf(ios::showbase | ios::uppercase);
```

Now the same numbers print as 0XC 014 12.
    Instead of the manipulators, you can also use ios flags dec, oct, and hex.

```
cout.setf(ios::hex);
```

12.3.5. Floating-Point Format

By default, floating-point numbers are printed in a *general* format that uses scientific notation when necessary to show the significant digits (6 by default).

```
cout << 123.456789 << ' ' << 123456789;
```

prints 123.457 1.23457e+008. (You can get an uppercase E by setting ios::uppercase).

You can explicitly choose either scientific or fixed format with the `ios` flags `scientific` or `fixed`.

```
cout << setiosflags(ios::fixed,ios::floatfield);
cout.setf(ios::scientific,ios::floatfield);
```

To reset to general format, you must use

```
cout << resetiosflags(ios::floatfield);
cout.unsetf(ios::floatfield);
```

To see a + sign for positive numbers, use `ios::showpos`. (This also works for integers.) To see trailing zeroes, use `ios::showpoint`. For example,

```
cout.setf(ios::fixed | ios::showpoint | ios::showpos);
cout << 123.456;
```

prints `+123.456000`.

You can change the precision from the default 6:

```
cout << setprecision(10) << 1.2345678;
```

or

```
cout.precision(10);
cout << 1.2345678;
```

prints `1.2345678`. In general and scientific format, the precision denotes the number of *significant* digits; in fixed format, the number of digits *after the decimal point*. (Not all implementations handle this correctly.)

```
double x = 123.45678;
cout << setprecision(2) << x << ' ';
cout << setiosflags(ios::fixed,ios::floatfield) << x;
```

prints `1.2e+002 123.46`.

The accessor `cout.precision()` and the mutator `cout.precision(n)` return the current precision.

Exercise 12.3.2. Read in 12 floating-point numbers and print them in a table format, preceded by month names, with the decimal points lined up and no trailing zeroes.

```
January    12.3
February    0.001
March    8100
 . . .
```

12.3.6. Output Operations That Respect Format State

Output routines for user-defined types should respect the format state. Consider the case of printing vectors. The following states are relevant:

- Field width
- Fill pattern
- Alignment
- + for positive values

We will not support internal alignment or leading zeroes.

It is easiest to preformat the output into a string and then send the string to the output stream. The stream will then apply width, alignment, and fill pattern to the string without further ado. To format to a string rather than directly to a stream, we use a *string stream*. String streams are discussed in detail in Section 12.7.

```
#include <float.h>
#include <strstream.h>
ostream& operator<<(ostream& os, const Vector& v)
{ const int BUFSIZE = 4 * DBL_DIG;
    // enough for two floating-point numbers and misc. characters
  char buffer[BUFSIZE];
  ostrstream strs(buffer, sizeof(buffer));
  strs.flags(os.flags()); // set same flags
  strs << "(" << v.x() << '/' << v.y() << ")" << ends;
  os << buffer;
  return os;
}
```

Exercise 12.3.3. Test the << operator for vectors and verify that it follows the stream state—in particular, floating-point format and alignment.

Exercise 12.3.4. Write an output-formatting routine for the Fraction class. Print fractions in the form -3/4. This is a bit trickier than appears at first sight. For example, if the stream has ios::showpos turned on, you need to leave it on for the numerator and turn it off for the denominator (since you don't want +3/+4). Just to show that it can be done, handle ios::internal properly.

12.3.7. A Critical Examination of the Format State Interface

Stream format state is an excellent example how muddleheadedness can creep into a library interface. Consider the name mismatches between operators and manipulators:

Attribute	Operator	Manipulator
Width	width	setw
Fill character	fill	setfill
Set flags	setf	setiosflags
Reset flags	unsetf	resetiosflags

It probably started out harmlessly enough with width and fill. Then someone added setf (why not setflags?) and unsetf. The manipulators then were named with set to distinguish them from the operators. Giving them different names is not strictly necessary but perfectly reasonable. But using set as a prefix is foolish, because it conflicts with setf (should the manipulator be called setsetf?) Probably setw was chosen over the longer setwidth because it is so common. It would be difficult to conceive of a charitable explanation for resetiosflags instead of the consistent unsetiosflags.

Exercise 12.3.5. Design a more rational naming scheme for these operators and manipulators.

All format attributes persist until changed, except for field width. It is not clear why field width is fundamentally different from, say, floating-point precision.

Exercise 12.3.6. Maybe *all* format attributes ought to reset to their defaults after use? Discuss the advantages and disadvantages of such an arrangement.

The C interface, while perhaps cryptic, does manage to present the options as they are relevant to the programmer, not the library implementor. The field width and precision, surely the most important attributes, are communicated concisely. To print a plus sign and leading zeroes in a decimal number, the C programmer writes "%+06d". The iostream equivalent is unbelievably cumbersome:

```
cout << setiosflags(ios::internal|ios::showpos|ios::dec)
  << setfill('0') << setw(6);
```

Another problem is general floating-point format. There really ought to be a flag ios::general for general floating-point format, just as there is a ios::dec flag for decimal integers.

Exercise 12.3.7. Write a function do_setformat(ios&, String) that scans a C-style format string and sets the format state accordingly. For example,

```
do_setformat(cout, "+06d")
```

sets the `ios::internal`, `ios::showpos`, and `ios::dec` flags and sets the fill character to `'0'` and the width to 6. (We will see in Exercise 12.4.6 how to turn this into a manipulator.)

According to [Kernighan and Ritchie], p. 243, the format string consists of flags (in any order), a number specifying the field width, a period followed by the precision (for floating-point numbers only), and a type. Flags and types are

–	Left justify.
+	Show + sign.
0	Show leading zeroes.
#	Use "alternate" format—leading 0 or 0x/0X for octal or hexadecimal numbers, or show decimal point and trailing zeroes for floating-point numbers.
space	If the first character is not a sign, prefix a space.
d	Decimal.
o	Octal.
x, X	Hexadecimal; X uses uppercase letters.
f	Fixed floating-point.
e, E	Scientific floating-point; E uses uppercase E.
g, G	General floating-point; G uses uppercase E.

Of course, this interface has its problems too, especially the "alternate" format. But it has one thing going for it—tradition.

12.4. MANIPULATORS

We have seen a number of *manipulators* (`endl`, `setw(n)`, and so forth) for formatting output. In this section, we will see what they are and how they work. Understanding how manipulators work is not central to using streams. Since the technique is complicated, you may want to skim over this material at first reading. The technique is interesting, because it shows how to design objects that manipulate other objects.

12.4.1. Function Pointers

It is necessary at this point to review the C++ syntax for function pointers. Addresses of C++ functions can be stored in variables and passed as function parameters. This is useful whenever an algorithm needs to leave the details of a computation open until its invocation.

Sorting is the traditional example. A sorting algorithm such as quicksort picks elements to compare and then rearranges them in some way until the sorting is complete. Except for the method of comparison, the algorithm is completely independent of the objects to be sorted. Sort functions are often written to carry out the comparison and rearrangement logic in a generic way, with a pointer to a specific comparison function passed as a parameter. Here we sort an array by ZIP code, the numerical (5-digit) postal code used in the United States:

```
int compare_zip(const Address& a, const Address& b)
{ return a.zip() - b.zip();
}

Array<Address> labels;
sort(labels, compare_zip);
```

A function name that, like `compare_zip`, is not followed by parentheses, denotes a pointer to that function. This is actually a pointer to the starting address of the function code in memory.

The syntax to describe such a function pointer is awkward, because the pointer-dereferencing operator (*) has a lower precedence than the function call operator (()). It is always best to make a type definition:

```
typedef int (*AddressCompFun)(const Address&, const Address &);
```

Then the prototype of the `sort` function is simply

```
void sort(Array<Address>&a, AddressCompFun c);
```

Without the type definition, the prototype is

```
void sort(Array<Address>&a,
    int (*c)(const Address&, const Address &));
```

an expression that rightly strikes fear in the hearts of C++ programmers.

Invoking a function through the function pointer is simple:

```
if ((*c)(a[i], a[j]) < 0) ...
```

This code executes the function whose starting address is stored in c.

Function pointers are useful when a wide variation of behavior needs to be specified for fixed object types. Virtual functions are a better mechanism to express a *narrow* range of behavior variation for related object types.

Exercise 12.4.1. Implement the `sort` function, using the quicksort algorithm. Test it with two different comparison functions: `compare_zip`, and `compare_city`.

12.4.2. Manipulators without Arguments

The `endl` manipulator, like every stream manipulator that does not take an argument, is a function that eats a stream reference and returns it:

```
ostream& endl(ostream& os)
{ os << '\n';
  os.flush();
  return os;
}
```

An ostream is prepared to accept a pointer to such a manipulator function:

```
typedef ostream& (*OManip)(ostream&);

ostream& ostream::operator<<(OManip m)
{ return (*m)(self);
}
```

The stream permits the manipulator to act on itself.

Exercise 12.4.2. Write a manipulator `tab` that sends a single tab character to an output stream.

Exercise 12.4.3. Write the code for a manipulator `skipwhite` that eats up any white space from an input stream. (Such a manipulator, called `skipws`, is actually defined in the iostream library.)

12.4.3. Manipulators with an Argument

Manipulators that take an argument are more difficult. Consider the `setw` manipulator that takes an integer argument. This manipulator acts on the `ios` class, the common base class of `istream` and `ostream`. It sets the width of either the next input field or the next output field.

The obvious extension of the previous method does not work:

```
ios& setw(ios& s, int w)
{ s.width(w);
  return s;
}

os << setw(10) << x;
```

The expression `setw(10)` is illegal, because the `setw` function takes two arguments. (We were lucky with functions taking a single argument—omitting the argument resulted in a legal object, a function pointer.) Instead, the value of the expression `setw(10)` must be an object that the stream can accept.

There are two possibilities for setting this up. We can define a class `setw` with a constructor `setw(int)`, or we can define a function `setw(int)` that returns an object of some class. The second approach is preferred, because it only introduces a new function for each manipulator, not a new class. We will need to introduce a class as well, momentarily, but it can be shared among manipulators.

The setw(int) function needs to return an object of some class. That class is shared among all manipulators with one integer argument. It is designed to remember

- The action to take on the stream
- The integer argument

Here is the class definition:

```
typedef ios& (*IosIntManip)(ios&, int);

class IosIntApplic
{
public:
  IosIntApplic(IosIntManip, int);
friend ostream& operator<<(ostream&, const IosIntApplic&);
friend istream& operator>>(istream&, const IosIntApplic&);
private:
  IosIntManip _manip;
  int _value;
};
```

The overloaded << operator applies the stored action on the ostream object, using the stored value as the second argument.

```
ostream& operator<<(ostream& s, const IosIntApplic& a)
{ (*a._manip)(s, a._value);
  return s;
}
```

The setw(int) function returns a specific applicator, specifying the width-setting action and the integer width to be set. The width-setting action is given by a function, named do_setw, with two arguments. It invokes the width operation of the ios class.

```
ios& do_setw(ios& s, int n)
{ s.width(n);
  return s;
}
```

Now we are ready to implement the original setw(int) function:

```
IosIntApplic setw(int n)
{ return IosIntApplic(do_setw, n);
}
```

Exercise 12.4.4. Explain, in gory detail, all steps that are involved in the execution of the expression

```
cout << setw(10);
```

Exercise 12.4.5. Implement a manipulator `tab(int)` that sends a number of tab characters to an output stream.

Exercise 12.4.6. Implement a manipulator `setformat(String)` that scans a C-style format string and sets the format state accordingly, as described in Exercise 12.3.7. For example,

```
cout << setformat("+06d") << n;
```

12.5. ERROR STATE

In real life, input and output operations do not always succeed. Output might fail for both hardware and logical reasons:

- A disk is full.
- A printer is disconnected.
- The file pointer has been set to an improper position.

Likewise, input might fail for a number of reasons:

- There is a physical problem with a device (for example, a disk has a bad sector).
- The end of file has been reached.
- The characters on the input stream are not in the expected format.

The error state of a stream keeps track of these problems. Each stream has three state bits, depending on whether the error originated in the device, the buffer, or the formatting layer:

`eofbit`	End of file (or other device error)
`badbit`	Stream buffer error
`failbit`	Formatting failure

A stream buffer error results when a stream is not attached to a physical file or device, or if the attached file or device has an error.

There are five operations that report on these states:

`good()`	No error and no end of file encountered. "The next operation might succeed."
`fail()`	An error condition has been encountered. "The previous operation has failed."
`bad()`	Stream buffer error encountered.
`eof()`	End of file encountered.
`rdstate()`	Returns all state bits.

These operations are somewhat confusing. It is important to note that good()
does *not* mean !bad() or even !fail(), and that fail() does *not* simply return
the value of failbit.

To say it outright, good() is pretty worthless. The good() operation won't
reliably report on the success of the last operation, because it fails if a value was
read successfully but was followed by the end of file. You can't use good() as a
predictor for the next operation. Even if the stream is happy now, it could still
fail before it completes reading the next input. The eof() function is not all that
useful—it is false if nothing but unread white space precedes the end of the file.
Call it only after input has failed. The distinction between a stream buffer error
and another error is not usually of great interest, and older implementations of
the stream library make other uses of badbit. Therefore, bad() is rarely called.

It is best to test the state of a stream *after* attempting to read from it.

```
int n;
cin >> n;
if (!cin.fail())
   // n successfully read
```

Since !fail() is the most useful information, it can also be accessed through
the conversion stream → void*.

```
cin >> n;
if (cin)
   // n successfully read
```

Errors on output are usually easy to handle. You may choose to test for
them and refuse to perform more output if an error occurs, or you may just
perform the output and let the lower-level routines refuse to actually send the
characters.

Errors on input are much more bothersome. Every programmer must cope
with end-of-file handling and detection of improper input formats. Here is a
function to read vectors in that copes with error conditions.

```
istream& operator>>(istream& is, Vector& v)
{ char ch;
  is >> ch;
  if (ch == '(')
  { double x, y;
    is >> x >> ch;
    if (!is.fail() && ch == ',')
    { is >> y >> ch;
      if (!is.fail() && ch == ')')
      { v = Vector(x, y);
        return is;
      }
    }
  }
```

```
    }
    is.clear(ios::failbit | is.rdstate());
    return is;
}
```

There are two possible causes for errors. The (,) characters may be missing, or the floating-point numbers between the (,) are not present. When an error is encountered, the function sets the `failbit`. The code for doing this is unbelievably clumsy. An operation, strangely called `clear`, sets all error state bits. We retrieve the current bits with `rdstate`, set the fail bit, and then store the result.

Note that the parameter v is unchanged if the read operation fails. This is the correct behavior. It would have been wrong to use

```
is >> x; if (!is.fail()) v.set_x(x); // DON'T
```

If input had failed later, v would be partially overwritten.

Exercise 12.5.1. Write a function to read fractions into a `Fraction` object. Fractions look like this: -3/4. Be sure to set the error state if there is a formatting error.

12.6. FILE INPUT AND OUTPUT

Getting a file stream for reading or writing with the default attributes is very simple. You supply the file name in the constructor of an `ifstream` or `ofstream`.

```
#include <fstream.h>
ifstream is("input.dat");
ofstream os("output.dat");
int n;
while (is >> n) os << n << endl;
```

`fstream` files are opened for both input and output.

When opening the file, you can set different attributes; for example,

```
ofstream os("output.dat", ios::noreplace);
```

The following attributes can be specified when opening a file:

in	Open for reading
out	Open for writing
ate	Open and seek to end of file
app	Append each write at end of file
trunc	Truncate to zero length
nocreate	Fail if file doesn't exist
noreplace	Fail if file exists
binary	Open in binary (nontext) mode

File streams can be opened and closed explicitly:

```
fstream fs;
fs.open("file.dat", ios::in | ios::out | ios::binary);
// ...
fs.close();
fs.open("file2.dat",ios::in);
```

File streams can read and write raw (binary) data and move the file read and write position. We refer to [Teale] for details.

12.7. STRING STREAMS

String streams read and write to C-style character arrays, not files. Unfortunately, they don't work directly with our String class. The following examples show how to use an intermediary buffer to negotiate between a string stream and string objects.

```
#include <strstream.h>

char buffer[100];
ostrstream os(buffer, sizeof(buffer));

os << setiosflags(ios::left) << setw(10)
   << "Month" << ':'
   << resetiosflags(ios::left) << setw(4)
   << 12
   << ends;

String result(buffer);
```

Now the result string contains the string "Month   : 12". The ends manipulator is essential to terminate the string correctly!

```
String input = "12/3/1945";

char buffer[100];
istrstream is(input.c_array(buffer, sizeof(buffer)),
  sizeof(buffer)));

is >> day >> ch1 >> month >> ch2 >> year;
```

A strstream can be used for both reading and writing.

C programmers will recognize string streams as the stream equivalent of the C functions sprintf and sscanf. String streams are very useful both for input and output. Input from human users is notoriously unreliable. It is generally necessary to gather the input a character, word, or line at a time and then to analyze it. After the input is placed in a string, an istrstream is a convenient mechanism for parsing and reading numerical values. Conversely, output should be gathered first in a string and then sent to a stream. Since the stream automatically applies formatting attributes such as field width, fill character, and alignment to strings, these need not be replicated. This technique was used in the vector output in Section 12.3.4.

Exercise 12.7.1. Write a function that scans a date in a string, in any one of the formats

```
2/28/1994
1994-2-28
February 28, 1994
28 February 1994
```

Translate it into a Date object. Here you see the advantage of reading from a string. It is easy to back up and rescan a string, but you cannot back up more than one character in a file.

Exercise 12.7.2. (For wizards) Write a StringStream class that can read from and write to String objects. Of course, the string should grow as needed to hold the results from writing. This is a nontrivial project. Consult [Teale] for detailed information needed to define your own stream classes.

12.8. CREATING A NEW STREAM CLASS

Not only can the stream functionality be extended by permitting input and output of user-defined types; it is also possible to add user-defined *devices*. Here we will extend output to a graphics screen.

The stream package divides the responsibility of printing data into two parts: formatting (in ios, the common base class of all stream classes) and buffering (in streambuf).

Buffering gathers characters in a buffer, to send them to an output device in a chunk, or stores them in a buffer, for reading, as they are delivered by an input device in a chunk. This is necessary for reasonable performance when interacting with files or devices such as serial ports.

The buffer interface is documented in [Teale]. New buffer types can be derived from a base class streambuf. Two virtual functions, overflow and underflow, specify the device-dependent actions of emptying the buffer when it is full and filling it up when it is empty.

For simplicity, we will perform no buffering and define overflow to transmit the character that caused the overflow (in other words, every incoming character) to the graphics screen.

We derive a new buffer class:

```
class GraphicStreambuf : public streambuf
{
```

```
public:
  GraphicStreambuf(GraphicsContext& gc);
protected:
  virtual int overflow(int c);
private:
  GraphicsContext& _gc;

  double _xnext;
  double _ynext;
};
```

The overflow function puts the character c on the graphics screen, at position (xnext,ynext), and advances that position. We are not actually doing buffering, and the overflow function will be called every time a character is ready for printing. It simply displays the character.

```
int GraphicStreambuf::overflow(int c)
{ char buf[2];
  buf[1] = 0;
  double x, y;
  switch(c)
  { case EOF:
      break;
    case '\n':
      buf[0] = 'X';
      _gc.text_extent(buf, x, y);
      _xnext = 0;
      _ynext += y;
      break;
    default:
      buf[0] = c;
      _gc.text(buf,_xnext,_ynext);
      _gc.text_extent(buf, x, y);
      _xnext += x;
      break;
  }
  return 1;
}
```

We derive a new stream class from ostream and place a GraphicStreambuf field inside it; see Figure 12.1.

```
class GraphicStream : public ostream
{
public:
  GraphicStream(GraphicsContext&);
```

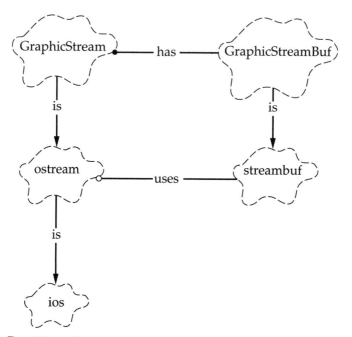

Figure 12.1. The stream class hierarchy, showing the added classes.

```
private:
  GraphicStreambuf _buffer;
};
```

The constructor informs the ostream base class of the location of the buffer:

```
GraphicStream::GraphicStream(GraphicsContext& gc)
: _buffer(gc),
  ostream(&_buffer)
{}
```

This stream class can be used like any other output stream:

```
GraphicsContext gc;
GraphicStream gs(gc);
gs << "Hello, World" << endl
   << setiosflags(ios::fixed)
   << setprecision(8) << -M_PI;
```

This is quite amazing and is a tribute to the modular and extensible nature of the streams package. We were able to hijack the formatting layer completely and link our own destination into the buffering layer.

Exercise 12.8.1. Add buffering to the graphic stream. Give the `streambuf` base class a character array—it will stash the characters into the buffer and call `overflow` when it runs out of space. Then empty the buffer. Consult [Teale] for an exact description of the interface, or, if you are adventurous, try to figure it out yourself by studying the iostream source code.

12.9. PERSISTENCE

A persistent object is stored in a file or other permanent medium rather than in computer memory. A program can save persistent objects, interrupt the computation, and reload the same data at a later time. In fact, the data can be reloaded by a different copy of the same program or transported to a different computer for further processing.

C++ does not have built-in support for persistence, but the support can be supplied in a library. We will discuss the design of a typical persistence library now. The following components are essential. A stream class, `PersistentStream`, derives from `fstream` for loading and saving persistent objects. To be persistent, an object must belong to a class deriving from the base class `Persistent`.

12.9.1. Persistent Pointers

Simply saving and restoring pointer values is meaningless. A pointer is a memory address, and it is in general impossible to reload an object into exactly the same location at which it is located when it is saved.

To see the complexities involved, consider the following example. A person has name and age. A vehicle has an owner and a driver, each represented as a pointer. Pointers are necessary for sharing information: One person can own several vehicles. The driver of one vehicle can be the owner of the same vehicle or another.

```
class Person : public Persistent
{
public:
  // ...
private:
  String _name;
  int _age;
  // ...
};

class Vehicle : public Persistent
{
public:
  Vehicle(Person*);
  void drive(Person*);
  // ...
```

```
private:
  Person* _owner;
  Person* _driver
};
```

We generate two person and two vehicle objects as shown in Figure 12.2:

```
Person* joe = new Person("Joe", 41);
Person* carl = new Person("Carl", 19);
Vehicle car(joe);
Vehicle truck(joe);
car.drive(carl);
truck.drive(joe);
```

Now we want to save both vehicles and restore them some other time:

```
PersistentStream ps;
ps.save("vehicles.dat");
car.archive(ps);
truck.archive(ps);
ps.close();

// much later

ps.load("vehicles.dat");
car.archive(ps);
truck.archive(ps);
ps.close();
```

Both saving and loading use the archive operation. When the stream is opened for saving, archive saves the information to disk. When it is opened for loading, archive restores the information from disk. This seems odd, but as we will soon see, it makes it a bit easier to implement persistent classes.

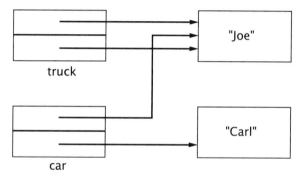

Figure 12.2.   Relationships between Vehicle and Person objects.

Consider saving `car`. It contains two pointers: one to `joe`, its owner, and one to `carl`, its driver. We must save these `Person` objects in order to restore the `car` object successfully. Now look at `truck`. Since we already saved `joe`, we must be careful not to save additional copies, but instead save each pointer as an instruction to restore it as a pointer to that object, wherever it will be in memory when the objects are read back in.

Let us assume that all pointers point to heap objects and that all pointers point to the start of an object, not to a field inside. We number all pointers that we save. When we save a pointer for the first time, we save the number, the type name, and the object to which it points. Subsequent saving of the same pointer only writes the number.

For example, here is how the two vehicles will be stored.[1]

```
1 Person
"Joe"
41
2 Person
"Carl"
19

1
1
```

When restoring a pointer, we read the number in. If it is one that we never encountered previously, we make a new object on the heap and remember the correspondence (*number, heap address*). Subsequent reads of a pointer with the same number are mapped to the same heap address.

Exercise 12.9.1. Describe the storage format if the `truck` object is stored before the `car` object.

12.9.2. Persistent Types

If a pointer may point to either a base or derived-class object, then we need to know the object's actual type when restoring it.

To understand the problem better, let us refine the previous example. Suppose classes `Car` and `Truck` derive from `Vehicle`, and the `Vehicle*` pointers `car` and `truck` actually point to objects of the derived classes:

```
Vehicle* pcar = new Car(joe);
Vehicle* ptruck = new Truck(joe);
// ...
PersistentStream ps;
```

---

[1] We are saving the files in text format to make them easy to read and debug. In practice, it would be more common to use binary format.

```
ps.save("vehicles.dat");
archive(pcar, ps);
archive(ptruck, ps);
ps.close();

// much later

ps.load("vehicles.dat");
archive(pcar, ps);
archive(ptruck, ps);
ps.close();
```

Now we are writing *pointers* to the stream. We use a regular archive function that calls the p->archive(ps) operation only if p is not null. Since the archive operation is virtual, the vehicles are saved as cars and trucks. When reloading, we have to know whether to allocate and fill a car or a truck object.

When saving a persistent pointer, the stream writes the type name of the object as a string. When reading it back, the stream reads the type name string. It then needs to have some way of creating an object of that type. The problem is that it needs to do this at run time, not at compile time.

For example, suppose we read the type name string "Truck". We now need to allocate a new Truck object. But type names are a compile-time phenomenon. At run time, there are only bytes and machine instructions, not types, much less type names.

We therefore need to build a correspondence between type names and types. We will set up, in a way that will be detailed later, a table that stores type name strings and objects of the corresponding type. For example, the entry corresponding to "Truck" is a Truck object. We invoke the clone function on the object, to get a copy, and fill the clone with the information from persistent storage.

12.9.3. Making Classes Persistent

Here we describe what you must do to make a class persistent in this particular library, but we defer a discussion on why it works until the next section. The requirements are typical for persistence mechanisms, but the details are different from one library to the next.

First, your class must derive directly or indirectly from Persistent. Next, you must supply a virtual archive operation that calls archive on the base class (if distinct from Persistent) and all fields. Simply call the global archive function on all fields. This works for fields of numeric types, classes derived from Persistent, and any combination of pointers and arrays of these types.

```
void Person::archive(PersistentStream& ps)
{ ::archive(_name, ps);
  ::archive(_age, ps);
}
```

```
void Vehicle::archive(PersistentStream& ps)
{ ::archive(_owner, ps);
  ::archive(_driver, ps);
}
```

Derived-class objects must save and restore their base class:

```
void Truck::archive(PersistentStream& ps)
{ Vehicle::archive(ps); // save base class
  ::archive(_weight, ps);
}
```

The third requirement is to place a call to a macro DECLARE_PERSISTENT inside the class and a call to a macro IMPLEMENT_PERSISTENT inside the module implementing the class.

vehicle.h:

```
class Vehicle : public Persistent
{
public:
  Vehicle(Person*=0);
  void drive(Person*);
  virtual void archive(PersistentStream&);

  DECLARE_PERSISTENT(Vehicle)

private:
  Person* _owner;
  Person* _driver;
};
```

vehicle.cpp:

```
IMPLEMENT_PERSISTENT(Vehicle)

void Vehicle::archive(PersistentStream& ps)
{ ::archive(_owner, ps);
  ::archive(_driver, ps);
}

// ...
```

Exercise 12.9.2. Add persistence to the Shape class and its descendants. Link in the persistence code, and verify that you can save and restore an arbitrary collection of shapes.

12.9.4. Implementing the Persistence Mechanism

If you are interested only in using the persistence mechanism, you can skip this section. It discusses the implementation details and touches on some rather technical aspects.

We chose to make the persistent streams bidirectional. The `archive` functions check whether the stream is currently saving or loading. We did this to make the persistent mechanism easy to use. Other implementations force the user to implement load and save operations separately:

```
void Person::load(PersistentStream& ps)
{ ::load(_name, ps);
  ::load(_age, ps);
}

void Person::save(PersistentStream& ps)
{ ::save(_name, ps);
  ::save(_age, ps);
}
```

Not only is this more tedious; it is also error-prone. If a new field is added to the class, and only one of the two operations is updated correctly, the results will be disastrous—saved objects cannot be reloaded. Having only one archive function completely solves that problem.

Of course, the global `archive` function is highly overloaded. There are separate functions for all numeric types, all of the same form. We show the `int` version.

```
void archive(int& i, PersistentStream& ps)
{ if (ps.is_saving())
     ps << i << endl;
  else
     ps >> i;
}
```

To deal with arrays, we use the template mechanism to define a parameterized family of archive functions. (Templates are discussed in Chapter 14.)

```
template<class X>
void archive(Array<X>& a, PersistentStream& ps)
{ if (ps.is_saving())
     ps << a.low() << " " << a.high() << endl;
  else
  { int l, h;
    ps >> l >> h;
    a.empty();
    a.grow(l, h);
  }
```

```
    for (int i = a.low(); i <= a.high(); i++)
        archive(a[i], ps);
}
```

To understand saving and restoring pointers, we need more information about the `PersistentStream` class. It keeps a map to track the correspondence (*address, number*) during saving and an array for the correspondence (*number, address*) during loading.

```
class PersistentStream : public fstream
{
public:
    PersistentStream();
    void load(String);
    void save(String);
    void close();
    Bool is_saving() const;

    void archive(Persistent*& x);

private:
    enum Mode { CLOSED, LOAD, SAVE };

    Persistent* find(int) const; // for loading
    void add(int, Persistent*);
    int find(const Persistent* p) const; // for saving
    int add(const Persistent* p);

    Mode _mode;
    Array<Persistent*> _toptr; // for loading
    Map<const Persistent*, int> _fromptr; // for saving
    int _maxnum;
};
```

Archiving a pointer is also split into a save and load part.

```
void PersistentStream::archive(Persistent*& x)
{ if (is_saving())
    // save part
  else
    // load part
}
```

Let us first look at the save part:

```
        if (x == 0) { self << "0" << endl; return; }
        int n = find(x);
```

```
if (n) self << n << endl;
else
{ n = add(x);
  self << n << " " << x->name() << endl; // write type name
  x->archive(self);
}
```

Null pointers are simply written as 0. For other pointers, we check whether we saved the object before. If so, we just save the associated number. If not, we add the pointer to the map and save the number, the type name, and the object by calling its virtual archive function.

Loading is more complex, because of the support for polymorphic types.

```
int n;
self >> n;
if (n == 0) { x = 0; return; }
x = find(n);
if (x == 0) // new entry
{ String name;
  self >> name;
  x = Persistent::clone(name);
  x->archive(self);
  add(n, x);
}
```

A 0 indicates a null pointer. For other numbers, we check whether we already read in the associated object. If so, we simply fetch its address. Otherwise we read the type name string and ask the type name repository, a shared object in the Persistent class, for a clone of an object of that type. We fill the clone object with the contents of the archive and remember its location.

It is interesting to note that the various archive functions exhibit all three kinds of polymorphism. A finite number of archive functions are supplied for numeric types; that is ad hoc polymorphism. Parametric polymorphism is used to define the archive functions for all Array<X> types. Pure polymorphism occurs with the virtual archive operations for all classes deriving from Persistent.

This completes the hardest part of the mechanism. One problem remains: the construction of the type name repository. The Persistent class keeps a shared map object that associates strings with objects for cloning.

```
class Persistent
{
public:
  virtual void archive(PersistentStream&) = 0;
  virtual String name() const = 0;
  virtual Persistent* clone() const = 0;
```

```
    static Persistent* add_type(String, Persistent*);
    static Persistent* clone(String);
private:
    static Map<String, Persistent*> _typemap;
};
```

Each persistent class adds a pair (class name, default object) to the map:

```
Persistent::add_type("Vehicle", new Vehicle);
```

These commands are hidden behind the preprocessor macros that must be added to each class. The macros define the trivial clone and name functions, as well as a static object whose initialization adds the map entry. Here are the macro definitions. Note that the trailing backslashes are necessary to continue the replacement text over several source lines.

```
#define DECLARE_PERSISTENT(X) \
    String name() const { return #X; }  \
    Persistent* clone() const { return new X(self); }  \
    static Persistent*_type

#define IMPLEMENT_PERSISTENT(X) \
    Persistent* X::_type = Persistent::add_type(#X, new X);
```

This is definitely wizardry, and we will not dwell on it. Macros like this are a common strategy to define routine code for a variety of desirable mechanisms. You may well encounter similar macros in other libraries. They often come in DECLARE/IMPLEMENT pairs.

12.9.5. Limitations of C++ Run-Time Type Support

We had to go through a great deal of trouble to implement persistent objects. Even with all the effort, the implementation is far from perfect. Persistent pointers must point to objects that

- Point to the heap
- Point to the beginning of an object
- Point to an object of a class deriving from Persistent

Pointers to fields inside other objects do not work. In particular, multiple inheritance creates a problem. (That particular difficulty can be overcome with a more complex implementation.)

Why was it so difficult? There are three reasons. All are connected with the weak support for classes at run time. The only run-time type support that C++ provides is the typeid operator. It returns a reference to an object of a standard class Type_info describing the object. Unfortunately, at the time of this writing, there are only two things you can do with a `Type_info` object: compare it against another `Type_info` object to see whether they denote the same type, and apply the `name` operation to obtain a string describing the type.

Given a class, there is no way of *iterating* through its bases and fields. We had to require that the class author provide the `archive` operation, simply by applying `archive` to each base and field. C++ does just the same when building a default constructor or copy constructor, but it doesn't reveal the necessary information for us to do it in other situations.

Given a pointer to a class object, there is no automatic way of getting a new heap object that is an identical copy of the current object. We implement this obviously useful capability through the virtual `clone` operation

```
X* X::clone() const { return new X(self);}
```

Given a string containing a type name, there is no way of getting the associated `Type_info` object or an object of the type. We had to build a map for this purpose.

Other object-oriented programming languages—in particular, Smalltalk—have much stronger support for classes. In Smalltalk each class is an object of a class `Class`, roughly comparable with the `Type_info` object representing a class in C++. In Smalltalk, the class object can be located given its name. To instantiate an object of a class, simply invoke a `new` operation on the class object. It is possible to obtain information about the superclass, fields, and operations of a class at run time. The Smalltalk browser, which is written in Smalltalk, uses this information.

Exercise 12.9.3. Another case in which the exact information on the fields of objects is important is *garbage collection.* In a *mark and sweep* garbage collector, objects that are known to be alive set a mark bit in the objects to which they have pointers. Recursively, all reachable objects are marked. Unmarked objects are unreachable and can be reclaimed. The advantage of garbage collection is that you can allocate objects as you need them and not worry about deallocation. You don't even need to supply destructors. "Garbage collection means you never have to say delete." As we will see in Chapter 13, simple data structures can be cleaned up with *reference counting,* but reference counts cannot deallocate cycles. Tough garbage requires a professional collector, which we will implement in this exercise.

Classes whose objects can be collected must derive from a base class `Collectable`, which contains the mark flag. The `Collectable` constructor enters the address of each collectable object in a set of pointers (`Set<Collectable*>`), and the destructor removes the addresses from there.

If we were able to locate `Collectable` pointers in an object at run time, we would be in good shape. Instead, we must ask each class that derives from `Collectable` to supply a function `mark`, which calls `mark` on all collectable pointers:

```
void Vehicle::mark()
{ mark(_owner);
  mark(_driver);
}
```

Now implement the collection phase. Iterate through the set of pointers to allocated objects. For each pointer, you must find out whether it points to the heap or the stack. There are a number of ways to do that. If you know that the stack is in one segment, you may be able to test the selector value. Or you can overload the new operator for Collectable to set a flag for heap-allocated objects. (See [Stroustrup], p. 215, for details.) For each stack object, call mark. That will recursively mark some of the heap objects. Then traverse the set of pointers again and delete all unmarked objects.

12.10. DESIGN HINTS

12.10.1. Polymorphic Output

Polymorphic output is easy to arrange. Have all classes derived from the common base class implement a virtual print(ostream&) operation. Then add a << operator as follows:

```
ostream& operator<<(ostream& os, const Base& x)
{ x.print(os);
  return os;
}
```

Since x is a reference, the print function is bound dynamically, printing the derived-class object to which x refers.

Using polymorphism for << means that it is not necessary to define a separate << operator for each derived class.

It is also common to add a second overloaded version to print pointers.

```
ostream& operator<<(ostream& os, const Base* p)
{ if (p != 0) p->print(os);
  return os;
}
```

That way, the object to which a pointer p points can be printed either as os << *p or as os << p.

12.10.2. Polymorphic Input

For input, it is a good idea to have a virtual read function and define

```
istream& operator>>(istream& is, Base& x)
{ x.read(is);
```

```
      return is;
  }
```

But this is not as polymorphic as you might like: You already have to *know* what to expect in the input, create a blank object of that type, and have it read from the stream.

True polymorphic input means that we create a new object, of the type that is actually present in the input stream, and then read it in. This cannot be the operation of a class, since there isn't yet an object on which to act.

There must be a way to find out the type of the next object in the input stream, so that the format of the contents can be properly parsed. Typically, the output routine first writes the type name and then the contents.

```
Array<Shape*> figure;
for (int i = figure.low(); i <= figure.high(); i++)
   os << typeid(*figure[i]).name() << " " << *figure[i];
```

To reverse this process, we read in the type name and then have to find a way to get an object of that type. Section 12.9.4 discusses a systematic way of doing that. For simple class hierarchies, an ad hoc approach works (barely).

```
istream& operator>>(istream& is, Shape*& x)
{ String name;
  is >> name;
  if (name == "Rectangle") x = new Rectangle;
  else if (name == "FilledRect") x = new FilledRect;
  else if (name == "Polygon") x = new Polygon;
  // ...
  else x = 0;
  if (x != 0) x->read(is);
  return is;
}
```

Each class must have a default constructor, because we first must make an object before we can fill it by reading the data.

An alternative is to give each class a constructor that takes an `istream&` argument. That is conceptually very clean—we express the fact that objects can be constructed from the data found in a stream.

```
x = new Rectangle(is);
```

This scheme has only one added complexity: If input fails, be sure to initialize the object to some default state (or raise an exception).

12.10.3. Dealing with Failure

Input can and will fail—certainly at the end of the file, but perhaps before because of an unexpected error in the input format. Of course, human input is completely unpredictable. Even computers' files do get corrupted occasionally.

There is no way of testing for failure except by doing it and seeing whether it worked. *After* each read, check for failure. You may then check for eof() to see whether the reason for failure is the end of the file or a formatting problem.

If you expect to read a certain input pattern but it is not present, report a format error by turning on the failbit. You may as well stop reading. All other input operations will do nothing, because the stream has now failed.

Before committing to change a value, be sure that all input operations have been successful. Changing half of an object and then leaving the other half unchanged is definitely rude, and it also may produce an object that doesn't conform to the class invariant.

Once an input stream has failed, it is very hard to "unfail" it. You can clear the failbit and take your chances, but that is pretty useless in practice. If you cannot tolerate failure, read the input file as a sequence of strings and then parse the strings.

For output operations, error handling is not nearly as important. The major reason for output failure is a device failure (disk full, printer out of paper) about which you cannot do anything anyway in an output routine. When the buffering layer detects the failure, the stream state is set to failure, and all further output is ignored. You can slightly speed up the process by checking for failure at the beginning of the output routine. Of course, after all output is completed, you must check whether the stream is still happy. If not, report failure to the client that requested the output.

C H A P T E R   13

MEMORY
MANAGEMENT

The topic of memory management has little relationship with the theme of object-oriented programming. Many advanced programming languages employ garbage collection, automatically reclaiming memory that is no longer used. However, even the best garbage collection methods are computationally expensive. C++ has no garbage collection capabilities, and the programmer is responsible for allocating and deallocating memory. Therefore, some knowledge of the C++ memory management model is necessary to implement robust classes that hide the acquisition and release of internal storage from the class user.

13.1. THE FREE STORE

13.1.1. Memory Areas

C++ programs can allocate objects in one of three memory areas:

- The run-time stack
- The static data area
- The heap or free store

Local variables that are declared inside a function are allocated on the run-time stack. Their *visibility* and *lifetime* coincide, from the point of declaration until the end of the enclosing block. At the end of each block, all variables declared in that block are popped off the runtime stack. Of course, the values are not physically removed. Instead, a stack pointer is adjusted, and the memory area will soon be overwritten with other stack variables.

All variables that are declared outside of functions, as well as local and class variables that are declared as static, are allocated in the static data area. Their visibility depends on the declaration. Local static variables have the same scope as any other local variables. Global and shared class variables are visible in one or more modules. They come alive sometime before main starts and persist until after main exits. Unlike all other variables, static variables of nonclass type are guaranteed to be initialized with zero.

The stack and static data areas suffice to allocate data whose size and amount is known at compile time. However, most nontrivial programs cannot foresee the exact amount of run-time memory required for each data type, because the generated data usually depends on user input or other external events. Any variable amount of data must be allocated on the heap or free store.

13.1.2. Heap Allocation

The new operator is used to allocate an object on the heap. The syntax is

```
X* p = new X( constructor arguments);
```

A new object is allocated on the free store and constructed as specified. The constructor arguments can be omitted to invoke the default constructor or for a type without constructors. The allocated object itself has no name, but a pointer to it is returned.

All blocks that are allocated from new must be recycled to the free store when they are no longer needed. A memory block that is no longer accessible but has not been returned to the heap is called a *memory leak*. This is not a concern for programs that run very briefly and allocate little heap memory, because the operating system reclaims all program memory on termination. But if a program with a memory leak runs sufficiently long, it will eventually exhaust the free store and cease to function properly. In writing reusable code, no memory leaks can be tolerated.

The delete operator is used to return a memory block to the heap. Its argument is a pointer to the object to be reclaimed.

```
delete p;
```

It is possible to allocate built-in arrays from the heap; however, that will never be done in this text, because the array templates are a more convenient way of managing variable-size arrays. Refer to [Stroustrup], p. 175, for details.

The heap keeps a list of memory blocks that are available for allocation and their sizes. It is easy to corrupt this information by passing an address to delete that was not originally obtained from new or by continuing to write onto a memory block after reclaiming it with delete. (However, deleting a 0 pointer is safe and guaranteed to have no effect.)

```
Employee joe("Joe User");
Employee* pj = &joe;
Employee* ph = new Employee("Harry Hacker");
Employee* pk = ph;
Employee* pn = 0;
delete pk; // OK
delete ph; // ERROR—deleting twice
delete pn; // OK—can delete 0
delete pj; // ERROR—cannot delete pointer to stack
```

It is a good idea to obtain pointers from the heap only (with `new`) and never from the stack (that is, never with &). It is also a good idea to set a pointer to 0 after invoking `delete` to reduce the risk of deleting it twice.

```
delete ph;
ph = 0;
```

Of course, this is not a complete safety guarantee. The same pointer value may be stored in a second pointer variable, and the programmer must still take care not to delete that value.

Corrupting the free list can lead to fatal consequences. Once the free list is damaged, a call to `new` may return a memory address that is already in use by another object. The resulting bugs tend to be difficult to reproduce, and the cause of the bug, namely the memory overwrite or faulty `delete` instruction, may well be far removed from the diagnosed symptoms. Encapsulating memory management is an important strategy to reduce the likelihood of such programming errors.

Exercise 13.1.1. Try corrupting the free list on purpose to see what happens on your system. Delete the same pointer twice. Then allocate pointers and check for duplicates or just for crashes.

13.2. DESTRUCTORS

13.2.1. Resource Management

Destructors are operations that are invoked automatically whenever storage for an object is reclaimed, just as constructors are automatically called when an object is created.

The construction and destruction activity is most easily envisioned for objects that exist on the run-time stack. When an object is allocated, space is set aside for it on the stack. At this point, the object has no well-defined value. Its storage is simply filled with the random bytes that happen to be on the stack as leftovers from previous program activity. It is the role of the constructor to turn the storage into an actual object, by initializing all data fields.

When program execution reaches the end of the block in which the object was allocated, the storage on the stack is abandoned. However, if a destructor is defined for the class to which the object belongs, the code of the destructor is executed first.

```
f(...)
{ ...
   { ...
     List m;
     ...
   } ← List destructor invoked on m
   ...
}
```

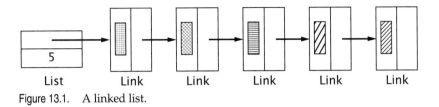

List   Link   Link   Link   Link   Link

Figure 13.1.   A linked list.

The purpose of the destructor is to relinquish any resources that the object may have acquired.

The most common resource that needs to be managed with constructors and destructors is heap memory. Consider, for example, a linked list (see Figure 13.1) of integers.

```
class List
{ // ...
private:

    class Link
    {
    public:
        int _info;
        Link* _next;
    };

    Link* _head;
    int _length;
};
```

A List object merely contains a pointer to the first Link. The integers that are conceptually stored in the list are physically contained in the Link objects. These Link objects are allocated on the heap, as more values are added to the list. The List destructor recycles the links back to the heap when the List object goes out of scope.

Destructors can perform other actions besides returning memory to the heap. Common actions include closing files, releasing locks, and reducing use counts.

An alternative to destructors are cleanup operations that are invoked manually. However, this is error-prone, because it is easy enough to forget to call the cleanup operation, or accidentally to call it more than once. In contrast, destructors are guaranteed to be invoked exactly once for each object.

Destructors are beneficial for code maintenance. Simple classes typically need no destructors. If a class evolves from a simple one to a more complex one, a destructor can be added. Existing code that uses the class need not be amended, just recompiled, and destructors are invoked automatically. If an explicit cleanup operation had been added instead, the existing code would have to be revisited to insert calls to that cleanup code.

13.2.2. Implementing Destructors

A destructor of a class X has the name ~X(). Like constructors, destructors are declared in the class definition. While a class can have many constructors, it can have at most one destructor.

```
class List
{
public:
  List();
  ~List();
  // ...
private:
  Link* _head;
  int _length;
};

List::~List()
{ Link* p = _head;
  while (p != 0)
  { Link* pnext = p->_next;
    delete p;
    p = pnext;
  }
}
```

Much like default constructors, destructors are invoked automatically and cannot be called by the programmer.[1]

Exercise 13.2.1. Define a class Figure that contains an array of shapes. An operation Figure::add(Shape*) adds a new shape. Since shapes are polymorphic, they are allocated on the heap:

```
fig.add(new Rectangle(...));
```

Make the destructor ~Figure delete all shapes.

13.2.3. Compiler-Generated Destructors

If one or more data fields or base classes of a class are objects of classes with a destructor, the compiler ensures that these data fields and bases are properly destroyed. Consider a class containing a data field of class List:

---

[1] This is not strictly true. There is a special syntax for explicitly invoking the destructor on an existing object, but it should *never* be used in normal C++ programs. It is useful only for implementing specialized memory allocation schemes.

```
class IndexEntry
{ // ...
private:
    String _phrase; // the phrase to index
    List _page_ref; // the pages on which _phrase occurs
    int _level; // the indentation level
};
```

Whether or not the IndexEntry class supplies a destructor, C++ ensures that the destructors of the String and List are invoked on the _phrase and _page_ref fields whenever an index entry object dies. Since _level is of type int, a numeric type that does not have a destructor, no special action is performed for that field. If no ~IndexEntry destructor is provided, the compiler will generate one that invokes the destructors of the individual fields. If a destructor is provided, the instructions to destroy the String and List fields are appended to that destructor.

Exercise 13.2.2. Write a class B whose default constructor and destructor print trace messages. Make a class C that contains two fields of type B. Supply no constructors or destructors to C. Allocate an object of type C and watch the trace message. Derive D from B and verify that creation of D objects triggers construction and destruction of the B base.

13.2.4. Destruction and Deletion

A destructor is invoked whenever the memory that an object occupies is abandoned. For an object on the stack, this happens on exit from the block in which the object is allocated. An object on the heap is destroyed when the memory block that it occupies is deleted.

```
Employee* pe = new Employee(...);
// ...
delete pe; // ~Employee invoked on *pe
```

It is common that the destruction triggers more deletions. Suppose a linked list is allocated on the heap and later freed:

```
List* pl = new List;
pl->insert(...);
// ...
delete pl;
```

The ~List destructor is invoked on the List object to which pl points, and afterwards the memory block in which that object resides is recycled to the free store. But the ~List destructor itself calls delete, this time on all Link objects that the linked list manages. In our example, the Link class has no destructor, and no special activity takes place before the links are reclaimed.

Exercise 13.2.3. Modify the Link class and add a ~Link destructor that calls delete _next. Modify the ~List destructor to delete _head only. What are the advantages and disadvantages of this approach?

This example makes it clear that we must be careful to distinguish between destruction and deletion. Destruction is the cleanup that occurs before the storage used for an object is abandoned, regardless of whether the storage is part of the stack, heap, or static data area. Deletion is the reclamation of storage to the heap. Deletion always involves destruction of the block to be reclaimed.

13.2.5. Virtual Destructors

Destructors can be declared as virtual. In fact, any class from which another class is derived ought to have a destructor and declare it as a virtual operation.

How does a class know whether another class will derive from it? If a class has any virtual function at all, it clearly intends to be a base class. In that case, be sure to add a virtual do-nothing destructor, if none was there, or to make the existing destructor virtual.

However, if a class has no virtual functions, it is costly to make the destructor virtual. It increases the size of each *object* by one pointer (to a table of virtual functions). For efficiency reasons, a virtual destructor is not usually added to classes like Date, List, or String, that have value semantics and are not envisioned as base classes for derivations.

Consider the following example.

```
class Employee
{
public:
  Employee(...);
  virtual void print(ostream&) const;
  // ...
private:
  int _id; // identification number
  // ...
};

class Manager : public Employee
{
public:
  Manager(...);
  virtual void print(ostream&) const;
  // ...
private:
  // ...
  List _superv; // ID numbers of supervised employees
};
```

```
Array<Employee*> staff;
// construct staff members
staff[1] = new Employee(...);
staff[2] = new Manager(...);
// ...
// print staff information
for (i = staff.low(); i <= staff.high(); i++)
  staff[i]->print(cout);
// recycle all allocated memory
for (i = staff.low(); i <= staff.high(); i++)
    delete staff[i];
```

Since the static type of staff[i] is Employee*, the compiler will invoke the Employee destructor, regardless of the actual type of the object to which staff[i] points. This is a problem, because the Employee destructor can clean up only a portion of the Manager object. In particular, the _superv list is not destroyed.

The remedy is to declare an empty virtual destructor in the base class.

```
class Employee
{
public:
  virtual ~Employee() {};
  // ...
};
```

The compiler-generated ~Manager is then automatically virtual as well, and the call

```
delete staff[i];
```

invokes the correct destructor, depending on the actual type at run time.

Exercise 13.2.4. Add sufficient detail to the Employee/ Manager example in this section to write a program that verifies that the Manager information is not properly destroyed without a virtual destructor. Check that adding a virtual ~Employee remedies the problem.

13.2.6. Pointers Have No Destructors

Only objects are destroyed, provided that their class supplies a destructor. Destructors are never automatically invoked on pointers.

```
f(...)
{ Employee* pe = new Employee(...);
  Employee e(...);
  // ...
} // ~Employee destroys e; *pe is not destroyed
```

This is to be expected. More than one pointer may refer to the same object, and the object should be destroyed only when it is no longer accessible by any pointer. In C++, the programmer must explicitly invoke `delete` at the proper time.

Similarly, when a reference goes out of scope, no destructor is triggered.

```
void print(List a, ostream& os)
{ // ...
} // ~List destroys a; os is not destroyed.
```

Exercise 13.2.5. Write a class B whose default constructor and destructor print trace messages. Call the functions

```
void fo(B b) {}
void fp(B* b) {}
void fr(B& b) {}
```

and compare the results.

13.3. ASSIGNMENT OPERATORS

Destructors are very useful for guaranteed cleanup without programmer intervention. However, their automatic invocation introduces a serious problem. Consider the code:

```
List a;
a.insert(...);
// ...
List b;
b.insert(...);
// ...

a = b;

// b goes out of scope
```

Suppose the lists look similar to Figure 13.2 before the assignment. The assignment a = b sets a._head to b._head and a._length to b._length (see Figure 13.3). Note that the old links of a are no longer accessible. As b goes out of scope, the destructor frees all links (see Figure 13.4). The a._head pointer now points to an unallocated link. Any further usage of a is an error. Even worse, the destructor for a will delete the invalid a._head pointer and corrupt the free list.

This example shows two problems: The original list was not deleted when a was replaced by another list, and the b list was deleted twice. Destruction appears to be incompatible with assignment.

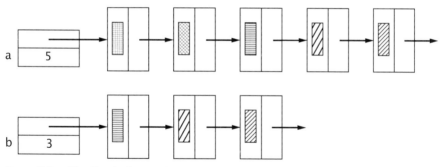

Figure 13.2.   The lists before assignment.

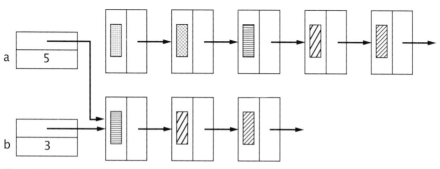

Figure 13.3.   The lists after assignment.

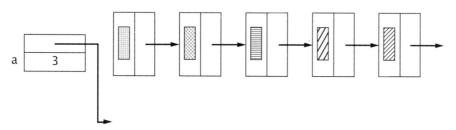

Figure 13.4.   The lists after destruction of b.

In C++, this problem can be solved by *overloading* the assignment operator. As we saw in Chapter 11, it is possible to define the meaning for essentially all C++ operators by defining special `operator` functions. In this section we wish to define only the assignment operator, `operator=`. A user-defined assignment operator has to carry out two tasks:

- Free the memory of the left argument.
- Copy the memory of the right argument.

Here is the assignment operator for the List class:

```
class List
{
public:
  List();
  ~List();
  const List& operator=(const List& b);
  // ...
}

const List& List::operator=(const List& b)
{ // guard against assignment to itself
  if (&self == &b) return self;
  // destroy the left-hand side
  Link* p = _head;
  while (p != 0)
  { Link* pnext = p->_next;
    delete p;
    p = pnext;
  }

  // copy the right-hand side
  _length = b._length;
  p = 0;
  Link* q = b._head;
  while (q != 0)
  { Link* n = new Link;
    n->_next = 0;
    n->_info = q->_info; // copy information
    if (p == 0) // first entry
      _head = n;
    else
      p->_next = n;
    p = n;
    q = q->_next;
  }
  return self;
}
```

Note that the assignment operator takes two arguments: the implicit argument self and an explicit argument b. It is customary to name the latter argument b or y, or even that, not a or x, to remind the reader that the first argument is implicit. The explicit argument is passed by constant reference to avoid copying it.

The assignment operator returns a reference to the left-hand side to allow multiple assignments

```
c = a = b;
```

The protection

```
if (&self == &b) return self;
```

guards against the assignment

```
a = a;
```

in which case the left argument should *not* be cleared. (Nobody would assign a = a on purpose, but it might happen in a conditional expression or through an alias.)

Any class with a nontrivial destructor needs a user-defined assignment operator that makes proper copies.

Exercise 13.3.1. Optimize the code for `List::operator=` to reuse existing links. Delete only the excess, and allocate only the difference. Then copy the information.

Exercise 13.3.2. Implement a doubly linked list `DList`, where each link points to both its successor and its predecessor. Write an assignment operator for `DList`. Cleaning up the old list is the same as in the singly linked case, but you must establish the back links in the copy.

13.4. COPY CONSTRUCTORS

13.4.1. Copying Function Arguments

In C++, objects can be copied with the assignment operator. Furthermore, objects can be copied into functions as arguments and out of functions as function results. These copies do not invoke the assignment operator, and they also conflict with destructors unless special action is taken.

In calling a function, all arguments of the call are copied into local variables of the function. These local variables are destroyed at the end of the function, just like any other local variables.

```
double average(List a)
{ double sum = 0;
  int n = a.length();
  // ...
  return sum / n;
} // ~List destroys a

List lst;
double avg = average(lst); // lst copied into a
```

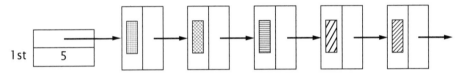

Figure 13.5.   The list before the function call.

It is helpful to look at the run-time stack. Before the call, 1st is located on the stack, as in Figure 13.5. When the function starts, its local variables, a, sum, and n, are initialized. The parameter a is initialized as a copy of 1st. That is, a._length is set to 1st._length and a._head is set to 1st._head, as shown in Figure 13.6.

When the function exits, all local variables are destroyed. Since numeric types have no destructors, sum and n are simply abandoned on the stack, but a is destroyed by ~List, deleting all links (see Figure 13.7). After the function returns, 1st._head is no longer valid. Furthermore, when the ~List destructor is invoked on 1st, an invalid pointer is passed to delete, causing corruption of the free list. This situation is just as serious as the assignment problem discussed in the previous section.

You may well wonder why the compiler does not use the code defined in operator= to assign a = 1st when the function starts. However, close inspection of the assignment code explains the problem. The assignment operator first frees the memory associated with the left-hand side of the assignment. However, the left-hand side, a, is completely uninitialized. In particular, a._head is a random pointer, and deleting it would be disastrous. The assignment operator can be used only to copy an object into another existing object, not to construct a new object.

In this situation, C++ requires the programmer to provide a so-called *copy constructor*, a constructor that initializes a new object as a copy of an existing one.

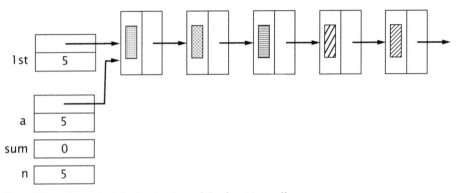

Figure 13.6.   The list at the beginning of the function call.

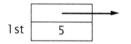

1st | 5

Figure 13.7. The list after
the function call.

Exercise 13.4.1. Place a trace message into the `List` destructor to verify that a function parameter variable of type `List` really is destroyed when the function exits. Try out what the program does when the list object is destroyed twice.

13.4.2. Implementing Copy Constructors

A copy constructor for type X takes a single argument of type `const X&` and builds a new object as a copy of the constructor argument. Here is the code for the `List` copy constructor:

```
List::List(const List& b)
{ _length = b._length;
  Link* p = 0;
  Link* q = b._head;
  while (q != 0)
  { Link* n = new Link;
    n->_next = 0;
    n->_info = q->_info; // copy information
    if (p == 0) // first entry
      _head = n;
    else
      p->_next = n;
    p = n;
    q = q->_next;
  }
}
```

Once a copy constructor has been defined, the compiler invokes it automatically to initialize function parameters with their call values.

Any class with a nontrivial destructor needs both a user-defined assignment operator and a user-defined copy constructor. When these memory management functions are defined, all destruction activity is matched by the appropriate copying actions.

Some data structures are very expensive to copy. Class designers can force class users to always copy pointers, not objects, by making the copy constructor and assignment operator *private*. The compiler then flags as an error any code that would require invoking either operation. No code should be supplied for these operations. This ensures that the linker will report an error if the class code itself invokes either operation.

Exercise 13.4.2. Place trace messages into the `List` default constructor, copy constructor, and destructor. Test the `average` function and verify that the constructors and destructors match.

Exercise 13.4.3. Explain the difference between

```
List b = a;
```

and

```
List b;
b = a;
```

Which memory management functions are involved in each case? If you are not sure, place trace messages in the List memory management functions and try it.

Exercise 13.4.4. Make the copy constructor and assignment operator of the List class private. Try calling the average function, and perform an assignment of lists. What error messages does the compiler produce?

13.4.3. Factoring Out Common Code for Memory Management Operations

The code of the copy constructor is, of course, the same code as the second half of the assignment operator. In fact, the assignment operator can always be regarded as invoking the destructor on the left-hand side, then invoking the copy constructor to copy the right-hand side. However, constructors and destructors cannot be invoked explicitly, and it is customary to factor out the common code.

```
class List
{
public:
  List();
  List(const List& b);
  ~List();
  const List& operator=(const List& b);
  // ...
private:
  void copy(const List& b);
  void free();
};

List::List(const List& b)
{ copy(b);
}

List::~List()
{ free();
}
```

```
const List& List::operator=(const List& b)
{ if (&self != &b)
    { free();
      copy(b);
    }
    return self;
}

void List::copy(const List& b)
{ _length = b._length;
    Link* p = 0;
    Link* q = b._head;
    while (q != 0)
    { Link* n = new Link;
      n->_next = 0;
      n->_info = q->_info; // copy information
      if (p == 0) // first entry
        _head = n;
      else
        p->_next = n;
      p = n;
      q = q->_next;
    }
}

void List::free()
{ Link* p = _head;
    while (p != 0)
    { Link* pnext = p->_next;
      delete p;
      p = pnext;
    }
}
```

Exercise 13.4.5. Write a Queue class with a copy constructor, destructor, and assignment operator. Use the copy/free factorization.

Exercise 13.4.6. Add a copy constructor and assignment operator to the Figure class of Exercise 13.2.1. To make a true copy of the shapes, you need to use the virtual clone function.

13.4.4. Copying Function Results

The copy constructor is used to copy function results out of the scope of a function into a temporary value in the scope of the caller. That temporary value is then used in further computations.

Consider a function that reverses a list without destroying its argument:

```
List reverse(List a)
{ List r;
  // ...
  return r; // List(const List&) copies r to scope of caller
} // ~List destroys r

List u, v;
v = reverse(u);
print(reverse(u), cout);
```

When the result r is computed, the function ends and must pass the result to the caller. An unnamed temporary list object is constructed from r using the copy constructor. Then the list destructor destroys the local variable r. The unnamed temporary object is used in the computation; in this example, it is assigned to v or passed to print.

Exercise 13.4.7. Write the reverse function. Explain the memory management functions that get triggered in the following code.

```
List a;
// add some values into a
a = reverse(a);
```

If you are not sure, place trace messages in the memory management functions and try it.

Exercise 13.4.8. Write a class B whose default constructor, copy constructor, assignment operator, and destructor print trace messages. Then consider the following code:

```
B f(B b)
{ B c = b;
  B d;
  d = c;
  return d;
}

int main()
{ B x;
  B y;
  y = f(x);
}
```

First try to determine all construction, destruction, and assignment activity. Then run the program to confirm your solution.

13.4.5. Memberwise Copying and Assignment

As we have seen in Section 13.2.3, the compiler generates destructors, or enhances programmer-supplied destructors, to ensure that all data fields are properly destroyed. In the same fashion, copy constructors and assignment operators are automatically generated. These operations simply apply copying and assignment field by field, a process referred to as *memberwise copying*.

That is good news for users of classes with nontrivial copy semantics. Such classes can be used in "plug and play" fashion as building blocks for other classes. High-level classes can use data fields of any type without having to understand their mechanics of copying and destruction.

To understand how memberwise copying and assignment is carried out, consider again the `IndexEntry` example.

```
class IndexEntry
{ // ...
private:
    String _phrase; // the phrase to index
    List _page_ref; // the pages on which _phrase occurs
    int _level; // the indentation level
};
```

The copy constructor is used to construct a new object as a copy of an existing object, typically to copy it into or out of a function. It performs this copy individually on each field. The `String` and `List` copy constructors are used on the `_phrase` and `_page_ref` fields. Plain assignment is used on the `_level` field, since the type `int` has no special copy requirements.

The analogous process is carried out in assignments. The assignment

```
IndexEntry a, b;
// ...
a = b;
```

is equivalent to the individual assignments

```
a._phrase = b._phrase; // uses String::operator=
a._page_ref = b._page_ref; // uses List::operator=
a._level = b._level; // plain copy of int values
```

For this reason, it is necessary to declare explicit copy constructors, assignment operators, and destructors only for low-level classes whose implementation directly manages some resource such as heap memory. Higher-level classes should rely on the compiler-generated memory management functions.

Exercise 13.4.9. Build the `IndexEntry` class and place a few entries into the `_page_ref` list of an `IndexEntry` object a. Then execute the code

```
IndexEntry b = a;
b = a;
```

Place trace messages in the `List` copy constructor and assignment operator and verify that the `List` subobjects are copied and assigned.

13.5. REFERENCE COUNTING

13.5.1. Avoiding the Cost of Copying

Classes have destructors to free the programmer from the burden of having to remember when to relinquish a resource such as free-store memory. Classes that have destructors then need copying and assignment operations to ensure that each object has its own copy of the information, because destructors cannot be allowed to clean up shared copies. But the cost of copying is substantial. Consider a function call

```
double average(List a)
{ double sum = 0;
   int n = a.length();
   // ...
   if (n > 0) return sum / n; else return 0;
} // ~List destroys a

List lst;
lst.insert(x);
// ...
avg = average(lst);
```

When the parameter a is constructed as a copy of `lst`, all links in `lst` are copied, as in Figure 13.8. The information is then inspected (but not modified), and the copied links are destroyed at the end of the function. This is quite inefficient.

For function arguments, a constant reference can be used to avoid call by value and the cost of copying:

```
double average(const List& a)
{ double sum = 0;
   int n = a.length();
```

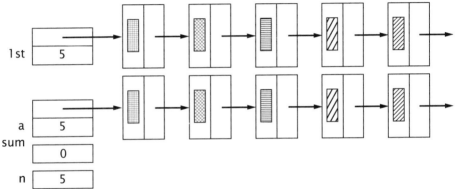

Figure 13.8.   A copy of the list is passed to the function.

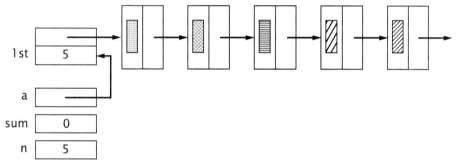

Figure 13.9.   A reference of the list is passed to the function.

```
// ...
return sum/n;
} // ~List destroys a
```

Now the address of 1st, not a copy of the 1st object, is passed to the function, as shown in Figure 13.9.

However, that technique fails for function return values:

```
List reverse(const List& a)
{ List r;
   // ...
   return r;
   // List(const List&) copies r to temporary in scope of caller
} // ~List destroys r

List lst;
List rev = reverse(lst);
```

Transferring the result r out of the scope of the function into the scope of the caller involves a copy into a temporary, followed by the destruction of r. That is, all links of r that were built up in the computation are first copied, then deleted.

There is no easy way of avoiding that copy. The function could be re-formulated

```
void reverse(const List& a, List& result);
```

but this can make the usage of the function less pleasant, and it is not an option for functions that define overloaded operators. We cannot have the function return a reference

```
List& reverse(const List& a); // DON'T
```

A reference to what? The function cannot return a reference to a local object, because the stack of the function is popped when the function exits. Neither can we, in good conscience, return a reference to an object on the heap, because the caller would then be obligated to delete that object when it is no longer needed.

Rather than trying to avoid the copy, we will learn how to reduce its cost.

13.5.2. Reference Counts

It is often said jokingly that any problem in computer science can be solved by an added level of indirection. Indeed, this will help us manage objects that themselves must manage resources. We achieve that by separating the information into

- An access class, sometimes called a *handle*
- A representation class, containing a reference count and the object data

The class user sees and copies only the access class. The representation class is invisible to the class user. Its class data is augmented by a field, called a *reference count*, that keeps track of the number of access objects sharing the same representation (see Figure 13.10).

When an access object is copied, the reference count is incremented, as in Figure 13.11. When an access object is destroyed, the reference count is decremented, as in Figure 13.12. Only when the reference count reaches zero is the representation object itself destroyed and the resources associated with the data released, as in Figure 13.13.

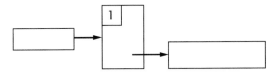

Figure 13.10.   The reference count after object creation.

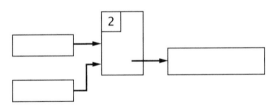

Figure 13.11.   The reference count after object copy.

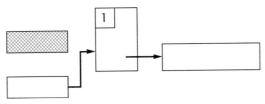

Figure 13.12.   The reference count after a destruction.

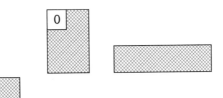

Figure 13.13.   The reference count after the last destruction.

13.5.3. Implementation of Reference Counts

Let us implement a linked list class using reference counts. The list representation carries the reference count and the fixed list data:

```
class ListRep
{
private:
  unsigned _rc; // reference count
  Link* _head;
  int _length;
  // ...
friend class List;
};
```

The access class contains only a pointer to the data representation:

```
class List
{
public:
  List();

  // ...

  List(const List&);
  const List& operator=(const List&);
  ~List();
```

```
private:
  void copy(const List& b);
  void free();

  ListRep* _rep;
};
```

As in Section 13.4.3, the copy and free functions are used to define the copy
constructor, assignment operator, and destructor:

```
List::List(const List& b)
{ copy(b);
}

List::~List()
{ free();
}

const List& List::operator=(const List& b)
{ if (&self != &b)
  { free();
    copy(b);
  }
  return self;
}
```

The copy and free functions manipulate the reference count field in the ListRep
class.

```
void List::copy(const List& b)
{ _rep = b._rep;
  _rep->_rc++;
}

void List::free()
{ _rep->_rc--;
  if (_rep->_rc == 0)
    delete _rep;
}
```

The ListRep destructor is invoked only when all access objects sharing the list
data are destroyed. It then deletes the links:

```
ListRep::~ListRep()
{ Link* p = _head;
  while (p != 0)
```

```
    { Link* pnext = p->_next;
      delete p;
      p = pnext;
    }
}
```

The `ListRep` constructor can be called only from `List`:

```
List::List()
{ _rep = new ListRep;
}
```

When a `ListRep` object is constructed, we set the reference count to 1:

```
ListRep::ListRep()
: _rc(1),
  _head(0),
  _length(0)
{}
```

Note that the `List` class contains a single data field—a pointer to the list representation. Objects of type `List` are similar to pointers, but there is an important difference. Since constructors, assignment operators, and destructors can be defined for classes but not for pointers, list objects can automatically update the reference counts.

The `List` user need not be concerned with the fact that reference counts are used to manage lists. In fact, the `List` user never sees the `ListRep` class. All operations are declared on the level of the `List` class:

```
class List
{
public:
  List();
  void insert(int);
  int remove();

  int head() const; // peek at head
  int length() const;

  // ...

  List(const List&);
  const List& operator=(const List&);
  ~List();
private:
  // ...
};
```

The class implementor has to go to some degree of inconvenience to code the operations, since all data fields must be reached by indirecting through the _rep pointer.

```
int List::length() const
{ return _rep->_length;
}

int List::head() const
{ ASSERT_PRECOND(_rep->_head); // cannot peek empty list
  return _rep->_head->_info;
}
```

Naturally, this is not a major concern, because it is outweighed by the benefits to the class user.

13.5.4. Copy on Write

The reference count implementation discussed so far has one disadvantage. Suppose a copy of a list is made and then modified:

```
List a;
a.insert(x);
List b = a;
z = b.remove();
b.insert(y);
```

The changes to the copy b also affect the original list a! Since both a and b share the same data (with reference count 2), any modification through either list object affects the other. This seems unintuitive, and while one might get used to it for simple lists, it really makes no sense when lists are used as building blocks for other classes. Consider, for example, an IndexEntry class

```
class IndexEntry
{
public:
  // ...
  void indent();
private:
  String _phrase; // the phrase to index
  List _page_ref; // the pages on which _phrase occurs
  int _level; // the indentation level
};

void IndexEntry::indent()
{ _level++;
  _page_ref.empty();
}
```

```
IndexEntry a;
// ...
IndexEntry b = a;
b.indent();
```

Then a._level and b._level differ by 1. We would expect that a._page_ref and b._page_ref also differ. But if the representations of the list are shared, the empty() operation empties both lists.

To overcome this problem, we will make a complete copy of the data in those operations that modify the object—that is, operations not declared as const. Of course, that copy is necessary only when the reference count is larger than 1.

A clone function performs the copy when necessary, by invoking the ListRep copy constructor.

```
void List::clone()
{ if (_rep->_rc == 1) return;
  _rep->_rc--;
  _rep = new ListRep(*_rep);
}

ListRep::ListRep(const ListRep& b)
{ _length = b._length;
  Link* p = 0;
  Link* q = b._head;
  while (q != 0)
  { Link* n = new Link;
    n->_next = 0;
    n->_info = q->_info; // copy information
    if (p == 0) // first entry
      _head = n;
    else
      p->_next = n;
    p = n;
    q = q->_next;
  }
}
```

The clone function is called in all destructive list operations.

```
int List::remove()
{ ASSERT_PRECOND(_rep->_head); // cannot remove from empty list
  clone();
  int r = _rep->_head->_info;
  Link* p = _rep->_head;
  _rep->_head = _rep->_head->_next;
  delete p;
```

```
    _rep->_length--;
    return r;
}
```

After the call to `clone`, the operation manipulates its own copy of the list data without disturbing any shared copies. This technique is called *delayed copy* or *copy on write*, because copying is delayed as long as possible. Objects share the information for reading purposes, and copies are made only when necessitated by a write operation.

Exercise 13.5.1. The `ListRep` class has a copy constructor (used in `List::clone`) and a destructor (used in `List::free`), but no assignment operator. Explain why that operator is not needed.

13.5.5. Guidelines for Implementing Reference Counts

Reference counts and copy on write are sophisticated techniques, but once mastered, they can be implemented in a routine fashion. Use the following guidelines.

1. You need two classes, X and XRep.
2. The X class defines all interface operations.
3. The XRep class contains all data fields.
4. The X class contains a pointer XRep* `_rep` and no further data.
5. The XRep class has a reference count unsigned `_rc`.
6. The XRep class has a copy constructor that makes an actual copy of the class data (but is invoked only in `clone` when the reference count is greater than 1) and a destructor that releases any resources (but is called only when the reference count goes to 0).
7. The X class has private `copy`, `free`, `clone` operators that manipulate the reference counts and invoke the XRep destructor and copy constructor as needed. This code is completely routine.
8. The X class has a copy constructor, assignment operator, and destructor that call `copy` and `free`. This code too is completely routine.
9. The X operations access the data fields by indirecting through the `_rep` pointer. This is merely tedious.
10. All destructive operations must call `clone`.

If this is so mechanical, why doesn't the compiler do it for us for all classes? As we will see in the next section, reference counting is a very useful technique in many practical cases, but it is not a universal solution for memory management.

Exercise 13.5.2. Implement the `Figure` class of Exercise 13.2.1 by using reference counting.

Exercise 13.5.3. Implement a queue of integers using reference counting.

13.5.6. Drawbacks of Reference Counts

Reference counting is an excellent storage management for many applications. It does, however, have three drawbacks.

Copying a reference-counted pointer consumes more time than copying a plain pointer. The updating of the reference counts with every construction, copy, assignment, and destruction exacts a performance cost. (Using inline functions makes a measurable difference and is strongly recommended.) In some programming situations, manual deallocation of heap objects or manual release of other resources is not too hard to do, and the gain in performance may be important enough to forgo the added automation and security that reference counts provide.

If some objects can have a huge number of pointers to them, one must be careful not to have the reference count "wrap around" beyond the largest representable value. Instead, these objects must be kept alive forever. Naturally, this situation is rare.

Most importantly, reference counts do not work for complex data structures. If there are cycles in the data structure, as in Figure 3.14, cycles of blocks may never be deallocated, because they "support themselves," although there are no external references to them. In practice, such data structures do occur frequently—for example, in graphs or networks. Fortunately, in many other applications the nature of the problem guarantees the absence of cycles. For example, in a word processor, paragraphs may contain words, equations, graphs, or tables, which themselves may contain other objects, but since each object is made up of strictly smaller ones, no cycle can appear.

To perform automatic deallocation of arbitrary data structures without programmer intervention, full garbage collection is required. Some research has been undertaken to add garbage collection to C++, but at this time no garbage collection facilities are available as part of the language. We recommend the use of reference counting when applicable, and well-encapsulated ad hoc memory management for cyclic containers such as doubly linked lists and graphs.

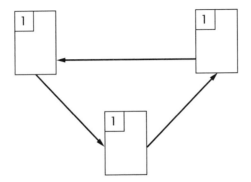

Figure 13.14.   A self-supporting cycle.

13.6. DESIGN HINTS

13.6.1. Agree on Responsibilities with the Class User

When you place a pointer as a data field in a class, you are taking on the responsibility of managing a resource: the memory to which the pointer points. You have to contract with the class user regarding the details. A number of contractual models are reasonable in different circumstances. The important part is that both the class user and the class implementor clearly understand their obligations. As class designer, you need to draft a contract that balances the user's need for convenience with the implementor's need for simplicity.

If the user gives you the pointer value as an argument to a constructor or operation, you must come to an agreement whether you or the user will delete it. If you initialize the pointer, you must either automatically delete it in a destructor or give the user a public operation (such as `free`) to do it manually. If you supply a destructor, you must also supply a copy constructor and assignment operator, or else extract the promise from the users that they will never make a copy of any object.

13.6.2. Avoid Data Fields That Are Pointers

The simplest way of avoiding the morass of destructors, copy constructors, and assignment operators is to use data fields that already know how to copy and destroy themselves. If *all* data fields are of that kind, then the compiler generates a complete and correct set of all memory management operations automatically for you.

Use a string class, not a `char*` pointer. Use a `List`, not a `Link*` pointer. Use an `Array<X>`, not an X* pointer. And, the single most often overlooked possibility: Use an X object, not an X* pointer.

It is impossible to avoid pointers completely in all classes. There are three valid reasons for using them:

- For sharing
- For polymorphism
- For 0|1 relationships

13.6.3. A Class That Has a Destructor Needs
Both a Copy Constructor and an Assignment Operator

If you decide to offer the class user the convenience of automatic cleanup by supplying a destructor, you must decide what to do for object copying. You can prevent it by making the copy constructor and assignment operator private. If you want to allow copying, implement the copy constructor. You can mechanically synthesize the assignment operator from the destructor and the copy constructor using the `free`/`copy` functions.

13.6.4. Polymorphic Types Must Have Virtual Destructors

If you delete a pointer that may point to a base or derived-class object, the base class destructor must be virtual, to ensure correct cleanup of the entire object, not just the base part.

This is a difficult design requirement. How do you know whether a class will have derived classes? If the class has virtual functions, you are sure it has been designed to serve as a base class. Then make the destructor virtual if it exists, or a add a do-nothing virtual destructor otherwise.

If a class has no virtual function, adding one or more virtual functions increases the size of *each* object by one pointer (to the so-called virtual function table). For classes that are small and unlikely candidates for derivation, such as Date, it seems worth the risk not to include a virtual destructor.

Conversely, if you derive from a base class, check that the base class has a virtual destructor.

PARAMETERIZED CLASSES

14.1. TYPE PARAMETERIZATION

If we want to find out how to implement a queue, we can consult a textbook on data structures and most likely will find code for a queue of integers. Of course, a queue of integers is rarely what one needs in actual programming situations. We may need to implement a queue of customers. A mechanical change, replacing all int with Customer, yields a queue class that stores customers instead. Actually one must be somewhat careful. The int in

```
int Queue::remove()
```

must be changed to

```
Customer Queue::remove()
```

but

```
int Queue::length() const
```

should remain unchanged. Of course, queues of objects of entirely different types will be needed in other applications. To avoid the mechanical (and somewhat error-prone) process of adapting and editing existing code, a mechanism is desirable that lets us code the operations for a queue of objects of an arbitrary type, from which queues for specific types can be obtained. In C++, the *template* mechanism serves this purpose.

A generic Queue<T> template has a type parameter T. When that parameter T is replaced with an actual type, say Customer, a class Queue<Customer> results. The process of obtaining a class from a template is called *template instantiation*, shown in Figure 14.1. The class Queue<Customer> behaves like any other class. Objects of that class are declared in the usual way:

```
Queue<Customer> cashier_queue;
```

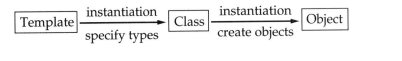

Figure 14.1. Template instantiation

Parameterized types are useful for all containers, such as arrays, linked lists, queues, or hash tables. More generally, templates are useful for all constructs that generalize to arbitrary types.

14.2. USING TEMPLATES

Using a template that has been implemented by someone else is very easy. Just plug in actual types for the type parameters to obtain a class, then use that class as you would any other. The `Array` template that was used throughout this book is a typical example. Other class templates are instantiated in the same way:

```
List<Shape*> display_list;

display_list.insert_tail(new Rectangle(...));

class Mailbox
{ // ...
private:
  Queue<Message> _msg;
};

void Mailbox::append(Message m)
{ _msg.insert(m);
}
```

It is the job of the compiler and linker to ensure that the code for all operations of the instantiated class is produced.

The instantiation type can be any legal C++type.

```
Queue<int>
Queue<Message>
Queue<Event*>
Queue< List<Vehicle*> >
```

Note the spaces in the last example. Omitting the spaces between the >s yields a syntax error:

```
Queue<List<Vehicle*>> // ERROR
```

The >> is parsed as a shift operator—tokenization occurs before any syntactic analysis.

Exercise 14.2.1. Verify that template arguments can have arbitrary type as follows: Build an array a of type Array< Array<double> >. Grow it to hold ten elements, and grow each array inside it to hold ten elements. You effectively have a matrix. Set the (*i*, *j*) element to be *i* + *j* * 0.01. Make a copy b of a. Print the elements in the copy.

Exercise 14.2.2. Write a class HashTable that implements a hash table of strings. To store the strings, use an Array< List<String> >. Use s.hash() to find the hash value of a string s.

14.3. IMPLEMENTING A CLASS TEMPLATE

14.3.1. The Class Interface

The class interface of a parameterized class is the same as that of a regular class, prepended by the keyword template and a list of the template parameters. For the queue example, we need two templates: one each for the link and queue classes.

```
template<class T>
class Link
{
public:
  Link(T, Link<T>* = 0);
private:
  Link<T>* _next;
  T _info;
  friend class Queue<T>;
};

template<class T>
class Queue
{
public:
  Queue();
  void insert(T t);
  T remove();
  int length() const;
private:
  Link<T>* _head;
  Link<T>* _tail;
  int _length;
};
```

The keyword class in

```
template<class T>
```

is a misnomer. T can be any type; it need not be of class type. For example, Queue<Event*> and Queue<int> are legal template instantiations, even though Event* and int are not classes. The designers of the language were merely reluctant to introduce another keyword type to describe this situation accurately.

14.3.2. Implementing Parameterized Operations

Each operation of a class template is prepended by the template keyword. The class name is qualified with the template argument list.

```
template<class T>
void Queue<T>::insert(T t)
{ Link<T>*P = new Link<T>(t, _head);
  if(_tail) _tail -> _next = p;
  else _head = p;
  _tail = p;
  _length ++;
}

template<class T>
T Queue<T>::remove()
{ ASSERT_PRECOND(_head != 0);
  T t = _head->_info;
  Link<T>* n = _head->_next;
  delete _head;
  _head = n;
  if (_head == 0) _tail = 0;
  _length --;
  return t;
}
```

The placement of the <T> is somewhat confusing. They are almost always necessary, but they must be omitted for the names of constructors and destructors.

```
template<class T>
Queue<T>::Queue()
 : _head(0),
   _tail(0),
   _length(0)
{}

template<class T>
Queue<T>::Queue(const Queue<T>& b)
{ copy(b);
}
```

Templates for operations can be inline-replaced.

```
template<class T>
inline int Queue<T>::length() const
{ return _length;
}
```

Exercise 14.3.1. Write a template Pair<X,Y> to store a pair of objects. Here is some sample code:

```
Pair<String, double> p("Harry Hacker", 3.3);
if (p.first() != "Carl Cracker")
  x = p.second();
```

You will need to prefix each definition with template<class X, class Y>.

Exercise 14.3.2. Write a template HashTable<T> to make a hash table of arbitrary class types. Assume that the class T has an operation hash(). Test HashTable<String>.

Exercise 14.3.3. Write a template Map<K, T>. A map stores correspondences between elements of type K and of type T. For example,

```
Map<String, double> salary;
salary.set("Harry Hacker", 33000);
double x = salary.get("Harry Hacker");
```

Implement the map as an array of Pair<K, T>.

14.3.3. Shared Data

Suppose we want the remove operation to return a "zero" element, rather than raising an exception, when it is invoked on an empty queue. We cannot simply return 0.

```
template<class T>
T Queue<T>::remove()
{ if (!_head)
    return 0; // DON'T
  // ...
}
```

If the type T is not an integral or pointer type, there may be no valid conversion from 0 to an object of type T. Instead, we may allocate a static object for this purpose:

```
template<class T>
class Queue
{
  // ...
private:
  static T _defval; // default value
};

template<class T>
T Queue<T>::remove()
{ if (!_head)
    return _defval; // OK
  // ...
}
```

A shared class variable is ideally suited for this purpose. If T is instantiated as a numeric or pointer type, _defval is guaranteed to be initialized with zero. If T is of class type, the default constructor is invoked to initialize it. It is reasonable to assume that the default constructor is most likely to construct a default object. If the class has no default constructor, then instantiation fails.

Shared class variables must be both declared and defined. The definition template has the form

```
template<class T>
T Queue<T>::_defval;
```

Exercise 14.3.4. Ensure that the Map<K, T>::get operation returns a default value if the key is not present.

14.3.4. Changing a Class to a Parameterized Class

Rather than developing a class template from scratch, it is usually easier first to write and debug an individual instantiation and then to add the template keywords and type arguments. For example, start with a queue of floating-point numbers (why not integers?)

```
class Queue
{
public:
  void insert(double t);
  double remove();
  int length() const;
private:
  // ...
};
```

After testing, replace all double with T and prepend template<class T> before the definition of the class and of each operation.

Exercise 14.3.5. Carry out this process to change a stack of floating-point numbers into a stack template holding objects of any type.

Exercise 14.3.6. Implement a Queue<T> template, representing a queue as a sequence of links with pointers to the first and last link. Of course, you will need to supply a copy constructor, assignment operator, and destructor.

14.4. TEMPLATE PARAMETERS

14.4.1. Multiple Type Parameters

Templates can have more than one type parameter. A common example is a *map* or *associative array*, a data structure for storing associations.

```
Map<String, int> age;
age.set("Harry Hacker", 10);
String name;
int a = age.get(name);
```

The map template depends on two types: the type of the key and of the value.

```
template<class K, class V>
class Map
{
public:
  void set(const K& key, const V& value);
  V get(const K& key) const;
  // ...
};
```

14.4.2. Nontype Parameters

Besides types, templates can be parameterized by integer values known at compile time. Arrays of fixed size are the most useful application:

```
template<class T, int LO, int HI>
class FixedArray
{
public:
  T& operator[](int);
  T operator[](int) const;
private:
  T _elements[HI-LO+1];
};
```

```
template<class T, int LO, int HI>
T& FixedArray<T, LO, HI>::operator[](int i)
{ ASSERT_BOUNDS(LO <= i && i <= HI);
  return _elements[i - LO];
}

FixedArray<Point, 1, 10> a;
```

These arrays are just like C arrays, but without the hassle:

- The [] operators perform range checking.
- The lower bound does not have to be 0.
- FixedArrays are copied by value.

Since the size of the array is known at compile time, it is allocated on the stack, without free store overhead.

Exercise 14.4.1. Implement the FixedArray template. Explain why copy constructor, assignment operator, and destructor are not needed.

14.5. FUNCTION TEMPLATES

In C++, we can define templates of both operations and regular functions. The classical example for the latter is

```
template<class T>
inline T max(T a, T b)
{ return a > b ? a : b;
}

unsigned long x, y, z;
z = max(x, y);
```

For function templates, instantiation is much more difficult for the compiler than for class templates. There are no <...> to aid the compiler in the selection of the template. In fact, there may be any number of overloaded nontemplate max functions defined as well, and the compiler may need to make a heroic effort to find the correct one. In practice, very few functions are general enough to be parameterized in this way.

The most useful application for function templates is to define functions that operate on class template instantiations when an operation template is not appropriate. For example, consider this template to print the contents of a queue.

```
template<class T>
ostream& operator<<(ostream& os, const Queue<T>& q)
{ // ...
}
```

```
Queue<Customer> q;
os << q;
    // invokes operator<<(ostream&, const Queue<Customer>&)
```

Exercise 14.5.1. Write an operator template

```
ostream& operator<<(ostream&, Array<T>)
```

that prints all the elements in the array. Assume that operator<<(ostream&, T) is defined for the type T.

14.6. SPECIALIZATION

Occasionally, templates for classes or functions generate the correct code for almost all cases. It is possible to override the template-generated code by providing separate definitions for specific types.
    For example, the max template

```
template<class T>
inline T max(T a, T b)
{ return a > b ? a : b;
}
```

does not work correctly on C character strings.

```
max("Harry", "Hacker")
```

instantiates max(const char*, const char*), which compares the addresses of the strings. To obtain lexicographic comparison in this case, we can supplement the template by a specialization:

```
const char* max(const char* a, const char* b)
{ return strcmp(a, b) > 0 ? a : b;
}
```

Specialization can be used either to correct the general template behavior in special circumstances or to supply more efficient implementations for certain types, typically for the simple built-in types.

14.7. INSTANTIATION

14.7.1. The Instantiation Mechanism

The template mechanism is designed to be easy for the programmer to use, but it is definitely not easy on the compiler. When a class template is used, the compiler must locate the template definition and construct the layout for the instantiated class. When one class template uses another, as for example the Queue template uses the Link template, that template too needs to be instantiated.

Whenever a template operation or template function is used in a program, the compiler must locate the template code, generate code with the actual types, and place that code with the program's object code. Since a template function may well call other template functions, this code instantiation must be carried out recursively until all needed code is generated. Finally, some mechanism needs to be in place to make sure that multiple copies of the same instantiated code do not end up in the executable program.

Some compilers simply generate code for *all* operations of an instantiated class, whether or not they are used in a program. That eliminates the need for recursively determining which operations are actually needed, but it unnecessarily increases the size of the executable program.

14.7.2. Instantiation Failure

In writing a parameterized class, the type parameters are not constrained. However, the code may not instantiate properly for some types. Suppose we attempt to build a queue of `ostream` objects:

```
Queue<ostream> osqueue;
```

A number of operations will fail to instantiate, among them

```
ostream Queue<ostream>::remove()
{ // ...
  return t;
}
```

To return an `ostream` object, a copy constructor is required, but the copy constructor for `ostream` is private and hence not accessible.

This does not prohibit us from writing the Queue<T> template. It merely means that we cannot instantiate it with the type `ostream`. If instantiation is attempted, the compiler will refuse. This is called *instantiation failure*.

Actually, the instantiation strategy of the compiler, which at the time of this writing has not yet been standardized, affects the success or failure of instantiation. If the compiler generates code for all operations as soon as it instantiates a class, failure will occur immediately when an object of type Queue<ostream> is allocated. If the compiler instantiates code only for those operations that are actually used, instantiation fails only if the Queue<ostream>::remove operation (or another operation requiring a copy constructor) is called.

Exercise 14.7.1. Try instantiating `Array<ostream>`. What error messages do you get?

14.7.3. Instantiation Requirements

The fact that we cannot build queues of `ostream` objects is not serious. To get objects into and out of containers, we must require that the objects have a copy constructor. (To queue streams, one can use a `Queue<ostream*>`.) This requirement is not an explicit part of the `Queue` template, but it is implicit in the code of its operations.

It is important to make the requirements for instantiations explicit by a comment in the template for the class definition:

```
template<class T>
class Queue
/* RECEIVES: T - any type supporting copy construction
*/
{
  // ...
};
```

Containers such as arrays and queues typically require support for copy construction (to get objects into and out of the container), assignment (to move items within a container), and default construction (to initialize empty slots).

Instantiation requirements can get more complex if objects in a container need to be identified. Consider the `Map` class:

```
Map<String, int> age;
age.set("Harry Hacker", 10);
// ...
age.set("Harry Hacker", 20);
```

The first insertion must add a new *(key, value)* pair. The second insertion with the same key must find out that the key is already present, and change the associated value. This requires a mechanism for comparing keys.

```
template<class K, class V>
class Map
{
public:
  void set(K key, V value);
  V get(K key) const;
  // ...
private:
  Array<K> _key;
  Array<V> _value;
};

template<class K, class V>
void Map<K,V>::set(k, v)
{ Bool found = FALSE;
  for (int i = _key.low(); !found && i <= _key.high(); i++)
  { if (k == _key[i]) found = TRUE;
```

```
    }
    // ...
}
```

The code for the `set` operation introduces an implicit requirement, namely that the type K support comparison with the `==` operation. If K is instantiated with `String`, this is not a problem. But K is more likely to be of some class type, for example

```
Map<Employee, double> salary;
```

If no `operator==` has been defined for the class `Employee`, instantiation will fail, perhaps surprising the user of the `Map` template.

To reduce surprises, it is important that the template document what it expects of its type arguments.

```
template<class K, class V>
class Map
/* PURPOSE:   a table of key/value associations
     RECEIVES: K - any type supporting copy construction and ==
               V - any type supporting copy construction
*/
{
    // ...
};
```

14.7.4. Specifying the Behavior of Instantiation Types

For large maps, linear search is unacceptable. Binary search requires that the keys support a linear ordering. In writing the template, code must be chosen to make instantiation succeed for the largest number of cases.

We could require that K support an operation

```
int K::compare(const K& b) const
```

that returns a negative number if `self` is less than b, zero if they are identical, and a positive number otherwise. The template code for the binary search can then use that operation:

```
if (_key[i].compare(k) < 0) ...
```

Alternatively, we can require that K support the < operator:

```
if (_key[i] < k) ...
```

Requiring an operation with a specific name (such as `compare` or `hash`) is a bad idea. It is then impossible to instantiate the template with nonclass types such as pointers. For example, instantiation of Map<Employee*, double> must fail, because key[i].compare(k) then invokes the dot operator on a pointer—a syntax error. Even for classes, it is generally not possible to add new operations. Restricting the use of the Map template to those classes that already have an operation named compare is undesirable.

The second solution, requiring an overloaded < operator, is better, since overloaded operators need not be operations and can be added without touching the definition of the key class. For example, if Map<Employee, double> is desired, it is easy to supply a suitable

```
Bool operator<(Employee, Employee)
```

However, for nonclass types, < is already defined. In particular, for pointers it denotes comparison of their memory locations (provided they point to the same array). It is not possible to override this behavior through overloading. If we rely on the < operation for binary search, instantiation will succeed if K is a pointer type, but the generated code will be wrong.

A third possibility is to require that the user of the Map function supply a regular function, not an operation, with a specific name, say compare. The template code uses that function

```
if (compare(_key[i], k) < 0) ...
```

This makes using the template somewhat cumbersome—a specific function for comparing elements must be coded. To instantiate Map<String, int>, the user must supply

```
int compare(String a, String b)
{ if (a < b) return -1;
  if (a > b) return 1;
  return 0;
}
```

It also means that all maps with a given key type must use the same ordering. In practice, it might be desirable to compare employees lexicographically by name in some situations and by ID number in others. But there can be only one function

```
int compare(Employee, Employee)
```

in a program.

The possibilities we considered—requiring an operation with a fixed name, an overloaded operator, or a function with a fixed name—attempt to solve the problem of defining a total ordering for the key type on the *template* level, in a uniform way for all possible instantiation types. A template designer may decide that this is not reasonable and have the sort order defined on the *class* or *object* level instead.

A class-level solution requires specification of a comparison function for each instantiated Map class. This is best done through specialization. The class template declares, but does not define, a static function for comparison:

```
template<class K, class V>
class Map
{
public:
  static int compare(const K&, const K&);
  // ...
};
```

When the template is instantiated, a specialized definition of the function must also be supplied.

```
int Map<String, int>::compare(const String& a,
  const String& b)
{ if (a < b) return -1;
  if (a > b) return 1;
  return 0;
}
```

This comparison function is used for all maps of type Map<String, int>.

Note one advantage of this method—the name of the comparison function is now in the name space of the Map template, not in the global name space.

Alternatively, an implementation can provide a choice of comparison functions at the object level. Each instance of Map<K, V> can have its own comparison function. The comparison function must be supplied in the constructor:

```
template<class K, class V>
class Map
{
public:
  Map(int (*)(const K&, const K&));
  // ...
};

int comp_id(const Employee& a, const Employee& b)
{ return a.id() - b.id();
}

Map<Employee, double> salary(comp_id);
  // construct with pointer to comparison function
```

Exercise 14.7.2. Implement three versions for a template HashTable<T>, in which you supply the hash function on the template, class, and object level. Show the instantiation of HashTable<String> in each of the three cases.

14.8. SMART POINTERS

14.8.1. Interface

Every programmer knows that pointer errors can cause severe problems and may be difficult to debug. As we will see in Chapter 15, pointers interact poorly with exceptions, because it is not possible to attach destructors to them. In this section we will implement a template that generates classes whose objects act like pointers, except that they are smart enough to clean up after themselves. We use reference counting to keep track of the number of smart pointers pointing to an object. The type SmartPtr<X> is a reference-counting pointer to X, a smart X*.

To make smart pointers behave like regular pointers, we overload the * and -> operators. To manage the reference counts, we supply the copy constructor, assignment operator, and destructor.

```
template<class X>
class SmartPtr
/* PURPOSE:  reference-counting pointer
      RECEIVES: X - any class type supporting copy construction
*/
{
public:
   SmartPtr(); // makes null pointer
   SmartPtr(const X& x); // makes pointer to copy of x

   X& operator*();
   const X& operator*() const;
   X* operator->();
   const X* operator->() const;

   SmartPtr(const SmartPtr<X>&);
   const SmartPtr<X>& operator=(const SmartPtr<X>&);
   ~SmartPtr();

private:
   // ...
};
```

This class implements a smart pointer to an object of type X. The object itself is located on the heap.

Here is how to use it. Don't call new to make a new object, because new returns a dumb pointer. Instead, use the following syntax:

```
SmartPtr<Employee> p = Employee("Harry Hacker", 2536);
```

Thanks to the overloaded operators, p behaves like a regular pointer:

```
cout << *p;
p->raise _salary(0.05);
```

You can copy them around and don't even have to keep track of the copy:

```
SmartPtr<Employee> q = p;
```

When you are done with p, simply forget it. Don't call **delete**; that's for deleting dumb pointers. When p and all of its copies have gone away, the object memory is automatically recycled.

These smart pointers have a number of advantages over regular pointers. They are guaranteed to be initialized as either null pointers or pointers to a heap object. Indirection through a null pointer is checked. No **delete** is ever necessary. Objects are automatically freed when the last pointer to them has gone away. (As always, reference counting cannot reclaim cyclic garbage.)

However, there is one significant problem with these smart pointers. Unlike regular pointers, they do not respect inheritance. Suppose Manager is derived from Employee. The compiler automatically converts a Manager* to an Employee*, but SmartPtr<Manager> and SmartPtr<Employee> are completely unrelated types. This makes smart pointers unattractive for polymorphic code.

14.8.2. Implementation

The following Wrapper class template wraps the object together with a reference count:

```
template<class X>
class Wrapper
/* PURPOSE: wrap X object with reference count
     RECEIVES: X - any type supporting copy construction
*/
{
private:
   Wrapper(const X& x); // sets _obj to copy of x

   X _obj;
   unsigned _rc;

   friend class SmartPtr<X>;
};
```

A smart pointer object points to a wrapper (see Figure 14.2).

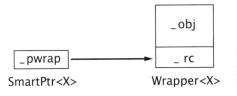

Figure 14.2. A smart pointer pointing to a wrapper object.

Copy constructor, destructor, and assignment operator manipulate the reference counts in the usual way.

```
template<class X>
class SmartPtr
{
  // ...
private:
  void copy(const SmartPtr<X>& b);
  void free();
  Wrapper<X>* _pwrap;
};

template<class X>
void SmartPtr<X>::copy(const SmartPtr<X>& b)
{ if (_pwrap) _pwrap->_rc++;
}

template<class X>
void SmartPtr<X>::free()
{ if (_pwrap)
  { _pwrap->_rc--;
    if (_pwrap->_rc == 0) delete _pwrap;
  }
}
```

The overloaded operators give access to the object inside the wrapper. Note the curious unary -> operator that returns a pointer to an object. The overloaded -> operator is special and quite different from all other operators. The expression p->m means to get the result from p.operator->(), which should be an expression on which ->m makes sense. The -> is actually taken twice: p->m is (p.operator->())->m.

```
template<class X>
X& SmartPtr<X>::operator*()
{ ASSERT_PRECOND(_pwrap); // cannot indirect through 0 pointer
  return _pwrap->_obj;
}

template<class X>
X* SmartPtr<X>::operator->()
{ ASSERT_PRECOND(_pwrap); // cannot indirect through 0 pointer
  return &_pwrap->_obj;
}
```

The const versions of these operators perform the identical actions but act on const SmartPtr<X>.

The default constructor makes a null pointer.

```
template<class X>
SmartPtr<X>::SmartPtr()
: _pwrap(0)
{}
```

Construction of a pointer to an object on the heap is not so simple. Because there is no way of replicating the constructors for the variable type X in the Wrapper<X> template, one must first construct a value on the stack, then copy it inside the wrapper.

```
template<class X>
Wrapper<X>::Wrapper(const X& x)
: _obj(x),
  _rc(1)
{}

template<class X>
SmartPtr<X>::SmartPtr(const X& x)
: _pwrap(new Wrapper<X>(x))
{}
```

Exercise 14.8.1. In the best tradition of C, our SmartPtr class imitates the implementation of real pointers, not their conceptual use. As we pointed out before, there are three distinct design reasons to choose pointers: sharing, 0 | 1 relationships, and polymorphism. It makes more sense to have three pointer templates: Shared<X>, Optional<X>, and Polymorphic<X>. Reference semantics is appropriate only for shared pointers. Optional and polymorphic objects would be more intuitive with value semantics. As we indicated, the template mechanism makes it awkward to do a credible implementation of polymorphic smart pointers. But it is easy enough to implement Optional<X>. The key here is value semantics. Consider an optional date, for example for death or termination.

```
Optional<Date> d1; // either blank or a date
Optional<Date> d2 = d1; // either blank or the same as d1
```

Implement the Optional<X> smart pointer template. Overload -> and * to gain access to the features of X. Use copy on write.

Exercise 14.8.2. Put the Optional smart pointer from the previous exercise to work. Implement a Link<X> for a queue to hold an X value and an optional pointer to the next link, Optional< Link<X> >. A Queue<X> contains an optional pointer to the head link. Implement the queue operations. The remarkable aspect of this queue implementation is that copying is automatic! No copy constructor, destructor, or assignment operator is required.

We don't advocate this approach for frequently used data structures like queues, because it is obviously not efficient. (For example, the automatic copy constructor is highly recursive.) However, it is reasonable for higher-level classes, where reliability and maintainability are more important than raw speed.

14.9. DESIGN HINTS

14.9.1. Clearly State Requirements for Instantiation Types

Virtually all templates require that instantiation classes be copiable and have a default constructor. Nevertheless, the requirement must be stated. If your template requires that the type argument be a class and not a numeric or pointer type, state that. Some templates require that the class argument derive from a fixed base class such as Persistent.

Be explicit about any operations, functions, or operator symbols that must work on objects of the instantiation type. Many templates require that os << x, x == y, or x < y be defined.

14.9.2. Minimize Dependencies on External Names or Operators

If your template performs output with << or comparison with <, it is useless for those operations that do not have << or < defined or, even worse, that have them defined to do something different from what you need in the template. The same holds for global functions like hash and compare. They can be defined only once. If you want to sort an array of employees in two ways, you cannot specify two global compare functions comparing employees.

If you compute a hash value with x.hash(), the template can be used only for class objects. If x is not an object, applying the hash operation is an instant syntax error. Even if x is of class type, the class may not have a hash operation. If the instantiator doesn't own the class, it is not possible to retrofit it. Unless your template is intended only for objects that inherit from some common base class, never invoke any operation on the instantiation objects.

The best way of specifying functions for comparison, hashing, printing, and other tasks is through function pointer arguments to the constructor or a specific operation (like sort). This is admittedly cumbersome for the user, but it maximizes the usability of the template.

14.9.3. Consider Building a Separate Template for Pointers

We can build *much* more efficient container templates if we know that the entries must be pointers. It therefore makes a lot of sense to offer a second template for that purpose. PtrArray<X> does just the same as Array<X*>, just more efficiently.

The efficiency gain comes from two areas. Construction, copying, and destruction of pointers is trivial: initialize, copy bitwise, and forget. It is *much* more efficient to call memcpy to move an array of pointers than it is to invoke a copy constructor for each entry in an array. Furthermore, we can use inheritance and derive a `PtrArray<X>` from an `Array<void*>`. That way, the array operations are coded only once, for the `void*` container. The X* container just makes inline calls to the base. This can dramatically reduce code size.

However, `void*` pointers should be avoided in the debug version. They make it impossible for the programmer to inspect the contents of containers during debugging. The best solution is to provide a debug version, with separate template code for each pointer type, and a release version, which maps to `void*`.

C H A P T E R   15

EXCEPTION
HANDLING

15.1. ERRORS AND EXCEPTIONS

Programmers must deal with error conditions and exceptional situations. Several error types are commonly encountered.

- *User input errors.* A user enters input that does not follow the syntactic or semantic rules of the application. For example, the user may ask to delete a filename that does exist, to drag the desktop into the trashcan, or to compile a program with syntax errors. An interactive program can typically inform the user of the problem and await further input. A program reading data from a file, such as a compiler, must report the error to a file or the display terminal and then either abort or try to go on processing.

- *Device errors.* Serial ports may be unavailable. A printer may be turned off. Such errors may cause a program task to be aborted or suspended until the problem is fixed. Devices may fail in the middle of a task. For example, a printer may run out of paper in the middle of a printout. It may be necessary for a program to abort just the print task and return control to the user, without exiting the program.

- *Physical limitations.* Disks can fill up, and available memory can become exhausted.

- *Component failures.* A function or class may perform incorrectly and deliver wrong answers or use other functions or classes incorrectly. Computing an invalid array index and trying to pop an empty stack are examples of this kind.

Most errors are unpleasant to handle. The programmer should not just abort the program with an assertion failure; the user may lose all work performed during the program session. Instead, the program must at least notify the user, save all work, and exit gracefully. But the code that detects the error condition is usually in no position to accomplish this. For example, the copy constructor of a linked list class may find that memory allocation fails because all memory is exhausted. Obviously, the list class has no information how to shut down an application. The transfer of control from the point of error detection to a competent error handler is the central problem of exception handling.

15.2. REACTION TO ERROR CONDITIONS

What should an operation do when it detects that memory is exhausted or when it is asked to do the impossible, such as popping a value off an empty stack? A number of strategies are available.

15.2.1. Returning an Error Code

Some data types, such as pointers, offer an easy way of distinguishing valid from invalid data. Suppose a function reads shapes from a stream. When the end of the file is reached, no further shape is available. This situation can be communicated easily by returning either a pointer to a new shape or a null pointer:

```
Shape* read_shape(istream&);
```

Similarly, a function returning a string may return the empty string to denote failure.

It is more difficult to return an error code if there is no obvious way of distinguishing valid from invalid data. A function returning an integer cannot simply return 0 to denote error—the value 0 might be a perfectly valid value. A function reading employee records may not easily return a null employee at the end of the file.

```
Employee read_employee(istream&); // return what at end of file?
```

It is always possible to write functions to return an explicit Boolean error code and return any result through a reference parameter:

```
Bool read_employee(istream&, Employee&);
```

Returning an error code is a good practice, especially for those operations that are known to fail eventually, such as reading data from a file or fetching elements from a queue.

15.2.2. Ignoring the Error

Suppose a queue of integers is implemented as a fixed-size circular array:

```
class Queue
{
public:
```

```
    void add(int);
    int remove();
    Bool is_full() const;
    Bool is_empty() const;
    // ...
};
```

What should the add operation do if the queue is already full? Presumably the precondition of add is !is_full(), and the operation can do whatever pleases it. It may choose simply to do nothing. (Since this particular operation has no return value, we could change it to return TRUE on success. Then again, if the caller didn't bother to check is_full() before adding to the queue, it isn't likely that the return value will be checked either.)

Doing nothing is not always easy, especially for functions that return a value. Consider the invocation of remove on an empty queue. The precondition of remove is !is_empty(), and the caller should always first check whether a queue is nonempty before removing a value from it. If the caller fails to do so, the remove function can return any value that it likes, such as 0 or INT_MAX.

For integers, such a value is usually easy to find, even though it is not distinguishable from a legal value. But suppose it is a queue of customers. The function cannot return 0 unless there happens to be a constructor Customer(int). It could return whatever object the default constructor generates, if there is a default constructor.

Of course, there are many situations when doing nothing is not feasible. If the copy constructor of a list class finds that there isn't enough memory to form the copy, it cannot simply ignore the problem. After all, it isn't the class user's error if memory is exhausted.

Doing nothing when asked to do the wrong thing can be a reasonable strategy. During debug mode, an assertion failure can be triggered instead.

Exercise 15.2.1. Implement the queue as a circular array of fixed size. Use the ASSERT_PRECOND assertion on underflow and overflow, but also supply a reasonable continuation of the operations in those cases. Test the error behavior with debugging on (the default) and debugging off (the NDEBUG preprocessor variable defined).

15.2.3. Setting an Error Variable

A time-honored error-handling strategy is to set a global variable when an error is discovered. For example, mathematical functions in the standard C library set an integer variable errno to the constant EDOM or ERANGE if a domain error (such as sqrt of a negative number) or range error (over- or underflow) is discovered:

```
double sqrt(double x)
{ if (x < 0)
    { errno = EDOM;
      return 0;
```

```
    }
    // ...
}
```

This is not a very useful mechanism. The error report contains only the type of error, not the name of the offending function or the value of the argument. Furthermore, if two errors occur in rapid succession, the second one will overwrite the reporting of the first one.

Properly monitoring the error variable is therefore dreadfully inconvenient. Each call to a mathematical function must be checked.

```
errno = 0;
y = sqrt(x);
if (errno != 0) // ...
```

In a correctly written program, domain errors on mathematical functions should never happen, or at least happen only in very exceptional situations. Monitoring an error variable requires that every call to a function that might report an error is complemented by a check against it, making the coding effort entirely disproportionate to the likelihood of the error.

Exercise 15.2.2. Try out `errno` by calling `sqrt(-1)` and `exp(1000)`. What is the value of `errno` when you evaluate `sqrt(-1) + exp(1000)`? (You may need to tell the run-time system to ignore floating-point errors rather than abort the program; use `signal(SIGFPE, SIG_IGN)`.)

15.2.4. Printing an Error Message

Printing a message reporting an error is reasonable in student programs and for debugging only. Users of commercial software programs get extremely perturbed when a product emits error messages that are incomprehensible to them and whose remedy is beyond their power. What would you do if your game program notified you "Warning: Cannot add to full queue" and then kept on playing, maybe with one less game piece?

Of course, users may be asked to cure those error conditions that are within their power to remedy, such as closing a disk drive door, turning on a printer, or, in a multitasking system, closing other applications or deleting unnecessary files to obtain more memory or disk space.

15.2.5. Aborting the Program

When debugging a simple program, there is nothing wrong with printing a diagnostic message and aborting. For real products, though, a simple abort is unacceptable. A user who has spent hours creating data with a program cannot afford to lose all work when a program aborts spontaneously on an internal error condition.

At the very least, a program should save all work on disk and remove any temporary files before aborting.

15.2.6. Jumping to an Error Handler

It is generally difficult to handle an error at the location of its discovery. When memory exhaustion is noticed in a constructor of a class, one cannot easily bail out and save all work right in that constructor procedure. Instead, the procedure must be abandoned, and error recovery must be initiated elsewhere.

C programs often use a nonlocal jump, implemented through the `setjmp` and `longjmp` functions, to transfer control to a body of code that can deal with errors and communicate with the program user.

However, these functions are incompatible with C++, because a `longjmp` simply abandons a portion of the stack without calling the destructors of stack objects. If those destructors merely close files and free memory, it is possible to use `longjmp` to go to a rescue point, save all work, and exit. But if some destructors manage other system resources that are not freed by the operating system on process death, that approach is not viable. Clearly, no retry is possible either.

C++ code should not use `setjmp/longjmp`. The C++ exception mechanism, which will be explained in Section 15.4, is the appropriate mechanism to transfer control to an error handler.

15.2.7. Raising a Signal

In many operating systems, processes can react to asynchronous error conditions such as a user abort request (by hitting [Ctrl+C], by killing a process, and so forth) or processor error (segment fault, illegal instruction, floating-point error). Using the `signal` function, a C program specifies a handler procedure to be called in such instances. (If no signal handler is specified, the program aborts.)

It is possible to raise a signal explicitly and transfer control to that error procedure, using the `raise` function, but this is not usually a good mechanism for error handling. There is very little a signal handler can do. Since it can be invoked asynchronously, the process may be in a completely unstable state, and it is doubtful whether the user's work can even be safely saved because the data structures may be left in the middle of an update, containing invalid references.

Signals should be used for their intended purpose only: namely, to handle catastrophic external events.

15.2.8. Raising an Exception

C++ has a convenient and safe mechanism to raise exceptions when errors are detected and to transfer both control and error information to code that is competent to deal with the situation. This exception handling scheme will be discussed subsequently.

15.3. ERROR HANDLER FUNCTIONS

As we saw in the previous section, an operation that finds an error condition can react to it in a number of ways. However, no one of them may be appropriate in all circumstances. For this reason, classes often support user-installable handler functions. A default handler provides some action, usually printing a message and aborting the program. However, the user can install another function—for example, to record the error message in a file and continue processing, or to raise an exception.

Here is a simple stack class with a user-installable error handler.

```
typedef void (*ErrorFun)(String);

class Stack
{
public:
  Stack();
  double pop();
  void push(double);
  Bool is_empty() const;

  static ErrorFun set_handler(ErrorFun);
private:
  Array<double> _s;
  int _sptr;

  static void default_handler(String);
  static ErrorFun _errfun;
};
```

A handler can be installed with the `set_handler` function. This function returns the old handler, and it is considered good form to restore the original handler on completion.

```
ofstream errfile; // file for error messages

void my_handler(String s)
{ errfile << "Stack: " << s << endl;
  exit(1);
}

ErrorFun old_handler = Stack::set_handler(my_handler);
// ...
x = s.pop(); // underflow calls my_handler
// ...
Stack::set_handler(old_handler);
```

The implementation is straightforward. The stack class contains a static variable that holds the pointer to the current error function. That variable is initialized to point to a default handler:

```
void Stack::default_handler(String s)
{ cerr << "Stack: " << s << endl;
  exit(1);
}
```

```
ErrorFun Stack::_errfun = Stack::default_handler;
```

The set_handler function returns the old handler and installs a new one:

```
ErrorFun Stack::set_handler(ErrorFun newerr)
{ ErrorFun olderr = _errfun;
  _errfun = newerr;
  return olderr;
}
```

Whenever an error is detected, the error handler is called:

```
double Stack::pop()
{ if (_sptr <= 0)
  { (*_errfun)("Stack underflow");
    return 0;
  }
  _sptr--;
  return _s[_sptr];
}
```

The pointer to the current handler and the set_handler function are shared class functions of the Stack class. All stack objects share the same handler. It would be possible to give each stack its own handler, but that does not appear useful in practice.

Exercise 15.3.1. Add an error handler to the Queue class of exercise 15.2.2. Test three handlers: doing nothing, aborting the program, and logging error messages to a file.

15.4. EXCEPTIONS

15.4.1. Raising an Exception

A feature for the structured handling of error conditions has recently been added to the C++ language.

When an error is encountered that cannot be handled at the point of detection, an exception can be raised with the command

```
throw e;
```

Here *e* can be any value, such as an integer or string,

```
throw "Stack underflow"; // not useful
```

but it is far more common to throw objects of special exception classes.

```
throw StackError(self, "Stack underflow"); // OK
```

Throwing objects of error classes is the right thing to do for two reasons. As we will see shortly, error handlers specify the type of the exception object with which they are willing to deal. One can usefully provide a handler for StackError, but it is unlikely that a handler for int or strings can do more than report the error and give up. And error objects allow the program to carry an arbitrary amount of information conveniently from the locus of detection to the error handler.

When a function throws an exception, a search for a handler is initiated. *The function does not return in the normal way*:

```
int Stack::pop()
{ if (_sptr <= 0)
     throw StackError(self, "Stack underflow");
  _sptr--;
  return _s[_sptr];
}
```

If an empty stack is popped and the throw statement is executed, the function execution terminates immediately. It does not return any value. That is good; the programmer need not worry about supplying a fake return value.

The caller of a function that raises exceptions cannot rely on the function call succeeding. If an empty stack is popped,

```
n = stack.pop();
cout << n << endl; // not executed if stack is empty
```

the operation does not return a value, and subsequent code is not executed. Instead, execution transfers to the error handler.

15.4.2. Handling an Exception

Exception handlers are specified with try blocks:

```
try
{ code
}
catch (StackError s)
{ // stack is empty, or other stack error
  // s contains error information
  handler code
}
```

The code in the try block is executed. That code may involve any sequence of statements, including loops or function calls. If anywhere during execution a stack error is reported, the code in the handler gains control.

It is not generally useful simply to wrap a `try` block around a function call that might raise an exception. Consider this call to pop.

```
try // DON'T
{ n = stack.pop();
}
catch (StackError s)
{ // ...
}
```

We can check for an empty stack with far less hassle:

```
if (!stack.is_empty()) n = stack.pop();
```

It is much more useful to check for errors that may occur anywhere in a subsystem:

```
try
{ read(is); // read in a file; parsing involves stack
}
catch (StackError s)
{ // report syntax error in input file
    // and close file
}
```

This example illustrates the transfer of control from the point of detection to a point of competent handling. The stack module can only report a stack overflow. It cannot close the input file. The error handler is located at a point where it is clear that the cause of the error is an improper input file. The handler has access to the input file and perhaps a user interface and can report the problem in a way that makes sense to the program user.

Exercise 15.4.1. Write a class `QueueError` and modify the queue class of Exercise 15.2.2 to throw an exception of that type on error. Catch the exception in `main`.

Exercise 15.4.2. In the queue class of Exercise 15.3.1, install a handler that throws a `QueueError` object.

15.4.3. Handling Multiple Exceptions

A `try` block can handle multiple exceptions:

```
try
{ code
}
catch (StackError s)
```

```
{ // stack is empty, or other stack error
  // s contains error information
  handler code
}
catch (MathError m)
{ handler code
}
```

If the code in the `try` block causes either a stack error or a math error, the appropriate handler is activated. If a different exception is raised, it must be caught by a handler elsewhere.

Exceptions are caught by their type—you throw objects and catch classes.

Exercise 15.4.3. Write two functions a (making an array error by accessing an out-of-range element) and q (making a queue error). In `main`, call randomly either a or q. Catch both `BoundsError` and `QueueError` and print a message in the handler.

15.4.4. Exception Hierarchies

Since exception handlers specify the type of the exception they are able to handle, it is often useful to layer exception classes using an inheritance hierarchy.

For example, we can derive specialized error types from `MathError` (see Figure 15.1):

```
class DomainError : public MathError { /* ... */ };
class RangeError : public MathError { /* ... */ };
```

A domain error signifies an attempt to evaluate a function at an argument that is not in its domain, such as the square root or logarithm of a negative number. A range error denotes over- or underflow of the result.

```
try
{ code
}
catch (DomainError& e)
{ // function applied to argument not in domain
  handler code
```

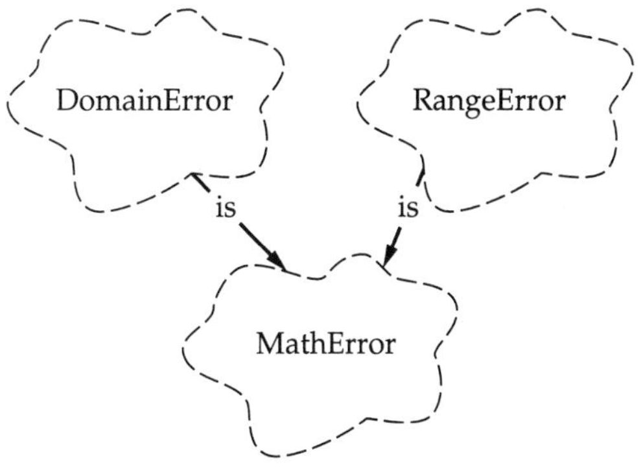

Figure 15.1. A hierarchy of math errors.

```
}
catch (MathError& e)
{ // some other math error
    handler code
}
```

All math errors that are not domain error type are handled by the second `catch` clause. Note that we catch the exception by reference, to avoid truncation to the base class. It is then possible to access derived-class information by invoking a virtual function.

Exercise 15.4.4. Derive `QueueOverflow` and `QueueUnderflow` from `QueueError`. Make a virtual function `print`. Throw the specific errors in the queue code. Catch them in `main` as `QueueError&` and invoke the virtual `print` operation.

15.4.5. Catch All and Rethrow

Occasionally, you want to catch any exceptions that fly past a certain point, just to take some cleanup or protective action.

```
try
{ // ...
}
catch(...) // some error occurred; this form will catch any exception
{ // evasive action
    throw;
}
```

The `throw` command without an argument inside a `catch` clause throws the current error again. You should rethrow any caught error that you don't know how to handle (or better, not catch it in the first place).

  If an exception is not caught anywhere at all, the program is aborted.

Exercise 15.4.5. Write a function `int read(ifstream& is, Queue& q)` that opens a file, reads integers from the file, and places them in the queue. If an exception occurs, close the file and rethrow the exception. If all numbers fit in the queue, also close the file and return the count of the numbers read.

15.4.6. Stack Unwinding

The most important action of the exception-handling mechanism is the "stack walk". All objects on the stack between the throw and catch point (see Figure 15.2) are properly destroyed by invoking their destructors. This activity is of crucial importance. Normally, objects on the stack are destroyed when execution reaches the end of the block in which they are declared. But when an exception is raised, the linear flow of execution stops and control is transferred to the nearest handler that can catch the type of the exception object. It is guaranteed that all destructors of abandoned stack objects are invoked.

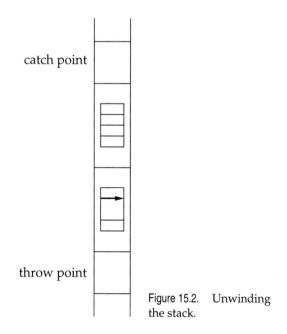

catch point

throw point

Figure 15.2.   Unwinding the stack.

In particular, if an error (say, out of memory) is detected inside a *constructor*, all subobjects that have already been constructed are destroyed, rolling back the entire construction process.

If a destructor that is invoked while an exception is pending itself raises an exception, the program terminates. It is therefore highly recommended that destructors never throw exceptions.

The stack walk must take great care to invoke destructors of previously constructed objects, because the program may continue indefinitely after the exception is handled. When a program aborts, the orderly reclamation of all resources is less important, but the purpose of exception handling is to have the handler provide a remedy and continue execution.

Exercise 15.4.6. Use the list class with tracing messages in the destructor from the exercises of Chapter 13 to verify that an exception causes proper destruction of all abandoned stack objects. Test the following situation:

```
f(List x) { /* throws exception */ }
g() { List a; f(a); }
main() { try { g(); } catch(...) {}}
```

15.4.7. Resource Acquisition and Release

The possibility of exceptions places an added burden on the programmer, who can no longer rely on the linear flow of program execution. Consider, for example, the following code. Here fs is a global variable of type ifstream.

```
fs.open("input.dat");
f(fs);
fs.close();  // may never happen
```

This code is wrong. The function f (or a function it calls) may throw an exception and never return! In that case, the close command is not executed.

It would be technically correct to catch any and all exceptions, close the file, and rethrow what was caught:

```
fs.open("input.dat");
try
{ f(fs);
}
catch( ... ) // some error occurred
{ fs.close();
  throw;
}
fs.close();
```

Applying this strategy in all similar situations would be extremely burdensome. Instead, it is recommended to structure code such that all resource relinquishment is performed through destructors.

For example, the destructor of a file stream automatically closes the file. Using a local file stream object solves the problem.

```
ifstream fs("input.dat");
f(fs);
```

The file is closed when execution reaches the end of the enclosing block or when an exception is handled in an outer block.

The same applies to memory allocation.

```
Employee* e = new Employee;
// ...
g(e);
delete e; // may never happen
```

The code should be reorganized so that the pointer is located inside a class whose destructor manages the memory deallocation. Smart pointers, such as those discussed in Chapter 14, are helpful in this situation.

The presence of exceptions therefore forces a programming style in which *all* resources are managed by constructors and destructors. *All* handles to those resources, and in particular all pointers to heap memory, should be fields of a class, not local variables of a function.

Exercise 15.4.7. Consider the following code.

```
Array<Shape*> figure;
while (!is.fail())
{ String s;
  is >> s;
  Shape* p = 0;
  if (s == "Point") p = new Point;
  else if (s == "Rectangle") p = new Rectangle;
  else ...
  if (p != 0) { p->read(is); figure.append(p); }
}
```

This code is not safe. Give at least three exceptions that might occur during the execution. What resources are lost when an exception occurs?

Exercise 15.4.8. Make the code of the previous exercise safe by catching every exception, releasing the acquired memory for shapes, and rethrowing the caught exception.

Exercise 15.4.9. Make the code of the previous exercise safe by using a Figure class instead of an array of Shape* pointers. The destructor of the Figure class must delete the memory for the shapes.

15.4.8. Bad Casts

In Chapter 9 we discussed the dynamic_cast operator to test whether a base class pointer actually points to a derived-class object:

```
Base* s;
// ...
Derived* r = dynamic_cast<Derived*>(s);
if (r != 0)
    // r equals s and points to a Derived object
else
    // s does not point to a Derived object
```

It is possible to cast references as well. But because there is no null reference, a failed cast throws an exception of type bad_cast. The test code is

```
Base& s;
// ...
try
{ Derived& r = dynamic_cast<Derived&>(s);
    // r equals s and refers to a Derived object
```

```
}
catch(bad_cast)
{ // s does not refer to a Derived object
}
```

Given that exceptions are supposed to be used for exceptional situations, this is actually a somewhat dubious strategy. The fact that s doesn't refer to the Derived object is not an error, just one branch in the control flow. An alternative is to perform a dynamic cast on the pointer &r.

Exercise 15.4.10. Write a function double area(Shape& s). If s is a rectangle or ellipse, return the area; otherwise, return 0. Use dynamic casts for references. Then reimplement the function by using dynamic casts for the pointer &s. Finally, suggest a better implementation that does not require type inquiry.

15.4.9. Exceptions Should Be Exceptional

There is some temptation to use the exception mechanism as a convenient way of getting from one program point to another. This should be resisted. Exceptions should be reserved for circumstances that are not expected to occur in the normal flow of a computation and whose occurrence creates a situation that cannot be resolved in the current scope.

Memory exhaustion is a good example where the exception-handling mechanism makes sense. One cannot predict in advance when memory is exhausted, and at the point of detection it is rarely possible to do much about it. For that reason, it is the default behavior of the new operator to raise an exception (of type xalloc) when it cannot comply with a request for memory.

Contrast that with the detection of the end of a file from which data is read. All files must come to an end, and the code reading the file in should be prepared to cope with that. The code doing the reading may be expected to query the stream state. Of course, in reading a file of a known format, an *unexpected* end of file, perhaps caused by a disk error, can legitimately be converted to an exception, whose handler rolls back the entire reading process and reports a corrupted file.

Similarly, when taking data from a queue, you should test whether the queue is nonempty before removing an element. It is considered poor style simply to take the element and trap the exception that is raised when removal from an empty queue is attempted.

Exceptions should be used to cope with unpredictable events only. If a problem can be predicted and handled in the current scope, a test should be coded instead.

Exercise 15.4.11. The penalty for not catching an exception is termination. Test what your run-time system does when an exception is thrown but not caught.

Exercise 15.4.12. Compare the cost of testing with the cost of catching an exception. In a timing loop, call `remove` repeatedly on a queue. In one run, test first whether the queue is empty. In another run, catch the exception that is thrown by removing an element from an empty queue instead.

15.4.10. Retry

Some programming languages provide special syntax to retry the statements in the `try` block after the problem has been cured in the handler. In fact, the Eiffel language forces the programmer either to retry or to propagate the exception outward. Giving up is not an option.

In C++, no special syntax for retry is provided, but it can easily be coded explicitly:

```
Bool success = FALSE;
while (!success)
{ try
    { code
      success = TRUE;
    }
    catch clauses
} //(*)
```

Unlike Eiffel, C++ does not force reentry into the `try` block, but it is a good programming strategy. When execution reaches the point (*), we are assured that the `try` block code has completed successfully. That makes it easy to provide meaningful assertions for the block. In contrast, when execution reaches the end of the `try` block itself, we only know that it got there, either by successfully passing through all statements of the code or by falling out of an exception handler that didn't propagate the error.

Exception handlers in `catch` clauses should always do one of the following three actions:

- Reraise the current exception or raise a different exception.
- Retry the `try` block code.
- Cure the exception completely in an alternative way.

Ignoring the exception but failing to propagate it is never sensible.

Exercise 15.4.13. Read a sequence of integers from a file into a queue, using the bounded queue of the previous exercises. If the queue overflows, retry by reopening the file and allocating a larger queue. (The queue constructor should allow a queue size.) Keep doing this until all data fits.

15.4.11. Exception Specifications in Prototypes

Exceptions bring a good deal of uncertainty to such mundane operations as calling functions. The function might throw an exception and never return in the normal way. If the function is supplied by a third-party vendor, the type of the raised exception might be unknown. Then no handler in the program can catch it, and the program will terminate.

It would be highly desirable if we knew that certain functions never throw any exceptions or throw only exceptions of a certain kind.

In C++ an optional mechanism—exception specifications—addresses this issue. Each function may be tagged with a list of exception types. A function so tagged promises never to raise any exceptions except those in the list:

```
int f(istream&) throw (StackError, MathError);
```

A function may guarantee not to throw any exceptions.

```
int f(istream&) throw ();
```

Unlike `const` specifiers, exception specifiers are not enforced at compile time. Instead, if an exception is detected at run time that is not of the type listed in the specifier list, the program terminates.

It is unfortunate that all functions without an explicit `throw` specifier are permitted to throw exceptions of any type. This makes it difficult to write functions with exception specifiers correctly, especially since exception handling is a new feature and existing functions are not declared with empty exception specifiers, even though they throw no exceptions. Consider this example:

```
int g(); // might raise any exception
```

If we want to call g in a function that guarantees to throw exceptions only from a specified list, then we must turn off any other exceptions that g might raise, or risk termination of the program.

```
int f(istream&) throw (StackError, MathError)
{ try
  { g();
    more code
  }
  catch(StackError) { throw; } // caller will handle error
  catch(MathError) { throw; }
  catch(...) { /* ... */ }
}
```

If g were known not to raise any exceptions (or to raise only exceptions of the type raised by f), we could just call it inside f without worrying about blocking unknown exception types.

Exercise 15.4.14. Provide exception specifications for all operations of the bounded queue.

Exercise 15.4.15. Write a function read(istream& is, Queue& q) throw ()
that throws no exception.

15.4.12. What Exceptions Should You Throw?

Since an unexpected exception can terminate the program, it is vitally important
that your code minimize the number of exceptions it raises and that you clearly
document the types of exceptions that can occur. Exception specifications are
the proper tool for that.

Never use exceptions to return the result of a computation. The caller of
a function can ignore a returned value without peril to the program, but an
uncaught exception results in termination.

Low-level code should limit itself to reporting the following kinds of
exceptions:

- Failure of precondition (for example, popping off an empty stack, inverting a
  singular matrix)
- Resource limitation (for example, out of memory, cannot allocate another font)
- Device failure (for example, drive door open, printer off-line)

High-level code should translate these detail exceptions into

- Subsystem failure

This enables the caller of the high-level operation simply to retry or abandon
the high-level operation rather than attempting to micromanage problems over
which it has no control.

15.4.13. What Exceptions Can You Catch?

There are two reasons to catch an exception:

- Catch those exceptions that you can handle.
- Catch *and rethrow* exceptions if you need to perform some action before a
  function terminates as an exception flies by it (but in this case it is usually
  better to reorganize code to have the termination action invoked automatically
  in a destructor).

Never catch and eat an exception that an outer block would handle more
competently.

When handling an exception, you have two choices. You can retry, perhaps
after prompting the user to remedy the cause of failure (close the disk drive,
turn on the printer, close other applications to provide more memory, erase a
file to create more disk space), or you can give up. The latter is usually the only
remedy when catching a failure of a precondition or a subsystem failure. There
is very little you can do to fix, for example, popping a value off an empty stack.
The cause could be external (for example, a corrupted input file) or programmer

error. It may be possible just to abandon the current operation (for example, not to read in the file). Or the program may need to be terminated after all work has been saved.

15.5. DESIGN HINTS

15.5.1. Catch Only What You Can Handle

If you don't know how to handle an error, don't catch it. Presumably there is a more competent handler in an outer scope.

Of course, you may need to perform some cleanup that is not included in destructors, as an exception flies by. It is appropriate to catch an exception, do the cleanup, and rethrow the exception.

15.5.2. Exceptions Are for Exceptional Circumstances

The punishment for an unhandled exception is the death penalty. Your program will die if one component throws an exception that nobody knows how to handle.[1] This simple fact should discourage you from using exceptions if there is another reasonable alternative.

15.5.3. Don't Rely on Exceptions If You Can Test

Don't rely on exceptions to report a failure that you could have tested. Test for an empty stack before popping an element. Don't just try and wait for the exception.

15.5.4. Don't Throw an Exception If You Can Continue

If you must choose between throwing an exception and continuing the computation, continue if you can. If you implement a stack and must do something about popping off an empty stack, return a default value. It is inconceivable that the default return value could cause a greater harm than the exception. Obviously, the immediate caller of pop didn't care—it would have been a simple matter to call is_empty first. The other callers are likely to have even less knowledge of the situation. At any rate, what *should* they do with the information? All they get to know is that somewhere inside, a stack was empty although it shouldn't have been.

It would be nice if all code were perfect, but frankly, most large programs have large numbers of minor and major flaws. Many of them are perfectly harmless, and it makes more sense to keep the program going rather than having an uncaught exception kill it.

---

[1]Admittedly, you can shut up any exception with catch(...), but you have lost the entire computation and have a program that may still be very sick.

There are situations where you plainly can't continue. You are flat out of memory; you must get more information out of a file, but you can't because of a stream error; you are stuck in the middle of a constructor. Then exceptions are appropriate.

15.5.5. Let Library Users
Choose How They Want Errors Handled

If you build that stack class, your users will not agree how nonfatal errors should be handled. Some want them turned into exceptions; others want them ignored.

You must humor both kinds of customers. First, make sure that the class interface makes it possible for the class user to test the preconditions of all operations and that all operations that cannot guarantee success *a priori* report an error status. Now the user who does not wish to catch exceptions has all the necessary tools to avoid them.

Then give the user a chance to install an error handler. The default handler throws the exception, but the user may install a null handler to indicate willingness to handle all nonfatal errors.

15.5.6. Constructor Failure

A constructor may fail for two reasons. The precondition may not be fulfilled; that is, it is being called with bad arguments. In that case, set the object to a default state and pass control on to the error handler. Or some essential resource may not be available. This is not the caller's fault, and there is no good way for the caller to test for failure, because constructors do not return values. This is a fatal error that should be turned into an exception.

15.5.7. Don't Lose
Resources During Exception Processing

The portion of the stack between the throw and catch point is abandoned before the exception is handled. All objects with destructors are properly destroyed, but pointers and handles to external resources are simply abandoned.

If possible, don't use pointers and handles on the stack but place them inside objects with proper destructors. If you don't have that luxury, you need to add code that catches any exception, relinquishes the resource, and rethrows the exception.

CLASS LIBRARY DESIGN

16.1. TREE-STRUCTURED LIBRARIES

16.1.1. Trees and Forests

Since class libraries gather together related classes, there is usually ample opportunity to exploit inheritance. Some class libraries carry this to the logical conclusion of providing a common base class for all classes, usually called Object or a similar name. Every class in such a library is derived directly or indirectly from the class Object. General-purpose libraries such as the NIH library ([Gorlen, Orlow, and Plexico]) contain Date and String classes, containers such as linked lists and hash tables, and control structures such as iterators. All these classes derive from Object. More importantly, library services are provided only to instances of classes that also derive from Object. The inheritance graph of the collection of all classes forms a tree with root Object.

Other class libraries, such as libg++ ([Lea]) or the Booch components ([Booch], ch. 9) are not organized in this fashion. Inheritance is used sparingly, and the resulting inheritance graph forms a collection of disjoint trees: a *forest*.

The choice of organization—tree or forest—has a profound impact on the user of a library.

16.1.2. Services Provided by an Object Root

If every class derives from Object, then Object can hold only the lowest common denominator of the properties of all classes that are in the library or to be used in conjunction with it. There are not many such properties. The following are commonly supplied:

- Writing to a stream
- Reading from a stream
- Computing a hash value (or 0 if hashing is not possible)

- Testing for equality with another object of the same class
- Aiding in run-time type information (which older versions of C++ do not support)
- Supplying debugging information

We will use the following minimal `Object` class for the remainder of this chapter.

```
class Object
{
public:
   virtual void print(ostream&) const = 0;
   virtual int hash() const = 0;
   virtual Bool is_equal(const Object&) const = 0;
};
```

The standard operators can be defined from these operations:

```
Bool operator==(const Object& a, const Object& b)
{ return a.is_equal(b);
}

Bool operator!=(const Object& a, const Object& b)
{ return !a.is_equal(b);
}

ostream& operator<<(ostream& os, const Object& a)
{ a.print(os);
   return os;
}
```

`Object` itself is an abstract class. No objects of class `Object` can be instantiated. *Every* class that wishes to interact with the library—for example, to have objects stored in a container—must override the pure virtual functions `print`, `hash`, and `is_equal`:

```
class Point : public Object
{
public:
   virtual void print(ostream&) const;
   virtual int hash() const;
   virtual Bool is_equal(const Object&) const;
   //...
private:
   double _x;
   double _y;
};
```

The print function is straightforward, and we return 0 as a hash value because we do not intend to put points into a hash table.

```
void Point::print(ostream& os) const
{ os << "Point(" << _x << "," << _y << ")";
}

int Point::hash() const { return 0; }
```

The is_equal function is more difficult. The explicit argument of

```
Bool Point::is_equal(const Object& b) const
```

is an Object&, not a Point&, because the signature of a virtual function cannot be redefined in the derived class. We must first test that the second argument really is a point, not an object of a completely different class. We therefore first test that b is indeed of the same type as self:

```
Bool Point::is_equal(const Object& b) const
{ if (typeid(self) != typeid(b)) return FALSE;
  Point& b1 = (Point&)b;
  return _x == b1._x && _y == b1._y;
}
```

(The typeid operator is a recent addition to C++. Many existing class libraries supply their own scheme for run-time type identification.)

Exercise 16.1.1. Derive Shape from Object. Define Shape::hash() to return 0, and have the various shapes inherit that behavior. But supply is_equal for all shapes.

16.1.3. Containers of Objects

A major reason for designing a class library with root Object is to provide services such as containers once, for the class Object. For example, a queue class would implement a queue of objects:

```
class Queue : public Object
{
public:
  void insert(Object* t);
  Object* remove();
  int length() const;
  virtual void print(ostream&) const;
  virtual int hash() const;
  virtual Bool is_equal(const Object&) const;
  // ...
};
```

In this example Queue is also derived from Object, since every class in a singly rooted library must directly or indirectly descend from the common root. That makes it easy to implement, say, a stack of queues. The virtual functions print, hash, and is_equal invoke the same operations on the items in the container:

```
void Queue::print(ostream& os) const
{ os << "Queue( ";
  for (Link* p = _head; p != 0; p = p->_next)
  { p->_info->print(os);
    os << " ";
  }
  os << ")";
}
```

Exercise 16.1.2. Write the code for Queue::is_equal and Queue::hash. For hashing, use some scheme to combine the hash values of the queue elements to form a hash value for the queue. Don't just add them up—that way, all queues with the same elements, but different orders of insertion, hash to the same value.

Exercise 16.1.3. Place some shapes in two queues and test whether they are equal.

Here we see a benefit of deriving everything from a common root. We can be assured that the protocol for printing, comparing elements, and computing hash values is uniform. That makes it easy to extend these operations to compound objects.

Let us discuss how to insert objects into a container and how to retrieve them. An object of any class derived from Object can be inserted easily.

```
Queue q;
q.insert(new Point(1.3, 2.0));
```

Of course, the queue must hold pointers to objects, not actual objects. (If the queue were to store actual instances of type Object, the derived-class information would be sliced away when placing a Point into the queue.)

Retrieving an object is not as easy. You must *remember* what kind of objects you stored in a particular container:

```
Point* p = (Point*)q.remove();
```

Of course, you may perform a run-time check:

```
Point* p = dynamic_cast<Point*>(q.remove());
if (p != 0) // ...
```

Programming errors are easy because insertion of any object is legal and cannot be checked by the compiler.

```
q.insert(new Circle(...)); // NO—q is meant to hold points only
```

This is a real disadvantage over a template Queue<T>. If q had been declared as a Queue<Point>, inserting a circle would have been detected at compile time.

On the other hand, *heterogeneous* containers are possible. Here is an example of a queue of both customers and employees. Run-time type inquiry is used to differentiate between the two classes when an object is removed.

```
Queue a;
a.insert(new Customer(...));
a.insert(new Employee(...));
// ...
Object* p = a.remove();
if (dynamic_cast<Customer*>(p) != 0) // ...
```

This has no analog in a forest-style library, in which Customer and Employee might not share a common base class.

Stored objects must usually be allocated on the heap. Do not try to insert the addresses of stack objects into a container:

```
Queue q;
// ...
Point pt(1.3, 2.0);
q.insert(&pt); // DON'T
```

The container may have a longer lifetime than inserted stack objects. The pointer to pt may be retrieved from the container long after pt has ceased to exist. If a mixture of stack and heap objects is inserted into a container, there is no way of telling which ones should be deleted.

```
q.insert(&pt);
q.insert(new Point(...));
// ...
Point* p = (Point*) q.remove();
p->plot(gc);
delete p; // only if p points to heap object
```

Since the container holds pointers to the inserted objects, no copies are made when the same object is inserted more than once.

```
Queue q;
Employee* e = new Employee(...);
q.insert(e);
q.insert(e);
q.insert(e);
e->raise_salary(0.05); // all three references to e are affected
```

This is rarely a good idea—it is now very difficult to ensure that the object to which e points is deleted exactly once.

Some class libraries provide an interface for inserting and removing container objects that attempts to mask the pointers.

```
class Queue : public Object
{
public:
  void insert(Object& t);
  Object& remove();
  // ...
};
```

This is a mistake. It makes the syntax for inserting and deleting objects awkward, forcing use of *new and delete &:

```
q.insert(*new Point(1.3, 2.0));
Point& p = (Point&)q.remove();
p.plot(gc);
delete &p;
```

It also invites programming errors that cannot be checked at compile time.

```
Point pt(1.3, 2.0);
q.insert(pt); // inserts address of stack object
Object ob = q.remove(); // slices returned object
```

Exercise 16.1.4. Insert a collection of shapes into a queue. Retrieve and plot them.

Exercise 16.1.5. Insert a random mixture of shapes and employees into a queue. Retrieve them, plot the shapes, and give the employees a raise.

16.1.4. Generic Containers

Containers are classes that hold objects of other classes. Examples are arrays, sets, and queues. It is tempting to capture their commonality by deriving them from a common base class, Container, as shown in Figure 16.1.

What operations might be common to all containers? Unfortunately, access protocol varies widely. For example, array elements are inserted at an integer position. There is no natural operation to remove an object, except by storing another one at the same slot:

```
void Array::set(int, Object*);
Object* Array::get(int) const;
```

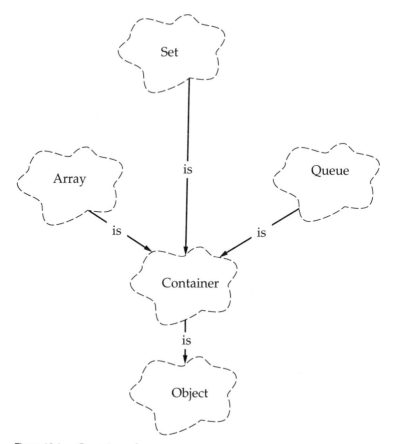

Figure 16.1.   Container classes.

Elements are inserted into a queue at one end and removed at the other:

```
void Queue::insert(Object*);
Object* Queue::remove();
```

Sets impose no particular order on their elements. They merely ensure that duplicates are not inserted:

```
void Set::insert(Object*);
```

Some kind of traversal mechanism is necessary to locate the elements in a set.

There seem to be few operations that are common to all containers! There is no sense in introducing a class if no meaningful operations can be found.

To find commonality, we must look further. Many containers support some form of linear traversal. Arrays can be traversed from the lowest to the highest index. To traverse a linked list, follow the links. Open hash tables that are implemented as arrays of linked lists are traversed by traversing each list

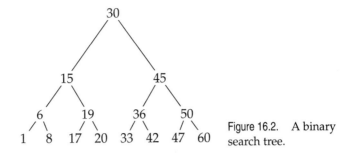

Figure 16.2. A binary search tree.

in turn. Unfortunately, tree structures are less amenable to a linear traversal. Consider a binary search tree, such as the one shown in Figure 16.2. (We use a tree of integers for this example. In a class library, it would be a tree of sortable objects.) Binary search trees are typically implemented from nodes that have pointers to the child nodes but not to the parent node.

```
class Node : public Object
{ // ...
private:
  Object* _info;
  Node* _left;
  Node* _right;
};
```

Finding the first element in the traversal is easy—follow the left children until the end. For the next step, however, it is necessary to back up. This requires that a stack of unused nodes be kept. Using such a stack, iteration through the tree can be achieved.

Perhaps with some degree of complexity in the implementation, we can therefore support a uniform iteration protocol for all containers:

- Reset iteration.
- Get current element.
- Advance to next position.
- Check for end of iteration.

This protocol can be packaged with the container class:

```
class Container : public Object
{
public:
  virtual void reset() = 0;
  virtual const Object* current() const = 0;
  virtual void next() = 0;
  virtual Bool at_end() const = 0;
  // ...
};
```

Of course, any particular container class must store the current position and redefine the iteration functions:

```
class Set : public Container
{
public:
  void set(int, Object*);
  virtual void reset();
  virtual const Object* current() const;
  virtual void next();
  virtual Bool at_end() const;
  // ...
private:
  int _current;
  Array<Object*> _hashtbl;
};

void Set::reset()
{ _current = _hashtbl.low() - 1; next();
}

const Object* Set::current() const
{ return _hashtbl.get(_current);
}

void Set::next()
{ do
    _current++;
  while (!at_end() && _hashtbl[_current] == 0);
}

Bool Set::at_end() const
{ return _current > _hashtbl.high();
}

class List : public Container
{
public:
  virtual void reset();
  virtual const Object* current() const;
  virtual void next();
  virtual Bool at_end() const;
  // ...
private:
  Link* _current;
  Link* _head;
};
```

```
void List::reset()
{ _current = _head;
}

const Object* List::current() const
{ return _current->_info;
}

void List::next()
{ if (!at_end()) _current = _current->_next;
}

Bool List::at_end() const
{ return _current == 0;
}
```

It is now possible to traverse a generic container whose exact type is unknown, by applying the virtual traversal functions.

```
void plot(Container& c, GraphicsContext& gc)
/* PURPOSE:   Plot a collection of points
     RECEIVES:  c - a container of Point objects
                gc - the graphics context on which to plot
*/
{ for (c.reset(); !c.at_end(); c.next())
    ((const Point*)c.current())->plot(gc);
}
```

As we will discuss in Section 16.2.4, it is actually advantageous to encapsulate the iteration mechanism in a separate Iterator class. That base class has virtual functions reset, current, next, and at_end. Each container derives a specific iterator from that base class. A container must be able to produce an iterator to itself.

```
class Set : public Container
{
public:
  class Iterator : public Container::Iterator
  {
  public:
    Iterator(const set&);
    virtual void reset();
    virtual const Object* current() const;
    virtual void next();
    virtual Bool at_end() const;
    // ...
```

```
    };
    virtual Iterator* new_iterator() const;
    // ...
};

Set::Iterator* Set::new_iterator() const
{ return new Set::Iterator(self);
}
```

Iteration through a generic container then proceeds as follows:

```
void plot(Container& c, GraphicsContext& gc)
/* PURPOSE:   Plot a collection of points
    RECEIVES:  c - a container of Point objects
               gc - the graphics context on which to plot
*/
{ Container::Iterator* it = c.new_iterator();
  while (!it->at_end())
  { ((Point*)it->current())->plot(gc);
    it->next();
  }
  delete it;
}
```

The interesting aspect is that we need not know the type of the container holding the points.

Exercise 16.1.6. Complete the implementation of the Set class and the set iterator.

16.1.5. Sorted Collections

Some containers, such as binary search trees and priority queues, require a total ordering on the elements to be inserted. Many classes do support a total ordering on their objects; for example, strings can be compared lexicographically, employees by their employee number. But many other classes do not permit an obvious ordering relationship. For example, it would be very difficult to compare two instances of class Queue, each holding elements from different classes. For that reason, it is not realistic to define an ordering relationship on the level of Object. Instead, many class libraries define a class Sortable as a base class for classes supporting a sort order:

```
class Sortable : public Object
{
public:
  virtual int compare(const Sortable& b) const = 0;
  /* return a negative number if self comes before b,
     0 if self and b are indistinguishable,
     a positive number otherwise
```

```
  */
};
```

Of course, the usual comparison operators can be defined in terms of `compare`:

```
Bool operator<(const Sortable& a, const Sortable& b)
{ return a.compare(b) < 0;
}
```

A *priority queue* supports rapid insertion of elements that arrive in arbitrary order, and retrieval of the smallest element from the head of the queue. This data structure is particularly useful for scheduling events. Events are generated in random order and have a time stamp, denoting when they are to be executed. The scheduler retrieves them in the order of execution. The implementation of a priority queue, using a balanced binary tree data structure (somewhat confusingly called a *heap*—no relation to the free store) is described in [Sedgwick].

A priority queue will accept only objects of a class derived from `Sortable`, because it must sort its entries.

```
class PriorityQueue : public Object
{
public:
  void insert(Sortable*);
  Sortable* remove();
  // ...
};
```

Let us define an `Event` class, which will serve as a base for deriving classes that describe types for different events.

```
class Event : public Sortable
{
public:
  Event(Time);
  virtual void process() = 0;
  // the action to take when processing this event
  int compare(const Sortable& b) const;
  // ...
private:
  Time _time;
};
```

`Event` is an abstract class. We make no effort to define the `print` or `is_equal` function. Instead, we leave that to the classes that derive from `Event`. We even add another pure virtual function, `process`, that must be defined by the derived classes.

We will, however, define compare to compare the time stamps. This turns out to be more difficult than you might think. The type of the explicit argument of compare is const Sortable&, not const Event&. In the is_equal function in Section 16.1.2, we tested whether self and b have the same type. If they don't, they cannot be equal. But for comparison, that does not work. We want the comparison to be carried out even if the objects to be compared are from different event classes. Only the time stamp matters for sorting, and the actual event class is immaterial. Here, the correct question to ask is whether b is an object of a class derived from Event:

```
int Event::compare(const Sortable& b) const
{ const Event* e = dynamic_cast <const Event*>(&b);
  ASSERT_PRECOND(e != 0);
  if (_time < e->_time) return -1;
  if (_time > e->_time) return 1;
  return 0;
}
```

It would not be correct to ask whether the type of b is Event (typeid(b) == typeid(Event)). There are no objects of type Event—it is an abstract class. Therefore, we use run-time type identification to inquire whether b is a kind of event.

This points to a real difference in behavior between object containers and sorted collections. Object containers can be truly heterogeneous. Elements may be compared, as in Set, but only with is_equal. Objects must tolerate comparison with objects of any other class through is_equal (and of course return FALSE). Objects of entirely different classes can be inserted into a set. Sorted collections do not work like that. Once the first element is inserted, the others must be comparable to it.

Exercise 16.1.7. Implement a binary tree class that contains sortable objects. The BinTree::print operation should print the tree in *inorder* (that is, first the left branch of each node, then the node itself, then the right branch).

Exercise 16.1.8. Add an iterator to the binary tree class to traverse the tree in inorder. You will need to keep a stack of parent nodes.

16.2. CONTAINERS

16.2.1. Container Types

A container type is an abstract type that specifies the protocol for insertion, removal, and traversal of elements in a container. Here is a description of the most common ones:

- A *list* is an ordered collection of elements. Elements can be inserted and removed at any position. Traversal presents the elements in order.

- A *stack* is an ordered collection of elements. Elements can be inserted and removed at one end only.
- A *queue* is an ordered collection of elements. Elements are inserted at one end and removed at the other.
- A *deque* (double-ended queue) is an ordered collection of elements. Elements can be inserted and removed at either end.
- A *bag* is an unordered collection of elements. The insertion position of an element cannot be specified. Multiple copies of identical objects can be inserted.
- A *set* is an unordered collection of elements, without duplicate copies of identical ones. In particular, there must be some way of testing whether two objects are identical.
- A *map* is an unordered collection of pairs (*key, value*). For each key, there can be only one associated value. Given a key, the associated value can be retrieved or removed. There must be some way of testing whether two keys are identical.
- An *array* is a special case of a map in which the key set is an interval of integers.
- A *keyed collection* is an unordered collection of elements of type T, together with a key function $k : T \rightarrow K$ mapping each element to a key of type K. Keys need not be unique. Given a key, the values with that key can be retrieved or removed with that key. An example is a set of employee records, keyed by the employee ID. A bag can be considered as a keyed collection in which each element is its own key.
- A *sorted collection* is a collection of elements on which a *total ordering* is defined. That is, given any two elements x and y, either x must come before y, x must come after y, or x and y are undistinguishable from each other. For example, strings are totally ordered by lexicographic comparison, and employee records can be sorted by their name or ID number. Other types, however, have no natural total ordering; for example, circles in the plane or sets of objects. The inserted elements can be traversed in sorted order.
- A *priority queue* is also a collection of elements on which a total ordering is defined, but only the smallest element can be retrieved or removed. The other elements need not be in sorted order. (As the smallest element is retrieved, the data structure reorganizes itself to place the next smallest element in front.)

These types are *abstract* types. They can be implemented by any suitable data structure. For example, a sorted collection can be implemented as a plain binary search tree or as a balanced tree such as an AVL tree, red-black tree, or 2-3 tree. A set can be implemented as a linked list or, with better performance, as a hash table.

The distinction between the abstract types and the concrete implementations is confusing for those types with common names. Technically speaking, a *list* is the abstract type, and a *linked list* is its most likely implementation. An *array* is an abstract type, almost certainly implemented as a block of consecutive elements in memory that is relocated when it needs to grow. Sometimes an effort is made to distinguish the two by referring to the latter as a *block* or *vector*, but the terminology is not at all standardized.

Most libraries of container classes present classes for the abstract types, such as Set, Map, and SortedCollection, internally realized with an implementation that is known to work well for most general purposes. Other libraries present classes for the concrete implementations, such as LinkedList, HashTable, or AVLTree, and leave it to the user to pick those with the performance characteristics that are best for a particular application. The latter approach is less convenient. If a linked list is first chosen in an application that conceptually requires a set, and later the amount of data is so large that a change to a more efficient hash table implementation becomes necessary, some amount of painful surgery is required to make that transition.

Some libraries try to give users the best of both worlds—control over both the abstract data structure and the concrete representation—by supplying multiple implementations such as SetAsLinkedList, SetAsBlock, or SetAsHashTable. That way, only the type name needs to be changed to switch from one implementation to another. The access protocol to the container remains unchanged.

To improve performance and reduce allocation overhead, it can be useful to store elements in a fixed-size block of memory. The size may be specified at compile time (through a template argument) or at construction time (through a constructor argument). Of course, as more elements are inserted into such a container, it fills up and further insertions become impossible. Strictly speaking, a stack made from a fixed-size array is not a proper implementation of the abstract type Stack; instead, it implements a *bounded stack*. Bounded containers have an added operation to test whether the container is full, in which case insertion of further elements is undefined, just as removal of elements from an empty container is undefined. Of course, in the real world, any implementation of an abstract type is bounded, since memory resources are finite. But exhausting memory is such a catastrophic condition that the continued survival of the program is in doubt, whereas reaching the bound of a bounded container is not at all unexpected, since bounds must be chosen tightly in order not to waste too much space.

Some libraries are careless about the distinction between bounded and unbounded containers. If your library gives you a StackAsBlock, you should check whether the memory block has a fixed size (maybe with some magic default) or whether it relocates to grow on demand.

16.2.2. Value and Reference Semantics

When an object is placed into a container, the container can hold either a *copy* of the object or a *reference* to the object. Implementation of either behavior can be found in existing libraries, but copying values is more useful. Making a copy is straightforward, and it does what you would expect from analogy with an array. The original object and the object in the container are distinct from each other.

```
Queue<Employee> q; // holds values
Employee e(...);
q.insert(e);
e.raise_salary(0.05); // copy of e in queue not affected
```

Value semantics requires that the object type permit copying. For example, a Queue<ostream> is not possible—the ostream copy constructor is private.

When containers hold object references, they store pointers to the inserted values only:

```
Queue q; // holds references
Employee* e = new Employee(...);
q.insert(e);
q.insert(e);
q.insert(e);
e->raise_salary(0.05); // all three references to e are affected
```

That is more common for libraries that are rooted in a single Object class (see Section 16.1). If the reference behavior is desired for container templates that hold values, it can be obtained by using a pointer type as template argument:

```
Queue<Employee*> q;
```

It is also common to support a separate template to hold pointers:

```
PtrQueue<Employee> q;
```

Just as important as the decision whether a container *holds* values or references is the decision whether it is *copied* by value or reference. When a copy is made of a container, the copy can either be a distinct value or refer to the same container as the original. Consider the following code, in which a copy r of a queue q is made:

```
Queue<Employee> q;
q.insert(e);
Queue<Employee> r = q;
r.insert(f); // is q also changed?
```

Should the change in r affect q? If the container is copied by value, then r is a copy of q, and q itself is not affected. Copy by value is the preferred semantics for C++, since it yields no surprises when containers are used as data fields of classes. But value copying is expensive, because each element stored in the container must be copied. (Reference counting and copy on write are particularly useful in this context.) For that reason, quite a few class libraries copy containers by reference or disallow copying altogether.

Copy by value is more general, since copy by reference can always be implemented with pointers.

```
Queue<Employee>* q = new Queue<Employee>;
q->insert(e);
Queue<Employee>* r = q;
r->insert(f); // q, r refer to the same queue
```

Exercise 16.2.1. In some implementations, pointer containers such as PtrQueue<T> "own" the pointers stored in them. When the container goes out of scope, the pointers are deleted. Explain why this makes copying the container difficult. Outline an implementation for a correct copy constructor and assignment operator. Implement the PtrQueue template.

Exercise 16.2.2. Containers can hold elements by value or reference, and they can copy by value or reference. Therefore, four distinct semantics are possible. Discuss the advantages and disadvantages of each, commenting on programmer convenience, possible surprises, and implementation considerations.

16.2.3. Insertion, Retrieval, and Removal

Containers show great variety with respect to their insertion and retrieval protocols. Stacks, queues, and deques have specific locations at which elements are inserted—the top of the stack, the tail of the queue:

```
s.push(x);
q.insert(x);
```

Arrays and maps require an *index* or *key* for insertion:

```
a.set(i, x);
m.set(k, x);
```

Bags, sets, and keyed collections are unordered; hence, no insert position can be specified:

```
b.insert(x);
```

Sorted collections and priority queues arrange elements according to their sort position, and no insert position is specified:

```
p.insert(x);
```

Lists are more complex than the other containers, because they support insertion by position. As part of its state, a list has a cursor that can be advanced. New elements can be inserted at the cursor position.

```
l.next();
l.insert(x);
```

Stacks, queues, deques, and priority queues have specific locations at which elements are retrieved—the top of the stack, the head of the queue:

```
x = s.top();
x = q.head();
```

Array elements are retrieved by specifying the index:

```
x = a.get(i);
```

Maps and keyed collections require a key for retrieval:

```
if (m.find(k)) // key is present
x = m.get(k);
```

For keyed collections, the find operation sets a cursor to the first entry matching the key. All entries matching that key can be retrieved with a current/find_next/at_end protocol:

```
for (c.find(k); !c.at_end(); c.find_next())
    c.current() is value with key k
```

Given a value, we can test whether it is present in a bag, set, or sorted collection. With a bag, we can inquire how many copies are present:

```
n = b.find(x);
```

The element under the list cursor can be inspected:

```
l.next();
x = l.current();
```

Arrays, maps, and lists permit modification of an element by returning a reference to a stored object:

```
if (a.low() <= i && i <= a.high()) a[i].change();
if (m.find(k)) m[k].change();
l.current().change();
```

For other containers such in-place change is not possible. Those containers use intrinsic properties, not an external position, to organize their stored objects. Changing an element's value may affect those properties and hence the position in the container.

Elements can be removed from the top of the stack or the head of a queue, priority queue, or sorted collection:

```
x = s.pop();
x = q.remove();
```

Elements are removed from maps and keyed collections by giving their key:

```
if (m.find(k)) // key is present
  m.remove(k);

if (c.find(k))
    c.remove(); // removes first match
```

To remove an element from a set, bag, or sorted collection, its value must be specified:

```
b.remove(x);
```

The element under the list cursor can be removed:

```
l.next();
l.remove();
```

16.2.4. Traversal

It is often necessary to carry out an operation on all elements in a container. Arrays can be traversed easily:

```
for (i = a.low(); i <= a.high(); i++)
  do something with a[i];
```

This simple method does not work with any other container. Imagine doing something with all entries in a map. Maps have keys, but unlike an array, we do not know for which keys k there are entries m[k]. Obviously we cannot try all keys. The container must support a separate traversal mechanism.

Linked lists can be traversed by moving the cursor from the beginning to the end:

```
for (l.reset(); !l.at_end(); l.next())
  do something with l.current();
```

Using the list cursor for traversal has one drawback: It changes the state of the list by moving the cursor position. Consider the following operator function:

```
template<class T>
ostream& operator<<(ostream& os, const List<T>& l)
{ for (l.reset(); !l.at_end(); l.next()) // ERROR
    os << l.current();
  return os;
}
```

The cursor operations modify the list state and hence cannot be carried out on a const object. It is important that printing a list not modify its state. Consider the following test print in a code segment that relies on the correct placement of the cursor position:

```
List<int> l;
// ...
l.reset(); // swap first two elements
a = l.remove();
cout << l; // test printout
l.next();
l.insert(a);
```

We need a way of traversing the list without moving the list cursor. Two methods are available: function application and external iterators.

The implementor of a container can easily write code that visits each stored element to apply a user-provided function. With such a service, printing a list can be implemented as follows.

```
template<class T>
ostream& operator<<(ostream& os, const List<T>& l)
{ l.apply(print_fun, &os);
   return os;
}
```

Here print_fun is the function to be applied at each node.

```
template<class T>
void print_fun(const T& t, void* p)
{ (*(ostream*)p) << t;
}
```

Since the apply mechanism must cope with arbitrary traversal actions, it provides for an application function with two arguments: the currently visited element and a generic pointer to another argument. In our example, the stream argument is transported to the print function as a void* pointer. If more than one argument is required, a pointer to a separate structure containing all argument values must be used.

The apply operation visits all elements without disturbing the list cursor:

```
template<class T>
class List
{
public:
   typedef void (*ApplyFun)(const T&, void*);
   void apply(ApplyFun, void*) const;
   // ...
};
```

```
template<class T>
void List<T>::apply(List<T>::ApplyFun f, void* p) const
{ for (Link<T>* n = _head; n != 0; n++)
    (*f)(n->_info, p);
}
```

Function application is somewhat cumbersome, because it is tedious to set up the auxiliary function. Furthermore, every node of the container is visited. It is not possible to stop the traversal when a particular element has been found. *External iterators* are better suited in that situation.

An external iterator is a class designed for traversing a container a step at a time. An iterator object can be attached to the container. It has its own cursor position, which can be advanced until the end of the container is reached.

```
List<Employee>::Iterator it(l);
while (!it.at_end())
{ do something with it.current();
  it.next();
}
```

A real advantage of iterators is that you can attach as many as you need to a given container.

What happens if an iterator happens to point a particular container element, and that element is removed? What happens to an iterator if the list through which it iterates is destroyed? It depends on the library. Some libraries are careful and adjust all iterators if the container to which they point is edited. Others are sloppy and only caution the programmer that using the iterator after such situations will have disastrous effects.

Class library designers must make a decision whether iterators can be used to inspect containers only or also to modify their contents. For example, should the list iterator be able to support insertion and removal at the current position? It depends. If we want to use an iterator to traverse a const container, its constructor must take a const reference to the container:

```
template<class T>
List<T>::Iterator::Iterator(const List<T>&)
```

After all, the iterator will be attached to a const object:

```
template<class T>
ostream& operator<<(ostream& os, const List<T>& l)
{ for (List<T>::Iterator it(l); !it.at_end(); it.next())
    os << it.current();
  return os;
}
```

If it is possible to carry out destructive operations like it.remove() through this particular iterator, the promise to leave the list unchanged can be broken.

There are two possible remedies:

- A library may supply two iterator classes: one for inspection and one for mutation.
- A single class can be provided, with two constructors, one taking a `const` reference, the other a non-`const` reference. The constructors set a flag to remember whether mutation is permitted. If a mutating operation is carried out and the flag is not set, an exception is raised.

The first approach uses a compile-time check, the second a run-time check.

Unordered containers, such as sets, bags, maps, and keyed collections, are traversed in a random fashion. These are often implemented as hash tables, and traversal just follows the vagaries of the hash function values.

Keyed collections typically have two kinds of iterators: one to iterate through all values in the collection and another to visit those matching a specific key.

In iterating through a priority queue, we may be assured that the first visited element is the minimum one. The remaining elements are visited in random order.

Of course, sorted collections are traversed in sort order. A binary search tree implementation makes function application easy: First apply to the left subtree, then to the root, then to the right subtree. However, providing an iterator that steps through the tree in sorted order is much more difficult. Such an iterator must keep a stack of visited tree nodes.

Exercise 16.2.3. Implement a queue as a sequence of links. Provide one implementation that has reference copy semantics and another that has value copy semantics.

Exercise 16.2.4. Implement a bag as a hash table template. The template needs to store pairs (*element*, *count*). Support `insert`, `find`, and `remove` operations.

Exercise 16.2.5. Implement a sorted collection as a binary search tree template. Supply `insert` and `remove` operations.

Exercise 16.2.6. Add an `apply` operation to the sorted collection that traverses the binary tree representation in inorder.

Exercise 16.2.7. Make a sorted collection of employee records. Apply a function to give every employee a raise of `p` percent, then apply another function to print every employee on a stream `os`. Combine the functions into one and apply that. Place the two required values (`p`, `os`) into an object of an ad hoc class and pass its address as the `void*` argument.

Exercise 16.2.8. Implement a keyed collection as a hash table template. Support an iterator that iterates through all entries with the same key.

16.3. FOUNDATION CLASSES

Foundation classes describe simple objects that are useful by themselves rather than serving as a basis for derivation or as a container for other objects. Examples are date, time, strings, fractions, and complex numbers. Objects of these classes should have the same look and feel as the numeric data types, such as integers and floating-point numbers.

16.3.1. Copy Semantics

Foundation objects should have value semantics for copying. That is, making a copy should yield a distinct copy, not provide another access to the same object. This is appropriate for foundation data types because it is the same behavior exhibited by numeric types. For example, a vector and a matrix should "feel" just like a scalar floating-point number.

16.3.2. Overloaded Operators

Comparison with == and != makes sense for all foundation classes. Those classes that naturally support a total ordering (strings, date, time, and fractions, but not complex numbers) should overload the relational operators <, <=, >, >=.

For objects that implement mathematical constructs, such as fractions and complex numbers, all arithmetic operators (+, -, *, /, +=, -=, *=, /=, ==, !=) should be provided. For strings it is traditional to overload + to denote concatenation.

It is best not to be tempted into introducing new overloads. One might argue that Date + int could result in another date a certain number of days away, or that Date - Date could report the number of days between two dates. There would even be a precedent for this: namely, C pointer arithmetic. But operations with meaningful names, such as add_days or days_between, are a better choice.

16.3.3. Default Objects

A default constructor should always be provided. Without one, no array of objects can be allocated. For many types this is not a problem. Complex numbers, fractions, vectors, or matrices default to zero; strings, to the empty string.

For other types there is no easy choice. What is a default date? The beginning of time, or January 1 of year 1? Surely that is never intended. Today's date? Obtaining it is somewhat computationally expensive. Default constructors should perform minimal work, because they are often invoked only to initialize an array that will be overwritten momentarily.

For geometric objects it is usually awkward to give a default value. What is a default rectangle? The unit square? In what coordinate system? What is a default font? 12 point Courier?

If no good default can be found, one can sometimes choose a value that is purposefully invalid and must be replaced with a real value before it can be used. For example, a default date might have the year set to 0. (Recall that there is no year 0: 1 B.C. is followed by 1 A.D.) Of course, one then has the burden of ensuring that the object is valid before executing any operations. This is analogous to pointers—the default null pointer is not a legal value for any pointer operations.

16.3.4. No Subclassing

Foundation classes are usually not designed to serve as the basis for derivation. It is difficult to envision a class that could usefully derive from Date. Such a class would have to describe a subset of dates that is distinguished in some way.

Even if subclassing is conceptually possible, it is rarely economical for foundation classes. Consider a class Matrix. One could derive a class SymmetricMatrix to describe the subset of matrices that are symmetric about the main diagonal ($a_{ij} = a_{ji}$). But using inheritance wastes storage. A custom implementation requires only about half the storage for symmetric matrices as for general matrices.

Since foundation classes are not designed for subclassing, they should not have virtual functions.

16.4. DESIGN HINTS

16.4.1. Naming Consistency

If a consistent naming scheme is important for a single class, it is even more so for a class library. If add adds an element to a binary tree, then the operation to add an element to a priority queue should also be add, not put. Be consistent with capitalization. Users get extremely annoyed when they have to use is_empty for some classes, isEmpty for others. In a nutshell, don't surprise the class users, and don't force them to look up details constantly.

Choose reasonable names. In one widely distributed class library, all containers have an operation getItemsInContainer. Contrary to what you may think, it does not simultaneously get all items in the container. Instead, it gets a *count* of the items. Surely some better name can be found for this operation—count comes to mind.

For very common names and operations, try to choose short but unabbreviated names. Your users will appreciate it. Use get instead of get_at. Try add instead of insert or ins. One library uses Set_of_p for a set of pointers. The "of" adds no information, whereas the "p" seems too cryptic.

Choose good pairs of names for complementary operations: get/set works better than get/insert.

16.4.2. Consistent Mechanisms

Use the same mechanisms to carry out related tasks in different classes. If the binary tree class uses a comparison function to compare elements, the priority queue should not use a < operator. If a set can be inspected with an iterator, an iterator with the same interface should be available to inspect a map.

16.4.3. Consistent Error Handling

A class library should present a consistent error model to the user. Recall the actions that an operation can perform when an error condition is detected:

- Ignore or work around the error.
- Return a status code.
- Place the object in an invalid state.
- Throw an exception.

Errors of the same severity should be handled in the same way by the various classes in the library. For example, if popping an empty stack simply returns a default value, removing an element from an empty queue should not throw an exception.

Exceptions that are thrown by different library classes should be related.

16.4.4. Memory Allocation

The golden rule is: If the library object allocates memory, the library object deletes it. If the library user allocates memory, the library user deletes it.

This is particularly true for containers. Users may insert the same pointer into multiple containers, and it would be a disaster if the container destructor always deleted all objects inside it. Of course, the container object needs to delete links or other auxiliary memory that it allocated.

Sometimes it makes sense for a container to delete its elements, but the behavior must be clearly advertised. For example, a dialog box object may contain a collection of polymorphic control objects:

```
ConnectionDialog::ConnectionDialog()
{ add(new EditControl(IDD_LABEL));
  add(new RadioButtonControl(IDD_TYPE));
  // ...
}
```

Then the dialog destructor may reasonably delete the control objects.

A popular graphical user interface framework features a rather bizarre convention to remind the programmer not to delete the objects. To add a button or other widget to a dialog box, you write code of the form

```
ConnectionDialog::ConnectionDialog()
{ new EditControl(self, IDD_LABEL);
  new RadioButtonControl(self, IDD_TYPE);
  // ...
}
```

Note that the return value of new is not used. The control element constructors call the surrounding dialog box (through the self parameter) and are added to a list of child controls. Since you aren't capturing the return value of new, you aren't tempted to delete it.

16.4.5. Tree or Forest?

Quite a few C++ class libraries are organized as trees. Many of them were influenced by Smalltalk libraries. In Smalltalk, *every* class derives from a base class Object.

In C++ the tree approach, with heavy reliance on a cosmic base class Object in the library interface, has an essential drawback. If an Object is falsely cast to a wrong derived class, the program behavior becomes unpredictable. In contrast, the Smalltalk run-time system checks, for each invocation of an operation, whether the responsible object can legally carry the operation out; if not, an error message is generated. Since C++ has no such checking, the cost of inevitable programmer errors is very high: Flaky programs are hard and expensive to debug.

Tree-structured libraries have a second disadvantage: They are hard to combine with each other. If two vendors offer libraries that are both rooted in a base class Object, then the libraries cannot be combined in the same project. (Name spaces offer a solution to this problem—see Chapter 10.) Even if the base classes have different names (TObject vs. CObject), it may be difficult to use them together. What should you do with a class that needs to interact with both libraries—derive it from both TObject and CObject? In Smalltalk, none of this is a problem: There is already a base class Object, and all other classes, in particular those of any library, always derive from it.

16.4.6. Copy Semantics

Value semantics are strongly preferred for copies. A copy should yield a new value, not another access to the original value. To share objects, for reasons of behavior or efficiency, use the mechanism provided by the language—that is, pointers.

It is expensive to copy bulky objects like linked lists, but the cost of copying can be greatly reduced by copy on write (see Chapter 13).

C H A P T E R   17

MULTIPLE
INHERITANCE

17.1. MULTIPLE BASE CLASSES

When deriving from a base class, we obtain two benefits: The derived class inherits the operations of its parent, and all virtual functions can be invoked polymorphically, on either base class or derived-class objects.

If deriving from one class is beneficial, it seems reasonable that deriving from more than one class would be even better. We inherit even more operations, and polymorphism can be exploited for each parent class. The process of deriving from two or more base classes simultaneously is called *multiple inheritance*.

In this section we will study the mechanics of multiple inheritance. For simplicity we use a somewhat contrived example. The Text class of Chapter 7 implements text that can be positioned anywhere on the screen. Let us implement this class by deriving from both Shape and String:

```
class Text : public Shape, public String
{
public:
  Text(Point, String);

  void move(double x, double y);
  void scale(Point p, double s);
  void plot(GraphicsContext& gc) const;
private:
  Point _start;
};
```

This seems like an excellent idea. As before, Text fits into the shape hierarchy. Text objects can be included in a list of shapes to be displayed or manipulated. Moreover, we inherit all the functionality of the String class, such as the ability of changing all characters to uppercase.

Operations from both Shape and String can be applied to Text objects:

```
Text t(p, "Hello, World");
t.to_upper(); // OK
t.move(x, y); // OK
```

From the point of view of object-oriented design, this seems a bit dubious. It is not clear that a text object *is* a string. The substitution principle would demand that a text object can always be used in place of a string object. However, not all inherited operations make sense for texts. For example, what is the meaning of concatenating two texts with different base points? We will discuss this concern in greater detail in Section 17.8.2.

In fact, we have resisted the temptation to derive Text from Point and String.

```
class Text : public Point, public String // DON'T
```

At first glance, this would seem to work very well. The scale and move operations for Point can be inherited without change to transform the base point of the text. But a text object *isn't* a point, and it is not a good idea to pretend otherwise just to save recoding two operations. It would be difficult to envision a situation in which we could meaningfully exploit polymorphism, applying a virtual function to an object that might either be a point or a text.

An object of type Text is made up of three parts, as shown in Figure 17.1: the inherited parts from both base classes, and those fields that were added in the Text class. Text objects can be converted automatically into either Shape or String objects. Suppose a function exists to test whether a string is correctly spelled.

```
Bool spell_check(String s);
```

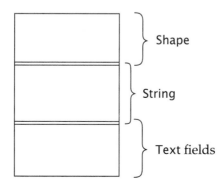

Shape

String

Text fields

Figure 17.1.   The layout of a text object.

It can be invoked to check the string portion of a text object:

```
Text t(...);
if (spell_check(t)) ... // OK
```

Multiple inheritance is useful to have the same object simultaneously used in multiple ways. For example, the same text object can be contained both in a list of (pointers to) shapes for redisplay and a list of (pointers to) strings for spell checking:

```
List<Shape*> shape_list; // for display
List<String*> string_list; // for spell checking
Text* t = new Text(...);
shape_list.insert_tail(t); // OK
string_list.insert_tail(t); // OK
```

When multiple inheritance is involved, the inheritance graph is no longer a tree (see Figure 17.2). In our example, Text has two base classes. The inheritance graph is a *directed acyclic graph* (DAG). There can be no cycles, because no class can be its own direct or indirect parent class.

A class can have any number of base classes, but duplicates are not allowed. For example,

```
class Car : public Tire, public Tire,
    public Tire, public Tire // ERROR
```

is illegal.

Exercise 17.1.1. Implement the Text class by inheriting from Shape and String. Test that a Text object supports both String operations (to_upper) and Shape operations (plot, move).

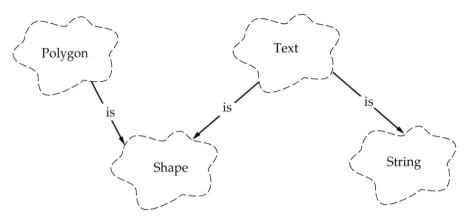

Figure 17.2. Multiple inheritance for Text.

17.2. REPEATED BASE CLASSES

Although it is not possible to derive directly from the same base class more than once, it is easy to produce scenarios in which a class has a common base class as an ancestor along more than one inheritance path.

Consider a TrafficSign class that is both a text and a polygon.

```
class TrafficSign : public Text, public Polygon
{
public:
  TrafficSign(Point c, int nvert, String t);
  // ...
};

TrafficSign sign(p, 8, "Stop");
sign.to_upper();
x = sign.circumference();
```

This is not necessarily a reasonable way of defining a traffic sign class, but it does show the phenomenon of repeated base classes, illustrated in Figure 17.3. A TrafficSign object contains two shape subobjects, shown in Figure 17.4.

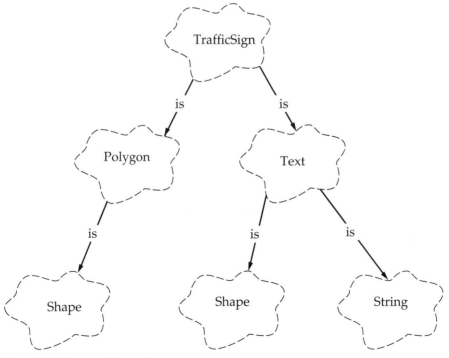

Figure 17.3.   Repeated base classes.

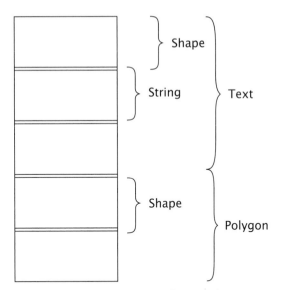

Figure 17.4.   The layout of a traffic sign object.

Since Shape is a class without data, this does not seem like a big problem. To make the matter more interesting, let us add a data field to Shape to specify a color:

```
class Shape
{ // ...
private:
  Color _color;
};
```

Then it is entirely possible that the two shape subobjects contain different color values, as shown in Figure 17.5. We may indeed want to have different colors for the polygon and the text, in which case the two color fields are just what we need. But the use of inheritance now becomes highly questionable. If TrafficSign inherits (indirectly) from Shape, each traffic sign *is* a shape. A shape of what color? The call sign.color() is ambiguous and does not compile (see Section 17.7). Conceptually, the traffic light objects no longer conform to the Shape protocol, and inheritance is out of place.

This situation is typical. Repeated occurrences of the same base indirect class are incompatible with the *is-a* relationship.

Exercise 17.2.1. Implement the TrafficSign class. Instantiate stop sign, yield sign, and speed limit objects. Verify that both to_upper and plot can be applied to traffic sign objects.

Exercise 17.2.2. We may take the point of view that the color of the polygon is the one we really consider important and that the text color is incidental. How

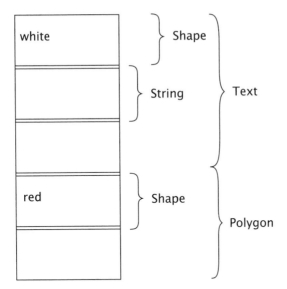

Figure 17.5.   Color fields in the shape subobjects.

would you model the `TrafficSign` class under those assumptions? (*Hint*: Do not use multiple inheritance.)

17.3. SHARED BASE CLASSES

Usually, it is not desirable to have repeated copies of a common indirect base class. Rather, all common bases should be merged into one.

Recall the `Person/Student/Employee/Professor` example from Chapter 7, shown in Figure 17.6. Let us model a teaching assistant. Teaching assistants are both students and employees:

```
class TeachingAsst : public Student, public Employee
```

`TeachingAsst` derives twice from `Person`: once through `Student` and once through `Employee`, as shown in Figure 17.7. Each object of type `TeachingAsst` contains two `Person` subobjects, each with fields for name and address. This makes little sense. Certainly we would want that information to be identical. Replicating the same data in two `Person` subobjects wastes storage and imposes a burden on the programmer to ensure that it stays the same.

With a bit of foresight, it is possible to merge multiple instances of a common indirect base into one. The direct descendants of the common base must prepare for that merging by specifying the inheritance as `virtual`:

```
class Student : virtual public Person
class Employee : virtual public Person
```

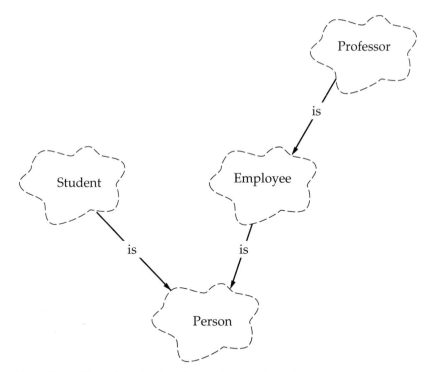

Figure 17.6. Hierarchy of university students and employees.

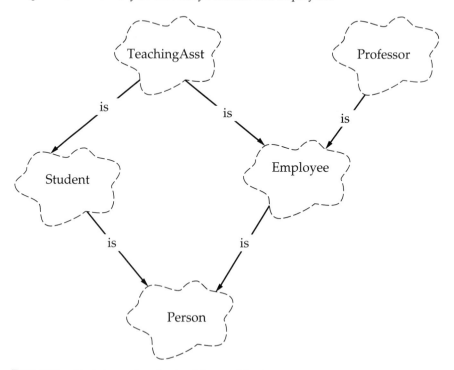

Figure 17.7. Deriving a class for teaching assistants.

class Student : public Person

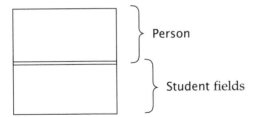

Person

Student fields

class Student : virtual public Person

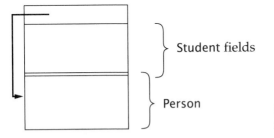

Student fields

Person

Figure 17.8.   The data layout with regular and virtual base classes.

The TeachingAsst class derives in the usual way from both parents:

```
class TeachingAsst : public Student, public Employee
```

Now all virtual bases are merged together.

The keyword virtual is not very descriptive. It has no direct connection with virtual functions. Virtual inheritance is similar to, but not quite the same as, regular inheritance. It affects the layout of the derived class, preparing the base class for merging in subsequent derivations. A better term might be "sharable". Specifically, a pointer is introduced in place of the base object, making it possible to locate the base object elsewhere in the class. Figure 17.8 illustrates the difference between regular and virtual inheritance.

Of course, the compiler must generate code to indirect through that pointer whenever a field of the virtual base class is accessed. The reason for making the virtual base movable becomes apparent when it occurs repeatedly. The TeachingAsst class contains two pointers to the same Person subobject, as shown in Figure 17.9:

```
class TeachingAsst : public Student, public Employee
```

Since the access to a Person field is automatically translated to follow the pointer, it does not matter that the Pointer subobject is now some distance away from the Student object. (In our illustrations, we have placed the shared bases at the end of the derived objects. Naturally, the exact layout depends on the compiler.)

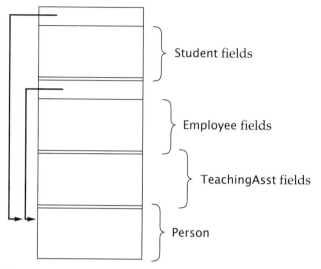

Figure 17.9.   A shared base class.

Shared common bases solve the base replication problem of multiple inheritance. The *is-a* nature of inheritance is preserved. A TeachingAsst is a Person in just one way, and it is the same person, whether first considered as a Student or first considered as an Employee.

From a theoretical point of view, it would be desirable if sharing of common bases was the default. Some programming languages, such as Eiffel, take just that route. For performance reasons, C++ requires manual intervention. Adding a pointer for *every* base class, just on the suspicion that some class may later use multiple inheritance and require merging of common bases, is indeed inefficient.

Shared base classes require foresight. The TeachingAsst class is the one creating the sharing problem, since it introduces the duplicate Person objects, but it can do nothing to solve it. Instead, a previous generation must have anticipated the problem and made Person a virtual (sharable) base.

Exercise 17.3.1. Implement the Student and TeachingAsst class. Place the same TeachingAsst object on a list of students and a list of employees. Give all employees a raise, and give all students a grade. Then print the teaching assistant object.

Exercise 17.3.2. Implement the TrafficSign class to merge the two Shape base classes. In particular, the color attribute applies to the entire sign. What changes do you need to make to the parent classes?

17.4. MIXINS

A common use of multiple inheritance is the addition of service protocols to class hierarchies. We have seen examples of such protocols in previous sections. Chapter 12 introduced a base class Persistent, and any classes that want to make use of the persistent storage mechanism must derive from that class. The container class library described in Chapter 16 is rooted in a base `Object`, and a class that desires storage in those containers must derive from `Object` or the descendant `Sortable`. A garbage collector may require that classes derive from a base class `Collectable`.

If only one of these service protocols is desired, single inheritance is sufficient:

```
class Person : public Persistent
```

This makes persistent storage available to `Person` and its descendants. (It also makes these classes responsible for implementing the necessary virtual functions.) Multiple inheritance is required if two or more protocols are added:

```
class Person : public Persistent, public Sortable
```

In this case, we do not use inheritance to express an *is-a* relationship between design level classes, but to add certain implementation mechanisms. The base classes `Persistent` and `Sortable` have either no or very few data fields. Their main contribution is to spell out an obligation for the derived class in terms of virtual functions that must be redefined, and in turn to enable certain mechanisms.

Derivation from such service classes is often called *mixin* inheritance. (Rumor has it that the term "mixin" originates from the disgusting habit of some ice cream stores to mix pieces of cookies or candy into a scoop of ice cream, at the customer's request.) Mixin classes do not typically share common bases, and it is unlikely that the sharing problem described in the previous section will apply. But if multiple inheritance is anticipated at a higher level, then the mixin inheritance needs to be virtual:

```
class Person : virtual public Persistent,
    virtual public Sortable
class Robot : virtual public Persistent,
    virtual public Sortable
class Android : public Person, public Robot
```

Exercise 17.4.1. If a class library has all classes derive directly or indirectly from a common base `Object`, should that be a virtual base class? Explain.

17.5. CONSTRUCTION

In the absence of virtual base classes, construction of multiple bases is straightforward. Simply construct all bases in the initializer list:

```
TrafficSign::TrafficSign(Point p, int nvert, String t)
: Text(p, t),
  Polygon(nvert)
{ // nvert calls to set_vertex
}
```

In general, the initializer list is a mixture of base and field constructions:

```
Text::Text(Point p, String t, Color c)
: String(t),
  Shape(c),
  _start(p)
{}
```

Shared base classes raise a knotty problem. An object must be guaranteed to be constructed exactly once. This is in conflict with the normal construction sequence of derived classes. Consider the construction of a teaching assistant object. TeachingAsst invokes the constructors of its bases, Student and Employee. The Student constructor in turn constructs its base, Person, and the Employee constructor constructs its base, Person. Unless special steps are taken, the Person subobject is constructed twice. That might be harmless, if the constructor merely zeroes out some fields, or it might be disastrous, if the constructor acquires some resources that later will not be released.

To avoid this problem, the normal construction sequence is suspended for virtual bases. Virtual bases are constructed separately from the rest of the object. The preferred method is to supply a default constructor for the virtual base and let the compiler invoke that. It is also possible to construct the virtual base separately from the *most derived* class:

```
TeachingAsst::TeachingAsst(Name n, Address a, double salary)
: Employee(salary),
  Person(n, a) // Person is an indirect virtual base
{}
```

That can be problematic. What is "most derived" today can be the base of further derivation tomorrow. A constructor that invokes the virtual base constructor cannot be invoked from the next derived class. This again shows that virtual base classes require a high level of planning and foresight.

Exercise 17.5.1. Derive another class GraduateAsst from TeachingAsst. What is the impact on constructors?

17.6. POINTER CONVERSION

Conversion of derived-class pointers to base class pointers is an essential feature of polymorphism. In single inheritance, pointer conversion between derived and base classes is simple. The address of a derived class object is automatically the address of its base class, because the base class is allocated before the derived-class fields. But if a class has more than one base class, this simple rule must fail for all but one of the base classes.

Consider the Text derived from two base classes. Suppose that the memory layout is as shown in Figure 17.10 (There is no guarantee for that—the compiler is free to sort the base classes in any order.) A pointer Text* p points

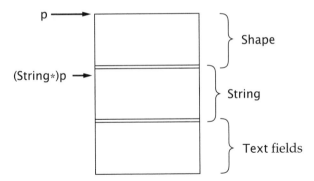

Figure 17.10.   Pointer conversion to a base class.

automatically to the Shape portion but not the String portion. However, all code that interprets p as a string must have the pointer adjusted to the string subobject. For example, p->to_upper() must receive the starting address of the String portion.

The compiler handles this automatically. When a pointer to a derived class is converted to a pointer to one of the base classes (either by an explicit cast or by a base class operation), the appropriate offset is added to the address:

```
Text* p;
String* q = p; // adds an offset
```

Occasionally the opposite cast is required: a String* pointer is known to actually point to a Text object. When performing the cast, the address is adjusted again.

```
String* q;
Text* p = (Text*)q; // subtracts offset
String* s = dynamic_cast<String*>(p); // subtracts offset
```

These adjustments are transparent to the programmer.

C programmers are used to the idea that pointer conversions and casts are "do-nothing" operations. In the presence of multiple inheritance, this is no longer true. In particular, the time-honored strategy of converting pointers to void* and casting back can lead to disaster:

```
Text* p;
void* r = p;
String* q = (String*)r; // does not point to a String!
```

As one might suspect, pointer conversion becomes more complex when virtual base classes are involved. Casting to a virtual base is permitted, as shown in Figure 17.11, and the cast follows the indirection:

```
TeachingAsst* t;
Person* p = t; // follows indirection
```

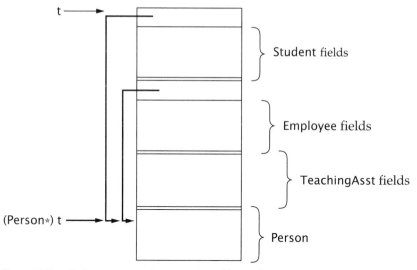

Figure 17.11.   Pointer conversion to a virtual base class.

The converse cast cannot be resolved at compile time. If a pointer points to a virtual base, there is no way of knowing where a derived class containing it is located. Consider a Person* pointer p that we know actually points to a Student s. The adjustment amount depends on the actual object into which p points. If p points into a plain Student object, the adjustment is smaller than if p points into a TeachingAsst object, as shown in Figure 17.12. Since the

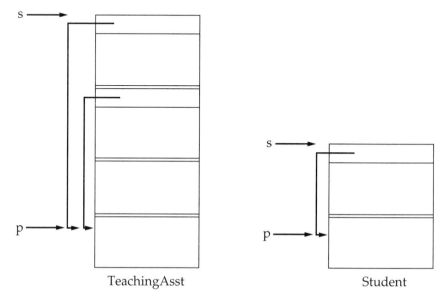

Figure 17.12.   Variation in the pointer adjustment amount.

adjustment cannot be determined at compile time, the static cast from a virtual base to a descendant is illegal:

```
Person* p; // we know it points to a student
Student* s;
s = (Student*) p; // ERROR
```

However, there must be some way of getting back. After all, if `Person` has a virtual function (say `print`) and `Student` redefines that virtual function, the call `p->print()` invokes `Student::print()` (or a descendant). The virtual function mechanism keeps a complete record of the necessary pointer adjustments. Provided the virtual base has at least one virtual function, we can use a dynamic cast to locate the derived-class pointer at run time:

```
s = dynamic_cast<Student*>(p); // OK
```

For that reason, it is a good idea to place at least one virtual function into a virtual base. A virtual destructor is a good choice.

17.7. AMBIGUITY RESOLUTION

17.7.1. Repeated Feature Names

When inheriting from two base classes, it is possible to inherit operations with the same signature from each class. For example, the `TrafficSign` class inherits a `plot` function from both `Text` and `Polygon`. This is fine *as long as you never call that function.*

Suppose `TrafficSign` does not define its own `plot`. Then the call

```
TrafficSign s(...);
s.plot(gc);
```

is rejected as ambiguous. You must specify which `plot` you mean:

```
s.Polygon::plot(gc);
s.Text::plot(gc);
```

17.7.2. Merging Features

The `plot` function that `TrafficSign` inherits from both base classes should actually be implemented in the derived class:

```
void TrafficSign::plot(GraphicsContext& gc) const
{ Polygon::plot(gc);
  Text::plot(gc);
}
```

Since `plot` is virtual in both base classes, the new `plot` overrides both of their `plot` functions. The `TrafficSign::plot` function is selected if a `TrafficSign` object is accessed either through a `Text*` or a `Polygon*`. Hence `TrafficSign::plot` merges the two virtual `plot` function hierarchies that are inherited from both ancestors.

Exercise 17.7.1. Write `TeachingAsst::print` to print both the student and employee information. How can you avoid printing the `Person` information twice?

17.7.3. Renaming

It is conceivable that a class may derive from two base classes, with virtual functions of the same name and signature but completely different functionalities. It is difficult to come up with realistic examples for this scenario, and we will look at a contrived example instead.

Suppose a class `Story` has a virtual operation `int plot()` that returns a number indicating a description of the story plot (1 = murder, 2 = alien invasion, and so forth). Suppose class `Window` has a virtual operation `int plot()` that plots the contents of the window and returns some number related to the drawing (1 = window hidden, 2 = window iconized, and so forth). We derive `StoryWindow` from both `Story` and `Window` to display the story in a window. (You were warned that this is a contrived example!)

We need to define `StoryWindow::plot()` to display the story text in the window:

```
StoryWindow* sw;
sw->plot(); // plots window with story contents
```

Having done that, we still can find out the story plot:

```
sw->Story::plot();
```

But now we have destroyed the virtual function hierarchy of `Story::plot` in a strange way. If s is a pointer to a story, the call `s->plot()` either checks for the plot or renders a window, since s may point to a plain story or to a `StoryWindow` object. We have merged the two inheritance hierarchies with the same function name, although they should not be merged.

Some object-oriented programming languages, such as Eiffel, let you solve such problems by renaming functions in a derived class. In fact, Eiffel forces you to rename any features that clash with others when you derive from multiple base classes. That neatly solves the problems discussed in this section, but it makes it more difficult to evolve the base classes. Adding a feature to a base class may break a derived class in existing code.

In C++, there is no explicit renaming feature, but renaming can be done by introducing intermediate classes, as shown in Figure 17.13.

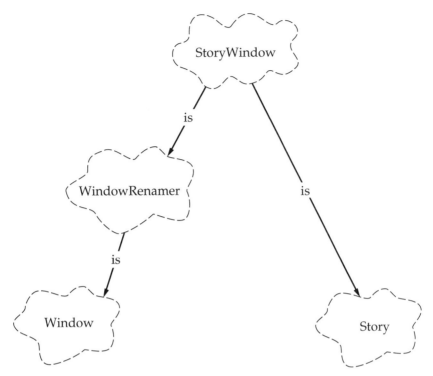

Figure 17.13.   The story window hierarchy.

```
class WindowRenamer : public Window
{
public:
   virtual void window_plot() const = 0;
   virtual void plot() const { window_plot(); }
};

class StoryWindow : public WindowRenamer, public Story
{
public:
   // ...
   virtual void window_plot() const; // plot text in window
};
```

Consider again the call s->plot() for a story pointer s. If s points to a plain story, then Story::plot is invoked. The same is true if s points to a StoryWindow. There is no problem, because that class has not redefined plot. Conversely, let w point to a Window that is actually a StoryWindow. The call w->plot() calls WindowRenamer::plot(), the closest function named plot on the path from the static type Window to the actual type StoryWindow. That function calls the renamed StoryWindow::plot_window.

This renaming is tedious and unintuitive. Fortunately, it is rarely, if ever, necessary. It is good to know that it can be done, because it guarantees that there is a way of combining any number of base classes, no matter what name clashes among virtual functions may exist.

Exercise 17.7.2. In the example, the call

```
StoryWindow* sw;
sw->plot();
```

invokes `Story::plot()`, making that version preferred over plotting the window. Redesign the `StoryWindow` class so that `sw->plot()` becomes ambiguous, forcing the programmer to choose between `sw->window_plot()` and `sw->story_plot()`. *Hint*: Introduce a `StoryRenamer` class.

Exercise 17.7.3. Suppose another window class derives from `StoryWindow` and changes the way the window is plotted. (A heart-shaped border for love stories?) What function does the derived class redefine? How can it be reached from the virtual `Window::plot()`?

17.7.4. Virtual Bases and Dominance

A feature of a virtual base class may be redefined along exactly one path without introducing an ambiguity. Suppose the class `Person` defines `id()` to return, say, the social security number, and suppose `Employee` redefines `id()` to return a different employee identification number, as shown in Figure 17.14. When `id()` is invoked on a `Student` object, it clearly refers to `Person::id()`. Hence, asking for the `id()` of a teaching assistant appears to be ambiguous:

```
TeachingAsst ta;
n = ta.id();
```

Is this the student identification number, `Person::id()`, or the employee number?

Suppose `id()` is a virtual function. Then we would expect that for every descendant of `Employee` the derived class version `Employee::id()` takes precedence over the base class version `Person::id()`. The social security number of the `Person` subobject of any `Employee` should never be the result of `id()`. Since `TeachingAsst` derives from `Employee`, it would be odd if the base class number could surface again in any way, even to create an ambiguity.

The *dominance rule* formalizes this reasoning. It states that a name in a virtual base class can be redefined along exactly one inheritance path without creating an ambiguity. This holds for any feature name—in particular, for both virtual and nonvirtual functions.

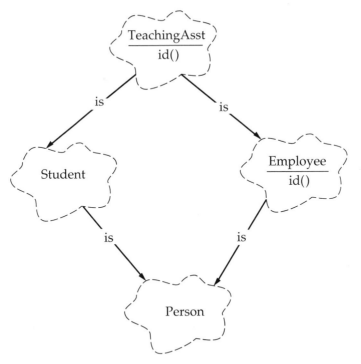

Figure 17.14. Dominance.

In our example, the call `ta.id()` is considered nonambiguous and refers to the redefinition `Employee::id()`. It does not matter whether `id` is a virtual function or not. Of course, if `Student` were also to redefine `id()`, an ambiguity would result.

The dominance rule applies only to *virtual* base classes. If `Person` were a nonvirtual base, then the call to `id()` would be ambiguous, because there would be two distinct `Person` objects: a student object with its notion of identification number, and an employee object with a different notion.

17.7.5. Repeated Bases

Consider the `TrafficSign` class that derives from `Text` and `Polygon`. Suppose we want to place a `TrafficSign` object onto a display list of shapes. Since `TrafficSign` derives indirectly from `Shape` (even twice!), it should be possible to convert a `TrafficSign*` into a `Shape*`:

```
List<Shape*> figure;
figure.append(new TrafficSign(...)); // ERROR
```

But the compiler does not admit this conversion. Looking at the data layout, shown in Figure 17.15, reveals why. Since there are actually two copies of a `Shape` object in a `TrafficSign`, the compiler does not know to which one you want to point.

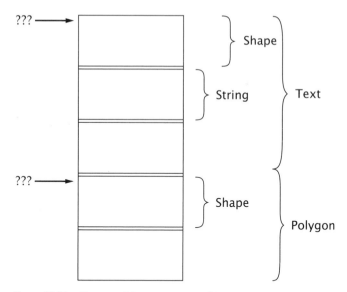

Figure 17.15.   Repeated bases cause ambiguity.

You can resolve the ambiguity by explicitly casting to one or the other direct base.

```
figure.append((Polygon*)new TrafficSign(...)); // OK
```

Since the direct bases of TrafficSign are distinct, casting to either selects a path to one of the repeated bases.

This ambiguity shows the conflict between repeated occurrences of a base class and the concept of inheritance as an *is-a* relationship.

17.8. IS MULTIPLE INHERITANCE USEFUL?

17.8.1. Multiple Inheritance Increases Complexity

Everyone will agree that multiple inheritance is far more complex than single inheritance. Virtual base classes are a difficult programming construct. The rules for ambiguity resolution are arcane.

There is one case in which multiple inheritance is simple: when inheriting from *disjoint* base classes. Disjoint base classes have *nothing* in common. There are no common base classes further down the hierarchy; hence, there are no repeated or shared bases. There are no operations with a common signature; therefore there are no name clashes, and no virtual functions are redefined along more than one path.

The most common case for this disjoint inheritance is the addition of mixins. When the protocol for a certain functionality, such as persistence, is expressed in a base class, and more than one functionality is desired for a particular class, then one simply derives from all these base classes. As long as there are no name conflicts, this is straightforward.

17.8.2. Conceptually Correct Multiple Inheritance Is Rare

Inheritance models the *is-a* relationship. It turns out to be quite uncommon for one class to be a special case of two separate classes.

Consider the Text class. Multiple inheritance was not forced upon us. Instead of inheriting from Shape and String, we could have used aggregation and used a data field of type Shape or String (or both). By deriving Text from Shape, we are able to place a Text object onto a list of Shape* pointers and apply *virtual functions*. That is a true benefit. By deriving Text from String, we were able to reuse the to_upper function without having to code

```
void Text::to_upper() { _string.to_upper(); }
```

Inheritance saved some editing. Since String has no virtual functions, we gain no advantage of polymorphism in this inheritance. Deriving Text from Shape, and adding a String data field, as we did in Chapter 7, is simple and does not give up much expressiveness.

Consider the TrafficSign class. Is a traffic sign a shape consisting of text and a polygon?

```
class TrafficSign : public Shape
{
  Text _notice;
  Polygon _border
};
```

A polygon with some text inside?

```
class TrafficSign : public Polygon { Text _notice; };
```

Text surrounded by a polygon?

```
class TrafficSign : public Text { Polygon _border; };
```

Both text and polygon?

```
class TrafficSign : public Text, public Polygon { };
```

All these seem reasonable. The *is-a* versus *has-a* test is inconclusive here. An advantage of using inheritance is the possibility of exploiting polymorphism. Do we envision a situation in which we have a container of objects, some of which are mere polygons, others traffic signs? A container of objects, some of which are plain text, the other traffic signs? Neither seems terribly likely. The

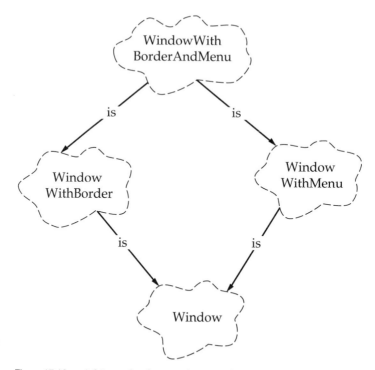

Figure 17.16.   A hierarchy for windows with menus and borders.

only meaningful base class is Shape. To plot traffic signs, they may well be located in a display list of shapes. In this case, inheritance from both Text and Polygon is the worst solution. A polygon is no longer a shape unless Shape is a virtual base class of Text and Polygon.

Some authors believe that this pattern is universal and that multiple inheritance has not proven to be a useful feature in actual programming. At the time of this writing, there seem to be no known examples that are generally acknowledged as compelling evidence of the usefulness of multiple inheritance. See [Cargill], ch. 9, for more information on this topic.

The literature contains lots of silly examples (like our StoryWindow). Figure 17.16 shows a common one ([Stroustrup], p. 207). On the face of it, it makes a lot of sense. A window with a border is a special case of a window; ditto a window with a menu; and windows that have both borders and menus are special cases of both. However, as a programming style, it must fail. Windows have other decorations, such as scrollbars, toolbars, and message panes. If we use inheritance, we end up with 32 classes and a bewildering collection of virtual base classes. It seems much better to model borders and menus as *attributes*. A window *has* a border (possibly of zero thickness), and it *has* a menu (possibly with no options).

We all use one library of classes that was built with multiple inheritance: iostreams. Figure 17.17 shows a part of the class relationship graph. Both

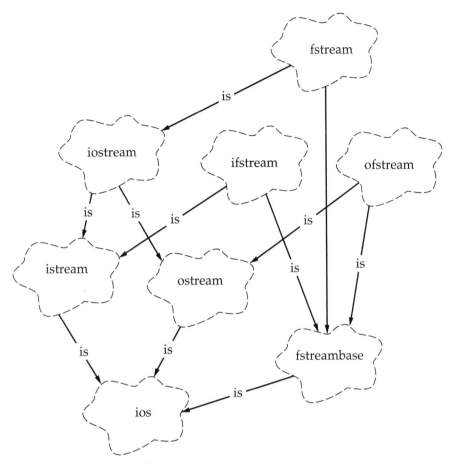

Figure 17.17. A portion of the iostream hierarchy.

istream and ostream derive from a class named ios that keeps track of format
and error state. It is not intuitively clear what an ios is, so it is difficult to say
what is more appropriate: does an istream *have* an ios, or *is* it an ios? The
class ios has no virtual functions, and polymorphism is not an issue. It does
make sense that an iostream is both an istream and an ostream. Since each of
them has an ios subobject, the inheritance from ios must be virtual.

This splendid idea has been completely given up for the other stream
classes. The file stream class for both input and output does not derive from
ifstream and ofstream, and neither does strstream derive from istrstream
and ostrstream, undoubtedly because of the complexity of factoring out yet
more common information into virtual base classes. Multiple inheritance can
be avoided altogether, at the cost of repeating some code, by having iostream
derive directly from ios. It is not necessary that this be done, but it *can* be done
easily. The fact that multiple inheritance is used in the iostream class library
does not prove that it is a necessary design feature.

The point is not that multiple inheritance should be avoided at all cost, merely that the gain from using it must be weighed against the cost of the added complexity.

Exercise 17.8.1. Derive `BarChart` both from `Shape` and from `List<double>`. Insert a few numbers and plot the chart. Deriving from the list saved us from having to code a protocol for insertion explicitly.

Exercise 17.8.2. Consider the `BarChart` of the previous exercise. Is a bar chart a shape? Do all shape operations (plot, print, move, scale) make sense for bar charts? Is a bar chart a list? Do all list operations (insert, remove, reset, length, and so on) make sense for a bar chart?

Exercise 17.8.3. The class library included with a C++ compiler contains a class `ShouldDelete`, which stores a flag to indicate whether or not a container of pointers should delete the objects it contains when it is destroyed. A base class `Container` derives both from `Object` and from `ShouldDelete`. Explain how the multiple inheritance can be avoided.

17.9. DESIGN HINTS

17.9.1. Beware of the Complexities of Multiple Inheritance

Multiple inheritance is much more complex than single inheritance. It is complex to program, and you might produce more errors in your code as a result. It is complex to implement, and your compiler writer might have had a less than perfect understanding of all the subtleties.

For those reasons, the advice to use inheritance for *is-a* design relationships only, not for convenience, holds even more strongly for multiple inheritance. In many cases, multiple inheritance is not terribly convenient.

17.9.2. Avoid Repeated Base Classes

Suppose a class D inherits from two base classes B and C. The easy case is if B and C have nothing in common.

If the base classes themselves have a common base A, that base should be a shared base, and virtual inheritance will be required to derive B and C from A.

If it is a repeated base, it is likely that not all inheritance represents an *is-a* relationship. A D object cannot be an A object in two ways.

17.9.3. Initialize Virtual Base
Classes with the Default Constructor

There are two ways to initialize a virtual base: with a default constructor, or explicitly from the "most derived" class. The notion of "most derived" is not stable. As soon as another class is derived, that one becomes the most derived class.

If you must initialize the virtual base explicitly from a derived-class constructor, also supply some other constructor for that derived class that doesn't initialize the virtual base. Otherwise, it is impossible to derive further classes from that class.

17.9.4. Place a Virtual Destructor into Each Base Class

Destroying an object with multiple bases is complicated by the fact that the destruction may be invoked through a pointer to any one of the bases. For example, a TeachingAsst object can be held in, and deleted from, a list of Student* or Employee* pointers. Either way, we don't just want the Student or Employee destructor called.

Place a virtual destructor (that is probably empty) into the Person base. That makes all derived destructors virtual. If there is more than one common base, place virtual destructors into all of them.

SIMULATION

18.1. CONTINUOUS AND DISCRETE EVENT SIMULATION

A good application of object-oriented programming is simulation. In fact, the first object-oriented language, Simula, was designed with this application in mind. We may simulate the activities of air molecules around an aircraft wing, of customers in a supermarket, or of vehicles on a road system. The goal of a simulation is to observe how changes in the design affect the behavior of a system. Modifying the shape of a wing, the location and staffing of cash registers, or the synchronization of traffic lights has an effect on turbulences in the air stream, customer satisfaction, or traffic throughput. Modeling these systems in the computer is far cheaper than running actual experiments.

Computer models are populated with objects that abstract and simplify real-world entities. Classes arise very naturally in the design. Customers enter a supermarket and join cash register queues, giving rise to a Customer class; vehicles populate a road. The simulation program may use classes Vehicle, Road, and TrafficLight. Inheritance is common: There are different kinds of vehicles, such as cars and trucks; supermarket shoppers fall into classes with different behavior, such as daily shoppers or weekly shoppers. We may know the percentage of cars and trucks or of daily and weekly shoppers, or we can study the effect of changes in that percentage on the system.

Simulations fall into two broad categories. *Continuous* simulations constantly update all objects in a system. A simulated clock advances in seconds or some other suitable constant time interval. Every clock tick, each object is moved or updated in some way. Consider the simulation of traffic along a road. Each car has some position, velocity, and acceleration. Its position needs to be updated with every clock tick. If the car gets too close to an obstacle, it must decelerate. The new position may be displayed on the screen.

In contrast, in *discrete event* simulation, time advances in chunks. All interesting events are kept in a priority queue, sorted by the time in which they are to happen. Once one event has completed, the clock jumps to the time of the next event to be executed.

To see the contrast between these two simulation styles, consider the updating of a traffic light. Suppose the traffic light just turned red, and it will turn green again in 30 seconds. In a continuous model, the traffic light is visited every second, and a counter field is decremented. Once the counter reaches 0, the color changes. In a discrete model, the traffic light schedules an event to be notified 30 seconds from now. For 29 seconds, the traffic light is not bothered at all, and then it receives a message to change its state. Discrete event simulation avoids busy waiting.

18.2. EVENTS

The implementation of discrete event simulation naturally leads to polymorphism. The event scheduler stores events, which have a time stamp indicating when they are to be executed. Each event has some action associated with it that must be carried out at that time. Beyond that, the scheduler has no concept of what an event represents. Of course, actual events must carry with them some information. For example, the event notifying a traffic light of a state change must know which traffic light to notify.

The base class is Event. An event has a time field to indicate its date of activation. When the event is activated, a virtual function process() is called. This virtual function may move objects around, update information, and, most importantly, schedule more events.

The event class is very simple:

```
class Event
{
public:
  Event(Time t);
  virtual void process() = 0;
  Time time() const;
  virtual ~Event() {}
private:
  Time _time;
};

Event::Event(Time t) : _time(t) {}
Time Event::time() const { return _time; }
```

Event is an abstract base class; we will derive actual events from it. Actual events may carry some data, and their process operation performs some action.

```
class TrafficLightChange : public Event
{
```

```
public:
  virtual void process();
  // ...
private:
  TrafficLight* _light;
};

void TrafficLightChange::process() { _light->change_color(); }
```

Events are compared by their time stamp and kept in a priority queue. (A priority queue is a data structure into which elements can be inserted in any order and removed in sorted order; see Chapter 17 for details on priority queues.)

After initialization, the simulation enters the *event loop*. Events are retrieved from the priority queue in the order specified by their time stamp. The simulated time is advanced to the time stamp of the event, and the event is processed according to its virtual process function:

```
PriorityQueue<Event*> event_queue;
Time now; // the simulated time
// initializations
while (event_queue.length() > 0 && now <= ENDTIME)
{ Event* event = event_queue.remove();
  now = event->time();
  event->process();
  delete event;
}
```

All further activity, including the scheduling of new events, takes place in the process operations.

18.3. A BANK SIMULATION

We will consider a simple example, a bank serving customers, as shown in Figure 18.1. Customers enter the bank. If there is a queue, they join the queue; otherwise they move up to a teller. When a customer has completed a teller transaction, the time spent in the bank is logged, the customer is removed, and the next customer in the queue moves up to the teller.

18.3.1. Exponential Distribution

Customer arrival is a *Poisson process;* that is, the time between two arrivals is exponentially distributed. An exponential distribution with mean μ can be obtained from a uniformly distributed random variable U in [0,1] by the transformation

$$E = -\mu \log_e U$$

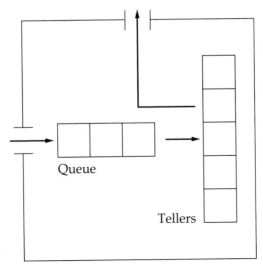

Figure 18.1.   The layout of the bank.

The following C++ function computes random values that are exponentially distributed with a given mean:

```
double expdist(double mean)
{ double r = rand();
  r /= RAND_MAX;
  return -mean*log(r);
}
```

(A more complex algorithm, due to Marsaglia, Sibuya, and Ahrens, is much faster than this simple method, because it avoids the call to the transcendental `log` function. See [Knuth], p. 128, for details.)

If a customer arrives at time t, we can schedule the next customer arrival at

```
t + expdist(M)
```

where M is the average time between two customer arrivals.

Processing time is also exponentially distributed, with a different average. In this simulation, we use

```
typedef double Time; // measured in minutes

const Time INTERARRIVAL = 1.0; // 1 minute
const Time AVG_PROCTIME = 5.0; // 5 minutes
```

That is, on average one minute elapses between customer arrivals, and customer transactions require an average of five minutes.

18.3.2. Customers

We only keep track of the time at which a customer enters the bank, for later computation of the average stay. Each customer object remembers the time of arrival:

```
class Customer
{
public:
  Customer(Time t);
  arrival_time();
private:
  Time _arrival_time;
};
```

We keep a class to accumulate statistics:

```
class BankStatistics
{
public:
  BankStatistics();
  void add(Time t);
  void print() const;
  double average_time() const;
private:
  int _ncust;
  Time _total_time;
};
```

When a customer leaves the bank, the time spent is added to the statistics:

```
void BankStatistics::add(Time t)
{ _ncust++;
  _total_time += t;
}
```

At the end of the simulation, we want to know the average time that customers spent in the bank:

```
double BankStatistics::average_time() const
{ if (_ncust == 0) return 0;
  else return _total_time/_ncust;
}

void BankStatistics::print() const
{ cout << _ncust
     << " customers. Average time "
     << average_time() << "minutes." << endl;
}
```

Exercise 18.3.1. In addition to the mean, keep track of the standard deviation of customer times in the BankStatistics class. (*Hint:* In addition to the sum of times, also accumulate the sum of squares.)

18.3.3. The Bank

We keep an array of tellers as well as a queue to hold waiting customers. The queue is not a priority queue but a regular FIFO (first in, first out) queue:

```
class Bank
{
public:
  Bank();
  void add(Customer*);
  void add_to_teller(int teller, Customer*);
  Customer* remove(int teller);
  void print() const;
private:
  enum { NTELLER = 5 };
  Array<Customer*> _teller;
  Queue<Customer*> _cust_queue;
};
```

Teller i is busy if _teller[i] holds a nonempty customer pointer, and available if it holds a null pointer.

When a customer is added to the bank, we first check whether a teller is available to handle the customer. If not, the customer is added to the waiting queue:

```
void Bank::add(Customer* c)
{ for (int i = 1; i <= NTELLER; i++)
    if (_teller[i] = 0)
    { add_to_teller(i, c);
      return;
    }
  _cust_queue.insert(c);
}
```

When a customer is added to an empty teller, something interesting happens. We know the customer will spend about five minutes with the teller. To obtain a variation of the time, we call t = expdist(AVG_PROCTIME). After time t has elapsed, the customer needs to be removed from the bank. Of course, we cannot wait around for that to happen, since other events will be going on in the meantime. Therefore we schedule a departure event to occur t minutes from now:

```
void Bank::add_to_teller(int i, Customer* c)
{ ASSERT_PRECOND(_teller[i] == 0);
  _teller[i] = c;
```

```
      Time t = expdist(AVG_PROCTIME);
      event_queue.insert(new Departure(now + t, i));
}
```

When the departure event triggers, it will notify the bank to remove the customer. We remove the customer and keep track of the total amount of time the customer spent in the waiting queue and with the teller. This makes the teller available to service the next customer from the waiting queue. If there is a queue, we add the first customer to this teller:

```
Customer* Bank::remove(int i)
{ Customer* c = _teller[i];
  _teller[i] = 0;
  stat.add(now - c->arrival_time());
  if (_cust_queue.length() > 0)
    add_to_teller(i, _cust_queue.remove());
  return c;
}
```

To show the current state of the bank, we print a dot for an empty teller and a C for a customer:

```
void Bank::print() const
{ for (int i = 1; i <= NTELLER; i++)
    cout << (_teller[i] == 0 ? '.' : 'C');
  cout << '<';
  int q = _cust_queue.length();
  for (i = 1; i <= q; i++) cout << 'C';
  cout << endl;
}
```

18.3.4. Arrivals and Departures

The classes Arrival and Departure derive from the base class Event. Departures remember not only the departure time but also the teller from whom a customer is to depart.

```
class Arrival : public Event
{
public:
  Arrival(Time);
  virtual void process();
};

class Departure : public Event
{
```

```
public:
  Departure(Time, int teller);
  virtual void process();
private:
  int _teller;
};
```

When a new customer is to arrive at the bank, an arrival event is triggered. The processing action of that event has the responsibility of making a customer and adding it to the bank. Furthermore, we must ensure that customers keep coming. When a customer arrives, we know that the next one is expected about a minute later; therefore, we schedule another arrival event:

```
void Arrival::process()
{ Customer* c = new Customer(now);
  bank.add(c);
  Time t = expdist(INTERARRIVAL);
  event_queue.insert(new Arrival(now + t));
}
```

To process a departure event, we remove the customer from the teller and reclaim the storage:

```
void Departure::process()
{ Customer* c = bank.remove(_teller);
  delete c;
}
```

Note that the new Customer allocation in Arrival::process is balanced against the deallocation in Departure::process.

18.3.5. Tying It Together

We have a number of global variables: the event queue and system time, the bank, and the statistics. (We will see later how to reorganize the code to eliminate the global variables.)

```
PriorityQueue<Event*> event_queue;
Time now;
Bank bank;
BankStatistics stat;
```

In the main program we need to set up the simulation, enter the event loop, and print the result at the end. The most important task in setting up the simulation is to get the flow of events going. At the outset, the event queue is empty. We will schedule the arrival of a customer at the start time (9 A.M.). Since

Arrival::process schedules the arrival of each successor, the insertion of the arrival event for the first customer takes care of the generation of all arrivals. Once customers arrive at the bank, they are added to tellers, and departure events are generated:

```
void main()
{ const Time STARTTIME = 9 * 60; // 9 A.M.
  const Time ENDTIME = 17 * 60; // 5 P.M.

  now = STARTTIME;

  event_queue.insert(new Arrival(now));

  while (event_queue.length() > 0 && now <= ENDTIME)
  { Event* event = event_queue.remove();
    now = event->time();
    event->process();
    delete event;
    bank.print();
  }

  stat.print();
}
```

Here is a typical program run. The bank starts out with empty tellers, and customers start dropping in:

```
.....<
C....<
CC...<
CCC..<
CCCC.<
C.CC.<
CCCC.<
CCCCC<
CCCCC<C
CCCCC<
C.CCC<
```

Due to the random fluctuations of customer arrival and processing, the queue can get quite long:

```
CCCCC<CCCCCCCCC
CCCCC<CCCCCCCCCC
CCCCC<CCCCCCCCCCC
CCCCC<CCCCCCCCCCC
```

```
CCCCC<CCCCCCCCCC
CCCCC<CCCCCCCCCCC
CCCCC<CCCCCCCCCCCCC
CCCCC<CCCCCCCCCCCCCC
CCCCC<CCCCCCCCCCCCC
```

At other times, the bank is empty again:

```
CCC.C<
CCC..<
CC...<
.C...<
.....<
C....<
```

This particular run of the simulation ends up with the following statistics:

```
457 customers. Average time 15.28 minutes.
```

If you are the bank manager, this result is quite depressing. You hired enough tellers to take care of all customers. (Every hour, you need to serve, on average, 60 customers. Their transactions take an average of 5 minutes each; that is 300 teller-minutes, or 5 teller-hours. Hence, hiring five tellers is just right.) Yet the average customer had to wait in line more than 10 minutes, twice as long as their transaction time. This is an average, so some customers had to wait even longer. If disgruntled customers hurt your business, you may have to hire more tellers and pay them for being idle some of the time.

Exercise 18.3.2. This particular run was not entirely typical. Run the simulation twenty times in a row, taking care to use different sequences of random numbers for each run. You will find that there is quite a bit of variation in the outcome.

Exercise 18.3.3. We populate our simulation with Customer* pointers, rather than Customer objects, for two reasons. First, it makes it simple to express the fact that each teller holds zero or one customer. More importantly, it allows us to introduce variations in customer behavior. Assume the bank is visited by a mix of 90 percent residential and 10 percent commercial customers. Assume that residential customers have simple transactions that take on average 4 minutes, but commercial customers deposit large amounts of checks and require an average of 10 minutes. Simulate a bank with these characteristics.

Exercise 18.3.4. For added realism, change the behavior of the bank by having more customers and fewer tellers during lunch hour (noon until 1 P.M.). *Hint:* Schedule a LunchHour event at noon to close some tellers and increase the arrival rate.

18.4. A SIMULATION FRAMEWORK

Let us consider the ways in which we might like to extend the bank simulation from the previous section.

1. We would like to run the same simulation repeatedly to average the results.
2. We would like to vary the parameters of the bank (number of tellers, arrival rate, and so forth) and analyze the effect of the changes.
3. We would like to vary the *structure* of the bank; for example, to have one queue per teller.
4. We would like to simulate an entity other than a bank, reusing as much of the general simulation code as possible.

Unfortunately, extending this application is difficult:

- There are many global variables and constants.
- There is high dependency ("use relationship") between classes, as illustrated in Figure 18.2.

Exercise 18.4.1. Change the structure of the bank to have one waiting queue per teller. Have a customer join the shortest queue if no teller is free. Would you expect the average service time to be longer or shorter than in the single-queue model? Run a number of simulations of both banks and compare the averages.

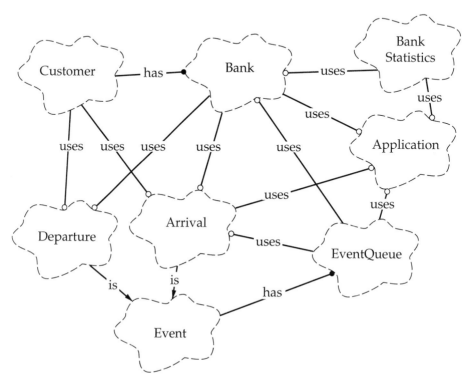

Figure 18.2.   Class relationships in the bank simulation.

18.4.1. Simplifying the Usage Relationship

It is time to reorganize the classes to manage the complexity of the system. An obvious choice is a Simulation class. It should contain the event queue and the simulation time. The event loop should be moved from main to a run operation of the Simulation class. To run the simulation multiple times, simply repeat the run operation.

The Simulation class is thus decoupled from the details of the bank and can be reused in other simulations:

```
class Simulation
{
public:
   void run(Time from, Time to);
   void schedule (Event* e);
private:
   Time _now;
   PriorityQueue<Event *> _event_queue;
};
```

Some actions need to schedule new events. For example, when a customer is moved to a teller, a departure event is generated and must be placed on the waiting queue. First, we need an operation to schedule another event:

```
void Simulation::schedule(Event* e)
{ _event_queue.insert(e);
}
```

A harder problem remains. The code for moving a customer to a teller is inside the Bank object. That code must be able to locate the simulation object to invoke schedule on it. There are three ways in which Bank::add_to_teller can call Simulation::schedule:

- Through a global variable
- Through an argument of add_to_teller
- Through a field or base class of Bank

Global variables are best avoided when possible. Making the Simulation object containing the event queue a global object is restrictive: The program will only be able to run one simulation at a time. For example, we cannot show two simulations in two windows.

Passing a reference to the simulation object as an argument to add_to_teller is workable. Of course, it requires that the caller of add_to_teller also have access to that object. It turns out that a number of operations must pass along the simulation object before it finally gets to add_to_teller, making the interfaces of these intermediaries somewhat unintuitive.

The simulation object could be a field or a base class of the Bank object. Given that our bank is not a real bank but a simulated bank, it sounds entirely reasonable to say that the Bank *is* a Simulation. We will choose inheritance:

```
class Bank : public Simulation
```

In general, we envision that other simulations also derive from the Simulation class:

```
class Factory : public Simulation
```

Now consider processing an event, say a customer arrival. The Arrival::process operation needs to know about the bank in order to add a new customer. Again, there are three ways it can access the bank:

- Through a global variable
- Through an argument of process
- Through a field or base class of Arrival

We would like to avoid the use of global variables. It appears unattractive to add a bank field to each Arrival event or to derive Arrival from Bank. We will choose to pass a pointer to the bank in each process call. The process operation is invoked in the event loop of Simulation::run:

```
void Simulation::run(Time from, Time to)
{ _now = from;
  while (_event_queue.length() > 0 && _now <= to)
  { Event* event = _event_queue.remove();
    now = event->time();
    event->process();
    delete event;
  }
}
```

The call to event->process() must be modified to pass the Bank object. Therefore, the simulation object must be able to locate the bank. But Simulation is a general, reusable class that knows nothing about banks. Fortunately, the convention is that the simulated entity *derives* from Simulation. The simulation object can therefore just pass a reference to *itself*.

```
event->process(self);
```

Because process is a virtual function of Event, another general class that knows nothing about banks, its signature now becomes

```
void Event::process(Simulation& s);
```

The corresponding function `Arrival::process` receives a reference to the bank object, but as the wrong type:

```
void Arrival::process(Simulation& s);
```

We know s must be of type `Bank&`, because our arrival events are generated only in bank simulations. We must cast to the derived class.

```
void Arrival::process(Simulation& s)
{ Bank& bank = dynamic_cast<Bank&>(s); // or bank = (Bank&)s;
  Customer* c = new Customer(bank.now());
  bank.add(c);
  Time t = expdist(INTERARRIVAL);
  bank.schedule(new Arrival(bank.now() + t));
}
```

The cast to the derived class is not pretty, but it is a consequence of using the `Simulation/Event` mechanism as a reusable base class.

After the redesign, the class relationships are much simplified, as shown in Figure 18.3.

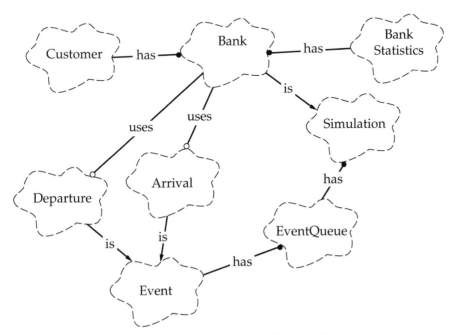

Figure 18.3.   Class diagram of the bank simulation after redesign.

18.4.2. Emergence of the Framework

Let us reconsider the original event loop:

```
_event_queue.insert(new Arrival(_now));
while (_event_queue.length() > 0 && _now <= to)
{ Event* event = _event_queue.remove();
  _now = event->time();
  event->process(self);
  delete event;
  bank.print();
}
stat.print();
```

It appears that it may be more difficult to move this code into
Simulation::run than we originally imagined. The Arrival event and
the calls to bank::print and stat::print are not at all generic but specific
to the bank problem.

We can generalize that every simulation run has the general form

initialize
```
while (_event_queue.length() > 0 && _now <= to)
{ Event* event = _event_queue.remove();
  _now = event->time();
  event->process(self);
  delete event;
```
  update
```
}
```
terminate

It now greatly helps to know that the bank (and any other simulation) will
derive from Simulation. We can simply make initialize(), update(), and
terminate() into *virtual* functions, which the derived class can redefine.

This is a powerful idea. The base class Simulation encapsulates the
general flow of action: initialize, loop to launch events, and update, terminate.
The derived class specifies how each individual action is to be carried out, but
it need not be concerned about the order of execution.

The simulation class now looks as follows:

```
class Simulation
{
public:
  simulation();
  void run(Time from, Time to);
  void schedule(Event*);
  virtual void initialize() = 0;
  virtual void update() = 0;
  virtual void terminate() = 0;
```

```
  Time now() const;

  virtual ~Simulation(){}

private:
  Time _now;
  PriorityQueue<Event *> _event_queue;
};
```

The initialization, update, and termination operations are defined as pure virtual. That forces the deriving class to specify an action. (A gentler alternative is to define them to do nothing.)

The event loop invokes these functions, not knowing what they will do.

```
void Simulation::run(Time from, Time to)
{ _now = from;
  initialize();
  while (_event_queue.length() > 0 && _now <= to)
  { Event* event = _event_queue.remove();
    _now = event->time();
    event->process(self);
    delete event;
    update();
  }
  terminate();
}
```

The derived class Bank redefines the operations:

```
void Bank::initialize()
{ schedule(new Arrival(now()));
}

void Bank::update()
{ print();
}

void Bank::terminate()
{ _stat.print();
}
```

The Simulation/Event classes form a simple starting point for simulation programs. By themselves they are not functional. Simulation has pure virtual functions initialize, update, and terminate. Event has a pure virtual function process. The implementor of a simulation must derive a simulation object from Simulation and one or more event types from Event. This setup yields an important benefit. A part of the design experience has been captured in the base classes and the requirements for derivation, and it does not have to be rediscovered for other discrete event simulation programs.

A collection of classes whose purpose is to serve as the basis for derivation, and whose nonvirtual operations impose an execution order on the virtual functions, is called a *framework*. A framework captures the general outline of the class structure and control flow typical to a problem domain. We will study frameworks in further detail in Chapter 19.

Exercise 18.4.2. Using the simulation framework, implement two bank types in the same program, one with a single waiting queue and the other with one waiting queue per teller. Run a number of simulations of both banks and compare the averages. The key requirement is to have all runs and computations in one program rather than restarting several programs.

Exercise 18.4.3. In this exercise, we will do a simulation of a biological system. Our world is a 10×10 array of cells. Each cell can be populated by at most two animals. There are four different species of animals, A, B, C, D. Animals get born, move, mate, and die according to the following rules:

1. When an animal is born, it has a 50% chance of being male or female. It will live for 45 days. Upon birth, it is placed on a random cell. If that cell is full (there are 2 other animals already there), then the new animal dies right away and does not enter the system.

2. When an animal is surrounded by 6 or more other animals, it dies of overcrowding. We count the animals in the current cell and the neighbors (including diagonal neighbors).

3. Once every 3 days each animal is checked for overcrowding and then moves in a random direction (with equal probability to north, east, west, south, northeast, northwest, southeast, southwest, no move). However, if the chosen direction is at the edge of the array of cells, or if it leads to a cell that is full, the animal stays put and tries again the next day.

4. If an animal gets into a cell in which another animal lives that is of the same species and of opposite sex, they mate. 15 days later this leads to 4 offspring.

5. The simulation starts with the birth of 16 animals of each species.

Use the simulation framework and schedule move and birth events. Make multiple runs and determine the expected eventual fate of the population.

Exercise 18.4.4. In this exercise, we will simulate traffic on a road containing traffic lights. Cars move in a single lane. The length of the road, the distance between traffic lights, the arrival rate of the cars, and the length of the simulation are specified in an input file. Cars have a location, speed, and acceleration. Every second, these values are updated.

Cars should not bump into another or cross a red traffic light. Therefore, cars must slow down once they get close enough to an obstacle. If no obstacles are close, cars should speed up to their ideal speed (28 m/s, approx. 30 mph). All distances are measured in meters, time in seconds.

Suppose dt is the time update interval (1 second for us). If the current acceleration is a, then the speed difference is $dv = a\,dt$, and the difference in position is $ds = v\,dt$. That is, every second compute dv, add it to v, then compute ds and add it to s.

That is good enough when we trundle along at constant acceleration, but we need to know what acceleration to apply when braking. If the current position and speed are s_0, v_0, and we desire to be at location s_1 with speed v_1, then

$$v_1 = v_0 + at$$

$$s_1 = s_0 + v_0 t + \tfrac{1}{2}at^2$$

You can solve these for a (and t). In particular, if a red traffic light is at s_1, then $v_1 = 0$.

Start braking if the next obstacle falls within a *brake horizon*—the minimum time needed to come to a complete stop plus some safety factor.

A typical compact car has maximum acceleration of about 2.5 m/s² and maximum braking deceleration of −8 m/s². You should cap acceleration at those values. Cars are 5 m long.

Traffic lights change color between red and green every 60 seconds. (We ignore yellow—this is California.)

Use the simulation framework and two events: to move cars and to change the traffic lights.

C H A P T E R   19

FRAMEWORKS

19.1. DESIGNING FOR INHERITANCE

We have seen many cases in which inheritance relationships between classes
were discovered in the design phase and then modeled in C++ with inheritance
and virtual functions. In this chapter we will go beyond that point of view and
discuss how to design classes that serve as the basis from which other, as yet
undiscovered, classes may inherit.

19.1.1. Protocol Specification

By specifying a set of virtual functions, a base class can impose a protocol
on its derived classes, relieving the derived-class designer from the task of
rediscovering the required functionality.

Consider a class Window to describe a window in a graphical user interface
environment. The base class Window is supplied as a basis for derivation. The programmer of an actual application derives classes, such as SpreadsheetWindow
and GraphWindow, from the class Window.

Suppose the contents of a window on the screen are corrupted, perhaps
because another window temporarily popped up before it and was removed,
or because the window was restored from its icon. Typically, graphical user
interfaces do not cache pixels of obscured or minimized windows but rely on
the ability of each window to repaint itself when notified in some way.

The details of the notification mechanism can be handled by the base class
Window. That class specifies a pure virtual function

```
Window::paint(Rectangle r)
```

whose task is to repaint the area of the window inside the rectangle r. Each class
that derives from Window must redefine paint to render its data in the form of
spreadsheet cells, a graph, or some other representation.

Since Window::paint is a *pure* virtual function, for which no definition
is supplied, each derived class must override this function. Similarly, the base

class will specify virtual functions for other actions; for example, reaction to keystrokes or mouse clicks. In this way, the base class enforces the services that a derived class must provide to fit into the windowing system.

Not all virtual functions need be pure. If a satisfactory default can be specified in the base class, the operation can be implemented at that level and overridden by only those derived classes for which the generic behavior is inappropriate. For example, to react to a timer event, `Window` may supply a virtual function whose action is to ignore the timer. Those classes that wish to take some action that depends on the system timer, such as animation, can redefine the virtual function. Most classes will be happy with the default.

Understanding the event flow in a graphical user interface environment requires expert knowledge. This knowledge can be mapped into the design of a base class or a set of base classes (a *framework*), which can be extended by a programmer who is an expert in the application domain but not in the user interface architecture. The base class specifies what services a derived class must provide to fit into the system. The application programmer overrides the virtual functions to display the application data or to handle user commands. These application-specific tasks cannot be undertaken by the basic `Window` class. Conversely, the application programmer is completely freed from user-interface issues, such as moving, sizing, and scrolling of windows.

19.1.2. Operation Sequencing

A base class that supplies virtual functions for derivation may call these virtual functions in other operations. For example, `Window` may have an operation that takes care of scrolling. That operation changes the coordinate origin, moves existing pixels, and then invokes the virtual `paint` function to render the portion of the image that has been scrolled in. The base class has no idea *what* is being painted, but it knows *when* the painting is necessary.

In this way, the base class imposes an order on the execution of the services that the derived classes supply.

19.1.3. Base Class Services

When a derived class carries out a concrete service, it may need information from the base class. Encapsulation forbids us from granting direct data access, so data must be supplied either through function arguments or through special operations.

For example, to redraw a portion of the screen in the `paint` operation, it is necessary to have a graphics context to paint on. When the base class calls `paint`, it can supply the graphics context as an additional argument.

It is impractical to use function arguments to communicate all information that a derived class may need. Instead, the base class typically offers operations that the derived class can call; for example, to find out the current window size or the current scroll offset.

When constructing a framework, it is our goal to design classes that serve as a basis for derivation of as yet unknown classes. It is particularly difficult to anticipate what information a derived class may need. Insufficient data access can render the base class useless as a platform for derivation, but if all implementation detail is exposed, the base class cannot evolve.

Exercise 19.1.1. Design a base class Chart that deals with data gathering and those services that you believe to be useful for specific charts, such as computing maximum, minimum, total, and averages. Then derive BarChart and PieChart from Chart.

19.2. PROBLEM DOMAINS FOR FRAMEWORKS

19.2.1. Simulation

The simulation code of Chapter 18 is an excellent example of a code framework. Base classes for the simulation and events enforce an application model that might not be obvious to a programmer unfamiliar with simulations. To construct a specific simulation, a programmer derives a class from Simulation and multiple classes from Event.

The overall control flow rests with the framework code, specifically the Simulation::run operation. It calls the initialize/update/terminate operations of the derived simulation class and the process operations of the event classes. These are the "hooks" for the programmer building a specific simulation.

19.2.2. Streams

We saw in Chapter 12 how to build a specialized stream class that sends output to a window rather than a file. We were able to create such a stream class because the iostream architecture is a framework.

The streambuf base class has virtual functions underflow and overflow. We supplied our own buffer whose overflow operation sends characters to a window. The framework does not care about the exact nature of the buffer but simply calls the virtual overflow function when necessary.

It is no accident that we were able to add our own stream class. The iostream package has been carefully designed as a framework to facilitate just this kind of extension.

19.2.3. Containers

[Booch], ch. 9, describes a framework for container classes. A base class Container serves to specify a standard protocol. A base class Iterator provides the reset/current/next/at_end iteration abstraction. A specific container class, such as a queue, is derived from Container, and QueueIterator is derived from Iterator.

Here the framework organization was chosen primarily for the convenience of the *implementor* of the container class library. Most programmers will simply use the existing container classes. They do not care whether these classes were built with a framework or not. The framework becomes visible only when a new container type needs to be implemented, but this is not likely to happen very often. The number of useful containers is fairly limited, and a good class library provides the standard data structures.

19.2.4. Application Frameworks

Frameworks for streams and containers form the basis for writing new classes. In contrast, the simulation framework is intended to build an entire *application*. Of course, the simulation code is just a simple example. Practical frameworks implement a lot more standard functionality, such as reading and saving files, displaying data, and gathering user commands.

Application frameworks are becoming increasingly popular. Programmers with experience in building applications of a certain type, such as simulation or financial trading programs, create the framework for an application. Experts in a specific problem, such as floor management in the Fremont factory or Swiss mortgage bonds, build their program on top of that framework. The same framework is used as the foundation of many different applications. The programmer using the framework is freed from having to reimplement routine tasks, such as reading and saving, and the user interface. This separation of the common from the specific makes the design of highly customized applications cost-effective.

19.3. A DIAGRAM EDITOR

19.3.1. The Problem Domain

In this section we will develop a very simple application framework. The problem domain that we address is the interactive editing of *diagrams*. A diagram is made up of nodes and edges that have certain shapes. Consider a class diagram. The nodes are cloud shapes, and the edges are either arrows or lines with circles. A different example is an electronic circuit diagram, where vertices are transistors, resistors, and capacitors. Connections are simply wires. There are numerous other examples, such as chemical formulas, flowcharts, organization charts, and logic circuits.

Traditionally, a programmer who wanted to implement, say, a class diagram editor starts from scratch and creates an application that can edit just class diagrams. If the programmer is lucky, code for a similar program, say a flowchart editor, is available for inspection; however, it may well be difficult to separate the code that is common to all diagrams from the flowchart-specific tasks, and much of the code may need to be recreated for the class diagram editor.

In contrast, a framework encapsulates those aspects that are common to all diagrams and provides a way for specific diagram types to express their special demands.

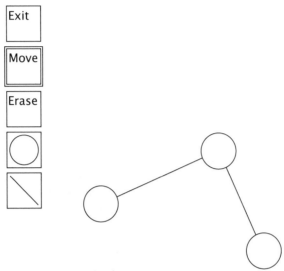

Figure 19.1.   Graph editor screen.

19.3.2. The User Interface

Many of the tasks, such as selecting, moving, and connecting elements, are similar for all editors. Let us be specific and describe the user interface that our very primitive editor will have. The screen is divided into two parts, shown in Figure 19.1. On the left is a collection of *buttons*. The first buttons are always the *exit, move,* and *erase* buttons. They are followed by one button for each node type and one button for each edge type. We will see later how a specific instance of the application supplies the icons for the buttons. Exactly one of the buttons is *active* at any time. On the right is the diagram drawing area. The mouse is used for drawing and for activating buttons. The mouse events consist of *clicking* (pushing down the physical button on the mouse and then releasing it) on a node, an edge, a button, or empty space, and *dragging* (pushing down the mouse button, moving the mouse to another location, and then releasing the mouse button). The mouse actions depend on the currently active button:

- If the currently active button is a node, clicking the mouse anywhere places a new node into the graph, centered at the mouse position. Dragging has no effect.
- If the currently active button is an edge, dragging the mouse from one node to another joins the two nodes by an edge.
- If the move button is active, dragging a node moves it to a new position.
- If the erase button is active, clicking on an edge erases it. Clicking on a node erases it and the adjacent edges.

   Of course, this editor is so primitive as to be barely usable. There is no provision to supply text labels for edges and nodes. There is no scrolling to handle larger diagrams. There is no cut and paste. These features can be handled by an extended version of this framework.

19.3.3. Division of Responsibility

When designing a framework, we must divide responsibilities between the framework and specific instances of the framework. For example, it is clear that the code to render a transistor-shaped node is not part of the general framework—only of the electric circuit instance.

Rendering the shapes of nodes and edges must be deferred. The same holds for *hit testing:* finding out whether a node or edge is hit by a mouse click. This can be tricky for odd shapes and cannot be the responsibility of the framework.

Drawing the icons on the buttons is an instance-level task, but rendering the button column is the job of the framework. This brings up a very interesting problem. The framework must have some idea of the node and edge classes in the application so that it can tell each type of node or edge to render its icon in a button. We will require that an application register all node and edge classes with the framework code.

Unlike Smalltalk, C++ does not recognize classes as objects that can be manipulated at run time. We use objects as stand-ins for their classes:

```
editor.register_node(new Transistor);
editor.register_edge(new Wire);
```

To render the button icons, the framework traverses the collection of sample nodes and edges and invokes plot_icon on each element.

Each node and edge is responsible for saving its data to a file and reading them back. As described in Chapter 12, reading of polymorphic objects is always difficult. In our case it is simplified by the fact that we have a complete set of possible types readily available through the node and edge registration. Each node and edge has a virtual function name(). In the file, we first save the name, then the object data. When reading, we search for the node or edge whose name we find, and then invoke its virtual read() function. Except for name(), read(), and print(), this activity can be implemented by the framework.

19.3.4. Framework Classes

The framework defines base classes Node and Edge with the following interface:

```
class Node
{
public:
  virtual String name() const = 0;
  virtual void plot(GraphicsContext& gc) const = 0;
  virtual void plot_icon(Rectangle r, GraphicsContext& gc)
    const = 0;
  virtual Node* clone() const = 0;
  virtual Rectangle enclosing_rect() const = 0;
  virtual Bool is_inside(Point p) const = 0;
```

```
      virtual Point boundary_point(Point exterior) const = 0;
      void move(Point p);
      Point center() const;
    private:
      Point _center;
    };

    class Edge
    {
    public:
      virtual String name() const = 0;
      virtual void plot(GraphicsContext& gc) const = 0;
      virtual void plot_icon(Rectangle r, GraphicsContext& gc)
        const = 0;
      virtual Edge* clone() const = 0;
      virtual Bool is_on(Point p) const = 0;

      const Node* from() const;
      const Node* to() const;
      void connect(Node* f, Node* t);

    private:
      Node* _from;
      Node* _to;
    };
```

These are abstract classes, and the programmer using this framework must derive node and edge types from these bases and override the virtual functions:

```
    class Transistor : public Node
    class Wire : public Edge
```

Interestingly enough, the abstract classes suffice to implement the `Diagram` data structure completely. The framework programmer does not have to modify it in any way:

```
    class Diagram
    {
    public:
      void add_node(Node*);
      void add_edge(Edge*);
      void remove(Point);
      Node* find_node(Point);
      void plot(GraphicsContext&) const;
      void print(ostream& os) const;
```

```
private:
  Array<Node*> _nodes;
  Array<Edge*> _edges;
};
```

The DiagramEditor class handles all user interaction and editing commands. The mechanics of mouse movement, rubber bands (outlines that show the position and dimensions of an object as the user changes them by dragging), and screen update are completely solved at this level and are of no concern to the programmer using the framework:

```
class DiagramEditor
{
public:
  void register_node(Node*);
  void register_edge(Edge*);

  void run(String infile);
  void read(istream& is);

  // ...

private:

  Array<Node*> _node_types;
  Array<Edge*> _edge_types;

  Diagram _diagram;
  // ...

};
```

The only obligation for the class deriving from DiagramEditor is to register the types of all nodes and edges before running the editor:

```
int main(int argc, char* argv[])
{ Args args(argc, argv);

  DiagramEditor editor;

  editor.register_node(new Transistor);
  editor.register_node(new Capacitor);
  editor.register_node(new Resistor);
  editor.register_edge(new Wire);
  editor.run(args.arg(1));
  return 0;
};
```

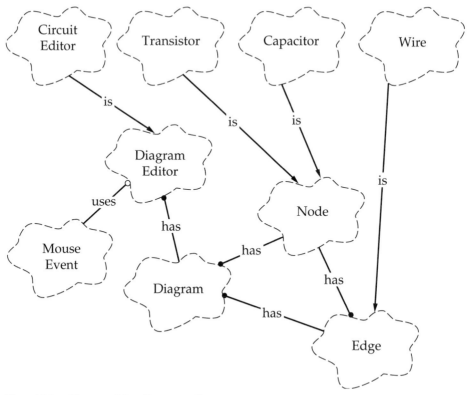

Figure 19.2.   Classes of the diagram editor.

The classes for this particular editor are summarized in Figure 19.2.

Let us summarize the responsibilities of the programmer creating a specific diagram editor:

- For each node and edge type, derive a class from Node or Edge and supply all required operations, such as plot, read, and hit testing.
- Register an object of each class with the editor when the program starts.

This is a curious programming style. Normally, a programmer supplies all the event flow of an application. In programming with an application framework, the event flow is controlled by the framework code. The programmer only adds bits and pieces of code that are invoked at the proper time.

19.3.5. Implementing Node and Edge Classes

We will implement one simple node and edge class to demonstrate the technique. Our nodes are circles, and our edges are simply straight lines that join them. (Other types of diagrams may prefer edges that are arcs or consist of line segments that are parallel to the coordinate axes.)

The routine operations for circles are name and clone:

```
String CircleNode::name() const
{ return "CircleNode";
}

Node* CircleNode::clone() const
{ return new CircleNode(self);
}
```

The plot operation draws circles in the diagram, and plot_icon is called to render the inside of the button:

```
void CircleNode::plot(GraphicsContext& gc) const
{ Ellipse(center(), RADIUS, RADIUS).plot(gc);
}

void CircleNode::plot_icon(Rectangle r, GraphicsContext& gc)
    const
{ Ellipse(r.center(), r.xsize() * ICON_RAD,
    r.ysize() * ICON_RAD).plot(gc);
}
```

The is_inside operation tests whether a point, namely the mouse pointer, touches the inside of the node shape:

```
Bool CircleNode::is_inside(Point p) const
{ return Ellipse(center(), RADIUS, RADIUS).is_inside(p);
}
```

When a circle is dragged to a new location, only the enclosing rectangle is displayed during the mouse movement. Mouse movement must give rapid feedback to the user, and a complex shape may not redraw fast enough. Therefore, each node must compute the rectangle enclosing it:

```
Rectangle CircleNode::enclosing_rect() const
{ Point c = center();
  Point d = c;
  c.move(-RADIUS, -RADIUS);
  d.move(RADIUS, RADIUS);
  return Rectangle(c, d);
}
```

The next operation is supplied because edges need it. Edges typically join not the centers of node shapes but points on the shape boundaries. Each node shape must be able to compute boundary points in any direction.

```
Point CircleNode::boundary_point(Point exterior) const
{ Point r = center();
  double a = r.angle(exterior);
  r.move(RADIUS * cos(a), RADIUS * sin(a));
  return r;
}
```

This completes the implementation of the CircleNode. Let us turn to the edge class. Again, name and clone are mechanical:

```
String Connection::name() const
{ return "Connection";
}

Edge* Connection::clone() const
{ return new Connection(self);
}
```

Rendering an icon is simple.

```
void Connection::plot_icon(Rectangle r, GraphicsContext& gc)
    const
{ Point c = r.center();
  Point d = c;
  c.move(-r.xsize() * ICON_RAD, -r.ysize() * ICON_RAD);
  d.move(r.xsize() * ICON_RAD, r.ysize() * ICON_RAD);
  Segment(c, d).plot(gc);
}
```

Joining two nodes is more complex. We must first compute the points on the boundaries of the node shape, then join them by a segment. The type of the nodes is not significant, as long as they report their center and boundary points. Even when other node types are added, edges will be drawn correctly:

```
void Connection::plot(GraphicsContext& gc) const
{ Point a = from()->boundary_point(to()->center());
  Point b = to()->boundary_point(from()->center());
  Segment(a, b).plot(gc);
}
```

For hit testing, we need to check whether the mouse pointer is close to the edge segment:

```
Bool Connection::is_on(Point p) const
{ Point a = from()->boundary_point(to()->center());
  Point b = to()->boundary_point(from()->center());
  return Segment(a, b).distance(p) < 0.1;
}
```

In this fashion, any number of node and edge types can be implemented. The effort that is required is minimal. Only those operations that are absolutely necessary, such as plotting and hit testing, must be coded.

Exercise 19.3.1. Build an editor to edit diagrams with circles and connections, by combining the specific CircleNode and Connection classes with the generic diagram editor framework.

Exercise 19.3.2. Add a RectangleNode node class and an Arrow edge class. Build the expanded editor. Identify the framework code rendering the buttons.

19.3.6. Generic Framework Code

In the last section we saw how to customize the framework to a specific editor application. In this section we will investigate how we can write the framework code without knowing anything about the types of nodes and edges.

The framework code is too long to reproduce here in its entirety, and some technical details, particularly of the mouse tracking, are not terribly interesting. Let us consider three typical scenarios: rendering the buttons, moving a node, and adding a new node.

Plotting the buttons is actually simple. As the result of the calls to register_node and register_edge, two arrays, _node_types, and _edge_types, contain the sample nodes and edges that were registered. We just ask each of them to render its icon.

```
for (int i = _node_types.low();
   i <= _node_types.high(); i++)
{ r.move(0, 1);
  r.plot(_gc);
  _node_types[i]->plot_icon(r, _gc);
}
```

Moving a node is more involved. When the mouse is clicked, we must first find whether the active button is "Move" and whether the mouse hit a node. If so, we remember the node for subsequent mouse move operations.

```
MouseEvent e;
// ...
switch(e.type())
{ case MouseEvent::LBUTTONDOWN:
    _start_node = _diagram.find_node(_start_point);
    if (_start_node != 0 && mode() == MOVE)
      _start_point = _start_node->center();
    else // ...
    // ...
}
```

When the mouse moves, we erase and redraw the enclosing rectangle to track
the node position. We draw the rectangles in XOR mode. To erase a rectangle,
simply draw it a second time.

```
switch(e.type())
{ // ...
  case MouseEvent::MOUSEMOVE:
    if (_start_node != 0 && mode() == MOVE)
    { Rectangle r = _start_node->enclosing_rect();
      r.move(_Last_point.x()-_start_point.x(),
        _last_point.y() - _start_point.y());
      r.plot(_gc); // erase old rectangle
      r.move(_current.point.x()-_last_point.x(),
        _current_point.y() - _last_point.y());
      r.plot(_gc); // draw new rectangle
    }
    else // ...
    // ...
}
```

When the mouse button goes up, we are ready to move the node to the final
mouse position and to redisplay the entire screen. The new display shows the
updated position of the node and its edges.

```
switch(e.type())
{ // ...
  case MouseEvent::LBUTTONUP:
    if (_start_node != 0 && mode() == MOVE)
    { _start_node->move(_current_point);
      display();
    }
    else // ...
    // ...
}
```

When adding a new node, we merely need to watch whether the mouse
button goes up while one of the the node buttons in the button bar is selected.
We now must add to the diagram a new node, whose center is the mouse
position and whose type matches that of the active button. This is where the
clone operation comes in. We have a pointer to one object of the desired node
type in the type registry. Of course, we cannot simply insert that pointer into
the diagram. If we did, all nodes of the diagram would end up identical. Instead
we invoke clone to get an exact duplicate, move it to the desired position, and
add it to the diagram:

```
switch(e.type())
{ // ...
```

```
case MouseEvent::LBUTTONUP:
  if // ...
  else if (mode() == NODE)
  { int i = _current_button - N_CMD_BUTTON;
    Node* n = _node_types[i]->clone();
    n->move(_current_point);
    _diagram.add_node(n);
    display();
  }
  else // ...
// ...
}
```

These scenarios are representative of the ability of the framework code to operate without an exact knowledge of the node and edge types.

19.4. GRAPHICAL USER INTERFACES

Writing an application in a graphical user interface is much more complex than reading commands from standard input and writing them to standard output. The programmer is no longer in control over the order of user input. The program user can click on buttons and windows in any order, close or size windows, pick menu commands, or enter keystrokes. The program must be able to perform the appropriate reaction to any events as they occur.

Furthermore, users have recently come to expect a great deal of comfort and convenience from their applications. A successful program must sport multiple windows, a toolbar with an array of buttons, and a status line, as well as fancy dialog boxes. Yet window management systems, in their effort to be user interface–neutral, give little or no support for these features.

Application frameworks are an effective tool for giving guidance to programmers. The framework defines the basics, such as the mechanics that are required to manage multiple windows, menus, and toolbar buttons for standard commands (File Open, Edit, Paste). Just as importantly, the framework supplies base classes that direct the programmer to a program structure that is compatible with the event flow of the graphical user interface.

We will discuss a number of features that are shared by both the Microsoft Foundation Classes (MFC) and the Borland Object Windows Library (OWL) for programming in the Microsoft Windows environment. A complete discussion of these systems would greatly exceed the scope of this book. Both products have good tutorial manuals, which are recommended for more information.

19.4.1. Multiple-Window Interface

Many applications use multiple windows to present information, as exemplified by Figure 19.3. A large window, the so-called *main frame* window, contains the other windows, the *child frames*. The main frame can be closed to quit the

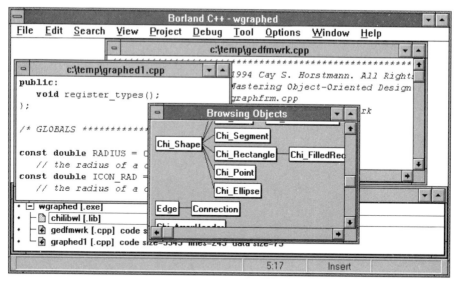

Figure 19.3.   Screen of an MDI application.

application or iconized to suspend the application. Each child frame can be closed or iconized, but that only reduces the number of active children. There are standard commands (Window Cascade, Window Tile) to arrange the child frames inside the main frame. When applied to the window shown in Figure 19.3, the Window Cascade command produces the result shown in Figure 19.4.

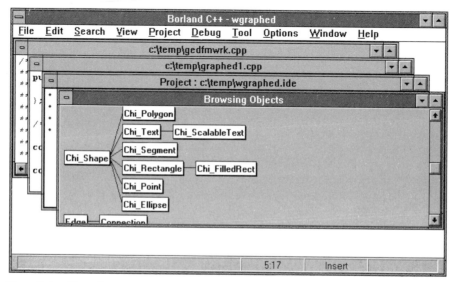

Figure 19.4.   The effect of the "Window Cascade" command.

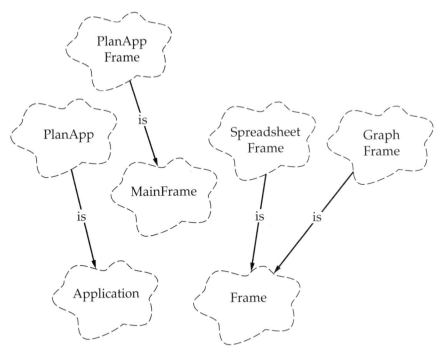

Figure 19.5. Application classes deriving from framework classes.

This command set for child frame manipulation works for every application that decides to follow the standard; that result is greatly appreciated by users, who only need to master the skill once. This interface is called *multiple-document interface* (MDI). The term "document" is misleading. It simply refers to any child type, not necessarily a word processor document. In a C++ compiler a "document" might contain

- Source code
- A list of error messages
- A browser graph
- A project graph

An application framework supplies two base classes,

```
MainFrame
ChildFrame
```

from which the application derives its own classes, as illustrated in Figure 19.5. Of course, only one class is derived from MainFrame, but for each different child type a different class may be derived from ChildFrame:

```
class PlanAppFrame : public MainFrame
class SpreadsheetFrame : public ChildFrame
class GraphFrame : public ChildFrame
```

As we will see presently, these frames do not do any display; they merely handle user interface chores. For example, one must derive from `MainFrame` to install a custom icon when the main frame is minimized.

19.4.2. Model/View Architecture

A particular challenge in multiple-window programming is the correct updating of all windows when the underlying data has changed as a result of user interaction in one window. Suppose the frame window contains a spreadsheet window and two graph windows, each displaying the spreadsheet data in different ways. When the user changes the value in a spreadsheet cell, both graphs ought to be updated. When the user drags the column in a graph, that should update both the associated spreadsheet cell and the other graph.

The same problem occurs with word processor or program code windows. In many programs it is possible to open two windows into the same file, to compare text in different locations. When the user types into one window, the other window needs to be updated.

This updating seems fiendishly complex and error-prone. A very elegant division of responsibilities, the so-called *model/view* architecture, makes it manageable. We distinguish between the underlying data, in the computer memory or a file, and the visual representations of that data on the screen. One set of data may be represented in multiple ways, such as the spreadsheet data as cells or a graph, or in multiple occurrences in the same way, such as the word processor document in two windows. The underlying data is called the *model*, and the visual representation a *view*. A single model can have multiple views. (Some frameworks refer to models as documents, which collides with the use of "document" in the multiple document interface, where a document means a view. We will stick to *model* and *view*.)

The model sits in memory and is accessible to the user only through its views. Views receive manipulation commands. A spreadsheet window receives keystrokes. A graph window receives mouse drags. If the keystroke or mouse drag signifies a request for data change, the view notifies the model. The model changes its data and forces refresh of all of its views. In the most basic case, the model simply marks the surfaces of all of its windows as invalid. Then the windowing system will ask each of the views to repaint itself. Each view then asks the model for the necessary data values and repaints itself from scratch. In particular, the view that received the user input is repainted in exactly the same way as all other views. This explains why multiple views into the same section of a word processor document get updated simultaneously.

Of course, for optimal response, an application cannot redraw all windows at every keystroke. There are several strategies for optimization. The model figures out the approximate difference between the old and the new information and keeps that region of each view that is known not to have changed. In a spreadsheet, only the current cell needs to be updated. In a graph, only one bar may need to be redrawn. In addition, the view that receives the user command can opt to redraw itself more efficiently than the other views. These strategies are usually sufficient to guarantee good performance.

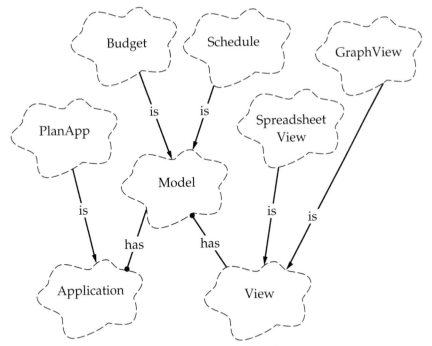

Figure 19.6.   Class diagram of the model and view classes.

A framework supplies two base classes:

```
Model
View
```

The programmer derives from these classes, as illustrated in Figure 19.6:

```
class Budget : public Model
class SpreadsheetView : public View
class GraphView : public View
class Schedule : public Model
class GanttView : public View
       // views the schedule as a Gantt chart
class PertView : public View
       // views the schedule as a PERT chart
```

19.4.3. User Interface Coordination

The windowing environment sends events to the application's windows, where the framework code captures them and distributes them to the interested parties. This is complicated by the fact that different events should be handled by different framework entities. Naturally, painting is performed by the views. Saving data is the responsibility of the models. Opening documents is carried out by the application object.

The framework understands the structure and routes user commands to the correct destination. For example, if the user selects "File Save" from the menu or clicks on the button with the "save" icon, the framework locates the model underlying the active view and notifies it to save its data.

The application framework ensures that the views fit to fill the inside of the frames. The user interface understands models. When the program user selects "File Open", the program presents a list of supported model types to pick from. The selected model gets opened with its default view, or the last view with which it was saved. For these reasons the framework must be informed of the relationships between models, views, and frames. For example, the application must know that a GraphView is surrounded by a GraphFrame and views the Budget model.

Here we run into an interesting problem. The desired correspondence is a correspondence between *classes*, not objects. The code executing "File Open" must have access to a list of correspondences between the model name ("Project schedule") and the model class (Schedule). When the user picks the name from the list, the class must be instantiated. C++ has a very weak support for "classes as objects", namely the typeid operator, which yields an object of type Type_info. Unfortunately, there is no operation to instantiate an object of a type whose Type_info is given. Existing frameworks use one of three work-arounds.

- Lists of names and function pointers can be assembled at compile time, using preprocessor macros:

```
MODEL_LIST_ADD("Project schedule", Schedule, ...)
```

- It is possible to define a more powerful analog to the built-in Type_info class using a template:

```
model_list.add("Project schedule",
ClassInfo<Schedule>(), ... );
```

- Finally, one can make objects stand in as factories for their classes, provided that they have a clone operation:

```
model_list.add("Project schedule", new Schedule, ... );
```

19.4.4. Responsibilities of the Framework User

The programmer using the framework to build an application must supply a number of classes, operations, and class relationships. A class (say PlanApp) must be derived from the base class Application to encapsulate the event loop. This is similar to the derivation of BankSimulation from the base class Simulation. In addition, for each model the programmer must derive from Model, and for each view the programmer must derive from View. If special icons and other user interface adaptations are desired, derivations from MainFrame and ChildFrame may be necessary.

The views must know how to paint themselves, using the data in the underlying model. The views must react to user input and translate user commands to operations that update the model. The models must know how to save themselves to disk and restore themselves from disk.

The framework must be told about the correspondences between views, frames, and models. This is typically done in the initialization of the application object.

The programmer using the framework enjoys two benefits. The framework handles the interaction with standard events; more importantly, the programmer reuses a successful design paradigm (model/view) without having to reinvent it.

Exercise 19.4.1. Use the Windows application framework that is included with your compiler to write a very simple application that reads in a set of data (strings and floating-point numbers) from a file and displays them in three views: as a text table, as a bar chart, and as a pie chart.

19.5. DESIGN HINTS

19.5.1. Using a Framework

When you use a framework, you take existing classes and build either more classes, or even an entire application, on the top. The framework contains *expert knowledge* on the interaction of system components. Having that expertise already embodied in code is the reason for using the framework.

You will need to find out how to fit the application-specific aspects in. There are several essential questions:

- What classes are provided as bases for derivation?
- How many classes can I derive from these bases?
- What virtual functions must I redefine?
- What virtual functions can I redefine, and what do they do by default?
- Are there special initialization requirements?

For example, in the simulation framework the base classes are Simulation and Event. Only one class can derive from Simulation, but multiple classes can be derived from Event. The Event::process operation must be redefined. Redefining the initialize/update/terminate operations of the Simulation is optional. Their default is to do nothing.

In the diagram editor, there are two base classes: Node and Edge. Both can serve as the base for multiple derived classes. A number of virtual functions, such as clone and plot, must be redefined. In addition, for proper initialization, all node and edge types must be registered.

19.5.2. Framework Design Challenges

In framework design, keep in mind who your customers are. Your customers are programmers. They build an application on top of the framework. *Their* customers are the users of the product.

Designing a single class is an order of magnitude harder than designing a single function, because one must *anticipate* what other programmers will do with it. Similarly, designing a framework is much harder than designing a class library or a single application, because one must anticipate what other programmers want to achieve.

The encapsulation of the framework implementation leaves little room for error. If a framework does not provide a hook for integrating an essential task, the framework itself needs to be redesigned or discarded. It is notoriously difficult to predict the complexities of real-world problems. A good rule of thumb for validating the design of a framework is to use it to build at least three different applications.

C++ LANGUAGE CODING GUIDELINES

A1. INTRODUCTION

This coding style guide is a simplified version of one that has been used with good success, both in industrial practice and for college courses. Of course, coding style preferences are intensely personal. However, having a uniform style within a group of programmers is enormously beneficial, and it can be achieved if every programmer is willing to compromise a little.

These guidelines plainly outlaw a number of constructs. This doesn't mean that programmers using them are evil, merely that the constructs are of marginal utility and that better ways of expressing the same functionality exist in the language. Experience has shown that it is beneficial to stay away from marginal features. Programmers who don't know them need not make an effort to master them, and programmers who do need not make an effort to make a choice. These guidelines also demand consistency in naming and layout. These are, of course, trivial details, but reducing gratuitous choice in unimportant matters enables programmers to spend their energy on solving real problems.

It is strongly recommended that programming teams and course instructors require adherence to this style guide (with suitable modifications for local taste) or one like it. Contact the author for a copy of this document in electronic form for modification and redistribution.

A2. MODULES

A2.1. Module Layout

Each C++ program is a collection of implementation files, or modules. The executable program is obtained by compiling and linking its constituent modules.

Each module has certain public information, such as the declaration of public classes and functions that are implemented in it. It also has private information, such as functions that are not called from outside, variables that cannot be inspected or modified from outside, and maybe local type declarations.

Unfortunately, C++ is not very supportive in this regard. All global data and functions are by default public. This guide requires that you declare all functions and global data as static unless they are exported to other modules.

The public interface of a module is specified in a header file having the same name as the .cpp file, but the extension .h. It contains extern declarations of all exported global variables, prototypes of all exported functions, and public type and class definitions.

Implementation and header files are organized as follows:

- Header comment block
- #include statements
- Constants
- Classes and type declarations
- Global constants and variables
- Functions
- Operations
- Test code

A2.2. Header Comment

Each module starts with a header comment block in the following format:

```
/*********************************************************
COPYRIGHT (C):      1992, All Rights Reserved.
PROJECT:            CS 151 Project
FILE:               wm.c
PURPOSE:            widget manipulation
VERSION             1.0
LANGUAGE:           Borland C++ 3.1
TARGET:             IBM PC
PROGRAMMER:         Cay Horstmann (CSH)
                    Jenny Koo (JK)
UPDATE HISTORY:
*********************************************************/
/* NOTES *************************************************
```

General comments go here, for example:

- *Command line options*
- *File formats*
- *Rules and conventions*
- *Pictures of the main data structures*

```
*********************************************************/
```

A2.3. Included Header Files

The next section lists all included header files:

```
/* INCLUDE *****************************************************/

#include <stdlib.h>
#include <string.h>
#include "cw.h"
#include " ..\util\keys.h"
#include "wm.h"
```

Sort header files in the following order:

- System header files <*xxx*.h>
- Local header files "*xxx*.h"
- The module's own header file

Follow the convention of using <...> for the files stored in the "standard place" of the compiler (for example, \borlandc\include), "..." for the files stored in the local directory. *Do not embed absolute path names, as in*

```
#include <c:\borlandc\include\stdlib.h> //   DON'T !!!
```

A2.4. The Class Section

This section contains the definitions of classes, enumerations, and types, in any order.

```
/* TYPES *******************************************************/
enum Weekday { MON, TUE, WED, THU, FRI, SAT, SUN };

typedef int (*DateCompareFun)(Date, Date);

class Date
/* PURPOSE: Store dates and perform date arithmetic
*/
{
public:
  // ...
};
```

A2.5. The Globals Section

Next come the definitions of global constants and variables. All global variables that are not declared in the header file *must* be declared as static—that is, private to the module.

The programmer is strongly cautioned against using global variables. In the author's experience, having more than three global variables in a module is excessive.

```
/* GLOBALS *******************************************************/

static const int days_per_month[] = { 31, 28, 31, 30, ... };
    // the number of days in every month (except for leap years)
const int JULYEAR0 = -4713;
    // Julian day 1 = Jan. 1, 4713 B.C.
```

A2.6. The Functions Section

This section lists all functions of the module. First, list prototypes (if any), then the functions. All functions without a prototype in the header file *must* be declared static—that is, private to the module.

You may sort the functions in any order, but you should sort them in reverse order of call. In particular, the module containing main has main last. If you follow this layout, you never need prototypes except in the rare case of a cyclic calling pattern among the static functions.

The functions are listed before the operations of classes because the operations need to know about the static functions, whereas the functions already know the operations from the class definitions.

Sort class operations by class. Separate operations of the same class by /*......*/ and operations of different classes by /*------*/ comment lines.

```
/* FUNCTIONS *******************************************************/

static long dat2jul(int d, int m, int y)
/* PURPOSE:   Convert calendar date into Julian day
   RECEIVES:  d, m, y—the day, month, and year
   RETURNS:   The Julian day number that begins at noon (Greenwich)
              of the given calendar date.
   REMARKS:   This algorithm is from Press et al., Numerical Recipes
              in C, 2nd ed., Cambridge University Press, 1992.
*/
{ // ...
}

/*---------------------------------------------------------------*/

istream& operator>>(istream& is, Date& date)
/* PURPOSE:   Read a date from a stream
   RECEIVES:  is—the stream
              d (OUT)—the date that is read in
   RETURNS:   is
```

```
*/
{ // ...
}

/*---------------------------------------------------*/

int main(int argc, char* argv[])
{ // ...
}

/*---------------------------------------------------*/

Date::Date(int d, int m, int y)
/* RECEIVES: d, m, y —the day, month, and year
*/
:  _day(d),
   _month(m),
   _year(y)
{}

/*.................................................*/

long Date::days_between(Date b) const
/* RECEIVES: b—a date
   RETURNS:  The number of days between this date and b
*/
{ // ...
}
```

A2.7. The Test Section

This section is optional but highly recommended. It contains a test stub to test the classes and operations implemented in the module. The test stub is enclosed in preprocessor directives for conditional compilation. It is compiled only for testing the module.

```
/* TEST ***************************************************/

#ifdef TEST_DATE

#include <stdlib.h>
#include <iomanip.h>

int main(int argc, char* argv[])
/* RECEIVES: month year
*/
```

```
{ int m = atoi(argv[1]);
  int y = atoi(argv[2]);
  Date d(1, m, y); // start date of the month

  cout <<  "Mon Tue Wed Thu Fri Sat Sun" << endl;
  Weekday w = d.weekday();
  for (int i = 0; i < w; i++) cout << "    ";
  while (d.month() == m)
  { cout << setw(4) << d.day();
    if (d.weekday() == SUN) cout << endl;
    d.advance(1);
  }
  if (d.weekday() != MON) cout << endl;
  return 0;
}

#endif
```

A3. CLASSES

A3.1. Class Header Comment

Each class declaration starts with a header comment:

```
class name [ : public base class [, public base class ]* ]
/* PURPOSE:
   STATES:
*/
{ // ...
};
```

The PURPOSE comment is mandatory. Describe the class in some way. You may phrase the description for an object of the class: "A mailbox stores and plays mail messages".

The STATES comment is very useful in understanding those classes that have clearly defined states that influence their behavior. For example, a bounded stack has two special states, "empty" and "full", that change the way that pop and push behave. Omitting the STATES comment implies that the class has no states that are observable through the public interface.

A3.2. Base Classes

Use only public inheritance. Use aggregation instead of private inheritance; that is, replace

```
class C : private B {};
```

with

```
class C { private: B _b; };
```

This requires no change in the interface of C. There is protected inheritance, but this style guide doesn't allow it.

A3.3. Class Layout

First list the public section, then the private section. (If you have a protected section, put it in between the two. This guide disallows protected data and is neutral on protected operations.)
Within each section, order features as follows:

- Local classes, enumerations, and types
- Constructors (except copy constructor)
- Mutators: non-`const` operations
- Accessors: `const` operations functions
- `static` and `friend` functions
- Memory management: Copy constructor, destructor, `operator=`
- Data fields
- Static (shared) class variables

This order is partially psychological, partially pragmatic. For the reader of a class, the *public* interface is the most important aspect and therefore must come first. The private section may change and should be of no great concern to most class users. In each section, we order items to answer the following questions:

- How can I make an object? (constructors)
- Then, what can I do to it? (mutators)
- Then, how can I find out what I did? (accessors)

We need to place the local types before these items because some of them may refer to them. And we place memory management functions (copy constructor, destructor, assignment operator) at the end because they are uninteresting for the class user. (*Note:* Do not supply these functions unless the default ones supplied by the compiler are inadequate.)
Each public feature and each data field that is not totally obvious from its name should have a one-line comment. You can omit comments for patently obvious functions like `print()`. More detailed descriptions will be found in the operations section:

```
class String
/* PURPOSE: character strings
*/
{
public:
  enum {NPOS = INT_MAX};
      // maximum number of positions in string
```

```
String (); // constructs an empty string
String (const char s[]);
String (char ch);

char& operator[](int i);
void set(int i, char ch); // change a character
// ...

int length() const;
Bool is_null() const;
char get(int i) const; // get a character
String substr(int from, int n = NPOS) const;
String operator+(const String&) const; // concatenate

friend String operator+(const char a[], const String& b);
static int compare(const String&, const String&);

String(const String&);
const String& operator=(const String&);
~String();

private:
  String(size_t len, const char s[], size_t slen);

  void detach();
  void unique();
  char* _str;
};
```

A3.4. Friends

The C++ compiler does not care where friend declarations are placed inside a class definition. The following rule is recommended:

A friend function that is used by the public is placed at the end of the public section. A friend declaration that serves for the implementation of the class is placed at the end of the private section. For example,

```
class List
{
public:
  // ...
  friend ostream& operator<<(ostream&, const List&);
private:
  Link* _head;
  friend class Iterator;
};
```

A3.5. Operations

In the declaration, do not omit the argument names of member functions; that is, don't use

```
class String
{
public:
    String remove(int, int); // NO
    // ...
};
```

Which int does what?

Do not use inlines in class declarations:

```
class Polygon
{
public:
    void set(int n, Point x) {_vertex.set(n, x); } // NO
    // ...
};
```

Instead, use

```
class Polygon
{
public:
    void set(int n, Point x);
    // ...
};

inline void Polygon::set(int n, Point x)
/* PURPOSE:   set a vertex of a polygon
    RECEIVES: n—position of vertex
              x—vertex
*/
{ _vertex.set(n, x);
}
```

Sure, it is torture to type all this for a trivial function (they don't call it "strong typing" for nothing), but there are a number of benefits. It is *much* easier to revoke the inline attribute. The inline source code doesn't clutter up the public interface. There is room for a decent comment for those functions that require it. For example, the foregoing operation would benefit from an explanation of the behavior if n is larger than the number of vertices of the polygon.

The only exception to this rule is that do-nothing inlines are permitted for default constructors and virtual destructors in the class definition.

```
class Customer
{
public:
  Customer() {};
  // ...
  virtual ~Customer() {}
};
```

A3.6. Data Fields

In a class, all data fields must be private. Prefix each field name with an underscore (_salary).

Use accessor and mutator functions to access and change the data.

```
class Employee
{
public:
  double salary() const;
  void set_salary(double s);
  // ...
private:
  double _salary;
  // ...
};
```

Use the naming scheme _field, field(), set_field() consistently. You do not need accessor and mutator functions for every data field. Do not start out with public data, promising to make the fields private later; that change is usually very painful. Do not use protected data, but make accessors and mutators protected instead.

A4. OPERATIONS AND FUNCTIONS

A4.1. Header Comment

Each operation and function has a comment of the following form:

```
/*    PURPOSE:   explanation
      RECEIVES:  argument 1— explanation
                 argument 2— explanation
                 .
                 .
                 .
      RETURNS:   explanation of return value
      REMARKS:   pre- and postconditions, exceptions, and so forth
*/
```

The PURPOSE comment is required, except for constructors, destructors, assignment operators, field accessors, and very trivial functions that are adequately described by their return value. The RECEIVES comment is omitted if the function takes no arguments. The RETURNS comment is omitted for void functions.

No purpose and return value comments are necessary for main. Explain the command line arguments in the RECEIVES section.

```
static long dat2jul(int d, int m, int y)
/* PURPOSE:   Convert calendar date into Julian day
     RECEIVES: d, m, y —the day, month, and year
     RETURNS:  The Julian day number that begins at noon of the given
               calendar date.
     REMARKS:  This algorithm is from Press et al., Numerical
               Recipes in C, 2nd ed., Cambridge University Press, 1992.
*/
{ // ...
}
```

Reference arguments that have no well-defined incoming value but are used to hold a result must be tagged as OUT.

```
istream& operator>>(istream& is, Date& date)
/* PURPOSE:   Read a date from a stream
     RECEIVES: is — the stream
               d (OUT)—the date that is read in
     RETURNS:  is
*/
{ // ...
}
```

A4.2. Declaration Attributes

Every function must have a return type. Use void for procedures.

Every accessor operation must be declared as const.

Every global function must be declared static unless its declaration is exported to the header file.

A4.3. Parameters

Parameter names should be explicit, especially if they are integers or Boolean:

```
Customer Bank::remove(int i, Bool b); // huh?
Customer Bank::remove(int teller, Bool display); // OK
```

Of course, for very generic functions, short names may be very appropriate.

For each array, pointer or reference argument, use const if the argument is not modified by the function. The function is presumed to *modify* all non-const pointer, reference, and C array arguments.

```
void Mailbox::add(Message& m); // will modify m
void Mailbox::add(const Message& m); // won't modify m
```

Never use pointers to denote C arrays. Pointer parameters are presumed to point to a *single* object:

```
void find(const Employee* e, int idnum);
   // e points to a single object (maybe derived from Employee)
void find(const Employee e[], int idnum);
   // e is a C array of objects (of exact type Employee)
```

Do not use pointers for reference arguments. Use references instead.

```
void swap(int* px, int* py); // NO
void swap(int& px, int& py); // OK
```

Do not use pointers to avoid the cost of call by value. If

```
int Bank::find(Customer c);
```

is considered too inefficient, use a constant reference instead.

```
int Bank::find(const Customer& c);
```

Of course, if all objects of the type are located on the heap, and you always access them with pointers, then a pointer parameter is OK. The only objection is to taking the address of a stack object in the call.

Do not write procedures (void functions) that return exactly one answer through a pointer or reference. Instead, make it into a return value:

```
void Bank::find(Customer c, Bool& found); // NO!
Bool Bank::find(Customer c); // OK
```

Of course, if the function computes more than one value, some of them must be returned through reference arguments.

A4.4. Function Length

As a rule of thumb, functions should not be longer than 30 lines of code. The function header, comments, blank lines, and lines containing only braces are not included in this count. For operations of classes, this limitation is rarely a problem. Functions that parse input with a long switch statement or if/else may end up being much longer, but then keep each branch to 10 lines or less.

A4.5. Constructors

It is considered good style to write constructors so that all data members are constructed outside the { ... } and only nontrivial actions are placed inside. For example,

```
Date::Date(int d, int m, int y)
/* RECEIVES: d, m, y—the day, month, and year
*/
:   _day(d),
    _month(m),
    _year(y)
{   ASSERT_PRECOND(valid());
}
```

A5. VARIABLES

A5.1. Comments

Every local variable, with the exception of really self-explanatory names and boring loop counters, must be commented when declared. Every global variable must be commented, without exception:

```
int nfont = 0; // the number of fonts currently loaded
```

A5.2. Initialization

Every variable must be explicitly initialized whenever possible.

```
int nfont = ft_load(); // the number of fonts currently loaded
```

It is almost always possible to do this in C++, by declaring the variable just before it is to be used for the first time. Remember that variable declarations and statements can be freely mixed.

Move variables to the innermost block in which they are needed:

```
while( /* ... */ )
{ int b = f();
   // ...
}
```

This is considered good style—much better than declaring all variables at the beginning of the function.

A5.3. Pointers

Follow the C++ convention of placing the * with the type, not the variable: in other words,

```
Shape* p;
```

not

```
Shape *p;
```

Of course, the compiler doesn't care. It ignores all white space, and we could equally well have written

```
Shape*p;
```

or

```
Shape
*
p
;
```

It seems to be more rational to declare p as a Shape* rather than declaring p as a thing whose * is a Shape.

You cannot declare *two* pointers like that:

```
Shape* p, q;
```

This declares a pointer p and an integer q. Don't declare two pointers in the same line, write

```
Shape* p;
Shape* q;
```

instead. Since you will need to write comments behind the declarations, this should never be a problem.

It is traditional, but extremely silly, to write the const for constant pointers and references as far as possible from the * or & to which they apply:

```
const Shape* s;
```

Instead, you should consider using

```
Shape const* s;
```

If more than one pointer or reference is required, that is the only way to preserve your sanity. A constant reference to a pointer (say for a hash function in a template) is

```
int hash(Employee* const&);
```

a reference to a constant pointer (say for a read function) is

```
void archive(Employee const*&);
```

A5.4. Global Variables

Global variables are those declared outside functions. When declared as `static`, they can be read and modified by all functions in the current module (hundreds of lines of code). When exported, they can be read and modified by all functions in the program (many thousands of lines of code). This is unreasonable in practice.

There is a simple strategy for minimizing global variables: Group related variables into classes. Don't use

```
int win_top, win_left, win_bot, win_right, cur_row, cur_col;
```

Instead, use

```
class Window
{ // ...
private:
  int win_top, win_left, win_bot, win_right;
  int cur_row, cur_col;
};

Window display_win;
```

Prime candidates for grouping are *arrays of the same length*. Don't use

```
int charwidth[NCHAR];
char* pixels[NCHAR];
unsigned char charcode[NCHAR];
```

Instead, use

```
class BitmapChar
{ // ...
private:
  int _width;
  char* _pixels;
  unsigned char _code;
};

BitmapChar display_font[NCHAR];
```

In fact, it makes sense to go one step further and declare a type `BitmapFont`:

```
class BitmapFont
{ // ...
```

```
private:
  String _name;
  Array<BitmapChar> _characters;
};
```

```
BitmapFont display_font;
```

In C++, it is often possible to replace global variables by shared class variables.

```
class Date
{ // ...
private:
  int _day, _month, _year;

  static const int days_per_month[12];
};
```

```
const int Date::days_per_month[12] = { 31, 28, ..., 31 };
```

This is considered good programming practice.

A6. CONSTANTS

A6.1. Constant Definitions

In C++, do not use #define to define constants:

```
#define NFONT 20 // DON'T
```

Use const instead:

```
const int NFONT = 20; // the maximum number of fonts
```

A6.2. Zero

Should you use '\0' and NULL, or just plain 0? This is up to you. It makes sense to use the "strongly typed" explicit symbols instead of 0. On the other hand, it is well within the spirit of C++ to use 0 as an *overloaded* symbol to denote the "right" zero value in various contexts.

A6.3. Enumerations

Use enum to define a number of related constants.

```
enum Color { BLUE = 1, GREEN = 2, RED = 4 };
```

Do not use a sequence of const or #define!

Avoid global enumerations. Whenever possible, make enumerations local to a class:

```
class Date
{
public:
    enum Weekday { MON, TUE, WED, THU, FRI, SAT, SUN };
    // ...
private:
    // ...
};
```

The programmer refers to these constants as Date::SUN, Date::MON, and so forth. The names SUN, MON, and so forth don't clutter up the global name space. That avoids nasty conflicts with other enumerations:

```
enum Workstation { SUN, DEC, HP, IBM, };
enum Exam { SAT, GRE, GMAT, };
```

When defining an open-ended number of enums, place a comma behind the last one:

```
enum Tokentype
{ NIL,
    // ...
    FRACTION,
    ROOT,
    MATRIX,
    TABLE,
};
```

It is legal, and it makes it easier to add another one.

It is often useful to have the compiler keep track of the total number of items:

```
enum Tokentype
{   NIL,
    // ...
    FRACTION,
    ROOT,
    MATRIX,
    TABLE,
    // add new token types above this line
    NTOKENTYPE
};
```

Now NTOKENTYPE keeps track of the number of token types defined. Be sure to include the comment, directing the person maintaining the code to insert new types before the counter.

In C++, it is common to use enum to define constants used inside classes. For example,

```
class Stack
{ // ...
private:
   enum { SSIZE = 20, };
   int _item[SSIZE];
   int _stackptr;
   //...
};
```

The seemingly more rational

```
class Stack
{ // ...
private:
   const int SSIZE = 20; // NO!
   int _item[SSIZE];
   int _stackptr;
   //...
};
```

is a syntax error.

A6.4. Magic Numbers

A *magic number* is an integer constant embedded in code, without a constant definition. Using magic numbers makes code amazingly difficult to maintain. They are strictly outlawed.

Even the most reasonable cosmic constant is going to change one day. You think there are 365 days in a year? Your customers on Mars are going to be pretty unhappy about your silly prejudice. Make a constant

```
const int DAYS_PER_YEAR = 365;
```

so you can easily cut a Martian version without trying to find all the 365's, 364's, 366's, 367's, and so on in your code. By the way, the device

```
const int THREE_HUNDRED_AND_SIXTY_FIVE = 365;
```

is counterproductive and frowned upon.

You can take it for granted that *all* array lengths will change at least twice (oops, meant to say, at least N_BUFLEN_CHANGE times) during the lifetime of the code. Declare the length of each fixed-size array as an individual constant. Don't use the same constant for two arrays unless, for compelling logical reasons, the two arrays *have to* have the same length.

A7. CONTROL FLOW

A7.1. The if Statement

Avoid the if...if...else trap. The code

```
if( ... )
    if( ... ) ...;
else
{   ...;
    ...;
};
```

will not do what the indentation level suggests, and it can take hours to find such a bug. Always use an extra pair of { ... } when dealing with if ... if ... else:

```
if( ... )
{   if( ... ) ...;
    else ...;
} // {...} not necessary, but they keep you out of trouble

if( ... )
{   if( ... ) ...;
} // {...} are necessary
else ...;
```

A7.2. The for Statement

Do not use the for loop for weird constructs (even though [Kernighan and Ritchie] contains an occasional abuse). Constructs such as

```
for (r = i = 0; s[i]; r += s[i++] - '0') r *= 10;
```

are not tolerated. Make it into a while loop. That way, the sequence of instructions is much clearer:

```
r = i = 0;
while (s[i])
{   r *= 10;
    r += s[i++] - '0';
}
```

Use for loops only when a variable runs from somewhere to somewhere with some constant increment/decrement:

```
for (i = a.low(); i <= a.high(); i++)
    a[i].print();
```

A for loop traversing a linked list can be neat and intuitive:

```
for (l.reset(); !l.at_end(); l.next())
    l.current().print();
```

A7.3. The switch Statement

The switch statement should be laid out as follows:

```
switch (x)
{   case a:
        ...
        ...
        break;
    case b:
        ...;
        return;
    case c:
    case d:
    case e:
        ...;
        ...;
        break;
    default:
        ...;
        ...;
        break;
}
```

Every branch *must* end in a break or return statement, even the last one. Fall-through is *not* permitted. You don't have to use a default, but if you do, put it at the end of the switch.

A7.4. Nonlinear Control Flow

Do not use the break (except in switch), continue, or goto statements under any circumstances.

It is always possible to avoid a break in a loop by adding another Boolean variable. It makes for a clearer loop, because you can easily verify the loop invariant.

The loop

```
for (i = a.low(); i <= a.high(); i++)
  if(a[i] == x) // found it
    break; // DON'T!
if (i > a.high()) // never found
  ...
```

can easily be rewritten as

```
Bool found = FALSE;
i = a.low();
while (!found && i <= a.high())
{  if( a[i] == x ) found = TRUE;
   else i++;
}
if (!found)
  ...
```

The break and continue commands are not stable. Adding more loops or statements at the end of a loop changes their meaning.

The goto command is for yacc output, not for code produced by humans.

The only nonlinear control flow statements that you may use are return and throw.

A8. LEXICAL ISSUES

A8.1. Naming Convention

The following rules specify when to use upper- and lowercase letters in identifier names:

1. All variable and function names and all structure members are in lowercase (maybe with an occasional upperCase letter or under_score in the middle); for example, font_cache.
2. All #defined macros, all enum constants, and all inline const are in uppercase (maybe with an occasional UNDER_SCORE); for example, CACHE_SIZE.
3. All typedefs and all C++ struct, class, union, and enum names start with uppercase and are followed by lowercase (maybe with an occasional UpperCase letter or Under_score); for example, FontCache.

Names should be explicit. Names should be reasonably long and descriptive. Use font_pointer instead of fp. No drppng f vwls. Local variables that are fairly routine can be short (ch, i) as long as they are really just boring holders for an input character, a loop counter, or the like. Furthermore, do not use ptr, p, pntr, pnt, p2 for five pointer variables in your function. Surely these variables all have a specific purpose and can be named to remind the reader of it (for example, pcur, pnext, pprev, pnew, pret).

A8.2. Indentation and White Space

Use tab stops every three columns. The default of eight columns wastes screen real estate.

Use blank lines freely to separate logically separate parts of a function.

Separate functions by comment lines like /*---------*/.

Use a blank space around every binary operator and ? :.

```
ch = i < IO_BUF_SIZE ? curChar : 0;  /* GOOD */
ch=i<IO_BUF_SIZE?curChar:0;/*BAD*/
```

Leave blank spaces after (and not before) each comma, semicolon, and keyword, but not after a function name.

```
if (x == 0)
f(a, b[i++]);
```

Every line must fit on 80 columns. If you must break a statement, add an indentation level for the continuation:

```
a[n] = ...........................................
    + ..................;
```

Start the indented line with an operator (if possible).

If this happens in an if or while, be sure to brace in the next statement, *even if there is only one:*

```
if( ...........................................
    && ..........................................
    || .......... )
{ ...
}
```

If it weren't for the braces, it would be hard to visually separate the continuation of the condition from the statement to be executed.

A8.3. Braces

Opening and closing braces must line up, either horizontally or vertically.

```
while (i < n) { a[i].print(cout); i++; }

while (i < n)
{   a[i].print(cout);
    i++;
}
```

Some programmers don't line up vertical braces but place the { behind the
while, arguing that it saves a line of code:

```
while (i < n) { // DON'T
    a[i].print(cout);
    i++;
}
```

Huh? Counting the lines above does not seem to support that theory.
    When the braces line up, it is easy to spot mismatches.

A8.4. Unstable Layout

Some programmers take great pride in lining up the names of class features:

```
class Date
{
public:
            Date(int d, int m, int y);
        long days_between(Date b);
    Weekday weekday() const;
            // ...
private:
        int _day;
        int _month;
        int _year;
};
```

This is undeniably neat, and we recommend it if your editor does it for you.
But don't do it manually on programmer's wages. The layout is not *stable* under
change. A return type that is longer than the preallotted number of columns
requires that you move *all* entries around.
    Some programmers like to format multiline comments so that every line
starts with **.

```
/* This is a comment
** that extends over
** three source lines
*/
```

Again, this is neat and a good thing if your editor has a command to add and
remove the asterisks. Otherwise, it is a silly thing to do, because it is a powerful
method of *discouraging* programmers from editing the comment. If you have to
choose between pretty comments and comments that reflect the current facts of
the program, facts win over beauty.

A8.5. The Preprocessor

It has been said that all usage of the preprocessor points to deficiencies in the programming language. C++ fixes some deficiencies. Do not use #define for constants or macros—use const, enum, and inline instead.

Do not use the #define facility to aid your transition from Pascal, as in

```
#define begin   {
#define end     }
#define repeat          do {
#define until( x )      } while( !( x ) );
```

Neat as they may be, these constructs are strictly outlawed. Your fellow programmers have better things to do than play preprocessor with your code.

A legitimate use for the preprocessor is conditional compilation; for example, #ifdef WIN31 ... #endif.

To comment out a block of code that may itself contain comments, use #if 0 ... #endif. (Recall that C++ comments do not nest.)

GLOSSARY

abstract class   A class without instance objects. An abstract class serves as a base class for other classes but is not specific enough to provide implementations for all operations.

accessor   A class operation that does not modify the object on which it is invoked. A **field accessor** is an operation that reports on the value of one field.

aggregation   The process of building classes out of component fields of simpler types.

analysis phase   The phase of a software project that concerns itself with an understanding of the problem domain and the problem to be solved, without considering any design or implementation strategy.

argument (of a function)   An actual parameter of a function call. The **implicit argument** of a class operation is the object to which the operation is applied. All other actual parameters of the operation are called **explicit arguments**.

assertion   A logical condition that is expected to be true when it is encountered during program execution.

assignment   The act of replacing the value of a variable with the value of an expression.

base class   A class from which another class derives. Also called **superclass** or **parent class**.

bag   An unordered collection of items. Unlike a set, a bag can hold multiple copies of the same item.

binding   Mapping a name to a specific feature. In **static binding** the selected feature is determined depending on the types of the variables involved in the selection process. In **dynamic binding** the type of the object, not the types of the variables referencing it, determines the selection.

buffering (in stream classes)   Storing characters in a buffer and transmitting the buffer contents from and to the external device when the buffer fills up, to reduce the frequency of device access.

call by reference   Passing as function argument the location of an object so that the function can modify it.

call by value   Passing as function argument a copy of a value.

casting   Forcing the compiler to change an object or pointer to another type. **Downcasting** means to force the compiler to change the type of a pointer to a base class into a pointer to a derived class. A **checked cast** is one that is checked at run time by making a type inquiry.

class   A collection of objects with the same operations and the same state range.

class library   A collection of related classes that address a common problem domain.

clone   A copy of an object that has the same value as the original. This is of interest only as a polymorphic operation, to copy an object of an arbitrary derived class that is reached through a base class pointer.

cohesion   The degree of connectedness of operations of a class; the degree to which the class describes a single abstraction.

constructor   An operation that turns raw storage into an object by initializing the fields and bases.

copy constructor   A special constructor to initialize an object as a copy of another of the same class.

copy on write   An optimization strategy in which objects share data and copying is delayed until one of the objects is about to make a modification. At that point, the modifying object makes a copy and stops sharing with the other objects.

copy semantics   The meaning of making a copy of an object. Under **value copy semantics** the copy of an object has an independent state. Modifying either the original or the copy has no effect on the other object. Under **reference copy semantics** the original object and the copy refer to the same data; a modification through either object affects the state of both objects.

coupling   The degree of interrelationships between classes.

CRC cards   A design technique for discovering classes by using index cards on which classes, relationships, and collaborators are recorded.

declaration   A description of a feature in sufficient detail to allow a reference to it in subsequent code, but lacking details required for the implementation of the feature.

deep copy   A copy of an object and all objects referenced by it.

deferred operation   A class operation of an abstract class of which no implementation is supplied. The operation must be redefined in derived classes. Also called a **pure virtual function** in C++.

definition   A description of the implementation of a feature.

derived class   A class that modifies another class (its base class) by adding fields and adding or redefining operations. Also called **subclass** or **child class**.

design phase   The phase of a software project that concerns itself with the discovery of the structural components of the software system to be built, without concern for implementation details.

destructor   An operation that turns an object into raw storage, carrying out any actions that are necessary before the object value is abandoned.

double dispatch   The invocation of a polymorphic function based on the types of two objects.

encapsulation   The act of hiding the implementation details of a class or module.

exception   An error condition that suspends normal program execution and transfers control to a handler.

feature   Any function, variable, constant, or type defined by a class or module.

field   A variable that is present in every object of a class.

formatting (in stream classes)   Translating between objects and their representation as a sequence of characters.

framework   A collection of classes that provides mechanisms for a particular problem domain. An **application framework** provides mechanisms for a particular application type. Actual applications are instantiated by deriving one or more classes from framework classes.

free store   The region of memory that holds objects with variable lifetime.

garbage collection   The reclamation of unused free store memory without programmer intervention.

global function   A function that is not an operation or shared function of a class.

global variable   A variable that is neither local to a block nor a field or shared variable of a class.

header file   A file containing the declarations of the public features in a module.

heap   (1) The free store. (2) A data structure to implement a priority queue.

heterogeneous collection   A collection of objects of different types.

identity   That characteristic that distinguishes an object from all others.

implementation file   A file containing the definitions of all features of a module.

implementation phase   The phase of software development that concerns itself with realizing the design in a programming environment.

inheritance   The definition of a derived class as an extension of a base class. The derived class specifies how it differs from the base class and keeps all base class features that it does not redefine.

initialization   Giving a specific value to an object that is being created.

inline constant   A constant that is compiled into a numeric value, not a reference to a storage location.

inline function   A function that is compiled into a sequence of instructions, not a call command.

invariant   A logical condition that is preserved by transformations. A **loop invariant** is preserved by the transformation effected by the loop instructions. A **class invariant** is preserved by all class operations.

instance   An instance of a class is an object of the class type. An instance of a template is a feature generated from the template. An instance of an application framework is an application made of classes deriving from the framework classes.

instantiation   The process of making an instance.

iterator   An object used to inspect or modify the contents of a container.

lifetime   The interval during which an object exists. The lifetime of a stack object extends from the point of definition until the end of the enclosing block. The lifetime of a dynamic object extends from the point of allocation until deallocation or reclamation by a garbage collector. The lifetime of a static object extends from the start to the end of the program.

map   A container that stores associations between key and value objects.

method   A class operation.

member   A feature of a class.

message (sending of)   Invoking an operation on an object.

mixin Inheriting from one or more abstract classes to add a specific service or protocol to a class.

model/view architecture A program design in which model classes are responsible for storing application data and view classes are responsible for presenting the data to the user.

module A collection of variables, constants, functions, and types that have common functionality.

multiple inheritance Derivation from two or more base classes.

mutator An operation that modifies the state of an object. A **field mutator** is a mutator modifying the value of a single field.

name space A mechanism for assigning unique (long) names to features and mapping them to convenient (short) names.

nested class A class defined in the scope of another class.

numeric type A type representing numbers, with special support provided by the programming language. In C++, the numeric types are char, int, float, and double and their signed, unsigned, short, and long variants.

object An entity in a programming system that has state, operations, and identity.

operation A function acting on objects of a class.

operator One of a collection of predefined symbols in a programming language from which expressions are built.

overloading Using the same name or symbol for a set of functions. The actual function is selected according to the types of the arguments.

parameter A function defines a set of **formal parameters**, variables that are bound to variables or expressions in every function call. The latter are called **actual parameters** of the call.

parameterized class A family of classes that has features depending on type variables. By binding the type variables to actual types, a specific class is instantiated.

persistence The continued existence of objects beyond the execution of a program.

postcondition A logical condition that an operation guarantees on completion.

polymorphism Associating different features to a name, together with a mechanism for selecting the appropriate one. **Ad hoc** polymorphism is name overloading. **Parametric polymorphism** refers to the multiplicity of names in parameterized classes. **Pure polymorphism** is the selection of operations through dynamic binding.

precondition A logical condition that the caller of an operation guarantees before making the call.

priority queue A container in which objects can be inserted in arbitrary order and are removed in sorted order.

reference An alias for an object.

reference counting A mechanism maintaining a count of the number of references to an object, with the objective of deallocating the object when the count reaches zero.

scope (of a feature) The portion of a program in which the feature name selects that feature.

shallow copy A copy of an object that shares references to other objects with the original.

stack unwinding Abandoning a portion of the stack and invoking destructors of all objects that are about to be abandoned.

shared base class   A class that is shared by several base classes of a multiply inheriting class. Called **virtual base class** in C++.

shared function   A function in the scope of a class that does not operate on a specific object. Called **static member function** in C++.

shared variable   A variable in the scope of a class that is not a field of a specific object. Called **static data member** in C++.

smart pointer   A parameterized class with overloaded operators that mimics a regular pointer and provides additional safety or convenience.

state   The current value of an object, which is determined by the cumulative action of all operations on it and influences the reaction to future operations.

stream   A data structure to translate between objects and character representations in an external device.

usage relationship   The relationship between classes that specifies that one class needs to be aware of the existence of another because it uses some service provided by the other.

virtual destructor   A destructor that is dynamically bound.

virtual operation   A family of operations that is specified in a base class and redefined in derived classes and can be dynamically bound in a call.

template   The definition for a parameterized class or a function, depending on type parameters.

template specialization   A definition of a template instance that overrides the form that would result from instantiating the template.

type inquiry   Determining the exact class of an object that is accessed through a pointer to a base class.

REFERENCES

[Aho, Hopcroft, and Ullmann] Alfred V. Aho, John E. Hopcroft, and Jeffrey D. Ullmann, *The Design and Analysis of Computer Algorithms,* Addison-Wesley, 1974.

[Bar-David] Tsvi Bar-David, *Object-Oriented Design for C++,* Prentice Hall, 1993.

[Beck] Kent Beck and Ward Cunningham, A Laboratory for Teaching Object-Oriented Thinking, *Proc. OOPSLA 1989, Sigplan Notices,* vol. 14, no. 10 (1989), pp. 1–6.

[Bentley 1986] Jon Bentley, *Programming Pearls,* Addison-Wesley, 1986.

[Bentley 1988] Jon Bentley, *More Programming Pearls—Confessions of a Coder,* Addison-Wesley, 1988.

[Booch] Grady Booch, *Object-Oriented Analysis and Design,* 2d ed., Benjamin-Cummings, 1994.

[Budd] Timothy Budd, *An Introduction to Object-Oriented Programming,* Addison-Wesley, 1991.

[Cargill] Tom Cargill, *C++ Programming Style,* Addison-Wesley, 1992.

[Cleaveland] J. Craig Cleaveland, *An Introduction to Data Types,* Addison-Wesley, 1986.

[Coad] Peter Coad and Edward Yourdon, *Object-Oriented Analysis,* 2nd ed., Prentice Hall, 1991.

[Coplien] James O. Coplien, *Advanced C++ Programming Styles and Idioms,* Addison-Wesley, 1992.

[Dewhurst and Stark] Steven C. Dewhurst and Kathy T. Stark, *Programming in C++,* Prentice Hall, 1989.

[Ellis and Stroustrup], Margaret Ellis and Bjarne Stroustrup, *The Annotated C++ Reference Manual,* Addison-Wesley, 1990.

[Ghezzi] Carlo Ghezzi, Mehdi Jazayeri and Dino Mandrioli, *Fundamentals of Software Engineering,* Prentice Hall, 1991.

[Goldberg and Robson] A. Goldberg and D. Robson, *Smalltalk 80—The Language and Its Implementation,* Addison-Wesley, 1983.

[Gorlen, Orlow, and Plexico] Keith E. Gorlen, Sanford M. Orlow, and Perry S. Plexico, *Data Abstraction and Object-Oriented Programming in C++,* Wiley, 1990.

[Horowitz] Ellis Horowitz and Sartaj Sahni, *Fundamentals of Data Structures in Pascal,* Computer Science Press, 1984.

[Kernighan and Ritchie] Brian Kernighan and Dennis Ritchie, *The C Programming Language,* 2nd ed., Prentice Hall, 1988.

[Knuth] Donald E. Knuth, *The Art of Computer Programming, Vol. 2: Seminumerical Algorithms,* 2nd ed., Addison-Wesley, 1981.

[Koenig] Andrew Koenig, *C Traps and Pitfalls,* Addison-Wesley, 1988.

[Lea] Douglas Lea, libg++, The GNU C++ Library, *Proc. Usenix C++ Conf.,* Denver, CO, 1988, pp. 243–256.

[Lippmann] Stanley B. Lippmann, *C++ Primer,* 2nd edition, Addison-Wesley, 1991.

[Louden] Kenneth C. Louden, *Programming Languages—Principles and Practices,* PWS-Kent, Boston, 1993.

[Martin] James Martin and James O. Odell, *Object-Oriented Analysis and Design,* Prentice Hall, 1992.

[Meyer] Bertrand Meyer, *Object-Oriented Software Construction,* Prentice Hall, 1988.

[Moore] Patrick Moore, ed. *The International Encyclopedia of Astronomy,* Orim, 1987.

[Murray 1989] Robert B. Murray, Building Well-Behaved Type Relationships in C++, *Proc. Usenix C++ Conf.,* Denver, CO, 1988, pp. 19–30.

[Parise] Frank Parise, ed. *The Book of Calendars,* Facts On File, 1982.

[Press] William H. Press, Saul A. Teukolsky, William T. Vetterling, and Brian P. Flannery, *Numerical Recipes in C,* 2nd ed., Cambridge University Press, 1992.

[Plum and Saks] Thomas Plum and Dan Saks, *C++ Programming Guidelines,* Plum Hall, 1991.

[Reynolds] John C. Reynolds, *The Craft of Programming,* Prentice Hall, 1981.

[Rumbaugh] James Rumbaugh, Michael Blaha, William Premerlani, Frederick Eddy, and William Lorensen, *Object Modeling and Design,* Prentice Hall, 1991.

[Sedgwick] R. Sedgwick, *Algorithms in C,* Addison-Wesley, 1990.

[Sewell] Wayne Sewell, *Weaving a Program—Literate Programming in WEB,* Van Nostrand Reinhold, 1989.

[Stroustrup] Bjarne Stroustrup: *The C++ Programming Language,* 2nd ed., Addison-Wesley, 1991.

[Teale] Steve Teale, *C++ Iostreams Handbook,* Addison-Wesley, 1993.

[Tufte] Edward R. Tufte, *Envisioning Information,* Graphics Press, Cheshire, CT, 1990.

[Wiener and Pinson] Richard S. Wiener and Lewis J. Pinson, *An Introduction to Object-Oriented Programming and C++,* Addison-Wesley, 1988.

[Wirth] Niklaus Wirth, *Algorithms + Data Structures = Programs,* Prentice Hall, 1976.

INDEX